Appreciatio[...]
All-in-One Ma[...]
75 Experts Share Tips and Wisdom
to Help You Get Ready Now

This is an incredible book! Personally, I have been married for 34 years and have helped hundreds of couples as a Mars Venus Success Coach and a Prepare-Enrich mentor for over 12 years. I can tell you that this book is destined to become ~THE~ marriage preparation manual. So many great experts have graciously shared their collective wisdom on how couples can best get along, keep love sizzling, minimize conflict, adjust their expectations, and realize their own personal growth within the realm of relationship. Ah, now if we can only get copies to every high school and college student in the world! And wouldn't it be great to see this gem of a book as a major motion picture? Magnificent job, Susanne, what a fabulous idea this is!

Melodie Tucker, Mars Venus Success Coach, Prepare-Enrich Mentor
and ProConnect Specialist; www.tinyurl.com/melodietucker

What a treasure! To put all this wisdom and years of research into a practical yet powerful book takes someone with Susanne Alexander's talent and heart! As a reader, rest assured you have the latest and greatest information to create the relationship you long for!

Pat Love, Ed.D., author of *The Truth About Love* and *How to Improve Your Relationship Without Talking About It*; www.patlove.com

This book contains wisdom from many sources, some of it serious, some amusing, all of it valuable and useful to couples preparing for marriage. It is like getting advice from a lot of experienced, knowledgeable counselors, all in one place. It would be valuable to any couple who wants to know what it will take to create and sustain a lasting marriage.

Tina B. Tessina, Ph.D., aka "Dr. Romance"
http://drromance.typepad.com/dr_romance_blog/; psychotherapist and
author of *Money, Sex and Kids: Stop Fighting about the Three Things That Can Ruin Your Marriage*; www.tinatessina.com

If we could give engaged and newlywed couples just one gift that would help ensure their success, it wouldn't be a toaster. It would be information about what to expect along their journey. We humans can do just about anything—climb Mt. Everest, walk on the moon, breast-feed twins—if we just know what to expect. This book delivers. It's filled with loving advice about what to expect in a normal marriage (or remarriage) plus offers heartfelt and helpful wisdom about how to handle the challenges that come with each stage, each milestone. It's a wedding gift that will keep on giving.

Diane Sollee, Founder and Director of www.SmartMarriages.com

From the moment we began reading this book, my partner and I started talking. We were both initially a little hesitant to jump into a marriage preparation book, partly because both of us had been previously engaged and the preparation process had not worked out well. But instead of feeling awkward reading it together, it helped us realize the strength and the depth in our relationship, affirmed that we were following the right path for us, and gave us concrete steps, goals, and suggestions for heading into a happy, fulfilling, and eternal marriage.

Talia Lindsley, in a serious relationship

There are a lot of books about marriage. Most of them are by one author, who, if you love, is great. But for those who aren't well read, have no idea where to begin, or simply want to absorb as much as possible, as efficiently as possible, on the topic of marriage, this book hits a home run. The wide variety of voices guarantees you WILL resonate and learn something new to bring into your upcoming or existing marriage.

Elizabeth Doherty Thomas, President of www.TheFirstDance.com, a wedding and premarital relationship website; www.ElizabethDohertyThomas.com

Imagine finding a book with the collected wisdom of some of the wisest relationship experts of the 21st century. At a time when messages of doom about marriage and enduring relationships abound, Susanne Alexander has created an amazing collection of solid advice for those who want to make relationships work. I have been a Marriage and Family Therapist for more than 30 years and married for 55 years, and I believe you don't find a soulmate, you learn to become one. The key is for both partners to be open to learning. Susanne's book, a treasure of information, includes a bibliography of contributors which alone is worth the price of the book.

Elva Anson, L.M.F.T, author of *Becoming Soulmates* and *How to Get Kids to Help at Home* (www.familyfirstbooks.com); blog: www.soulmatetips.blogspot.com

There is a wealth of wisdom between these covers from a vast array of the country's leading relationship experts. Follow the research cited and advice advocated in this book and your marriage will NOT become 1 of the 2 that currently end in divorce! DON'T get married without it!

Sherry Amatenstein, L.M.S.W., author of
The Complete Marriage Counselor; www.marriedfaq.com

All too often, married couples find it difficult to get beyond the wedding in their relationship with each other. When the luster of the fairy tale wedding starts to wear off and the difficult part of making a marriage work begins, many newly married couples flounder—they stumble—and sometimes, they fall. But, this can all be prevented by engaging in marriage preparation with resources such as All-in-One Marriage Prep. Using this book will improve your chances of getting it right the first time around.

Drs. Charles and Elizabeth Schmitz, America's #1 Love and Marriage Experts and Authors of the Best-Selling Book *Building a Love that Lasts: The Seven Surprising Secrets of Successful Marriage;* www.simplethingsmatter.com

If couples would spend as much time and research preparing for married life as they do for planning a wedding or buying a car, we would witness many more happy marriages. Marriage, when entered into with wisdom and understanding, becomes a fortress for well-being. This book, with the accumulated wisdom of over 75 experts, offers essential insights and practical advice to prepare any couple contemplating their future together to be equipped for the challenge. This will certainly assist in my counseling as a Family Doctor.

Brenda Maxwell, M.D., M.Sc., Ed. Cert., C.C.F.P., F.C.F.P.

A brilliant book! Filled with engaging anecdotes and experts' advice, plus self-assessment quizzes that are enjoyably and ultra-effectively short and sweet, this book is a Must Read for any couples planning to marry in the near future. Pre-marital discussions must cover the serious topics—not just the design of a wedding cake or selecting napkin colors for the reception—to make a marriage not just survivable, but a place where both partners can thrive and grow and like each other as well as love each other. Susanne Alexander's new book is a priceless gift for the future bride and groom, helping them prepare for that happily ever after.

Sharon Naylor, author of over 35 books, including *Love Bets;* www.sharonnaylor.net

An incredible smorgasbord of relationship wisdom from a broad array of experts on every conceivable aspect of the tricky task of making your own marriage a real success. Planning to wed? Read this first!

Ralph Jones, co-author, *World Class Marriage,*
www.worldclassmarriage.com

This is the type of book/guidance I have been looking for. It is so well-organized, and the language is understandable and enjoyable to read. I think this is the "gold" at the end of the rainbow! The section on step families is remarkable. It truly highlights the things that are so very important that I never thought of, because I was not fully aware and in the "it will work because we love each other so much" mind set. There were very touchy things that were discussed with great respect and guidance on the matter. There are so many different writing styles, topics, and points of view that you never get bored with the text—it flows and is not confusing. There are ALWAYS solutions, guidance, and success stories, even if you do encounter problems.

F. D., in a serious relationship

While we must all pass a test to get a license to drive, there is no course that couples must take before receiving a marriage license. The experts in this book all make impassioned pleas for doing the necessary preparation before walking down the aisle, and their insightful advice should be required reading for anyone who is serious about getting and staying married.

Jodie Gould, a.k.a. "The Husband Whisperer" and author of
Date Like A Man: To Get The Man You Want; www.jodiegould.com

Marriage advice is only GOOD if it actually helps the relationship and is only CREDIBLE if the person giving advice knows what they're talking about. All-in-One Marriage Prep *gives today's seriously dating, engaged, or newlywed couple GOOD and CREDIBLE marriage advice on anything and everything they need as they embark on the marriage journey.*

K. Jason and Kelli Krafsky, co-authors of *Facebook and Your Marriage*
(www.FBMarriage.com) and author of *Before "I Do"*
(www.FullMarriageExperience.com)

Linda ♡ Fr...

All~in~One Marriage Prep

75 Experts Share Tips & Wisdom to Help You Get Ready Now

May you have a bless...
journey before and after

Susanne M. Alexander

SUSANNE M. ALEXANDER
Relationship & Marriage Coach

7-9-1...

All-in-One Marriage Prep

Barringer Publishing, Naples, Florida, June 2010
www.barringerpublishing.com
Independent Book Editing: Autumn Conley (autiej@gmail.com)
Cover and Layout Design by Lisa Camp

ISBN: 978-0-9825109-9-5

Library of Congress Control Number: 2010908310

Printed in U.S.A.

In Honor and in Memory

In honor of the contributions of the experts to *All-in-One Marriage Prep*, and in memory of Craig A. Farnsworth, Susanne Alexander's husband, a portion of the profits from this book will go to The Dibble Institute for Marriage Education (www.dibbleinstitute.org). This organization helps young people gain the knowledge and learn the skills necessary for healthy, successful romantic relationships and marriages. Others are welcome to donate to the organization as well. Contact: Kay Reed, Executive Director, kayreed@dibbleinstitute.org, 800-695-7975.

❤ ❤ ❤

❤ ❤ ❤

Find Us on the Internet!
The website for this book is www.allinonemarriageprep.com.
Additional information is available at
www.marriagetransformation.com.

Table of Contents

Introduction

~~

Welcome to This Marriage Preparation Journey!
Susanne M. Alexander, Lead Book Editor

All of us involved in the project of creating this book are very delighted you are joining us on the adventurous journey of preparing for a happy, lasting marriage. We are here to help build your knowledge, skills, and confidence. Welcome! It may help you to hear a little of my personal story, how the book came to be, and what will help you in using it.

My Preparation and Marriage Journey

Marriage and preparation for it is becoming a recurring theme in my life, ever gaining focus and importance. At the age of nineteen in the mid-1970s, I married for the first time. We did no preparation at all, unless you count a brief, ineffective meeting with my parents. The marriage was full of painful difficulties, and we finally divorced when our daughter was eighteen.

In the late 1990s, a good friend was ending his marriage, and we discovered we had potential as a couple. Determined to do better at preparation than both of us had for our first marriages, we participated in personal transformation training, discussed our readiness to marry thoroughly with both of our parents to be sure we had their wholehearted support, met once with a counselor, read a book or two, attempted to build relationships with each other's adult children, and spent time writing down what we were committed to creating together in a marriage. Craig Farnsworth and I married in August of 1999, and we created a very excellent marriage. So, still limited preparation, but a significant step forward.

A few months after the wedding, someone approach us who was impressed with how well we had prepared for our marriage. She asked us to teach teenagers how be ready to marry. Flattered and excited to help, we created an eight-page handout and met with them. In the two years that followed, we led a few more workshops with teens and adults, and our handout grew each time. Two close friends provided inspiration, having reaped some valuable lessons in marriages that lasted mere months.

Becoming a Relationship and Marriage Coach

In late 2002, we had the brainstorm of publishing a book on this very topic because there was obviously a need for it. I was a business journalist, so I knew a little of writing, but we really had no clue how to write and publish a book, and our relationship knowledge was based largely on our experiences and some spiritual principles in support of marriage. I told Craig at the time, "Now, we aren't going to let this book change our lives, sweetheart!" Little did we know! After selling almost 2,000 copies in a few months, a light bulb went on that maybe there was a need for knowledge beyond what we ever imagined.

It was that realization that made us get serious about it all. We sought training as marriage educators/coaches with PREPARE-ENRICH. We found Smart Marriages®, the international coalition for people involved in relationship and marriage education (www.smartmarriages.com), and received more training at their annual conference. We established a company called Marriage Transformation LLC (www.marriagetransformation.com), and I began to work full-time for it while Craig supported us with his day job! I wrote more books, often with wonderful co-authors, and developed a specialty in character. We got better at publishing and began doing many workshops and coaching couples. We were flying high with a great booth at the Smart Marriages® Conference in 2007, with Craig in particular interacting with everyone.

Major Life Changes

And then, life happened. Three weeks after the conference, Craig had emergency surgery to remove a brain tumor, which turned out to be cancerous. My daily work went into slow motion as we dealt with surgeries, radiation, chemo, and multiple hospitalizations. My work virtually stopped when he needed full-time caregiving by the summer of 2008, but our marriage deepened and strengthened as we went through the process as partners. Craig's spiritual strength grew throughout the illness and as he came closer to the end. We created two books together as we planned for his funeral and dealt with hospice care at home. Our roles as spouses focused on helping each other and our children prepare for the end of his life here and his shift into a spiritual life as his soul went on to the next stage of his journey. The transition happened on July 1, 2009, and this book is dedicated to the progress of Craig's beloved soul.

All-in-One Marriage Prep Begins

At that point, understandably, being a relationship and marriage coach became very questionable for me. My partner in the business was gone. After months of physical and emotional recovery, I began to realize that I still felt passionate about this work, probably nudged along in that direction by my new "guardian angel!" I decided to focus more on unmarried individuals and couples, and the idea for this book arose.

What I didn't expect was how personally connected to the content I would feel while editing everyone's submissions and writing my own. Threads of learning from my first marriage showed up. Many blessings from my experiences with Craig wove into edits and in my own sharing. And, because Craig very strongly insisted that I prepare myself to remarry, I felt as if I was intimately engaged in marriage preparation for whatever the future holds. For me, bringing this book together was very much about an emotional completion of the past linked with preparing for the future. And, of course, I was very focused throughout on providing a useful tool for you as well.

Our Commitment to You

As you read through the wisdom from the wonderful and committed experts in this book, you will benefit from our collective life experiences and training. We are a diverse group, including both genders and various ages, races, cultures, and religious faiths. We have all gone through different relationship experiences, training, and career paths. Each expert shares their own perspective in their own voice, sometimes with strong opinions or humor included. Most stories and tips will be helpful to you, though you may not find all of them personally applicable. Please take what is useful to you now, apply it, and leave the rest for someone else who needs it. Keep it all in mind for the future though; these experts are also resources for you in your marriage. Each expert's biography beneath the articles gives you access to sources of further information.

What we have in common as a group of experts is our passion about the joy of marriage done well and our view, supported by research, that preparing for marriage enhances your ability to succeed. Please know that we sincerely want you to have excellent marriages. We have done our very best to give you much of what will help you do just that.

> **Susanne M. Alexander** is a Relationship and Marriage Coach specializing in character and certified by PREPARE-ENRICH. She is President of Marriage Transformation LLC, based in Cleveland, Ohio, (www.marriagetransformation.com), which has the mission of helping people create happy, lasting, character-based marriages. She is the author or co-author of *All-in-One Marriage Prep: 75 Experts Share Tips and Wisdom to Help You Get Ready Now; Can We Dance? Learning the Steps for a Fulfilling Relationship; Marriage Can Be Forever—Preparation Counts!; Pure Gold: Encouraging Character Qualities in Marriage; Happy at Home, Happy at Work;* and *A Perfectly Funny Marriage* cartoon book. Susanne has conducted workshops for individuals and couples in the United States, Canada, and China. She has been quoted in or written articles published in: *Washington Woman, Marriage Partnership, Inc., Ladies Home Journal, Newsweek, Chicago Sun Times, The Washington Times, NBC Online,* Yahoo.com Personals, Match.com, Hitched.com, ParentsConnect.com, and more. Susanne is a member of the American Society of Journalists and Authors. She has one married daughter, three married stepchildren, and three grandchildren. You can contact her at 800-501-6682 or Susanne@marriagetransformation.com.

Editor's Note to Couples: We are observing a cultural shift that has been underway for some time, from primarily women being involved in learning about how relationships work to more and more men being involved. Our request for this book is that you study it as a couple, equal partners in your commitment to gain the knowledge and skills needed for a healthy, happy, successful marriage that will benefit both of you and your families.

Foreword

~~

The Value of Relationship and Marriage Education
Julie M. Baumgardner

A man walks into an attorney's office and tells the lawyer he wants a divorce. The attorney asks him if he has a case. The man responds, "No, sir, I have a John Deere." A bit amused at the man's reference to a brand of tractor, the attorney then asks, "Does your wife beat you up?" to which the man replies, "Oh no! I get up every morning around five a.m. She sleeps until six or seven." The questioning went on for a few more minutes with the same type of mismatched responses. When the attorney could see he was getting nowhere, he finally asked, "Mister, exactly why do you want this divorce?" to which the man replied, "Me and my wife, we just don't communicate."

While this is comical and seems improbable, the truth is, couples struggle to communicate more than you might think. This type of scenario plays out in many marriages, especially in those for which there was no premarital preparation. With more than 2 million couples getting married annually in the United States alone, many who will tell you they want it to be for a lifetime, what can these couples do to help decrease the chances they will be part of the 40 percent of new marriages that end in divorce?

The Case for Premarital Education

More than a decade of research indicates that one of the smartest moves for couples preparing for marriage is to make sure they participate in premarital preparation—and by that, we aren't talking about planning the color scheme, reception, or where flowers will be placed. Studies have shown that couples who learn communication skills, learn how to effectively resolve conflict, learn how to resolve problems (which is not the same as conflict resolution), and hone their decision-making skills all stand a greater chance of their marriage making it over the long haul.

Premarital preparation involves training through such methods as attending skills-based classes, meeting with a Mentor Couple, or obtaining counseling that prepares couples for a successful marriage. Many preparation options also cover topics like intimacy in marriage, dealing with in-laws, handling finances, understanding and agreeing on expectations of marriage, and developing the qualities that lead to a satisfying marriage relationship. You will notice that many of the experts in this book and their programs and books are resources for you in this vital preparation process.

Marriage education pioneer David Mace once said, "Marriage is the deepest and potentially the most gratifying of all human relationships, but it is also one of the most demanding. Unfortunately, couples seldom enter into marriage with anything more than a little advice from their parents and a new set of china."

The Benefits of Premarital Preparation

"Premarital education has four overarching benefits for couples," said Dr. Scott Stanley, a marriage researcher at the University of Denver and co-founder of the Prevention and Relationship Enhancement Program (PREP; www.prepinc.com). "It allows couples to slow down for a time to allow for fostering discussion. It allows time to process the fact that marriage is a very important matter. It helps couples gain access to marital resources and providers, and it can lower the risk for subsequent marital distress and/or termination of relationships for some couples."

When couples slow down, it reduces impulsive decision making and provides ample time for reflection. The couple has time to clarify expectations with each other and to digest the magnitude of the decision to marry. The slowing-down process can also help them to look at their relationship without rose-colored glasses.

When couples have the time to process the fact that marriage is important and there are others in the community who want their marriage to be a success, their choice to marry tends to take on deeper meaning. They also realize that marriage is a long-term investment.

The latest research indicates that couples who participate in premarital programs experience a 30 percent increase in marital success over those who do not participate. They report:

- Improved communication
- Better conflict management skills
- Higher dedication to their mate
- Greater emphasis on the positive aspects of the relationship
- Improved overall relationship quality

"When you are engaged, everything seems like it is perfect," said Amber Brown, a newlywed who participated in one of the programs offered through my organization. "It is hard to imagine that you are going to need the skills and information presented in premarital education classes because you are so in love. But the truth is, if you listen and let it sink in, later on when the newness wears off and you see things about each other that are nerve wracking, something in your brain tells you, 'Wait…I know how I should respond to this.'"

Tony and Amber attended a premarital education class because Amber thought it would be helpful. "She pulled me there," said Tony. "I thought I had more important things to do. Plus, I didn't want to talk about personal stuff in front of other people. The reality is, now that we have been married for more than a year, what I learned in that class was like good pre-game practice."

Most men would never think of showing up for a game without knowing the playbook, or drive their car for 60,000 miles without taking it in for a tune-up, yet when it comes to marriage, they are willing to blindly jump in with both feet without a playbook or instruction manual.

As the newness of their marriage has worn off, Tony and Amber have come to terms with the fact that while they love each other, they definitely have their differences. "We did not live together before we got married, yet we knew we each had habits that could create challenges in our marriage," Amber said.

"I like to save money," said Tony. "She, on the other hand, likes to spend money on things I don't understand. When we attended our premarital class, finances was one of the topics. That was the first time we really talked about our finances and living on a budget. That was definitely an eye-opening experience for both of us."

"I am a neat freak," said Amber. "I don't think Tony really understood what that meant until after we were married. Both of us work, so I would spend most of Saturday cleaning the house by myself. At the end of the day, I would be furious with him for watching sports on television instead of helping me.

The skills we learned in our class helped us resolve this issue so it didn't create a chasm in our marriage. It was worth it to him to hire a housekeeper twice a month!"

Potential Problem Areas

Research shows that couples will face their most serious challenges during the first five years of their marriages. Listed below are the top ten potential problem areas:

1. Finances
2. Debt brought into marriage
3. Balancing work and family
4. Frequency of sex
5. Household expectations
6. Constant bickering
7. Communication
8. In-laws
9. Lack of time spent together
10. Husband's employment

Good premarital preparation covers these topics and more. Most participants in premarital education find it to be fun and informative. Oftentimes, spouses-to-be learn things about each other they never knew. The reality is, couples don't know what they don't know. They may think they are going into marriage with a good set of skills, but if they have nothing to gauge that by, it is hard to know if the skills they have in their tool box are constructive or not. If they have come from single-parent homes or are children of divorce themselves, their set of coping, relationship, and decision-making tools is likely inadequate.

Reflecting Back After Marriage

The latest research indicates that couples who participate in premarital preparation during the year before their marriage and some type of marriage enrichment the year following their wedding stand to benefit the most. These couples tend to enter into marriage with their eyes wide open to the possibilities for difficulties, but they are committed to staying together and making the relationship work.

"What we have realized over the first year of our marriage is that our premarital education class provided us with the resources and the foundation to do marriage well," said Amber Brown.

Since 93 percent of Americans rate a happy marriage as one of their most important objectives in life, doesn't it make sense to do those things that research shows will help you obtain this goal?

Julie M. Baumgardner, M.S., C.F.L.E., is the President and Executive Director of First Things First, an award-winning, grassroots initiative based in Chattanooga, Tennessee. The organization is dedicated to strengthening marriages and families through education, collaboration, and mobilization. Julie has conducted hundreds of workshops and frequently speaks nationally on family, parenting, and marriage issues. She also teaches community leaders how to build grassroots initiatives. Julie's weekly column on family issues in the *Chattanooga Times-Free Press* reaches thousands. Julie serves on the boards of a number of community and national organizations, such as The Marriage CoMission, The Coalition for Marriage, Couples and Families, Laugh Your Way to a Better Marriage, and The National Healthy Marriage Resource Center. She and her husband Jay have been married for more than twenty years and have one daughter. Julie can be reached at www.firstthings.org, julieb@firstthings.org, or 423-267-5383.

Chapter One
Preparing As a Couple
~ ~

You are beginning a journey that will ideally forge you into being strong partners. There are aspects of marriage preparation that each of you can and will do on your own, as you each have your own interests and learning styles. However, preparing together will build your knowledge of one another and your strengths as a couple. You will benefit from reading selections from the book and discussing and practicing the expert suggestions together.

The selections in this chapter will get you thinking more deeply about this preparation process and introduce you to some practical ways to engage in preparing yourselves as a couple.

♥ ♥ ♥

You Have Chosen—Now Prepare!
Greg Hunt and Priscilla Hunt

Why didn't someone tell me that before I got married? It's a common cry in a population where half of all marriages turn out badly.

David R. Mace and his wife Vera are co-founders of the Association for Couples in Marriage Enrichment (ACME, now known as Better Marriages). David states, "The Boy Scout motto is 'Be Prepared'...The major area of life for which we are most poorly prepared is, unfortunately, marriage and family living. Preparation for marriage is preparation for the one experience in life on which our happiness most deeply depends." [1]

Imagine explorers setting off to make a journey through unknown territory with no food, map, or compass (preparation). How likely are they to survive, let alone make it to their hoped-for destination? If there was ever an unknown territory, it is the budding relationship between two unique individuals.

According to Mace and the principles of Better Marriages, the following are the steps to getting your marriage off to a great start:

1. **Your Past:** Explore your personal history. Take a close look at yourself. Who are you? How did you come to be who and what you are? What do you want from life? What are the things that have shaped you to this point—your family background, interests, spiritual development, vocational development, sexual experiences and attitudes, and physical and mental health? Now, share your insights with your partner. Open up your inner self and reveal the kind of person you know yourself to be. Listen to your partner's insights about their own self-discoveries. Discuss what it might mean for the two of you to spend the rest of your lives together in marriage, the most intimate, most demanding, of all human relationships.

2. **Your Present:** Take a look at your compatibility. What drew you to each other? How will you feel about these aspects after marriage? What are your temperamental and personality similarities and differences? What do you have in common—age, culture, habits, education, spirituality, or personal tastes? Identify first the things you share in common. Then discuss the areas of difference and disagreement. Explore how much acceptance and tolerance you can contribute to keeping the peace when tensions arise over these differences—because they will!

3. **Your Future:** Examine your expectations for your relationship. Be realistic and specific. "Be happy" isn't concrete. Offer *details* about family, leisure time, finances, sex, and more. Building a marriage, like building a house, requires a blueprint and lots of decisions along the way so the finished product matches what you envisioned. Based on your agreed-on expectations, set goals for your relationship. Begin to put into writing the details of how you plan to attain the marriage you desire.

There are, indeed, many practical matters to discuss when it comes to marriage, but, in addition to the practical matters, there are the less clearly defined and more important matters of your feelings and attitudes toward each other. The sharing of these feelings and attitudes can lead to your inner lives being in tune with one another's. When you experience inner harmony and unity, you'll be able to cope with all the twists and turns that life will throw your way.

Learn all you can about yourself and your partner *before* marriage. After the wedding, you will then both continue to learn and adapt through the years.

You have chosen your partner for life. In the words of the French writer, André Maurois, "I have chosen. From now on, my aim will be not to search for someone who will please me, but to please the one I have chosen."[2]

1 Mace, David R., *Getting Ready for Marriage,* Abingdon Press (Nashville, TN), 1972.

2 Maurois, Andre, *The Art of Being Happily Married,* Harper (New York, NY), 1953.

Greg and Priscilla Hunt are dynamic speakers and are known for their lively, fun presentations. The Hunts are a certified Leader Couple and Specialists in Marriage Enrichment with Better Marriages (www.BetterMarriages.org). They are Seminar Directors for PREPARE-ENRICH, Instructor Trainers for Couple Communication, and certified Trainers for Mentoring for Better Marriages. They have been involved in marriage education and enrichment since they married in 1976. Priscilla is the Executive Director for Better Marriages, a non-profit since 1973, whose aim is educating couples for vibrant, lifelong relationships. After thirty-three years in pastoral ministry, Greg is now a consultant and writer, working in the areas of leadership, relationships, and spirituality. The parents of two adult children and grandparents to two granddaughters, Greg and Priscilla live in the metropolitan area of Kansas City, Kansas.

© 2010 G. Hunt; P. Hunt

❤ ❤ ❤

How to Recognize Your Soulmate
Kathryn Elliott, Ph.D., and James Elliott, Ph.D.

We know, we know. When you look at your track record of relationships or those of people close to you, it may look like a string of shipwrecks, failures, and just plain bad choices. But in the face of all that, we have one thing to say to you: *Your history is NOT your destiny!* How can we say that? Because we know relationships are our grand opportunity for learning…and for growth. Kathryn didn't know that before she met Jim. So, she gave up for a while on finding a good man. Little did she know that her destiny was on its way, and our marriage has brought fulfillment beyond our wildest dreams.

To gain the wisdom your history has to teach you, it will help to understand some concepts. The first one we want to give you is *soulmate*. We define soulmate by the quality of the relationship the partners share. The second is *voltage*—the level of closeness you want in a relationship. A *high-voltage soulmate relationship* is one where you connect at the core depth level; the level of soul.

It is not a matter of magic. Rather, a soulmate relationship can be created through skills. These are the skills we have discovered in our own marriage and taught thousands of people to use in crafting their own relationships characterized by intense emotional closeness. Such closeness is based on a foundation of values, particularly honesty, forthcomingness, cherishing, love, and inner freedom.

The voltage levels that partners choose—and it is a choice—is purely a preference. Low-voltage partners may feel they are soulmates. That is, they value each other highly. However, they prefer less closeness in their relationship. In contrast, high-voltage soulmates choose to take their relationship to a level of deeper emotional closeness, utilizing such skills as requesting, beholding, and extravagant expressions of love. Beholding is seeing each other without judgment as you are and holding each other's essence as sacred. If you long for a lot of emotional connection and talking through your feelings about the relationship, then you want a high-voltage soulmate relationship.

If you'd rather have a relationship that stays more on a surface level, then you prefer low-voltage. It's important that you find someone who wants the same level of voltage that you do. When you think back on your history, you'll find that some (or maybe even most) of your failed relationships were because of a voltage mismatch.

The third concept you'll need is *valuing* your partner. How can you tell if this is your soulmate? One way is by how highly you value the person. If they are on a pedestal in your mind; if you have them high, high in their importance to you—that's a great indicator. Why? Because someone who fulfills that soulmate longing you have will be the person who holds transcendent value for you—not just ordinary caring or warmth for them, but something beyond that. You look at them and just feel awe that they are in your life.

We want to make clear that in a soulmate relationship, there is *mutuality* in valuing. The valuing needs to be happening on both sides, by both partners. That means there are two pedestals—or maybe one pedestal that both partners are nestled on together! So, when you're looking for a soulmate, be sure to check that your partner wants to be with you as much as you want to be with them. Be sure you introduce each other with pride to relatives and friends and that you both want a lot of closeness. That's how soulmates are.

And that brings us to the heart of the matter. Your soulmate quest is not a matter of luck or even providence. It needs to be a carefully thought-out process. There's a song from an old musical called *State Fair* that goes like this: "I know what I like. And I like what I saw. And I said to myself, 'That's for me!'" Jim and I sing this to each other all the time, because the words capture the essence of where we were when we found each other. Kathryn had been clarifying the qualities she wanted in a partner, learning from previous partner experiences what qualities were important to her and which ones weren't. Jim had developed a list of fifty-six criteria for a life partner!

When we first saw each other, we said, "Looks good. That's for me!" and then we spent the next few months getting to know each other in-depth, discovering in the process that we met each other's criteria. If you're wondering, "Is there only one person in all the world for me?" we don't know the answer to that, but we do know that your quest for a soulmate should be guided by your own particular criteria for what is most important in a partner. Will some divine intervention be involved in finding your soulmate? Perhaps. But, for your part, be ready to recognize who is a good match for you.

Checklist for a High-Voltage Soulmate Relationship

This checklist contains the criteria or qualities needed in both partners in order to create a high-voltage soulmate relationship:

1. I like to talk to my partner about our relationship. ☐ T ☐ F

2. I like to make up quickly after an argument. ☐ T ☐ F

3. I like to read self-help books on relationships. ☐ T ☐ F

4. I like to tell my partner "I love you." ☐ T ☐ F

5. When we have a problem, I want to discuss it as soon as possible. ☐ T ☐ F

6. I would be willing to get into counseling or marriage preparation with my partner. ☐ T ☐ F

7. I like to talk about my feelings. ☐ T ☐ F

8. I like to listen to my partner talk about their feelings. ☐ T ☐ F

9. I like to tell my partner about their good qualities. ☐ T ☐ F

10. I like to analyze our conversations and arguments. ☐ T ☐ F

Scoring:

If you circled every **T**, you definitely want a high-voltage soulmate relationship. If you circled only a few Ts or none at all, you may want a low-voltage relationship. Let the knowledge of your voltage desires guide you in determining that you are a match.

Kathryn Elliott, Ph.D., and James Elliott, Ph.D. are therapists and soulmates. Since childhood, they had each longed for closeness and spent much of their adult lives searching for it in a partner. In 1989, at the start of their doctoral program, they found each other. They've enjoyed the great gift of spending the last twenty years married, working as therapists and creating and practicing Anthetic Therapy, their unique approach to individual and couples therapy, as well as learning how to be soulmates. They share their love story, love letters, and unique skills on their website, www.soulmateskills.org. You can gain more ideas for creating your own soulmate relationship in the Elliotts' book, *Disarming Your Inner Critic*, and they are currently authoring *Soulmate Skills.*

❤ ❤ ❤

Prepared Marriages Are a Better Option
Krsnanandini Devi Dasi and Tariq Saleem Ziyad

Janine and Jasper feel like they are a "match made in heaven." Both are motivated, hardworking sports enthusiasts who met at a basketball game. Both are twenty-six and sometimes marvel at their common interests and goals. After three years of "going together," they agree that it's time for them to make a more serious commitment to one another by getting married. Of course, this makes Janine's religious grandmother happy. She, however, with mature wisdom, firmly suggests that the enthusiastic young couple get some comprehensive, premarital counseling or relationship skill building from trained and dedicated marriage and family educators before they tie the knot.

Grandma knows well the story of too many couples, who in the early bloom of their relationship were "so in love," only to have their marriage end in bitter, acrimonious divorce. She offers to pay for premarital education sessions as a gift. Janine and Jasper accept and register to take a twelve-hour premarital skills-building program.

Will You Have an Arranged, Romantic, or Prepared Marriage?

In some Eastern countries, many people have arranged marriages. Parents, older relatives, and/or close family friends find mates for their loved ones. In most Western countries, however, two individuals meet and marry based on a romantic attraction. While both of these marital options have history (people have gotten married in one or the other of these ways for hundreds of years), a "prepared marriage" is usually a better way for couples to have a greater chance at a lifelong, satisfying marriage.

Prepared marriage includes spending time and resources to acquire or reinforce healthy relationship skills *before* you get married. **Preparation,** the "action or process of making something ready for use or service," is a prerequisite for a healthy marriage. Like Janine and Jasper, any couple that makes a choice to prepare for marriage is making wise use of time and money. It is far more depleting and costly to repair a damaged or troubled marriage.

Why Prepare?

Seeking premarital education or relationship skills-building from experienced, caring marriage educators or counselors helps couples assess their strengths and growth areas, acquire the healthy relationship skills they need, and get a more realistic perspective of what it takes for a marriage to work. Premarital education is the best preparation for success in family life.

More and more, clergy from many different religious traditions are requiring couples to get premarital education before they will perform a marriage. They are tired of the revolving door of marriage and divorce. They see the negative effects of marriage break-ups in their spiritual communities, as well as how these negatives affect children and society in general. So, either the clergyperson will provide the premarital education or refer a couple to someone else.

The high rate of divorce and its social and economic consequences demands that we consider what to do *beforehand* to prevent costly marital break-ups. Why should a couple spend thousands of dollars on a one-day wedding without at the very least getting the necessary preparation to have a lifelong marriage? When you think about it, many social and professional activities necessitate training, so why not marriage? Consider driving a car, being certified as an auto mechanic, getting a position as a bank teller, becoming a foster/adoptive parent, becoming a teacher, nurse, doctor, social worker, journalist, or postal worker. All of these things require training by people who have experience in the area, and marriage is no different.

Let's take a look at another couple who made the "prepared" choice:

Ayesha and Braj are thinking about getting married. They've had a rough relationship since meeting two years ago at a mall. They come from different religious backgrounds, and neither of their families is very favorable about their upcoming union. Braj has two children from an earlier relationship. With these serious challenges, their relationship is straining like a rubber band stretched to its limit. Still, neither Ayesha nor Braj wants to end the relationship. A friend suggests that they seek premarital education, and after initial reluctance on Braj's part, they look for somewhere to go for help. A family friend—a social worker—directs them to a website that identifies some local marriage and family education professionals.

What to Expect in Premarital Education Sessions

Like most qualified marriage and family educators, the professionals who work with Ayesha and Braj asked them to first fill out a *premarital inventory*. A premarital inventory is an excellent tool that provides an unbiased assessment of a couple's strengths and weaknesses or growth areas. The most commonly administered inventories are PREPARE-ENRICH, Foccus, and Relate. Many inventories can now be taken online and a report generated for the educator or counselor.

When couples respond honestly to a series of statements, their own answers reveal a wealth of information about how differences in personality characteristics, marriage expectations, family background, communication skills, insecurities, sexual concerns, parenting styles, leisure choices, spirituality, and more affect their relationship.

Premarital inventories are not compatibility tests. They are not intended to test whether you should marry someone or not; in fact, inventories are not tests at all. Instead, they are instruments that immediately point to areas that you need to strengthen, to serious relationship concerns, and to other information pertinent to your future marriage. There are no right or wrong answers—just truthful ones.

After taking the premarital inventory online, Ayesha and Braj worked through five, two-hour sessions, getting information and becoming more skilled in communication, resolving conflict, setting couple goals, identifying their family values, setting realistic expectations, recognizing baggage from the past and putting it in its proper place, financial planning, and parenting. They also created a couple and family mission statement. In one of the sessions, Ayesha was surprised to find out just how much her parents' divorce had affected her perception and expectations of marriage.

Choosing a Professional to Provide Premarital Education

There are several types of professionals committed to providing premarital education to couples. These include:

- Marriage and Family Therapists
- Trained Mentor Couples
- Clergy, such as Ministers, Rabbis, or Imams
- Marriage Educators
- Certified Family Life Educators

Those who offer premarital education and marriage enrichment sessions may vary according to education, training, experience, and commitment. Ask them about their qualifications. Find out if they utilize premarital inventories in their services. Check out their websites. If it's important to you, ask to see feedback evaluations from previous clients or references. Finally, have a heart-to-heart conversation with them to ensure you can trust them to prepare you for a lifelong healthy marriage. Do you sense they are someone you can confide in? Inquire about the process they use in their premarital education services.

You can find these professionals by going online or by asking about premarital education classes at churches, temples, mosques, or social service centers in your area. You can ask some folks you know who are married if they can refer you to people who offer premarital education—and consider asking them to mentor you as well.

By getting premarital education, couples can be *proactive before marriage* and have a much greater likelihood of walking down the aisle into healthy, strong marriages. The alternative is *reacting* by trying to fix weak or challenged marriages after the fact. That's why more and more family service providers are recommending premarital preparation.

Krsnanandini Devi Dasi and **Tariq Saleem Ziyad** are Co-Directors of Dasi-Ziyad Family Institute based in Cleveland, Ohio, an agency that provides a number of curricula, courses, and workshops (www.dzfi.org). Their educational services have empowered hundreds of couples, families, and individuals with healthy relationship skills. Krsnanandini holds degrees in Education and Sociology. Tariq has degrees in Psychology and Business Management. Dasi and Ziyad are Certified Family Life Educators (CFLEs), Certified Family Wellness Instructors, PREPARE-ENRICH Coaches, members of the National Council on Family Relations, and co-authors of several magazine and newspaper articles about healthy families, parenting, relationships, and marriage. This husband-and-wife team is the 2008 recipient of the Nguzo Saba Award for promoting community and family unity from the Imani Foundation. Featured in the popular book, *Cleveland Couples: 40 Inspiring Stories of Love and Commitment* by Kathy Dawson, Krsnanandini and Tariq have nineteen children altogether. She is the biological mother of ten of them—enough to keep them "working to empower families for a long time."

© 2010 K. Devi Dasi; T. Ziyad

♥ ♥ ♥

Marriage Preparation Essentials
Linda Bloom and Charlie Bloom

Great marriages don't just happen; they are created. The creation process involves the cultivation of personal strengths, skills, and a system of good support. It's a significant undertaking, but worth far more than the effort it requires to succeed. Anyone with sufficient motivation and a willingness to do the work required for a successful relationship is capable of achieving an excellent marriage. This is regardless of their background, personal history, personality, or predisposition. Most of us possess adequate raw material to start with what we have, and through experience and effort, our inner resources expand and deepen.

There are, however, some issues and concerns that can and should be addressed prior to marriage. While it may not be possible to anticipate all potential concerns, there are some questions that are relevant to nearly all marriages. These topics are essential to the establishment of alignment and agreement regarding foundational matters. These issues don't need to all be fully resolved prior to the marriage, but unless they are at least brought up and put on the table, it is likely that at a future point they will become a source of distress and disturbance to both partners. Examples of these issues are:

1. **Children:** Is there an agreement about having children? When? How many? Who will take care of them? How long will one or both of you stay home? If there are problems with fertility, is adoption an option? If you have a change of heart about any of these questions, how will you negotiate your prior agreements?

2. **In-laws:** What is your policy regarding family visits on holidays? How will you deal with aging or dependent parents?

3. **Work:** How will you determine whose job dictates where you live? Are

all promotions and raises in salary acceptable, even if they require more time away from the family?

4. **Money:** What are your expectations of each other for financial contribution to the family? What is the maximum one person can spend without consent from the other? Do you want a budget?

5. **Friendships:** Is it okay for each of you to have friends of the opposite sex? How much time is considered okay for both of you to spend with your friends? How do you deal with it if one person feels neglected in the relationship?

6. **Sexuality:** How will you handle differences in levels of sexual desire? How open are each of you to different sexual techniques? Is there a willingness to seek professional help if there is a sexual problem? If so, when? How will you deal with it if one person wants to get help and the other doesn't?

7. **Separateness and Togetherness:** What would be the ideal amount of time spent together and apart for each of you?

8. **Privacy:** What is your policy regarding communication about personal and marital concerns with other people?

9. **Love:** What are your preferred ways of expressing love and having it expressed to you?

Here is an example of a couple discussing Number 7, Separateness and Togetherness:

Ted and Suzanne have been together for three years. Ted is an introvert and thrives when he has large portions of time to himself. Suzanne is extroverted; she loves talking and connecting to people, most especially Ted. There is much that is wonderful in their relationship, but at times, the differences in their levels of desire for connection and solitude show up as problematic. They both know this issue has the potential to become a deal breaker if it is ignored. Although they don't know exactly how, they are both determined to come up with a means of reconciliation that works for them both.

One day, the couple sits down for a talk. Ted begins by telling Suzanne how difficult it is for him to be in a busy, noisy, demanding work place all week and how badly he needs quiet time in the evenings and on the weekends. Suzanne then expresses to him how much she misses him during the work week. She speaks of being lonely for his touch, for conversation, and for connection with him. They each speak with vulnerability and respect, without coerciveness or judgment.

Eventually, Ted and Suzanne are able to work out an agreement for dividing their free time on their weekends to allow for their differing needs to be fulfilled. Suzanne agrees to support Ted in his desire for solitude. Ted makes a commitment to be mindful of Suzanne's need for connection and to include time for the two of them to spend together on a regular basis on his list of priorities and concerns. They both commit to give the relationship the attention and time it needs to thrive.

Most couples put more time and effort into planning for the wedding than into their preparations for the life they are going to share. Putting more energy into marriage preparation promotes the establishment of a firm foundation for marriage. And when you do, the likelihood of creating a deeply fulfilling partnership increases dramatically.

Linda Bloom, L.C.S.W., and **Charlie Bloom**, M.S.W., are Psychotherapists and Marriage Counselors who teach communication seminars and relationship workshops throughout the world. They are co-authors of the best-selling book, *101 Things I Wish I Knew When I Got Married, Simple Lessons to Make Love Last,* and *Secrets of Great Marriages: Real Truths from Real Couples About Lasting Love,* published in 2010. They offer educational and counseling services to individuals, couples, and organizations. Their website is www.bloomwork.com, and they can be reached at 831-421-9822 or by email at lcbloom@bloomwork.com. They live and practice in Santa Cruz, California.

❤ ❤ ❤

Making Marriage Work Twogether
Yolanda "Yanni" Brown

A wedding is a big step toward building the rest of your life with someone. However, stabilizing your foundation before you say your wedding vows is vital to combat the ups and downs that a marriage will inevitably go through. Building that foundation involves constant conversations between the two of you, along with simultaneous mutual give and take in *your* relationship. Understand the benefits of your relationship as your own private entity; it's your relationship, and it should work for *you!* Once you've decided to say "I do," please understand that at some point you will really want to say, "I've changed my mind." But it's important that you talk it out—and most of all, work it out!

Communication is important, but it's even more important that the communication include compassion, consideration, and compromise for the good of your relationship. Always remember what is important is the constant give and take to preserve the overall relationship. Pick your battles wisely, because everything is not worth an argument! If one of you tends to leave clutter around but is considerate and does other positive things, maybe compromise and acceptance are wise. You are going to have disagreements, but have them fairly. Express your issues and concerns, but more importantly, discuss resolutions and be willing to compromise!

Get your household finances in order! Disastrous and chaotic finances are a sure-fire way to get into trouble quickly. If the finances are messed up, it will inevitably mess up your relationship. Plan a wedding you can feasibly afford. Remember that you still have to live after you marry. A budget for your relationship is just as critical as a budget for your life. I suggest you set up four bank accounts for after the wedding: a joint account for ALL of the bills, a joint savings account that requires both signatures to withdraw, and then each couple should have their own accounts for the special things they like to do or purchase without needing to account for the spending with the partner. Trust me, this helps!

Whether you are waiting for sex until after marriage or have become physically intimate beforehand, making love better means that you are creating the foundation of friendship and sex whenever you are together. Foreplay begins with your conversation and actions toward one another! It often doesn't start in the bedroom.

As you consider marrying one another, discuss how you plan to be spontaneous in your marriage and build your intimacy. After the honeymoon comes the children, the bills, the extended work hours, and before you know it if you aren't vigilant, your INTIMACY is gone out the window. Infidelity has the power to destroy what you have built, and what you won't do for each other, someone else will. Above all else, be committed to your commitment!

Create simplicity in your lives and your schedules so you will have quality time with each other. Date night is always a winner, but spicing things up is even better! What are your expectations and requests about your love life after marriage? Consider being creative, even when you don't feel like it;

taking action can get you in the mood. Men like when their wives initiate lovemaking, and women appreciate when their husbands pitch in and help make their home life easier.

If you want to enhance your intimacy, consider doing the following fun and romantic actions as you are courting one another (and remember to keep doing them after you're married!):

- Have a movie night for two. Get creative and print movie passes, as well as pick up all of your favorite snacks such as popcorn, candy, and other treats that you may like and enjoy.

- Cooking together can always add spice to your relationship. You can prepare your favorite dishes together. Add in foods to stimulate the senses such as honey, ginger, or pineapple, and enjoy great conversation, intimacy, and an opportunity to connect with one another and share some laughs and great conversation.

- Set up a day to celebrate your mate and let them know just how important they are and how much you appreciate them. If you are not sexually involved, this could include sending flowers or a plant to a home or office, writing a love letter, doing their errands, and taking them out to a favorite restaurant. If you are sexually intimate with each other, consider chocolate kisses on the pillow in the morning, a romantic invitation on scented paper, or enjoying an evening with a relaxing bubble bath, soothing music, and fresh rose petals on the bed to set the mood.

Your marriage has to work for the two of you! Be very careful how much input you seek from family and friends, both before you marry and afterward. While it's great to have a sounding board and a cheering squad, remember that your primary focus is developing and maintaining an amazing friendship and relationship with your partner and then your spouse.

Finally, as a married couple, know that on this journey you WILL be tested. Remember that you are a team, and you are in this love together. Twogether, you can withstand!

If you ask **Yolanda "Yanni" Brown**, "What's love got to do with it?" she answers without hesitation, "Everything." As CEO and Founder of Kiss & Make Up with Intimate Evenings, this forty-two-year-old Certified Relationship Educator and romance aficionado has made the celebration of LOVE her business. Yanni helps women, as well as committed, engaged, and married couples as they navigate through the challenges that accompany love, life, and the pursuit of happiness. Yanni is currently working on her own book, and she can be reached at: yanni@intimateevenings.com; www.intimateevenings.com; P. O. Box 118211, Chicago, IL 60611, 312-719-6632.

❤ ❤ ❤

Having a Healthy Couple Relationship
Ana Morante

Marriage is a very important institution, and it's possibly one of the most difficult things that any couple will do in their lives. It's very important to get ready for something of that caliber.

Self-Preparation

To have a healthy couple relationship, it's not as much a matter of *finding* the right person as it is actually *being* the right person. We should ask ourselves, "Am I the type of person that I would like to be married to?" To have a good, solid, healthy couple relationship, we have to start with ourselves. We have to start recognizing who we are, and, within that, we have to see what our gifts are and find the good things within ourselves that strengthen us.

We all carry baggage from our pasts. Maybe it is from the way we were raised or from the family we came from. When we are not aware of that baggage, it can get in the way of us enjoying our lives and actually performing the way we want to. One of the first things I suggest before even considering entering a serious relationship is take a look at yourself and find out what your strong points are, the things you are proud of. Also, it's important to find some of the areas of challenge that you need to face or work on.

Difficulties come when people enter relationships and do not feel good about themselves. They want to feel loved and accepted by someone else, yet they cannot do it for themselves! That puts a lot of expectations and pressure on the other person. Most of the time, those expectations lead to disappointment, because nobody can give us what we need to give to ourselves. Therefore, good marriage preparation starts with looking at yourself and seeing the areas you need to work on to feel more content…and you must be willing to do that work.

Committing to Being a Couple

Once we enter a couple relationship, one of the most important tasks is the commitment we make to it. Your lifestyles are going to change, especially if it's a relationship you expect to be long term. There is a vast difference between lifestyles when you go from being single to being married, and you have to be willing to face and make adjustments.

One of the first and most difficult changes is that from now on, you must be able to see life from a different perspective. Rather than just thinking about "me," now you need to think in terms of "we." When there is a disagreement, the best deal is going to be the one that works for BOTH of you. This usually brings a lot of challenges, because many times, some of the needs you both have are going to be in conflict. To address this transition successfully, you need three main skills:

- The ability to speak up for what you want and need
- The ability to listen to what your partner wants and needs. Listening doesn't necessarily mean you agree, but at least you can see your partner's point of view.
- The ability to cooperate and work toward finding a solution you can both live with.

When we are able to speak up for our needs and listen to the other person, we are in a better position to be able to cooperate so that we can find agreements that work for both of us. The best deal is the deal where we both feel like winners and where we are both able to satisfy our needs.

Editor's Note: The above is excerpted and edited from an interview between Susanne Alexander and Ana Morante on March 10, 2010.

Ana Morante, L.M.F.T., C.F.L.E., is a bilingual Marriage, Family, and Child Therapist, helping people in both Spanish and English. She is dedicated to strengthening couples and families and assisting in the creation of the best environment possible for children. She has a private practice in San Jose, California, and is a certified Parent and Family Life Educator and a Family Wellness Partner and Trainer. Ana has been married for sixteen years and has two daughters and a stepson. She can be reached through www.familywellness.com.

♥ ♥ ♥

The Value of Mentor Couples
Robert A. Ruhnke, D.Min.

After years of working to improve large group programs in my Catholic diocese (such as Pre Cana and Engaged Encounter), I came to the conclusion that it is *more effective and efficient to work with couples individually*. While no system is perfect—and this is not to say that large group programs have no value—the "couple-to-couple" mentor system continues to validate itself as a better process. As you are dating, courting, and considering marrying, I strongly encourage you to find a Mentor Couple to work with.

Case Study

As an example, let's look at Heidi Hicks and Tony Battle, a couple who would sail through any marriage preparation course and probably walk away saying, "That was great." I dealt with them off and on as their pastor and specifically talked with each of them about the value of prayer. When they became officially engaged, I sent them to Jerry Velasquez and Mary Velasquez, Ph.D., a married couple who were willing to be their mentors. After Heidi's and Tony's wedding, I asked for their feedback:

> Before we met our Mentor Couple, we were nervous. From talking to other couples who had gone through marriage preparation (not Father Rob's version), we thought this experience would be embarrassing and uncomfortable. We also felt like we knew everything about one another, so there would be no surprises! We got a lot out of our meetings. Not only did we become friends with a great couple with whom we shared similar values and morals, but Tony and I also learned things to make our marriage better.
>
> Mary and Jerry shared ideas with us that will stick with us forever. They made us a better couple just by being honest and sincere with us. They are a couple to model our relationship on. We did find out new things about one another. Some of the questions in the book are questions I normally would not have thought to ask before, but the answers to these questions are important. Tony and I were surprised about a few answers, but in a good way!

It has been most helpful to know that we have couple friends who we can talk openly and honestly with. They have been through the same issues and things we have. It is helpful to know we are normal, and other couples have the same problems. The *most important thing* Tony and I have learned from our Mentor Couple is to pray together. We never felt comfortable about this before. Mary and Jerry taught us that praying together is important. We now say our prayers together every night. We would definitely like to stay in touch [with our Mentor Couple]. They are like an extra support system. Sometimes you just can't tell your family about problems in your marriage, because they tend to take sides. Mary and Jerry have never done this, and we trust their judgment and advice.

This case study demonstrates that the couple-to-couple format allows for much deeper honesty and vulnerability. The engaged couple is very likely to learn skills (prayer, for instance) which were "only theory" prior to their sessions together. Heidi comes from a family that has no inhibitions about praying and talking about prayer. But it is clear from this feedback, that Heidi and Tony *were not able to pray together before they "learned" this from Jerry and Mary.* I think that is very significant. I know prayer was very familiar to Heidi and how much I had talked about prayer when giving private instruction to Tony. I also knew how much I had specifically talked about the value of praying together, but none of my instruction "taught" Heidi and Tony how to pray together. *It was the sessions with Jerry and Mary that made a significant difference!*

Robert A. Ruhnke, C.SS.R., M.Th., D.Min., was ordained a Catholic priest in 1966. In 1975, as Family Life Director for the Archdiocese of Galveston-Houston, Texas, he began to train married couples to function as sponsors (mentors) for couples preparing for marriage. In 1996, he began Marriage Preparation Resources (www.marriagepreparation.com) to make himself available to churches that wanted to set up the For Better and For Ever marriage preparation program, which he developed. He is also available online to assist those seeking information about Christian marriage and other personal/faith concerns and questions. Father Ruhnke currently lives in San Antonio, Texas.

❤ ❤ ❤

Marriage Advice for Premarital Couples
Matthew Turvey, Psy.D.

Before my wife and I tied the knot, we did three important things: we prayed; we got the blessing of our parents; and we prepared. Our preparation involved taking a PREPARE-ENRICH relationship inventory (This is fitting, I know, since I now work for the organization!).We also sought the advice and wisdom of all the older happily married couples we could find. We wanted to benefit from their experience on their marital journey. Almost fifteen years later, the following are the results of what we learned then and from our experiences since then:

- Remember that marriage is a lifelong journey. It won't always be easy, pretty, fun, or romantic. When two imperfect people team up in holy matrimony, it's always a bit of a mess. Nobody's perfect. Give your spouse the benefit of the doubt. Practice generosity every chance you get. Unless you have some pretty definite evidence otherwise, always assume your spouse has your best interests in mind.

- Have some fun. Laugh every day. Get away from the kids and the in-laws every once in a while. Protect your marriage above all else.

- Have good sex. Kiss a lot. Hug even more. Be there for your spouse when they need you.

- Don't sweat the small stuff. Live a little. Be silly every Tuesday. Don't take your spouse too seriously, but you better be serious about your marriage.

- There's no perfect marriage, no perfect spouse, no perfect relationship advice, so stop thinking you'll find it someday. A strong marriage is full of mistakes, but a strong marriage means being intentional and learning and working to fix those mistakes.

- If you start thinking someday that the grass is greener on the other side, that's because somebody over there is taking the time to water it, weed it, mow it, trim it, and make it his baby. Always remember your marriage can be that green.

- Never give up on your spouse, your marriage, your kids, or your family. Life's too short for giving up. Your marriage can last and be a wonderful place of hope, satisfaction, and fun.

I've come to believe that marriage preparation is different for every couple. You will make the best choices for you from the wide variety of options that includes such things as counseling, coaching, skills training, education, assessments, religious teaching, and mentoring. Please commit to and do something. Be intentional about investing in your relationship before marriage, and in your marriage partnership after the wedding. Who knows…maybe someday you'll be the older happily married couple that young couples seek out for marital advice and wisdom.

Matthew Turvey, Psy.D., L.P., is the Vice President of Outreach for PREPARE-ENRICH (www.prepare-enrich.com). He is a licensed psychologist with a specialization in Marriage and Family Therapy and oversees many of PREPARE-ENRICH's strategic partnerships and marketing efforts. He is the author of several articles on marriage and family topics, especially relational wellness in the workplace. Dr. Turvey has been married for almost fifteen years to his beautiful bride Nicole, and together they have three young children that keep them hopping, tired, and forever laughing.

© 2010 M. Turvey

❤ ❤ ❤

Exercises to Help You Prepare for Marriage
Sue Atkins

Applying the Values of Your Wedding Ceremony

Grab a cup of coffee and a pen, turn off your mobile phone, and make sure you won't be interrupted for the next thirty minutes or so.

Find six sheets of paper each, and write on them the headings below, one at the top of each sheet. Note: These headings are taken from one of the common marriage ceremonies. You may have chosen something different for yourselves, so choose to work on the values noted in it instead, if you prefer.

Headings:

1. To have and to hold

2. From this day forward

3. For better, for worse

4. For richer, for poorer

5. In sickness and in health

6. To love and to cherish

Take as much time as you need to write under each heading what you *think* each one is about. Focus on all the things you hope, dream, and wish for yourself and your partner. Be totally honest with yourself about your doubts and fears. Just relax and breathe deeply and slowly and allow whatever comes up inside of you to come out on paper. This is an excellent way to gain clarity, direction, and focus about what marriage and having a family means to you.

If you need help thinking of what to write down, consider the questions below.

To have and to hold. What does being a couple mean? What are your beliefs about faithfulness, loyalty, respect, and sharing? How much time do you want to spend together and apart? What things will you share, and what things should be private?

From this day forward. What are your feelings about commitment? How do you feel about divorce? How might the relationship change over the years? Where do children fit into your plans? How many children do you want? Do you share the same views on religion, education, and discipline for the children? How will you feel and what will you do if you can't have children?

For better, for worse. How will you increase and keep intimacy going in your relationship? How will you manage differences? What will you do if big issues arise? How do you habitually handle problems now, and how will that differ after marriage?

For richer, for poorer. What difference will marriage make for you financially? Will your attitudes toward employment change? Do you have the same values about working, borrowing money, saving, and spending? How are you likely to respond if one or both of you become unemployed? What do you feel about staying home to look after children, carrying on working, or childcare? Whose "job" is it to bring up the children? How will you share getting up in the night, staying off work, or changing nappies (diapers)?

In sickness and in health. How will you support each other during illness? During ill health among other family members? What does spousal help look like for you at times of sadness and difficulty?

To love and to cherish. How will you both demonstrate and express love in your marriage? How often do you need to have these demonstrations and expressions happen? How important will sex be in your relationship? What are your expectations for frequency and quality?

Once you've finished, take some time to talk through together what you've written. Think about where some of your feelings and expectations have come from. What is truly realistic in your marriage? What are you committed to do together to make things happen?

If doing this exercise leaves either of you feeling uncomfortable or with concerns about your relationship, try getting a sense of clarity about why you love your partner and what you want and expect from your relationship. Then find some quiet time to talk through your feelings, worries, anxieties, or concerns with a trusted friend or a trained counselor.

A high-level marriage isn't just a ring and a piece of paper; it's the way you treat each other every day. Make sure you are clear about the general direction you are going, because when your toddler keeps you up four nights in a row looking for her Cinderella handbag, you need to have the bigger picture very clearly in your head about where you are both going and how and why you are going there together.

Looking Back from Your Rocking Chair

Begin by imagining you're well into your nineties and your children have grown up and had families of their own. Picture this very clearly in your mind.

Now, visualize yourself surrounded by your wonderful family and then ask these questions:

- How does it feel having all your family together?
- What would your son or daughter say is the best thing about having you as a parent?
- What do they love most about you?
- How do they describe you to their children?
- How do you want them to describe you to their children?
- How would that description make you feel?
- If you could ask your future self just one question, what would it be? What would be the answer?
- What have been the highlights in your family relationships?
- What steps can you take to make sure those outcomes happen?

Now, visualize your children clearly in your mind. Then ask yourself the following questions:

- What type of parents do you want them to be?
- What values do you want them to demonstrate?
- When they look back at their childhoods, what do you want them to remember?
- What memories have you built in them that will last forever?
- What wonderful stories about their childhoods will they share with their own children?
- What steps can you take from now on to make sure those outcomes happen?

Creating Memories

Building happy family memories definitely doesn't depend on how much money you spend on your kids or whether they've got the latest technological gadgets. Positive memories depend on the time and attention and love you give your children. It depends on the funny moments, the traditions, and the being-together times.

So, take some time and consider what memories you want your children to have. Write your thoughts down. This will help clarify and focus you on what you want to achieve.

Now, take a deep breath and smile. It's time to go create memories together today and plan for new ones in the future.

Sue Atkins is a Parent and Relationship Coach based in Lingfield, Surry, England. She is the author of *Raising Happy Children for Dummies*, and she is the Judge for National Family Week "Family of the Year." Sue also appears regularly on *BBC Breakfast TV* and *The Jeremy Vine Show* on BBC Radio 2, which has over 6,000,000 daily listeners. To receive her free newsletter bursting with practical tips and helpful advice, go to www.positive-parents.com or buy her *Parental Journey* audio CD and ideas book at www.positive-parentsclub.com/The_parental_journey_audio_CD_and_ideas_book.htm.

♥ ♥ ♥

Preparing Teens for Marriage
Ana Morante

The first way to help our teenagers prepare for marriage is by modeling a good, strong marriage for them to witness. Children learn much more from what they see than from what they hear. They see our behaviors on a daily basis. If they see people who are able to respect, love, and care for themselves and do the same thing for their spouse and their children, that's what the children are going to be used to, and that's what they're going to look for in a partner.

It is also wise for parents to treat children the way you would like their future partners to treat them. Many times—especially during times of stress—parents don't think and just act or react too quickly. If we get frustrated and hit the kids or make derogatory remarks, we need to ask ourselves, "Do I want my child to be treated this way by their partner when they get into a relationship?" If the answer is "no," we need to stop that behavior and start modeling what a healthy, respectful, loving relationship is like. Sometimes, parents may realize they need help to behave differently. Getting help for oneself is another great life skill to model for our children.

It is also important to share your values with your children, what you see as important for you in your life. Especially with teenagers, it is very helpful to listen. By the time our kids are teenagers, they have already had plenty of opportunities to listen to us and to see our behavior. They pretty much know who we are and what we are about. Their task at this point is to start figuring out who they are and who they want to be—and be with. The best way to help them in that process is by listening to them. When we listen, they have to talk, and when they talk, they have to think. "Think, before you act" is one of the most important things we can teach our kids, and listening helps them to think.

When we listen to our children, we allow them the opportunity to put together everything they've seen so far from us and from other people in their lives, including other family members. They will also think about what they've seen in the movies and the media in general, and they'll start processing all of it and weighing it against their own life path. They will begin thinking, "What is it that I want now for my life?"

In order to show teenagers what they should want out of a happy marriage, we need to show them a happy marriage in the first place.

Editor's Note: The above is excerpted and edited from an interview between Susanne Alexander and Ana Morante on March 10, 2010.

Ana Morante, L.M.F.T., C.F.L.E., is a bilingual Marriage, Family, and Child Therapist, helping people in both Spanish and English. She is dedicated to strengthening couples and families and assisting in the creation of the best environment possible for children. She has a private practice in San Jose, California, and is a certified Parent and Family Life Educator and a Family Wellness Partner and Trainer. Ana has been married for sixteen years and has two daughters and a stepson. She can be reached through www.familywellness.com.

Chapter Two
Pacing and Timing Togetherness

~ ~

Are you feeling like you are racing toward intimacy and marriage? Or, are you already deeply involved in trying to behave like a married couple? This section will help you to see the wisdom in participating in the relationship-strengthening and commitment process at an even pace. We will help you take relationship and courting steps in a certain order to maximize your success. If you are already out of step with the recommended order, not to worry—you will just proceed as best as you can while making wise choices from here on out.

In addition, there are selections addressed to people who are considering marrying at a younger age and for those at an older and more mature stage in life. Happy and successful marriages can happen at any time in life.

♥ ♥ ♥

Pace It!
Emily Luschin

Nathan is getting ready to pop the question. He's trying to maintain his usual cool, but his excitement is palpable. Both he and Sarah will graduate from law school this spring. After that, they'll be heading off to Los Angeles to work in big law firms.

"We're excited to start work this fall. I've already talked to some lawyers about confidentiality rules for spouses. We've also found some awesome apartments close to each other downtown. We think it might be fun to get married in Los Angeles, but we'll probably do it in Seattle where Sarah's family is…."

Nathan is talking a mile a minute. I glance over at Sarah. She's chatting with another conference attendee. There's no ring on her finger…yet.

As a marriage researcher, I can't help but ask myself, how did they reach this point? They are at a crossroads in their relationship and in their careers. Where does Nathan's confidence come from? How is he so sure he wants to marry Sarah? They could easily go their separate ways. Why go together, let alone for life?

To answer these questions, I reflect on their story. They've known each other for two and a half years and dated for about two. They took classes together, studied together, ate dinner together, attended Jewish High Holy Day activities together, and commiserated during final exams. They have built a deep friendship around common interests, they enjoy each other's company, and they share the same outlook and life goals. In Nathan's own words, "I'm totally comfortable with Sarah. It's awesome to have someone I can talk to about everything, who talks to me about everything. Only…" he pauses and grins, "…you don't get away with anything. She knows if I'm complaining too much about a professor, because she's been there."

Suddenly it becomes clear. According to the research, Nathan and Sarah have done it right. From the beginning, they have *paced* their relationship. They pace it even now. Pacing has enabled them to judge more clearly where they want the relationship to go. It has ultimately freed them to choose with greater confidence.

Pacing is essentially building a relationship through a *smart, logical progression.*[1] The theory behind pacing is that committed, successful relationships don't just appear out of thin air. They are built over time. They are built because they require investment and energy. They require time because this building occurs over an extended period of days, months, and years. The question is always how to build a relationship well and with confidence. Are there "best practices" in building strategies to maximize relational success and prepare for marriage? Is there a "best way" to pace the building process?

The answer is yes! Research points to a number of ways couples can pace the building of their relationship. Below are a handful of examples that can help you as you prepare for marriage:

1. **Develop a shared history.** An important part of pacing is developing common memories and a shared history. You build this connection over time as you date and get to know each other. Not taking time to develop a shared

history can put your future marriage at risk. Warning signs that you may not have spent enough time on this process (as outlined by Dr. Neil Clark Warren[2]) are:

- Deciding to get married very quickly after meeting
- Deciding to get married too young
- Starting married life with too narrow an experience base
- Being too eager to get married

Marrying as a teenager is the highest known risk factor of divorce.[3] However, from about age twenty-one to twenty-seven, the risk of divorce plateaus. After twenty-seven, the risk declines slightly, and after thirty, the risk of divorce plateaus again.[4] These declines are due in large part to maturity.[5] Dr. Warren and others point out that in our society, adolescence can often last until the middle twenties.[6] *Too young* means getting married before forming your own identity. This includes emotionally separating from parents and defining your individual goals and needs.

Because this history-building process takes time, don't rush into marriage. To broaden your experience base, be sure to spend time together in a variety of settings and circumstances. For example, a college friend liked to take the girl he was seeing on an all-day hike. Besides having fun together, the experience showed him how she responded to a new circumstance, strenuous activity, fatigue, and stress, especially if they left early in the morning.

Doing a variety of things together often lets you learn new things about each other. Over time, you might discover some qualities or quirks you wouldn't have noticed otherwise. You might even reconsider a prospective spouse. My friend Greg is a good example. He and his now-wife dated for four months before getting engaged. Most of their dates involved hiking, which he loved and she seemed to enjoy as well, but after they got married, she refused to go hiking. He could have spared himself disappointment if he had taken the time to get to know her better through a variety of experiences, including but not limited to hiking. He might have still chosen to marry her, but he would have had a more solid, varied foundation. Another wife joked that she wished she'd dated her husband for more than nine months, because she would have discovered his annual love affair with tennis! Developing a shared history will spare you some potentially unpleasant surprises after marriage, help you be certain of your choice of marriage partner, and build a stronger foundation of connection for marriage.

2. Choose not to have casual sex (sometimes referred to as "hooking up"). Following this pacing principle may seem like a tall order. The hook-up (casual sex) culture is alive and well, as explored in Elizabeth Marquardt and Norval Glenn's study of the dating experiences of women on college campuses.[7] But despite its ubiquity, choosing not to hook up will allow you to pace your relationship and maximize your chances for relational satisfaction. The reason is that sex—casual or not—is extremely bonding.[8] Research has found that during sexual intercourse, powerful chemicals are released into the brain, including oxytocin for women and vasopressin for men. Both of these chemicals create a powerful, partly biochemical bond between partners.[9] Before marriage, choosing not to hook up gives you time to consider whether and how you want to bond with another person. After marriage, choosing not to have sex with anyone other than your spouse strengthens the trust, safety, and bond of your relationship.

3. Choose not to live together until you're engaged, planning to marry, or are married. Many couples believe living together (cohabiting) before marriage is smart. The intent is to "test out" the relationship to see if there is compatibility and readiness for marriage. This is actually a myth. In fact, couples who live together before marriage—without plans to marry or an engagement—are more likely to divorce.[10] Also, "serial cohabitation" (having more than one cohabiting partner in succession) increases your risk of divorce.[11] You can increase your chances for marital success if you choose to live together only after you plan to marry, are engaged, or are married.

4. Ask each other direct and detailed questions. Asking the right questions is part of getting to know each other well.[12] This is an important part of building an enduring relationship. The more you learn about each other, the better you can judge if you want the relationship to progress toward marriage. Some helpful questions to ask and discuss with each other are:

- What are your likes and dislikes?
- What are your hobbies?
- How much do you work or prefer to work?
- What are your dreams, ambitions, and goals?
- How do you respond to me emotionally, including when you're upset or frustrated?
- What do we have in common?

- What do we enjoy doing together in our free time?
- How much time do we prefer to spend together and separately?

When you start seriously thinking about marriage, other questions to consider include:

- Why do we want to marry generally? Why do we want to marry one another specifically? What does marriage mean to us?
- What do we want to accomplish in our lives?
- How will we manage our money?
- What are our financial goals?
- Do we want to have children? How many?
- How long should we wait before we have children?
- How do we plan to approach disciplining children we will have? Already have?
- How do we handle disagreements? What causes them to escalate into conflict? How could we improve?
- How much time do we want to spend with our in-laws and/or extended family?
- How will we express and share our spiritual/religious beliefs?
- How will we divide up housework?
- How do we want to spend our time away from work? Our vacations?
- What are our beliefs and commitments about being faithful to each other?
- What do we see as our future goals?

5. **Enroll in a research-based relationship skills education class.** Relationship education classes are fun and informative (and not group therapy). They can equip you with research-based skills and knowledge to form and sustain a healthy, successful relationship. Classes are available for every age and relationship stage, including high school students, singles, courting and engaged couples, newlyweds, new parents, and empty-nesters. To find classes in your area, go to Smart Marriages®: The Coalition for Marriage, Family, and Couples Education at: www.smartmarriages.com/app/Directory.BrowsePrograms.

6. **Take a research-based online relationship inventory/assessment.** Relationship inventories are for everyone, whether single, dating, engaged, or married. They provide personalized couple advice and online or in-person relationship assessments. Research on the RELATE program found that couples consistently report higher relationship satisfaction after reviewing their personalized reports.[13]

Pacing is a broad, yet powerful relationship principle. It includes everything from asking the right questions about your partner and the relationship, to equipping yourself with research-based skills and knowledge, to choosing the timing of sex. Doing all of these things allows you to judge more clearly whether you know one another well enough to marry and directs where you want the relationship to go. Taking time to know one another well also provides more confidence in making relationship decisions. Pacing frees you to build a stronger relationship now in preparation for marriage later!

1 A prolific scholar on this subject is Dr. John Van Epp. For further reading, see *How to Avoid Falling in Love with a Jerk*. New York: McGraw-Hill, 2008.

2 Warren, Neil Clark. *Finding the Love of Your Life*. Wheaton, Illinois: Tyndale House Publishers, 1998.

3 Popenoe, David, and Barbara Defoe Whitehead. "Information Brief: Ten Important Research Findings on Choosing a Marriage Partner—Helpful Facts for Young Adults." The National Marriage Project. www.virginia.edu/marriageproject/pdfs/pubTenThingsYoungAdults.pdf (accessed March 16, 2010).

4 Heaton, Tim B. "Factors Contributing to Increasing Marital Stability in the United States." *Journal of Family Issues* 23, no. 3 (2002): 392-409.; Lehrer, Evelyn. "Age at Marriage and Marital Instability: Revisiting the Becker–Landes–Michael Hypothesis." *Journal of Population Economics* 21, no. 2 (2008): 463-484.

5 Lehrer, Evelyn. "Age at Marriage and Marital Instability: Revisiting the Becker–Landes–Michael Hypothesis." *Journal of Population Economics* 21, no. 2 (2008): 463-484.

6 Oppenheimer, Valerie K. "A Theory of Marriage Timing." *The American Journal of Sociology* 94.3 (1988): 563-591.

7 Glenn, Norval and Elizabeth Marquardt. *Hooking Up, Hanging Out, and Hoping for Mr. Right: College Women on Dating and Mating Today*. An Institute for American Values' Report to the Independent Women's Forum. 2001.

8 Bush, Frieda McKissic, and Joe S. McLlhaney Jr. *Why Isn't Anyone Telling Our Kids About the Other Dangers of Casual Sex?* Presentation at The Family Research Council, Washington, DC. March 25, 2009. 42-44.; Bush, Freda Mckissic, Jr, and Joe S. Mcilhaney. Hooked: New Science on How Casual Sex is Affecting Our Children. Chicago, IL: Northfield Publishing, 2008.

9 Ibid

10 Demaris, Alfred, and K. Vaninadha Rao. "Premarital Cohabitation and Subsequent Marital Stability in the United States: A Reassessment." *Journal of Marriage and the Family* 54 (1992): 178-190; Wu, Zheng. *Cohabitation: An Alternative Form of Family Living (Studies in Canadian Population)*. New York: Oxford University Press, USA, 2001. 149; Dush, Claire, Catherine Cohan, and Paul Amato. "The relationship between cohabitation and marital quality and stability: Change across cohorts?." *Journal of Marriage and Family* 65 (2003): 539-49; Kline, Galena, Howard Markman, Scott Stanley, Michelle St. Peters, Sarah Whitton, Lydia Prado, and P. Antonio Olmos-Gallo. " Timing is everything: Pre-engagement cohabitation

and increased risk for poor marital outcomes." *Journal of Family Psychology* 18 (2004): 311-18.

11 Teachman, Jay. Premarital sex, premarital cohabitation and the risk of subsequent marital dissolution among women. *Journal of Marriage and Family* 65 (2003): 444-55.

12 Stritof, Sheri & Bob. "Questions for Engaged Couples—Questions to Discuss Before You Get Married." Marriage —THE starting place for exploring marriage and marriage issues. http://marriage.about.com/od/engagement/ss/engagedissues.htm (accessed March 22, 2010).

13 "Home - The RELATE Institute." www.relate-institute.org/ (accessed March 17, 2010).

Emily Luschin, M.Ed., is an affiliate scholar at the Institute for American Values (www.americanvalues.org). She began working in the field of marriage and family as a Research Assistant on the National Healthy Marriage Resource Center in the School of Family Life at Brigham Young University. Thereafter, Emily was a program analyst for the Administration for Children and Families, Department of Health and Human Services, where she founded and served as Managing Editor of the *African American Healthy Marriage Initiative Newsletter* (2006-2007). She teaches marriage and relationship education classes and is a Certified Gottman Educator. Her publications include the *Healthy Marriage Initiative Activities and Accomplishments 2006* and *Military Service and Marriage: A Review of the Research*. Contact information: Institute for American Values, 1841 Broadway, Suite 211, New York, NY 10023; Telephone: 212-246-3942. Emily lives in Tokyo, Japan, with her husband and daughter.

♥ ♥ ♥

The Law of Relationship Order
Krsnanandini Devi Dasi and Tariq Saleem Ziyad

Before you get married, there is a key relationship principle you should follow to get the best results and avoid a negative, unhealthy relationship or marriage break-up. This dynamic relationship principle is the "Law of Relationship Order," and it is illustrated below by using a math analogy.

In mathematics, there is a law or principle called the "Order of Operations." It states: In a relationship of numbers, when more than one number is to be connected in some way through any of the following operations—addition, subtraction, multiplication, or division—there is a definite order in which these numbers must connect in order to get the correct answer or result.

In this mathematical law, we find the sequence in which operations *must* be performed when more than one operation is involved:

- When there are parentheses, do the operations within the parentheses first.
- Then multiply, working from left to right.
- Then divide, working from left to right.
- Then add, working from left to right.
- Finally subtract, again working from left to right.

To see how this works, try computing this formula: 4 + (10 x 2)

1. What result do we get when we don't follow the Order of Operations, simply going from left to right?

4 plus 10 = 14; 14 times 2 = 28

This answer is incorrect. Why? Because we did not follow the Order of Operations.

2. What answer do we get when we do it the right way and follow the Order of Operations? We first perform the operation inside the parentheses and then figure out the equation, from left to right.

10 times 2 = 20; 20 plus 4 = 24

This is the correct answer. Why? Because by following the Order of Operations, we get it right.

Similarly, the Law of Relationship Order, a fundamental principle of human relationships, can be stated as outlined below.

The order in which **healthy** relationships develop is that two people:

- First, get to *know* each other, especially each other's character
- Then, develop *trust* between one another
- Next, make sure you can *depend* on each other
- Next, make a *commitment* to one another
- Last, engage in *intimate physical touch* only *after* the commitment of marriage.

In other words, in people connections, as in math connections, there is a sequence, an order, that people need to follow to have healthy, successful relationships with positive outcomes. The process is as follows:

1. **Know:** You meet someone, observe, and become familiar with their ways, habits, and characteristics. You will consider a wide range of aspects about the person such as: Are they courteous, polite, mean, or irritable most of the time? What is their relationship with God? How often do they become angry? How do they treat their mother, father, and other elders? What are their hobbies? Do they live a structured or haphazard life? How do they handle money? Do they owe major debts? Are there any exes to worry about? Do they have children? How do they treat strangers? Can they laugh at themselves? Are they a clean person? Do they abuse drugs or alcohol? Do they have a sense of humor? What are their feelings about things that are important to you? Also, carefully consider how you met the other person. Was it through a trusted friend or relative, at a library, school, grocery, or other public place, or was it at a bar where people may be more likely to put on a false face?

2. **Trust:** Building a healthy relationship means this person's habits, activities, words, and actions are based on principles and behavioral patterns you can count on. Do you have confidence in the integrity and honesty of this person? For example, can you depend on them to tell the truth, be clean, have compassion for others, and consider you first sometimes? Also, at this stage, find out the honest opinion of some of your family members and friends about this person.

3. **Depend:** Dependability is a deeper expression of trust. It indicates a teammate attitude, a partner you can rely on to get things done. This is someone you can depend on who provides emotional and practical support. At this stage, you should know that this person is dependable, that you can rely on them to be honest, to keep their promises, and to have certain ethical or moral principles of behavior. In other words, you can trust this person to act in socially healthy or mature ways most of the time. Do they accept responsibility for taking good care of you by being respectful and emotionally supportive? And for treating you with dignity, love, and appreciation? Can you ask them to look out for someone very dear to you and be almost certain they will take good care of your loved one? If you are having a problem, can you depend on this person to make their best effort to help you? Romance and attraction aside, is this person your friend?

4. **Commitment:** After you have come to know someone and can assure yourself that this person is worthy of your trust and you can depend on them,

then you can mentally, emotionally, and verbally commit yourself to a deeper relationship. Generally, commitment refers to forming an engagement that leads to marriage.

5. **Intimate Physical Touch:** After you know someone well, can trust and depend on them, and you realize you can make a marriage commitment to this special someone and that they can make a commitment to you, then and only then should there be intimate touch. Degrees of intimate touch range from holding hands, embracing, kissing, and finally sexual intercourse. We recommend that sexual intercourse be reserved for *after* marriage.

At this point, you are probably saying to yourself, "Who follows this Law of Relationship Order in today's world?"

Put in the words of the ditty that we learned as children:

"First, comes love" (Know, Trust, and Depend on one another)

"Then comes marriage" (Commitment)

"Then comes the baby in the baby carriage" (Results from Intimate Touch)

Unfortunately, in our contemporary society, many, many people neglect this process and do the steps out of order. Men and women intimately touch each other long before they know each other well or feel they can trust or depend on one another. "Hooking up," one-night stands, having multiple partners, and cohabitation are commonplace, especially in Western culture. Sometimes people hastily marry a person before they really know them, before they have learned whether they can count on that person, before they have developed trust in them, and prior to having a solid commitment to one another that will last.

The result of neglecting the Law of Relationship Order has been disastrous for relationships, producing high divorce rates, out-of-wedlock children, bitterness, and enduring emotional scars. Therefore, be determined to proceed with a deeper commitment for relationship success from this point on by following the Law of Relationship Order when you are in a relationship that you want to lead to marriage.

Krsnanandini Devi Dasi and **Tariq Saleem Ziyad** are Co-Directors of Dasi-Ziyad Family Institute based in Cleveland, Ohio, an agency that provides a number of curricula, courses, and workshops (www.dzfi.org). Their educational services have empowered hundreds of couples, families, and individuals with healthy relationship skills. Krsnanandini holds degrees in Education and Sociology. Tariq has degrees in Psychology and Business Management. Dasi and Ziyad are Certified Family Life Educators (CFLEs), Certified Family Wellness Instructors, PREPARE-ENRICH Coaches, members of the National Council on Family Relations, and co-authors of several magazine and newspaper articles about healthy families, parenting, relationships, and marriage. This husband-and-wife team is the 2008 recipient of the Nguzo Saba Award for promoting community and family unity from the Imani Foundation. Featured in the popular book, *Cleveland Couples: 40 Inspiring Stories of Love and Commitment* by Kathy Dawson, Krsnanandini and Tariq have nineteen children altogether. She is the biological mother of ten of them—enough to keep them "working to empower families for a long time."

❤ ❤ ❤

Marrying Young
Mark Gungor

A multitude of studies and surveys have been released in the past several years touting the idea that there is a perfect or ideal age for people to marry. Some of these same studies and surveys also claim there is a certain education level, income level, geographic area, and religious preference that determines whether or not you will be happily married or even stay married at all. And while most people don't pay much attention to some of these "ideals," they do seem to grab a tight hold on the age at which you marry as being an indicator of future marriage success.

When the possibility of someone marrying at a younger age arises, there tends to be strong objections from all directions. Many decry the potential marriage of eighteen- to twenty-two-year-olds as a terrible idea since the couple is "too young," but it wasn't long ago that such a marriage would not have been thought of as unusual. And, it's vital that we now seriously consider going back to supporting young marriages. It's common for people to think that waiting or delaying marriage until you are almost thirty years of age is the best possible option. They believe you need to get your college degree, have enough money, and sow all your wild oats before you can possibly consider settling down into marriage.

We know that sexual activity before marriage increases the likelihood of a divorce. We also know that couples who live together have an even higher rate of divorce. (Two very under-reported studies that have also been done!)

But then, we tell young people today that they should wait until they are almost thirty to marry—an age that will most likely guarantee they will have been already sexually active or even have lived with someone already. How is that going to help build successful marriages? Waiting until this age only encourages young people to pick up all kinds of emotional and physical baggage when they are out there doing it all wrong, going from one relationship to another.

Even in the Christian community (a group who should know better), we push and encourage delayed marriage. Parents often threaten their young people with negative consequences if they marry young. "We won't pay for your education!...You'll have to pay for your own wedding!...We'll disown you!"... We pull all financial and emotional support from the young couple, and then when they fail, we rush back to them with "I told you so..." What these couples need is exactly the opposite. They should have all the support and help that a family can give. After all, you would think parents would actually want their kids to succeed in their marriages.

Mormons bring an interesting perspective to marriage. Only 6 percent of those who follow the demands surrounding a temple marriage end up in divorce. Only 6 percent! But it's not just a question of getting married in a certain place. Leaders claim the success rate is linked to the Church requiring the candidates for marriage to be people of character—people who stick to their commitments of love and of asking for help, when they need it. What is so striking is that many of these marriages happen between couples who are still in their teens!

One cold—and often very sad—reality that couples face when they get married at an older age is issues with infertility. Often men and women have their lives and futures perfectly planned so that they can finish college, travel, experience all life has to offer, wait until they have enough money to buy the big house in the suburbs with the mini-van in the driveway, and then get married and think about having children. The truth is, their bodies may not have gotten the memo on how the plan is supposed to go. If you wait until you are almost thirty to marry, and then wait even longer beyond that to have children, you could end up in a world of pain and disappointment, just like so many couples today whose bodies simply are not cooperating with the "just wait" plan. So, many heartbroken would-be-moms and dads go through endless doctor visits, procedures, and way too much money for the treatment of infertility. We should be encouraging young adults to start their families when their bodies are created to make and birth healthy babies. And make no mistake: This should be a strong consideration when you look at studies on how age of *both* the mother and the father impact the health of a baby. Even genetics and biology tell us that waiting is not the best idea.

Then, there is an additional threat when people wait so long for marriage and children: the elimination of the role of grandparents. The culture of divorce that has been ripping and tearing at our family structure has, so far, failed to destroy us. Though the documentation of the damage divorce does to people and particularly their children is sufficiently solid, homes (though patched and sown together) have been able to hold together to some degree. This has been due in large part to the presence of grandparents. These are wonderful people who love their grandchildren unconditionally and whose age, wisdom, and financial resources play a key role—in some cases, *the* key role—as stabilizers in those children's lives. Those who delay marriage (and subsequently child rearing) are denying themselves one of the greatest joys men and women have cherished for millennia: an extended family where parents get to participate in the lives of their grandchildren.

For centuries, men and women became grandparents when they were in their late forties and early fifties, allowing them plenty of time to enjoy and participate in their grandchildren's lives. Then, in their seventies and eighties, they witnessed the arrival of their great-grandchildren. People who delay marriage and family today, however, do not realize how greatly they are cheating themselves by making it virtually impossible to experience the richness of having multiple generations alive and interacting as a family. And for what? An extended adolescence? To drink more beer or to experiment with more sexual partners? To focus on their careers and a chance to make money more quickly than their parents did?

The longer you live in your self-centered, all-about-you lifestyle, the more selfish you will become. Do you really think it's easy to break ten or fifteen years of ingrained and entrenched habits to make room and accommodate a new spouse? It's not so easy! Why not marry younger and build your life *together* rather than getting everything exactly the way you like it and think it should be before you try to fit your spouse and potential children into it. We can say all these external variables contribute to and cause divorce, but it's not true. Marriages do not fail because of age, money, or education—many of the underlying arguments for delaying marriage. Such thinking is utter nonsense. Marriages fail for one reason and one reason only: One or both people become selfish. To imply that young, poor, or high-school-only graduates are incapable of real commitment is an insult to them. We have young, poor, high school graduates in the armed forces working with great commitment, some giving the highest measure of commitment by sacrificing their very lives.

By following this ridiculous notion of delayed marriage, we will succeed in destroying ourselves from within. Young people need to be encouraged to do this right. Stop the serial dating, don't wait until they are pushing thirty, and stay sexually pure until marriage. Families need to stop cutting their kids off and realize that their assistance is also vital to help their young adults build strong, healthy marriages. It's time to reverse the trend and help young people learn the skills to be successful at relationships and marriage.

Mark Gungor is one of the most sought-after speakers on marriage and family in the country. Each year, thousands of couples attend his "Laugh Your Way to a Better Marriage"® seminars. His take on marriage issues is refreshingly free of both churchy and psychological lingo. Mark is Pastor of Celebration Church in Green Bay, Wisconsin. He speaks for churches, civic events, business meetings, and even the U.S. Army. Mark has been featured on national broadcasts such as *Focus on the Family* and ABC News. His daily Internet radio show is heard worldwide, and his weekly television show *Love, Marriage, and Stinking Thinking* is available on TBN and Sky Angel. Learn more about Mark and his marriage seminars at www.laughyourway.com. Mark and his wife Debbie recently celebrated their 37th wedding anniversary and have two married children and four grandsons.

❤ ❤ ❤

Later-Life Love
Greg Hunt with Priscilla Hunt

Imagine a thirty-something minister standing at the altar with a seventy-something couple, supplying them with wisdom before they say, "I do." The picture has a certain comic, Norman-Rockwell quality to it. The young officiant speaks, and as he speaks, his two seasoned elders look at him and listen with patient self-restraint, perhaps even amusement.

That's the preposterous position I found myself in with Jon and Martha. Drawn into their remarkable story of love, it fell to me to bless them on their wedding day and, as I always did, to offer advice to the couple before leading them in their vows.

My wife Priscilla and I had a longstanding relationship with Martha through our church. She called one day to tell us she had reconnected with her high school flame. She and Jon had first fallen in love as schoolmates in Depression-era Missouri, but their parents had come between them, thinking them wrong for each other. Then came World War II…and other loves. Both married others and had families of their own; they lost touch with each other as life moved on.

Years later, after each had lost a spouse and on the occasion of a fiftieth high school reunion, they rediscovered each other and reignited their love. Within days, Jon was making plans to move across country to be with Martha. They decided to fulfill their adolescent dreams and get married.

Priscilla and I genuinely delighted in this fairytale story of rekindled love. In our role as pre-marriage support people, we didn't want to do anything to squelch their joy. Nonetheless, we knew that their "in-love" feelings, as with all newlyweds, would eventually give way to ongoing life. They would have to learn each other's ways and adjust to each other's idiosyncrasies. They would have to intertwine two separate lifetimes of life, work, family, friends, and faith. We talked about all of this during pre-marriage appointments, and we assured them we would continue to support them after their wedding, come what may. They humored us when we told them marriage might not be totally smooth, unable to imagine that anything could strain the love they felt.

Jon and Martha did fine for a month or two after the wedding, but then the complications became real and deep-running. Anger and conflict became relentless features of their marriage. Jon, the regimented military man, found it difficult to adjust to Martha's artistic sensibilities. Martha, accustomed to her autonomy, chafed at Jon's controlling ways. He wanted to travel, while she enjoyed a more sedentary existence. Their differences threatened to smother the serendipity of their re-found love.

Genuinely concerned for the future of their relationship, they came to us for confidential conversation, and we met off and on the rest of their lives. Determined to make their marriage last, they re-learned and un- learned the lessons of two lifetimes. Their married life together had a ragged quality they hadn't anticipated, but they persevered, and it did end well. Martha and Jon were at each other's side to the very end of Jon's life.

Although older couples are often skeptical, later-in-life marriages must deal with the same realities any marriage faces. They also have unique characteristics that deserve special attention. Below is a short checklist of things for life-seasoned couples to consider and discuss before saying their wedding vows:

1. Consider things every couple deals with as they build a life together:

    a. Relationship goals

    b. Similarities and differences of personality and temperament

    c. Communication skillfulness

    d. Conflict resolution skillfulness

    e. Handling of finances

    f. Expectations related to family and friends

    g. Expectations related to work and leisure

    h. The place of sexuality in your relationship

    i. Your wants for your spiritual and religious life as a couple

2. Learn one another's habits and consider your level of compatibility. Though personal habits are subject to change as long as we live, they tend to become increasingly ingrained over time. It is wise to ensure that you can accept and live with each other the way you are now.

3. Talk honestly about current and potential future health issues. These will have an impact on everything from sexuality to use of leisure time.

4. Consider the family systems you will be weaving together. What part will they play in your lives? What are your roles as parents, stepparents, and grandparents? What relationship boundaries do you need to establish together? What pre-marriage discussion topics are important to address with your families?

5. Be honest and realistic about your current finances and estate matters. Where will you live? How will you handle the assets and debts you bring to the marriage? What legal steps are wise to take to clarify these matters? How can you discuss these matters with your families?

6. If you have been married previously, talk sensitively about your previous marriages. What did you value most in them? What were your greatest challenges? What are the most important things you learned from being in these relationships? How have your previous relationships influenced your hopes and fears for your new relationship? Don't neglect to consider the role of grief: Have you and your partner gone through the grieving process and reached true acceptance related to your previous partners, or does a former partner cast an unhealthy shadow over your current relationship?

7. Dream some dreams together. Talk imaginatively AND realistically about what you would like to experience together with the rest of your lives. In keeping with the idea that living things are growing things, make plans that will stretch you and enhance your zest for life.

Later-life love can be a wonderful thing; but it doesn't happen automatically. You can build an enduring marriage if you take the time for mutual discovery, honest talk, and ongoing growth in the areas of relationship that matter most to you.

Jon and Martha waited until after their marriage to launch this process and wished they had done it beforehand. We promised we would tell their story to encourage other couples to get the sequence right. It's the best way for a fairytale romance to end well.

Greg and Priscilla Hunt are dynamic speakers and are known for their lively, fun presentations. The Hunts are a certified Leader Couple and Specialists in Marriage Enrichment with Better Marriages (www.BetterMarriages.org). They are Seminar Directors for PREPARE-ENRICH, Instructor Trainers for Couple Communication, and certified Trainers for Mentoring for Better Marriages. They have been involved in marriage education and enrichment since they married in 1976. Priscilla is the Executive Director for Better Marriages, a non-profit since 1973, whose aim is educating couples for vibrant, lifelong relationships. After thirty-three years in pastoral ministry, Greg is now a consultant and writer, working in the areas of leadership, relationships, and spirituality. The parents of two adult children and grandparents to two granddaughters, Greg and Priscilla live in the metropolitan area of Kansas City, Kansas.

❤ ❤ ❤

Marrying Successfully Later in Life
Mark Gungor

As you consider marrying, you look forward to having a stable, secure, and mature relationship. You want a relationship where difficult issues have been resolved (or at least you have agreed to not resolve them), where the understanding and rules of the relationship have been firmly established, and where both parties feel secure and understood. Unfortunately, there is one ingredient that is essential for a relationship to become a mature marriage, and that is time.

Even if you do everything right, time is the only way to grow your relationship from a weaker, immature one to a solid, mature one. This can be particularly frustrating for couples who are marrying or re-marrying later in life. If you are in your forties, fifties, or sixties, you undoubtedly have achieved a great degree of maturity in your personal life. You now have found that special other person, fallen in love, and want to tie the knot.

You look around yourself and see that many of your friends in the same age bracket have wonderful marriages that are secure and mature. You also assume that since you are of a mature age, you, too, should have a mature relationship. Be aware that instead, yours may be a struggle. When your marriage is new or only a few years old, those in your age bracket have often been married for twenty, twenty-five, or thirty-plus years.

It's wishful thinking that since you are both mature adults you should be able to fast track your relationship into the mature type of marriages you see in those around you. It doesn't matter how old YOU are—your relationship is new. In fact, one of the great struggles of getting married later in life is that even though you may be forty-seven years old, you will have the relationship of a twenty-something-year-old who just got married. And that can be very frustrating. It's one thing to have a marriage of a twenty-year-old when you are twenty; it's quite another when you are pushing fifty. And the truth is, the younger couples are likely to be able to adapt to their marriage problems and each other more easily than the two of you at your age. What can you do?

First of all, you have to adjust your expectations. The only way you will have the marriage of a couple who has been married for thirty years is to stay married for thirty years, period. Just get used to that fact.

Secondly, stop comparing your marriage with those thirty-year marriages around you. Sure, the couples are the same age as you, but their relationship is a lot older than yours, and there is just no way you can compete with that. It would be like being fifty and comparing your body to that of an eighteen-year-old. I don't care how much you work out, cry, and pray, you will never have a young body again. Such comparisons are only likely to create a sense of depression and failure. It is the same when you compare your marriage to those of your peers who have been married a long time.

When you marry later in life, it may seem like the one thing you don't have is time, but like a fine wine, time is the only way you can get what you truly want. So, get as comfortable as you can with the notion that you are marrying later in life. Realize that staring at the water won't make it boil any faster, and sit back and allow what years you do have together to sweeten your relationship. Finally, be thankful to God for the relationship you do have (you could be alone). Enjoy what you have, and "let patience have her perfect work" in you.[1] Time is too valuable to waste wishing things were different.

[1] *The Bible,* James 1:4 (NKJ)

Mark Gungor is one of the most sought-after speakers on marriage and family in the country. Each year, thousands of couples attend his "Laugh Your Way to a Better Marriage"® seminars. His take on marriage issues is refreshingly free of both churchy and psychological lingo. Mark is Pastor of Celebration Church in Green Bay, Wisconsin. He speaks for churches, civic events, business meetings, and even the U.S. Army. Mark has been featured on national broadcasts such as *Focus on the Family* and ABC News. His daily Internet radio show is heard worldwide, and his weekly television show *Love, Marriage, and Stinking Thinking* is available on TBN and Sky Angel. Learn more about Mark and his marriage seminars at www.laughyourway.com. Mark and his wife Debbie recently celebrated their 37th wedding anniversary and have two married children and four grandsons.

Chapter Three
Preparing As Individuals

~ ~

Hmmm...does this chapter seem out of order for you? You are already a couple, right? What we find as we are working with couples is that sometimes once couples begin preparing for marriage together, the need for some individual self-preparation work arises. As you do activities and have discussions as a couple, please pay attention to when you feel an inner nudge (or receive feedback from each other!) that there is personal work to do.

We guide you here through assessing the effects of your individual pasts on your function in the relationship, being responsible for yourself, doing self-assessment and maturity checks, and understanding how to make good judgments about each other's readiness for marriage.

❤ ❤ ❤

Creating an Intimate, Loving Relationship
Margaret Paul, Ph.D.

You may have had many different types of relationship experiences in your life. While each has probably taught you valuable life and relationship skills, you may also have developed attitudes and behaviors that are interfering with you now with a new partner. For example, you may have fears of intimacy, you may have learned bad habits for maintaining a relationship, or you may not know about loving yourself as well as your partner. I can help!

Intimacy Challenges

Are you ready to have the wonderful experience of emotional intimacy in your life? We all want to feel close and connected with someone, but there are very real fears that may be keeping you from opening to emotional intimacy with your partner.

What is the first fearful thought that comes to you when you think of feeling close to someone? Perhaps these:

- "I'm going to be rejected" or "I'm going to be abandoned."
- "I'm going to be smothered, engulfed, or controlled. I will lose myself."
- "If I lose the person I love through death, I won't be able to handle the pain."

These are the fears that lie behind the fear of intimacy. It's not the intimacy itself, but the bad things that can happen that are sometimes part of an intimate relationship. These fears come from the pain of having been rejected in the past, of having lost yourself in a relationship, or of having too much loss without knowing how to handle the resulting grief. These experiences may have been so painful that you are afraid to experience them again. They may prompt you to keep your partner at a distance instead of letting them get close to you.

Is this pain inevitable in an intimate relationship? Yes and no. The pain of rejection is not inevitable, but if you are constantly expecting it, you are likely to unwisely interpret many of your partner's words or actions as "rejecting." Losing yourself in a relationship is not a certainty either and is highly unwise for you. You cannot be a full partner to someone else if you are lost in the process. The pain of losing a loved one through death may happen and is always a huge challenge, but would you really rather live a life without love than face this challenge? Besides, you can learn strengths and coping skills between now and then to help you if or when such an event happens.

Let's pause for a moment and actually look at the actions you could take if you really wanted to create a terrible relationship. It's a bit humorous, but also sad. I want better for you.

Creating a Terrible Relationship

Steps to follow:

1. **Take no responsibility for your own feelings.** Make sure you do not take responsibility for your own feelings and your own sense of safety and security. Make sure you ignore your feelings enough so that you create an empty black hole inside that needs to be filled up by sex, things, or someone else's love or attention.

2. **Find someone to do it for you.** Look for someone to fill your emptiness, someone to make you feel loved, happy, safe, and secure. A good way to determine if your partner is the right person for you is if they come on REALLY strong, promising you the world, or at least great sex.

3. **Once you find the right person, be sure to behave in one of the following ways:**

    a. Completely give yourself up. Completely put yourself aside, focusing all your attention on the other person's feelings and needs. Your hope is that if you are wonderful enough and sacrifice yourself enough, the other person will give you the love you are seeking. Be sure to completely ignore your own feelings and needs, no matter what the other person does. Be the best caretaker to your partner that you can be to try to have control over getting their love and approval.

    b. Demand the other person live up to your expectations. Start slow, gradually building to becoming more and more demanding of the other person. If they don't meet your expectations, be sure to criticize, blame, chastise, berate, threaten, ignore, yell at, belittle, lecture, debate, and argue with your partner. Your job is to gain control over getting the other person to completely give him or herself up. Your aim is to get them to focus only on filling your emptiness and needs with their love, approval, attention, sex, devotion, time, and adoration. Be the best taker you can be, making sure to keep your partner feeling guilty and responsible for your feelings of security and self-esteem.

4. **Be the victim.** As your relationship starts to decline, move more and more into thinking and behaving as a victim of the other person's choices. This will lead to more fights or to distance, lack of passion, lack of fun, and a complete inability to communicate about anything, even minor situations. In any discussions, be sure to seek to be right, win your point, and make your partner wrong. After all, this is a competition to determine who is the good one and the right one. Or, just collapse and give in—a great way to be a victim.

5. **Withdraw from your partner.** Start to spend less and less time with your partner, spending it alone or with other people, or in front of the TV. Convince yourself that your misery is completely your partner's fault and

that you picked the wrong person again. NEVER EVER take any responsibility for your own feelings, needs, behavior, and choices. Never forget that you are the victim.

6. **Get your partner into counseling.** Seek counseling to get your partner to change. Do NOT enter counseling to deal with your own controlling behavior of being a taker or caretaker. Rather, be sure to tell the therapist everything your partner does wrong, using the therapist's office as just another arena to prove that you are right and your partner is wrong, or that you are the good one and your partner is the bad one.

If you noticed that you agreed with any of the actions above, getting help is wise.

Healing and Loving Yourself

One of the primary keys to healing your fears and allowing intimacy to develop with your partner is developing your loving adult self.

Consider the damage to your relationship from this potential occurrence: You are in a relationship with someone you really love. Unexpectedly one day, your partner gets angry with you, shuts down to you, or threatens to leave you.

If you are operating from the ego, wounded part of yourself, your reactions might be:

• "What did I do wrong?" (Taking it personally and feeling rejected).
• "What do I have to do to fix this?" (The beginning of losing yourself).

Then you might also get angry or shut down to avoid feeling rejected, or you might scurry around trying to make things right, taking responsibility for your partner's feelings. Out of your fear, you try very hard to control your partner.

Instead, if you are operating from your loving adult self, your responses might be:

"My partner is closed right now and trying to blame me or punish me for something. My heart hurts from being treated this way, but I know their behavior has nothing to do with me. I cannot cause another person to act this way, nor am I responsible for how they choose to behave. If my partner leaves, I will feel very sad—even heartbroken—but I can manage this feeling with deep compassion and tenderness toward myself. Now, I wonder how I can best take loving care of myself until he or she opens up?"

As a loving adult, you would not take your partner's behavior personally and feel rejected by it, nor would you give yourself up trying to get your partner to open up. You might ask your partner what's wrong, with an intention to learn. If he or she opens up, then you can have a productive conversation. If not, then you would compassionately tend to your own heartache and do something loving for yourself: take a walk, call a friend, read a book, and so on.

You would not fear being left by your partner, as you would not be abandoning yourself. You would know that you will take loving care of yourself.

Developing your loving adult self is a process that takes consistent practice. When you shift your intention from trying to control another person and prevent them from rejecting you and instead focus on taking loving care of yourself, you gradually develop your loving adult. The more powerful your loving adult self is, the less you fear intimacy. You no longer fear rejection because you no longer take others' behavior personally, and you no longer fear losing yourself because you no longer give yourself up to avoid rejection. As a loving adult, you learn how to manage loss so you don't have to avoid love.

When We Are Loving to Ourselves, We Are Loving to Others

Contrary to what many people believe, being loving to ourselves is not at all about being selfish. Being loving to ourselves means we are taking full responsibility for our own feelings and needs so that we are not needy, selfish, and demanding of others to do this for us. It is when we are not loving ourselves that we selfishly make others responsible for giving to us the love that we are not giving to ourselves. We try to have control over getting their love.

Being loving to ourselves never means we disregard others' feelings and needs. It doesn't mean we ignore the effect our behavior has on others. We are being selfish rather than loving when we do not consider the consequences of our actions on others.

At the same time, being loving to ourselves means we do not allow someone's needy and demanding behavior to determine our choices. For example, if you want to do something important to you, and your partner is angry because they want you to attend to them rather than do what brings you joy, it is your partner who is being selfish by not supporting you. By doing what truly brings you joy, you are being loving to yourself, and you are also being loving to your partner. You are giving them an opportunity to learn and grow into being a more loving, supportive, and personally responsible person. If you abandon your own joy, you are abandoning yourself and robbing your partner of growing opportunities. This is not truly loving.

When We Are Loving to Others, We Are Loving to Ourselves

It is not loving to ourselves to be unloving to others—to be harsh, blaming, angry, judgmental, mean, or unkind. We can never feel happy with ourselves when we are treating others in unkind ways.

Being loving to others means being kind, understanding, compassionate, empathic, supportive, and open to learning about their feelings and beliefs. Being loving is about supporting our own and others' highest good with kindness, caring, understanding, and compassion. It does NOT mean we take responsibility for their feelings and needs. We can care about their feelings and needs. We can also care about the effects our behavior has on them without taking responsibility for how they are treating themselves and what they are telling themselves that is causing their own distress.

When loving others, we have to accept that it is their own treatment of themselves and their own beliefs that cause their pain—not our choices. We enable others rather than love them when we take responsibility for their happiness and pain. The challenge here is to care about others' feelings and needs without taking responsibility for them.

When we care about and take responsibility for our own pain and joy, and compassionately care about others' pain and joy without taking responsibility for them, we are being loving to ourselves and others. Learning to do this is what relationships, marriage, and life are all about!

Margaret Paul, Ph.D., is a noted public speaker, best-selling author, workshop leader, relationship expert, and Inner Bonding® facilitator. She has counseled individuals and couples, as well as led groups, classes, and workshops since 1968. She is the author and co-author of eight books, including the internationally best-selling *Do I Have To Give Up Me To Be Loved By You?*; *Healing Your Aloneness*; *Inner Bonding*; and *Do I Have To Give Up Me To Be Loved By God?* She is the co-creator, along with Dr. Erika Chopich, of the Inner Bonding® healing process, recommended by actress Lindsay Wagner and singer Alanis Morissette, and featured on *Oprah*, and of the unique and popular website www.innerbonding.com. Their transformational self-healing/conflict resolution software program, SelfQuest®, at www.selfquest.com, is being donated to prisons and schools, as well as sold to the general public. Margaret has three children and three grandchildren.

❤ ❤ ❤

The Value of Self-Responsibility
Molly Barrow, Ph.D.

One aspect of being mature within a relationship is the ability to take responsibility for your own life and behavior. Being responsible also includes "cleaning up" after yourself when your words or actions cause harm instead of good.

If you blame someone else, the world, your partner, or God because you are not happy, then you will remain absolutely glued to your excuses and blaming. To get control of your own life means you stop whining and blaming others.

If you want things to be different, then YOU must be the one to do it. Other people are busy with their own lives, including your partner. Others will walk right over you and not even notice that you were waiting for someone to make you happy, to fix your pain, or to balance your checkbook.

Repeat often, "I gladly take responsibility for changing my life."

Take your hits like a winner, make the best of a situation or leave it, then whistle while you work. What is the point of a defeated attitude that is mostly concerned with looking innocent? "I didn't do it." Would you want those words to be a synopsis of an entire irresponsible life? After today, be eager to say "I *did* it!" regarding your life decisions.

It's time to maturely address any incomplete situations from your past, mistakes made without follow-up apologies, or damaged relationships with parents, siblings, or friends. The less baggage you keep in your life, the less negative energy you bring into your relationship with your partner, and the happier you both will be.

No one wants to come near a big baby, much less take the time to assist you in achieving your personal goals if you just sit there hoping for change and doing nothing about it. Do you feel powerless? You are powerful! The power to change is already in you. Choose to take responsibility for you, stand up, move forward, and clean up any mess yourself.

Molly Barrow holds a Ph.D. in Clinical Psychology and is the author of *Matchlines for Singles, Matchlines for Couples, How to Survive Step Parenting,* and the *Malia and Teacup* self-esteem building series for young readers. An authority on relationship and psychological topics, Dr. Barrow is a member of the American Psychological Association, Screen Actors Guild, and Authors Guild, and is a licensed mental health counselor. Dr. Barrow has appeared as an expert in the film *My Suicide*, the documentaries *Ready to Explode* and *KTLA Impact*, NBC news, PBS *In Focus*, and on WBZT talk radio. She has been quoted in *O Magazine*, *Psychology Today*, *Newsday*, *New York Times*, *CNN*, *The Nest*, MSN.com, Yahoo.com, Match.com, *Women's Health*, and *Women's World*. Dr. Barrow has a radio show on www.progressiveradionetwork.com and is a columnist for www.Menstuff.org. Dr. Barrow has a counseling practice in Naples, Florida, and is happily married with a wonderful family including three children, one daughter-in-law, and two precious grandsons. Her website is www.drmollybarrow.com; Blog is: http://drmollybarrow.blogspot.com/; Twitter is: www.twitter.com/drmollybarrow; Live & Archived Radio Shows are: www.progressiveradionetwork.com/the-dr-molly-barrow-show/

❤ ❤ ❤

Do You Have a Tail?
John Buri, Ph.D.

Do you have a tail? You know, one of those flawed areas in your life that people who are close to you are able to see but only you have a tough time noticing?

I often encourage people that if one person tells you that you have a tail, then you can usually ignore it. If two people tell you that you have a tail, then it's wise to begin wondering. And if three people tell you that you have a tail and one of those people is someone who loves you and knows you well, then you had better go home, pull down your pants, and check your rear end in the mirror.

I am often surprised by how little self-insight happens for most of us before we get into a serious relationship. If we have roommates, they are probably able to see our tails, but typically they will not point them out unless those shortcomings are a source of irritation to them. For example, if someone continually leaves their dishes for others to clean up and hardly ever lifts a hand to clean the apartment (clearly a tail), roommates will typically say something only after they have become fed up with the behavior.

But in reality (for most of us), the only times we are ever confronted on a regular basis with the fact that we may have a tail (or maybe many tails) is when we end up in a serious relationship. In such instances, the person we love is able to clearly see the tail(s) and is actually in a position to talk with us about it. Now, let me ask you a question. If your partner notices that you have a tail and wants you to change, should you change to please that person?

Case in point: I grew up in an alcoholic home. If you know anything about alcoholic homes, you know they tend to be a bit chaotic, unpredictable, and unreliable. You can't always count on people to be there when you need them. As a result, I learned early on that if I got really close to others and depended on them, I was setting myself up for disappointment and hurt.

Now, there are many ways that a person who grows up in such an environment can protect themselves from the disappointment of being let down by the ones they love. For example, they can become indifferent—"If I just don't care, then I can't be hurt as much." Or they can numb themselves, first with an endless stream of entertainment and later with their own attachments to alcohol, drugs, and sex. The goal is to do anything that will keep them from feeling the pain of not being able to count on those who claim to love them. Or they can rebel and keep the source of the pain at a distance by repelling it in anger.

My response was not any of these. My response was to become highly self-sufficient. If I didn't rely on anyone else, I was less apt to be disappointed when they weren't there for me. This response to my alcoholic home environment worked really well in nearly every area of my life such as school, academics, sports, and work. But then I got married.

It wasn't very long after our wedding before my wife wanted more closeness between us, more interdependence, and more of me relying on her and her being able to rely upon me. Essentially, she wanted a "two shall become one" sort of marriage, with me as a husband, not a roommate. I was faced with a decision: Should I change to please my wife? I suspect that you have been faced with the same sort of decision: Should you change to please your partner? The answer is NO! Don't ever change to please your partner. Whatever change does happen will be forced, half-hearted, AND short-lived.

So, then I wondered: Should I change to please myself? If you have found yourself in this type of situation where someone has wanted you to change, then you know the answer to this one. The truth is that I was actually quite pleased with the way I was; being self-sufficient had worked out very well in my life. So, I didn't have any desire to change to please myself.

So then why change? The answer was surprisingly obvious (once I saw it). I needed to change in order to become a better person. Just because I had experienced a dysfunctional home life did not make it any less true that as human beings, we are meant to have a life of connection, interdependence, relying on others, and having them be able to rely on us. In short, we are intended to have a life of love.

Was it easy to come to grips with the fact that I had a tail and needed to change? NO! If you know anything about people, you know that self-sufficiency was not the last tail that I ever had to deal with in my life, and you no doubt also realize that there are still other tails for you to deal with. If you are aware of these realities, you also know that once a person is no longer open to pulling down their pants and checking for tails, they get stuck in the ruts of life and stop growing. It is then that the human spirit begins to resign itself to the way things are rather than the way things *could be.* It is then that the human spirit begins to shrivel up.

Life would be so much easier if it was static and unchanging, and we could simply sit back day after day and enjoy its passing, but that is not the way life is. Instead, life is more like the flow of a river, and each day its currents tug and pull on us as individuals and as couples. Sometimes the currents of life are mild, gently pulling us downstream. But at other times, they are like rushing water, and we have to row madly just so we aren't swept downstream. This is one of the beauties of love—having someone to row—and grow—with.

John Buri, Ph.D., is a professor of Psychology at the University of St. Thomas in St. Paul, Minnesota. He and the love of his life, Kathy, also his high school sweetheart, have been married for thirty-eight years and have six children and six grandchildren. Dr. Buri has taught a university course on the Psychology of Marriage and the Family for the past twenty-five years. He is the author of the marriage book *How To Love Your Wife,* as well as over fifty research articles and book chapters. He is a frequent speaker on topics of dating, marriage preparation, marriage enrichment, parenting, and family life. Dr. Buri can be reached at jrburi@stthomas.edu.

❤ ❤ ❤

Are We Mature Enough for Marriage?
Paul Coleman, Psy.D.

There is no doubt that you and your mate will be opposites in some area. He's a bit of a slob, you're a neat freak; he's introverted, you're extroverted. In fact, research findings are quite clear that every couple will have several areas of *permanent disagreement* that can never be "fixed," only managed. But such differences between mates obscure what are really deeper, more profound similarities. The truth is, you will attract—and be attracted to—someone who is at your same level of psychological maturity and adjustment.

Psychological maturity is a broad term that defines how well and in what manner a person copes with life and is able to relate well to others and the environment. There are numerous factors that determine your current level of maturity and adjustment, most notable being the quality of your early family life, the types of losses or challenges you've had to face so far in your life, your degree of optimism or pessimism, and even biology (some people have a nervous system that makes them more or less vulnerable to stress).

It is wise to assess how mature you both are and whether you are mature enough to handle the responsibilities of marriage. If you are not mature enough, then assess whether you have the support structure in place with family and counseling to help you as your marriage progresses through challenges.

Rules for Assessing Maturity and Adjustment

There are four rules to keep in mind as you do the assessment. They are:

1. You will attract and be attracted to a person who is at—or very slightly above or below—your level of adjustment.

2. The level you are at will determine how well or poorly you manage your relationship and cope with life's stressors.

3. There are three broad ranges of emotional maturity: low, mid-, and high. You may possess traits that can be found in all three ranges but one range will be primary.

4. If you grow in your maturity, the level you are currently at will determine how encouraging or how resistant your partner will be to your growth. People in the lower levels of adjustment, for example, are threatened by a partner's healthy psychological growth.

The Scale of Emotional Maturity

Emotional maturity ranges on a continuum from very low to very high. There is no absolute, universally recognized scale of adjustment, so I will create one here that captures the essential qualities of maturity and psychological adjustment at various levels. Your task is to honestly assess where you fit on the following continuum:

Levels 1-5   Lower Range of Adjustment

Levels 6-10   Mid-Range (Average) Adjustment

Levels 11-15   Highest Levels of Adjustment

As a consequence of Rule One above, if you are at a Level Six, for example, you will probably be attracted to someone who falls within the four-to-eight range of maturity. That means someone who is at a Level Fourteen—even if he or she is physically attracted to you—would not become emotionally involved with you. Neither of you would feel the "chemistry." (Similarly, a college sophomore would not be attracted to, say, an eighth grader. If there were such an attraction, we would conclude that the eighth grader was extremely mature or—more likely—that the college sophomore was extremely immature.)

If you are attracted to someone within your emotional maturity range who is nonetheless a bit higher in maturity, it suggests a desire on your part to either grow—or to be taken care of. If you are attracted to someone who is one or two steps below you, it suggests that you are comfortable being in a relationship where you are the leader or the rescuer—where you can have a little more control. At the highest levels of adjustment, small differences in adjustment (she is a thirteen; he is a twelve) mean very little. Higher functioning people usually desire to propel forward to even higher levels of growth. At the lowest levels of functioning (he's a four; she's a three) small differences can also mean very little—each person is quite stuck. It's at the mid-range levels where differences of one or two levels allow the most opportunity for dramatic change—higher or lower.

Levels 1-5: Low-Maturity People

At this Low-Maturity level, anxiety and fear rules the day. There is a great deal of insecurity and neediness. As such, a person may keep very emotionally distant from a partner or may crave closeness in almost an addictive manner. Here, the world is seen in black and white terms: He loves me or he doesn't;

she is attracted to me or she isn't; if she loved me she would do what I want. Under very low stress, such couples might get along, but any stress can prompt arguments or disengagement as their personal insecurities erupt.

A person at this low level will rarely accept blame for any problem or will do the opposite—almost always accept blame. As such, reality is distorted and mature problem solving is impossible, because the "problem" is not being seen properly. The couple perceives that the "solution" will never work. Highly controlling or abusive people are at this level—as are those who are easily controlled. People here need a great deal of reassurances they are loved and wanted. At these levels, there may be many psychological symptoms—chronic anxiety, depression, inability to "bounce back." (People at high levels of adjustment are not immune to symptoms; they can become depressed or anxious too. However, they are able to cope with those symptoms better and tend to bounce back much more quickly.)

At the lowest levels, there are double standards. Neither side can see how the very things they complain about ("You don't appreciate me…you're too controlling…you're too rejecting," and so on) are things they are guilty of themselves. For example, one may spend freely and doesn't wish to be questioned about their spending but will micro-manage the partner's spending.

At this level, relationship interactions rarely look like adult-to-adult but rather like child-to-child or parent-to child. The couple squabbles, fights over who is right and who gets their way, or they lecture in an "I know best" manner. Rarely do they possess good communication skills, and even if they do possess them, their underlying needs for love or control override their ability to have a thoughtful, compassionate, give-and-take conversation. Winning (or its opposite—submitting) overrides a respectful give-and-take. Healthy hobbies and reasonable outside interests are usually threatening to the other partner, and there is often use of emotional blackmail—"If you cared about me, you wouldn't spend time with your friends…."

Level 6-10: Mid-Range Maturity People

The Mid-Range level is where the majority of couples tend to fall, because often one must have experienced more of life's challenges in order to develop and grow. People at the low end of the Mid-Range category still possess some of the traits of the Low-Maturity group. Someone at the high end of the Mid-Range (a score of nine or ten) may possess some of the qualities of people at the High-Maturity range.

Mid-Range people can think through problems and are not as emotionally reactive to situations. However, their insight is limited, and they are still prone to blaming others at times ("Look what you made me do!...I shouldn't have yelled at you, but you made me do it!"). They can put bad feelings aside when needed and realize that relationships mean sacrificing one's needs at times. However, they still are not balanced in how much they take care of others versus how much they give. They might put aside their needs a bit too much for the sake of others—or might give to others a bit too little for the sake of themselves.

Usually Mid-Range people cope well with adversity, but under higher stress, they may become less cooperative, more stubborn, or more emotional. These people can assert themselves when needed, although they have a tendency on occasion to speak either a bit too harshly or not assertively enough. They might care how others feel and have compassion but may get too caught up in another's drama. They might get caught in the middle between warring parties, trying to be a rescuer or peacemaker. If they feel let down by someone, they are likely to feel hurt and take it personally.

Mid-Range people may feel pressure to do what they think others want them to do rather than taking a firm stance, and many are people pleasers. They are usually responsible people—sometimes actually over-responsible— and therefore get hurt or tired more easily. They may be taken advantage of by others. Mid-Range people are good examples of how one's strengths (thoughtful, understanding, hardworking, and so on) can become weaknesses if stretched too far (an overly-thoughtful person can "think too much" and worry about being wrongly perceived; an overly-compassionate person can get walked on or may "enable" unhealthy behaviors in others.)

In relationships, these couples can slog through difficult times, although become a little war-torn perhaps. But, they are capable of coming through with the relationship still reasonably strong. They often want what's best for their partners and encourage hobbies and outside interests.

Level 11-15: High-Maturity People

High-Maturity, well-adjusted people can see many sides to an issue. They are not likely to take things personally when others let them down or things don't go the way they want. They accept life on its terms rather than bemoan the fact that life isn't always fair or that bad things can happen to good people. They tend to be humble. It isn't that they stop seeing the true value of themselves so much as they never stop seeing the true value of others.

People in this range listen well with open minds. They have a strong sense of who they are and what they believe and yet will listen in a manner that makes them open to being changed. They take responsibility for their actions and choices. They are compassionate but are not rescuers. In fact, they are very likely to allow people to make mistakes and learn from them instead of trying to protect others from making mistakes.

High-Maturity people handle disagreements well. They do not feel threatened by differences of opinion and can remain calm even when others do not. They don't insist others think and feel the way they do. They don't control; they don't feel a sense of entitlement. In negotiations with a partner, they try to come up with a plan that meets both sets of needs when possible. They do their best and let the outcome happen naturally. They would never remain in a relationship with someone who has strong misgivings about the relationship. They want to be with someone who *wants* to be with them—not with someone who has to be persuaded.

High-Maturity people can live comfortably with mixed emotions. They understand that you can love someone and be angry at them; that you must balance generosity with self-interest; and that one can have convictions but be open to greater truths. They seek truth and don't like to deny or pretend. They don't play mind games in relationships. They will readily admit faults when they know them to be true. They don't manipulate or control others. They understand that love cannot be coerced.

Personal and Relationship Growth

Ideally, for each of you as human beings, your personal goal is to try to grow to the highest level of maturity and adjustment that you can. In your relationship and marriage, a related goal is to support your partner's efforts to grow. It doesn't matter where you start from—it is still wise to raise your maturity and adjustment levels before marriage. Ensure that you are choosing a partner who will become a spouse that encourages you to be the person you were meant to be within a relationship that fosters growth, trust, and love.

Paul Coleman, Psy.D., is a Psychologist and Relationship Therapist in private practice. He is the author of a dozen books including *The Complete Idiot's Guide to Intimacy* and *We Need to Talk: Tough Conversations with Your Spouse*. He has appeared as an expert on the television shows *Oprah* and *Today*. Dr. Coleman and his wife Jody have been married for twenty-seven years, and they have three children. He can be reached at www.paul-coleman.com.

♥ ♥ ♥

The Buffalo Wing Principle
Amy Spencer

We've all made that checklist for what we want in the right person, right? Maybe we've done it on paper, on a napkin, with friends, or just in our minds. Well, I'm here to tell you what to do with that list: Crumple it up and throw it away!

Why? Because it's not a *person* you're looking for at all. It's a *relationship*. Here's what I mean: Do you think you want someone hot? No, actually, *you don't*. What you want is a relationship in which you feel madly attracted to your partner. It doesn't matter how this person looks empirically—whether they're tall or slim or dark-haired or blue-eyed—and it doesn't matter if other people think they're hot or not. What matters is that *you* feel attracted to them. Here's another example: Do you think you want someone with a good sense of humor? *You don't*. What you want is a relationship in which the two of you crack each other up.

So make a new list, and this time, fill it with how you want to *feel* in the right relationship. Or, if you've already met a wonderful someone, ask yourself: Do I feel like my best self in this relationship? Do I feel comfortable and appreciated and loved and sexy and strong with my partner? Do I feel like my most natural, authentic self, that I'm with someone who gets me and supports me being me? And—this is also important—do you feel this is a relationship in which *you* can be the most loving, supportive, and happy partner in return?

As you're making that mental list of how you want to feel, remember that who we *think* we want may be different than who we really need. Relationships aren't head-to-head match-ups; they're dances—fluid and moving and working off one another. I remember going to a Monday Night Football Happy Hour with a date a decade ago. When we got our buffalo wings and he reached for the round one, I said, "Wow, that's so cool! I like the flat ones, and you like the round ones. We're perfect for each other!" Never mind that I, ahem, jumped the gun a little on that one and probably scared the guy off.

What's important is that as odd as the idea was, there was some truth to it. You don't need to like the same exact things in a relationship. You just need to fit together as a nice, complementary unit. Your partner can be the wine to your cheese, the round chicken wing to your flat one. In real life, he or she can be the straight man to your goofy sense of humor, the adventurous one to your channel surfing from the couch. So what if you like different movies, books, or music! What's important is that you work well together as a twosome.

So think about that as you choose the right partner for yourself. It's not about who they are as a person; it's about the relationship you have when you're together and the relationship you want to have after marriage. How do you feel when you're with them? Do they let you be the best you? Whether you're sharing a plate of buffalo wings or a household, what's most important is that you work well in your dance with each other.

Amy Spencer is the author of *Meeting Your Half-Orange: An Utterly Upbeat Guide to Using Dating Optimism to Find Your Perfect Match* (Running Press, 2010, www.meetingyourhalforange.com). She created the website *The Dating Optimist* (www.thedatingoptimist.com) and the iPhone application "Half-Orange Optimisms." Amy writes for *Glamour, New York*, CNN.com, *Cosmopolitan, In Style, Real Simple, Harper's Bazaar,* and Match.com. She was previously the host of a Sirius satellite radio relationship call-in show called Sex Files on the Maxim channel and has appeared on Fox, E!, CBS, NBC, VH-1, and others. Amy has also been featured as a Relationship Expert on Howard Stern's Sirius channel Howard 100 News. Amy is married and lives with her "half-orange"—her husband—in Venice, California.

❤ ❤ ❤

How to Marry a Winner
Krsnanandini Devi Dasi

"How," a client asked me recently, "do you marry a winner?" She said this out of much frustration, after witnessing the devastating divorces of her older brother and sister and after just breaking up with a young man she termed a loser. "I don't see a lot of happy marriages," she continued. "I want to get married—please don't misunderstand me. I think I'm ready for marriage, but I am so afraid of marrying the wrong person, somebody who turns out to be a terrible disappointment."

This client wanted to know how to choose the right mate—one that would go the long haul, be a champion, and make it to the finish line and do so with enough grace and just enough charm to attract her attention for a lifetime. Just what can you do to ensure that you and the person you marry will have a lasting, successful relationship? You can prepare to find the right mate by preparing to BE the right mate.

Prepare yourself first. Then, when you meet and get to know someone you are serious about, get premarital education or relationship skill-building. However, don't stop working on yourself at that stage either. Athletes train for a marathon, students study for academic examinations, and drivers study to pass their driving tests. People who want to get married should prepare themselves by engaging in self-reflection and self-improvement, get clear on what marriage really means, and become adept at communication and conflict resolution skills. This is the process of marital fitness or readiness.

Steps in the Self-Preparation Process

Here are suggested steps in the process of preparing yourself to be an excellent marriage partner:

1. First, write a list of the most vital qualities you want in a mate. Don't hold back, and be very honest about what is really important to you. For example, if you want a husband who loves children, put it down. If humor is important, say so. If financial solvency is a value, write it down. If spirituality is a requirement, list it.

2. Review this list and check off the qualities that you personally have. That's right. You and your mate have to have many similar qualities and values. This is an indispensable step in preparing for the right spouse—the realization that it's really about working on you!

3. Accept and be clear that you want to get married and begin to act and prepare for that marriage. Visualize what it would be like to be married successfully. Imagine that you are a magnet, attracting a compatible and winning person into your life. The power of your attraction builds as you improve yourself, and the more likely it is you will draw your mate to you.

4. If you were anticipating the arrival of a very special guest at your home, you would prepare by cleaning, decorating, and cooking. Similarly, a spouse with winning qualities is very desirable to you, so envision yourself getting ready for their arrival.

5. Examine your diet and your lifestyle to see where you can grow and improve. Then take specific actions to improve your life. Complete that degree, take that yoga class, de-clutter your house (or your room or your car), find a more fulfilling job, or sit down to study the spiritual books that you've procrastinated on for so long. In other words, identify some personal and professional goals and implement them.

Characteristics of a Winner

Hundreds of clients weighed in on qualities they would assign to successful, caring people who contribute positively to their spouses, families, and communities. The winners are:

Trustworthy	Affectionate
Respectful	Generous
Truthful	Compassionate
Clean	Willing to compromise
Supportive	Selfless
Considerate	Good listeners
Patient	Self-disciplined
Creative	Resourceful
Industrious	Determined
Courteous	Forgiving
Responsible	Friendly

Winners also:

- Honor their commitments
- Plan their work (set goals) and work their plan
- Have a zest for life
- Treat elders and authorities with respect
- Have the capability to laugh at themselves
- Generally have optimistic, positive attitudes

Remember to Include the Spiritual

Physical or intellectual attraction may be nature's way of making us connect in the first place, so we move forward into family life to keep the species going. However, it's our spiritual foundation that motivates us as individuals to act with integrity and gives us the strength to honor our commitments.

For any union to be vibrant, lasting, and successful, it must be built on spiritual principles. The most prominent of these principles are: Truthfulness, Compassion, Cleanliness, and Self-discipline. If you practice these principles and only accept a partner and spouse who does so as well, you will have a strong, durable, empowering foundation on which to build and keep your marriage.

Realizing and acting upon your eternal connection to God, the Universal Creator, and Source of everything is as much a part of your preparation for marrying a winner as everything previously discussed. Consider worshipping together, praying with one another, or engaging in meditation practices together. Find spiritual communities where you can volunteer your time together. All of this will strengthen your bond together, as well as give you opportunities to assess whether the winning characteristics are present.

Finally, let's conclude with the following quotation from Zig Ziglar, a popular motivational speaker. His words are some of the most profound comments ever made about choosing the right partner. Although this quotation refers to consideration after the fact, wondering if you've chosen the right person after you've already married, it is still applicable to the topic of marriage preparation. Take time to reflect on it, digest it, and incorporate it into your thinking as you prepare to choose and marry your partner. Pay particular attention to the last two sentences, for they are the most significant:

> …[M]any people have a lot of wrong ideas about marriage and what it takes to make that marriage happy and successful. I'll be the first to admit that it's possible that you did marry the wrong person. However, if you treat the wrong person like the right person, you could well end up having married the right person after all. On the other hand, if you marry the right person and treat the person wrong, you certainly will have ended up marrying the wrong person. **I also know that it's far more important to *be* the right *kind* of person than it is to marry the right person. In short, whether you married the right or wrong person is primarily up to *you*.**[1]

The key to marrying a winner is to be one yourself, and when you are gifted with children, be a winner again by training and preparing your sons and daughters for healthy marriages of their own.

---

1 Zig Ziglar, *Courtship After Marriage*, pp. 11-12; bolding added

Krsnanandini Devi Dasi is a Certified Family Life Educator, Certified Family Wellness Instructor, PREPARE-ENRICH Coach, and Co-Director of Dasi-Ziyad Family Institute (www.dzfi.org). However, of all the education, credentials, and professional experience that Ms. Dasi brings to her work in healing and strengthening individuals, couples, and families, she is most grateful for her connection with her spiritual mentor and teacher, Swami Bhaktivedanta. While she is thankful for being able to serve in these professional capacities, Ms. Dasi attributes her passion, dedication, and commitment to the inspiration and gentle, empowering wisdom that she received from her beloved teacher. She currently serves as Senior Minister of the Cleveland, Ohio, Hare Krishna community and is supportive of her husband's work in the Muslim community.

♥ ♥ ♥

Preventing the Past from Derailing Your Future Marriage
Beverly Rodgers, Ph.D., and Tom Rodgers, Ph.D.

Our nation now has the oldest and the largest singles population in its history. Singles are waiting to marry or choosing alternatives like non-married co-parenting or cohabitation in record numbers. Marriage is being reduced to a sentimental ceremony or avoided all together. We hear from singles that they are afraid to marry. But there is hope, and it doesn't have to be this way.

Singles tout reasons like the high divorce rate among their parents and friends, thinking marriage is out of date, and fear of failure. There are specific wounds children of divorce need to address, such as an inability to trust and a sense of inevitable doom in relationships. We have found that *knowledge of how to have a successful marriage can overcome couples' fears.* To have a successful marriage, it is vitally important that you know the following:

1. What you fight about is often not what is really bothering you. Typically, there are deeper roots to your anger that need to be identified and understood.

2. If you understand and heal your past and recognize and address when issues from the past are triggered in the present, it will make for a better future.

Let's delve deeper into these concepts.

Know What You Are Really Fighting About

Relationship experts say most marital fights are not what they seem to be about. The chronic conflict over a husband not cleaning up his crumbs and dishes from the counter may not be about the kitchen at all. In the same way, your partner's criticism about you not being on time for dates is likely about something else. There could be a deeper root in both cases.

Biblical guidance about anger says, "A wise man controls his anger. He knows that anger causes mistakes."[1] In addition, "A gentle answer turns away wrath, but harsh words cause quarrels."[2]

Anger theorists teach that in order to moderate or control anger, it requires understanding that it is not a primary emotion. Anger is a secondary emotion, usually felt in response to a more primary feeling. This means anger is generally more of a response rather than the root of a particular situation. Submerged under anger are the four primary feelings that help define or give purpose to our angry expression. Chances are, if you are feeling anger, you can trace it to any one or more of these four GIFT emotions:

Guilt

Inferiority (or Inadequacy)

Fear

Trauma or pain

We have developed GIFT as an acronym for these underlying emotions to help you easily trace them to their origin. We feel it is a GIFT to you and to your partner or spouse to identify the root(s) of your wrath. If you respond to your partner's or spouse's words or actions with anger, it tends to create a defensive or angry response from them in return. Healthy communication and problem solving are thwarted, and the conflict goes unresolved. The GIFT exercise instead helps you to trace the root emotions of your anger. This will then assist you in communicating your frustration and irritation more honestly and effectively.

We have seen that if one partner reacts in anger, the other is much less likely to really listen. If, however, that same person shares what is really bothering them (guilt, inferiority, fear, or pain), then their partner is much more apt to listen and make changes in words or actions.

At first, you may resist believing that anger is really veiling one or more of these four basic feelings. Let's look at an example to help you understand. When someone cuts you off in traffic, how do you feel? It likely moves you to angrily even the score. Perhaps you pull in front of them, call them names, or rudely gesture at them. You feel disregarded, less than, cut off, and put down. Does this sound like inferiority to you?

Another example may be when a relative calls whining and complaining that you have not talked to them in a while. Many times you respond with anger, when what you really feel is defensiveness and guilt. Think about what makes you mad in your relationship. Now, look for the root. Isn't it found in your GIFT?

Dealing with Your Past Makes for a Better Future

All of us enter relationships and marriages with wounds from the past. In the Soul Healing Love Model, we call them "soul wounds." Some are huge and traumatic—like divorce or the death of a parent—and some are more minor, but they still affect us in our relationship interactions.

The problem with these wounds, especially the traumatic ones, is that they are stored and processed in our brain stem, our *old brain*. This is the most primitive part of our brain, and it functions in a very archaic fashion, often getting us in trouble if we do not heal the wounds stored there.

To help you understand how this works, the human brain is divided into two basic parts: the cerebral cortex, which we call the new brain; and the brain stem, or *old brain*. Humans are the only mammals that have a new brain. It helps us take in information, organize it, and make decisions. It gives us the ability to observe ourselves and evaluate our own behavior.

The difference between humans and animals is that we can objectively critique and assess what we do. Of course you can't picture a dog barking frantically at the paper delivery boy and then saying, "I bet I really looked stupid doing that." Sometimes when we do something really embarrassing, such as losing it in the grocery store because the checkout clerk is entirely too slow, the gift of seeing ourselves in our mind's eye may not be so wonderful after all. But we have the ability to do just that, so we have access to changing our words, actions, and future.

The primitive *old brain* is a part of our autonomic nervous system, the source of our fight-or-flight response. It floods our body with chemicals when it senses fear or real or perceived danger. Painful memories from childhood can trigger the urge to engage in battle or flee, and we can have physiological responses such as sweaty palms, heart palpitations, and perspiration. These memories may not be conscious during a reaction.

Sometimes the triggering event in the present simply reminds the *old brain* to feel the same way as in the past, and it takes careful thought and discussion to determine the initial stored event.

Another key aspect about the *old brain* is that it is *atemporal,* which means it has no sense of time. So, a trauma that occurred at age five can be relived at age twenty-five with the same emotions that you felt as a child. For example, maybe you badly burned yourself as a child on an appliance while your alcoholic parents were away from home drinking. As an adult, you could have an *old brainer* response that refuses to allow that type of appliance in your home. In a similar way, you may have experienced trauma in an earlier relationship or previous marriage that is stored in your *old brain.* Perhaps you were sexually abused. When your current partner touches you, it can trigger an *old brainer,* causing you to react and withdraw in fear.

While *old brainers* may not seem so serious when it comes to appliances, having such negative feelings and sensations about love and relationships can be very interpersonally perilous, especially if you choose to marry. They can cause *reactivity*—using more emotion in a current situation than it deserves—because a soul wound is being triggered.

Let's look at some more examples. Perhaps an abusive parent hit you in a particular spot on your body. Every time your partner touches you there, you become angry (with fear and trauma/pain underneath). If you can figure out together what is happening, it opens up the possibility that your partner's gentle touch and affirmation of safety might help heal the wound. If your mother often neglected to fix dinner for the family, any disruption in your partner or spouse taking you to a restaurant or cooking and serving a meal, could trigger an *old brainer.* If you overreact, get enraged, yell, threaten, accuse, or pout, then you are experiencing *reactivity.*

Typically, if one partner or spouse becomes reactive, there is a greater likelihood that will trigger *reactivity* in the other. It is easy to see how these experiences can become volatile and destructive to your couple relationship. We often see that one partner or spouse becomes fearful, angry, and overly emotional, which causes them to draw false conclusions. The other will then become angry and fearful and hurl a few false accusations too; we call this *interactivity.* When couples are experiencing *interactivity,* they are both triggered and have a hard time calming down and communicating effectively.

Digging Deeper Exercise

The following Digging Deeper Exercise will help you prevent and respond to *reactivity* and *interactivity* in a healthy way. It allows you to do several things:

- Remember and assess memories stored deeply in your *old brain* and identify words and actions that trigger them in your current relationship
- Understand the feelings these memories and triggers evoke, or more basically, "Why am I so reactive?"
- Connect those feelings to early childhood wounds
- Separate family-of-origin issues from patterns in your relationship or marriage
- Determine what you really need from your partner or spouse

In order to do the Digging Deeper Exercise, you will need to answer these simple (although not easy) questions:

1. *What are the words or actions that my partner or spouse does or does not say or do that trigger my anger?* Answer: When my partner does this_____, I feel angry, and beneath that is (guilt, inferiority, fear, or trauma/hurt).

2. *What is the event from my childhood that is triggering my feeling (guilt, inferiority, fear, or trauma/hurt)?*

3. *What do I do when I feel this feeling?* Do you yell and criticize? Do you withdraw and pout? Do you lecture or try to control? If you had to repress feelings from childhood, then you may spew them out onto your partner or spouse with a vengeance. You will want to understand these emotions so that they do not cause harm to others.

4. *What do I really need?* It is important to dig even deeper when you are determining your needs. You may need healing, so the resolution may involve your partner or spouse in helping you understand and accept the original wound. You may also need to request that your partner or spouse speak or act in a new way that helps to reduce *old brain* triggering. This work opens up the possibility of a more profound relationship between the two of you, through expressions of understanding, validation, and empathy.

Building a Growthful Marriage

Marriage is a crucible of growth and vital personal development. Before marriage, you will determine what will help you both prepare for this lifelong process. This will help you build a healthy, lasting marriage together.

1 *The Bible,* Proverbs 14:29 (NIV)

2 *The Bible,* Proverbs 15:1 (NIV)

Beverly Rodgers, Ph.D., and **Tom Rodgers**, Ph.D., have been Christian-based Counselors and married to one another for over thirty years. They own and operate Rodgers Christian Counseling and the Institute for Soul Healing Love in Charlotte, North Carolina. Both have their Ph.D.s in Clinical Christian Counseling. Dr. Bev also has a Masters Degree in Marital and Family Therapy, and Dr. Tom also has two Masters Degrees, one in Counseling and one in Human Development. Together, they have written *Soul Healing Love, Adult Children of Divorced Parents, The Singlehood Phenomenon,* and *Becoming a Family That Heals.* They have appeared on television on *A Time for Hope, His Side Her Side, The American Family, NBC Nightside,* and *Marriage Uncensored.* They have also been featured speakers on radio shows on NPR, the BBC, and *Focus on the Family.* Together they facilitate relationship workshops for couples, singles, and families across the globe. The couple has two grown daughters. They can be contacted through their websites: www.soulhealinglove.com and www.becomingafamilythatheals.com.

Chapter Four
Adjusting Expectations
~ ~

One of the exciting parts of courtship is getting to know one another very well. You seem to never run out of questions for each other. There is an art to posing questions well, however, and to discovering what you each expect from marriage. This chapter will help you with those subjects.

You will explore whether you think relationships and marriage are the "hard work" people often say they are. Other experts will then help you with understanding how to be intentional with creating a marriage that turns out well.

♥ ♥ ♥

The Art of Asking Questions
Susanne M. Alexander, Stanis Marusak Beck, and Michael J. Beck, Ph.D.

Posing and answering questions about issues that will affect your relationship offers an opportunity for personal reflection, as well as in-depth discussions with each other. Asking questions and engaging in the discussions that follow them will assist you to explore your marital readiness and compatibility. When you ask questions of each other, you are reflecting interest and fostering understanding of yourselves and your relationship. Questions to your partner keep you connected and sensitive to each other's needs and interests, a vital element in any loving relationship.

Sometimes your discussions as a couple may feel like mini-therapy sessions as you explore past issues in your lives and help each other to find healing. You can use discussions for tapping into your relationship roots, gaining understanding and empathy, and strengthening your emotional bonds with each other. Honesty is vital—be careful that you do not simply answer the questions in the way you think your partner wants you to answer them.

Sometimes parents or friends can also be helpful in asking key questions, so you can listen to each other answer another person.

You may have difficulty with someone asking you questions, particularly personal and intimate ones. Many people start out in life asking many questions in their eagerness to discover the world, but over time, they may start to associate questions with examinations in school or being in trouble with someone. Answering questions may also lead you to feel vulnerable. However, questions and answers and the process of exploring them actually provide an opportunity for you to understand your own thought processes and the emotions that are triggered during discussions. Being vulnerable and willing to ask and answer questions—especially difficult ones—will be facets of a successful marriage for you.

The range of topics for the two of you to discuss can be very broad. However, it is wise to at least explore life experiences, memories, and beliefs; goals and fantasies; sex; emotions and dreams; and previous romantic and family relationships. It can be wise to include discussions about your experiences and successes with handling problems, your spiritual lives, your views of gender equality, parenting choices and philosophies, and how to handle money as a couple. Remember to set up a quiet, calm, and safe space for any discussions that will be about very emotional or difficult topics for one or both of you.

A note about posing and answering questions about sex: The way a person experiences sex often shows their level of maturity. A person who spends an inordinate amount of time self-stimulating or viewing pornography, for example, generally wouldn't have that much interest in their partner and may not be interested in creating a family. In addition, when someone can talk about sex freely, they usually talk candidly about other topics as well.

Remember that questions are not intended to lead to arguments or the effort to prove that a point of view is the "right" one; they are to provide a time to share and to listen. If you are apart during your courtship, you may also choose to pose and answer questions with each other via email or some other form of electronic communication. Be prepared to answer any question yourself that you are willing to pose to your partner!

Being heard unconditionally goes a long way toward healing old wounds. This is a simple cure couples can give each other by just asking the right questions and/or being active listeners. Interruptions, criticism, and defensiveness sabotage the process and have a damaging affect. Couples need

to be open-minded and sincere, with a sense of humor, in order for this type
of connecting communication to be most effective.

> **Susanne Alexander** is a Relationship and Marriage Coach. She used to work full-
> time as a freelance journalist and is insatiably curious, so her books tend to be full
> of questions. (www.marriagetransformation.com)

> **Stanis Marusak Beck**, M.S.W., A.C.S.W.-R, M.A., a Clinical Social Worker, is
> currently on the faculty of the Long Island Center for Modern Psychoanalysis.
> **Michael J. Beck**, Ph.D., is founder of the Institute for Psychotherapeutic Studies,
> where he taught, wrote, and supervised mental health professionals for a number
> of years. They co-authored *365 Questions for Couples* with their daughter Seanna
> Beck. They have been married since 1967. They live in New York and have two
> adult daughters. She can be reached at 631-587-1924. Dr. Beck can be reached at
> mjbeck3391@att.blackberry.net.

❤ ❤ ❤

Before You Walk Down the Aisle
Julie M. Baumgardner

Have you ever decided to do something and been so head-over-heels
convinced that you had all the answers that you either didn't seek advice from
anyone or you ignored valuable wisdom shared with you? On more than one
occasion, I have listened to couples talk about being so starry-eyed in love
that in spite of what others tried to tell them, they truly believed love would
carry them through their marriage journey.

After attending a number of weddings, I was curious about what type of
advice newlyweds wished they had received once they realized they didn't
know it all.

One woman shared that after living together, she and her husband had
been married ten months. They thought the only thing that would be
different after they married were the rings on their fingers. Now they know
that could not be further from the truth. She wishes someone had told
them not to live together before marriage and how steep the learning curve
is in the first year when the commitment is different.

Many couples preparing for marriage assume living together is the next
step before walking down the aisle. It seems logical to them to test drive

the marriage to determine compatibility and save money at the same time. However, research shows there is no substitute for the real thing. The best way to prepare for a great marriage relationship is to spend time together getting to know the love of your life and participate in marriage preparation to learn skills for healthy communication, conflict management, problem solving, goal setting, and more. It is wise to talk with couples who have been married for a number of years and ask them their secrets for keeping their marriages on track or getting back on track after troubled times. It is also a good idea to thoroughly discuss areas where you don't yet agree and come up with solutions. Dealing with these issues before you tie the knot could be one of the best investments you make in your relationship. As you do all of these things, ask yourself how committed you are to the relationship. The key to a healthy, lasting marriage is commitment to making it work.

Another young newlywed admitted that she and her husband really didn't talk about finances before they walked down the aisle. Even though they had their paychecks automatically deposited and bills set up for automatic payment, she actually had no idea what was in their checking account at any given time. "Not too long after we married," she said, "I decided to spend a little extra on payday. Little did I know, I almost caused us to bounce checks because it was the first of the month, the time when many of our largest bills are paid. To this day, we still haven't established a budget."

Research shows that money is one of the least important relationship factors when couples are considering marriage; however, it is the number one thing that creates distress in marriage. Many couples go deep in debt trying to furnish their home, drive nice cars, and generally keep up with the lifestyle of others. Instead of trying to immediately have what your parents accumulated over many years, participate in a money-management seminar that will teach you how to budget your money. Most money experts agree there are three cardinal rules to follow when it comes to managing your money: spend less than you make, avoid going into long-term debt, and save some for difficult times.

One couple shared that even though they love each other, adjusting to having someone else around and having to consider their thoughts, feelings, likes, and dislikes is a huge change. Topics up for discussion and negotiation include how they get ready in the morning with only one bathroom, when to go to bed when one of them is a night owl and the other isn't, what to spend money on, how to do the laundry, who cleans the bathroom, how often to see in-laws and extended family members, when to have visitors, and when to schedule date nights.

Learning how to do the marriage dance without stepping on each other's toes is a skill that takes time to master. The best approach is talking about all of these issues both before marriage and immediately as they arise after the wedding. Keeping your frustrations to yourself will only create friction in your relationship and cause you to harbor resentment. Marriage is where you learn it isn't all about you and your wants and desires. It is learning how to let another person be a part of your life. You have to figure out how to give, receive, and compromise—and this process must begin long before the wedding day.

One bride said she wished she had known she would have to sacrifice who she was for the sake of her marriage. Pre-marriage education would have helped her avoid this trap. Healthy marriage isn't about sacrificing who you are when you come together as one. Coming together should make you better as individuals and better as a team. Talking about career expectations, having and rearing children, and individual and collective goals before you marry will be helpful. There are seasons in marriage when you choose to make sacrifices because it is honoring to your relationship. This doesn't mean one person does all the sacrificing all the time.

Finally, almost every couple I spoke with talked about keeping expectations realistic. It is wise before marriage to talk about what you expect from each other after marriage and agree on what is realistic and how to accomplish what is important. Just because you marry someone doesn't mean they are going to be able to meet your every need, make you happy, and be perfect all the time. There will be disagreements, and you will make mistakes. Believe it or not, there will be times when you don't feel head-over-heels in love. That doesn't mean you married the wrong person. Nobody is perfect. Everyone has needs and opportunities for growth. Instead of focusing on your own needs and your spouse's weaknesses, focus on your spouse's needs and strengths and on your own opportunities for growth. Even after more than twenty years of marriage and being immersed in information about how to be successful at it, I still have to keep myself in check when it comes to my expectations of my husband and our marriage.

Getting your marriage off to a great start takes at least as much preparation time as you put into your wedding day—preferably more. The couples I spoke with have high hopes for a long-lasting, healthy marriage. If that is your goal, make it a point to start investing now in your relationship. The return on your investment will be worth it!

Julie M. Baumgardner, M.S., C.F.L.E., is the President and Executive Director of First Things First, an award-winning, grassroots initiative based in Chattanooga, Tennessee. The organization is dedicated to strengthening marriages and families through education, collaboration, and mobilization. Julie has conducted hundreds of workshops and frequently speaks nationally on family, parenting, and marriage issues. She also teaches community leaders how to build grassroots initiatives. Julie's weekly column on family issues in the *Chattanooga Times-Free Press* reaches thousands. Julie serves on the boards of a number of community and national organizations, such as The Marriage CoMission, The Coalition for Marriage, Couples and Families, Laugh Your Way to a Better Marriage, and The National Healthy Marriage Resource Center. She and her husband Jay have been married for more than twenty years and have one daughter. Julie can be reached at www.firstthings.org, julieb@firstthings.org, or 423-267-5383.

❤ ❤ ❤

Are Relationships Hard Work?
Don Ferguson, Ph.D.

One of the many unnecessary burdens we place on young couples is the ancient wisdom that relationships are hard work. Much like the opposite fairy tale that marriage will lead to happily ever after, this description places the partners at a disadvantage from the beginning. This concept of hard work makes the best thing that could happen to you sound like a life sentence of drudgery.

We often seem to speak about marriage as if it were something to be endured, and we convey that only with the skills and strength of ancient heroes will they succeed. Worse, partners may already suspect that they do not have the skills and ability to be heroic in their marital endeavors. The world is going to throw every possible challenge and obstacle at the couple, and they are best advised to recognize that it is their relationship that can make life easier, rather than suggesting that it is their relationship that will require such tremendous effort.

We have so much wisdom and research available from people like John Gottman, Sue Johnson, Daniel Wile, and many others that inform us that increasing fear and apprehension in relationships only makes things worse. We know from studies of relationships, work functioning, trauma, and other areas that when we provide people a sense of competence, power, and control, they are much more likely to rise to the challenges of difficult or even dangerous situations. Instead, when we impose a sense that the goal is something extraordinary and rare, requiring unusual effort and skill, we may already be facilitating a bad ending.

A relationship requires attention. Whereas young lovers may not believe they have skills with which to build effective communications, enhance intimacy, expand trust, and prove dependability, they all do possess skills for paying attention. In fact, during the days of early love when the couple is affected by high levels of the hormone oxytocin and neurotransmitter dopamine, paying attention to the loved one is the most natural thing on Earth. Every waking moment is filled with thoughts of that person, and the most prominent drive experienced is to connect with and please the partner.

If the couple believes there is a magic formula for building relationships that they are expected to find and master, they will unfairly limit themselves. In hopelessness and fear of exposure for their lack of competence, they will hunker down and show less of themselves to each other. We all, however, have skills for loving a partner in ways that make the other feel loved. As Gary Chapman describes in his books about the Five Love Languages, these skills, along with the ability to receive such attention well, are vital for relationship and marriage success. The perception of what kinds of attention actually provide comfort and relief will be different for each of us as well, and this is where experimentation can help the couple.

Rather than issuing dire warnings to young lovers that they are in for hard work, why not enthusiastically propose that they are entering a series of learning-in-action experiments? Within these experiments, they will talk to, touch, give things to, listen to, and admire each other in thousands of ways and then do a quick scan and communication to see which behaviors actually result in feelings of love, comfort, and relief. In such experiments, any approach or behavior with positive motives is neither good nor bad but is merely a question placed to the partner: "Did that feel good?" The partner can then provide feedback and guidance: "It feels best when you not only look at me when I am talking about something serious but also hold my hand; I love it when you tell off-color jokes, but never in front of my parents"; and so on. We might also add that during these experiments, life is going to throw everything at them that tests their commitment to one another. That is where the work comes in—not in struggling with each other, but in building their strength as a couple to fend off attacks from the outside world.

When someone thinks relationships must be hard work, they might insist that the other partner should work hard to win them. From such peculiar roots spring the ideas of playing hard to get and not giving one's partner valuable information. Some even write books encouraging such behavior. If indeed your goal is to have a relationship based on mistrust, deception, and wild guesses, then this is certainly the way to go. On the other hand, many partners would do almost anything to make their loved one happy if they just had a little information. The attitude that "if they really loved me they would know what I need" is nonsensical in its assumption that partners are skilled mind readers, and it is also the surest way to rip the fun out of a relationship.

So, if you are preparing for marriage, please enter an agreement to experiment, to exchange information, and have some fun together as you learn and grow. At the same time, know that the hard work you may have heard about will be lessened if you stick to some basic agreements. The simpler you make these agreements, the better. Perhaps rule number one should be to pay loving attention to your partner in some manner—no matter how small—every single day. Rule two might be to not have discussions or activities with a friend or coworker that you want to hide from your partner. If, for example, you are feeling misunderstood by your partner, under this rule, you tell them and not someone else. When in doubt, go back to rule number one. See! That's not so hard.

Don Ferguson, Ph.D., Psychologist and author of *Reptiles In Love: Ending Destructive Fights and Evolving Toward More Loving Relationships* (2006, Jossey-Bass/Wiley) has been a teacher, trainer, and practitioner in the field of relationships and group therapy for over twenty-five years. He has presented hundreds of seminars and training sessions to clinicians, businesses, government offices, and other organizations. Visit his website www.inrelationships.com for more information on his methods and workshops. In 2009, Dr. Ferguson opened Infinite Relationships, LLC, where he and colleagues offer intensive evaluations, evening seminars, weekend workshops, education, and psychotherapy groups, as well as other forms of individual and couples therapy.

♥ ♥ ♥

Expectations vs. Intentions
Greg Hunt and Priscilla Hunt

When Bill and Christy decided to marry, they did so with excitement and uneasiness. Their love for each other was strong, and they had no trouble imagining a lifetime together. At the same time, both of them had come from families where the parents divorced after years of conflict. They knew the stress and grief of love gone wrong. They wanted something better, but they also wondered whether they had it in them to succeed.

Were they doomed to repeat the patterns of their past? Was it fair for them to hope for something better? These questions have to do with expectations, and expectations are powerful. We tend to get what we forecast, good or bad. Our expectations predispose us and set forces into motion that bend the future toward what we hope or fear.

What are your expectations about your relationship? Do you expect your chosen partner to be the perfect match and that you'll both ride off into the sunset, living happily ever after? On the contrary, do you expect that your relationship will end up just like disaster stories you've seen with your own eyes—cruel words ricocheting off of walls, deciding to call it quits after putting up with each other for twenty years? Or, do your expectations fall somewhere between these two extremes, with a sense that though you won't always get things right, you will find a way to experience a largely satisfying lifetime together?

Don't underestimate the power of these expectations!

At the same time, don't overestimate their power, because there's a force that's even stronger than expectations: the force of intentions.

Intention has to do with the willpower you possess to take control of your unwritten future and make it a triumph over the past. It comes as a reminder that you don't live your lives as victims of fate. Intention also has to do with the responsibility you share to shape the relationship you want. It comes as a reminder that dreams come true if you act to make them happen.

Both before and after you marry, you must be intentional about growth in your relationship. Decide now to learn everything you can about yourself and your partner, as well as how to build your skills and strengths. Read relationship books. Attend relationship classes. Take advantage of relationship inventories/assessments. Meet with a Mentor Couple, coach, or counselor. Subscribe to relationship newsletters. Seek input from spiritual leaders and pray together for guidance. Join relationship groups. Develop relationship skills. And most of all, put into practice what you learn! It's not enough to know it—you must *choose* to do it.

If you *expect* to hit some rough patches but have intentionally equipped yourself and your relationship to handle them, you'll be able to navigate anything that arises. You'll also know what your resources are and be able to ask for appropriate help as needed. If you intend to learn more and more about yourself and your partner as years go by and follow up those *intentions* with action, your relationship will stay fresh and current. If you *expect* that the investment of time and energy in marriage pays off and add *intention* to your expectations, you will do whatever is required to develop a strong, healthy relationship.

It's all about expectations versus intentions. Your relationship can be everything you intend it will be. At the same time, be prepared to work for it. It's never too early to start, and it's never too late to begin.

Greg Hunt and **Priscilla Hunt** are dynamic speakers and are known for their lively, fun presentations. The Hunts are a certified Leader Couple and Specialists in Marriage Enrichment with Better Marriages (www.BetterMarriages.org). They are Seminar Directors for PREPARE-ENRICH, Instructor Trainers for Couple Communication, and certified Trainers for Mentoring for Better Marriages. They have been involved in marriage education and enrichment since they married in 1976. Priscilla is the Executive Director for Better Marriages, a non-profit since 1973, whose aim is educating couples for vibrant, lifelong relationships. After thirty-three years in pastoral ministry, Greg is now a consultant and writer, working in the areas of leadership, relationships, and spirituality. The parents of two adult children and grandparents to two granddaughters, Greg and Priscilla live in the metropolitan area of Kansas City, Kansas.

Chapter Five
Deepening Friendship

~ ~

The concept of being friends as well as spouses is gradually becoming part of the culture of marriage. Friendship brings deep and enduring gifts to your partnership that will help sustain you through the normal challenges that arise in everyone's lives and marriages.

These selections will help you with seeing the benefits of the friendship between you, understand what friendship between partners looks like, and discuss how being friends will enrich your marriage.

♥ ♥ ♥

Compatibility and Friendship
John Van Epp, Ph.D.

Love Can Be Blind

Marc flopped back on the couch and with a sigh of despair exclaimed, "How could I have been so blind? These things were staring me in the face!"

He continued to describe one experience after another which, at the time they happened, seemed trivial and unrelated. Now, in hindsight, they were weaving together in a tapestry of clear and distinct patterns.

After a long reflective pause, Marc concluded, "I really thought I knew her—but I guess I didn't after all."

The "love is blind" phenomenon is often generated by getting to know lots of *good stuff* about a partner, but just not the *right stuff*. In studies on the first five years of marriage, unrealistic expectations of a spouse are one of the most common sources of conflicts. Research has also revealed that couples who explore specific areas of their relationship prior to marriage have better quality relationships and a lower risk of divorce.

Romance and Friendship

Ted Huston, Ph.D., a Professor of Human Ecology and Psychology at the University of Texas at Austin, conducted a long-term study of married couples to understand the premarital predictors of couples who were still happily married thirteen years after their weddings. Huston found a number of pathways that led to disillusionment, unhappy marriages, and divorces. But the couples who were the most likely to feel happy and in love more than ten years into marriage were those who dated with strong romantic feelings while also taking their time to establish stable friendships, where they grew to deeply know and trust one another.

No matter whether you were swept off your feet the first time you laid eyes on each other, or shot with Cupid's arrow long after you were in your relationship, one thing is for sure: You must have *compatibility with chemistry.* In a study of almost 10,000 married adults from thirty-three countries, mutual attraction and love feelings were unanimously at the top as the essential prerequisites for partner choice.

Although chemistry is absolutely essential, be aware that chemistry alone can be misleading. Too often, this intoxicating attraction can be a poor judge of character, seeing only what it wants to see. So, be sure you also have a healthy dose of compatibility.

I was invited to interview individuals and couples who were being filmed for a romantic relationship program. I spent the day asking a series of questions to a range of participants, from those who were single and in early adolescence to those who had been married for many years. I decided to have a few questions that I would ask every participant just to see if the answers would vary according to age and status. By the end of the day, a remarkable discovery occurred: Every participant gave exactly the same answer to one of the questions. The question was, "If you had to identify the most important thing in your marriage (or future marriage) what would it be?"

Every participant stated that the number one quality was a *deep, best-friend relationship.* They described an image of great friends spending their lives together—creating a home; going shopping; taking walks; attending movies, sporting events, plays, and other recreational activities; and laughing and crying together. No matter what crossed their paths, they would create a lifestyle where they faced it together.

A Final Compatibility Check

That is true compatibility—sharing a considerable number of similarities between your personalities, values, and overall lifestyle, and blending together your differences in ways that create gains for each of you. A sure test of your compatibility is to ask yourself, "Do I feel that being with my partner makes me a better person?" and "Am I feeling secure and enriched by what I am giving and receiving in this relationship?" You both *absolutely* have to feel wonderful about what you put into and get out of your relationship.

Great chemistry is fundamental, but developing a deep and genuine friendship with rich compatibility is essential.

John Van Epp, Ph.D., President/Founder of *Love Thinks, LCC* is the author of *How to Avoid Falling in Love with a Jerk* (McGraw-Hill), which blends in-depth research with humorous stories to provide a map for making healthy relationship choices. His twenty-five years of clinical experience and extensive research in premarital, marital, and family relations have paved the way for his teach-out-of-the-box courses, PICK (How to Avoid Falling for a Jerk) and Marriage LINKS to be taught in thousands of churches, singles organizations, educational settings, and social agencies in all fifty states, ten countries, and by more than 2,500 military personnel. Van Epp and his innovative Relationship Attachment Model, book, and relationship courses were awarded the Smart Marriages® Impact Award in 2008, and they have been featured in *The Wall Street Journal, Time, Psychology Today, O Magazine,* and *Cosmopolitan.* Dr. Van Epp has appeared on the *CBS Early Show, The O'Reilly Factor, Fox News,* and *Focus on the Family.* He has been happily married for over thirty years and is the proud father of two daughters. His website is www.lovethinks.com, and he can be reached at vanepp@nojerks.com.

❤ ❤ ❤

The Key to a Successful Courtship and Marriage? Ask a Dolphin!
Paul Coleman, Psy.D.

Years ago, my wife, children, and I visited a large seaside aquarium where one of the attractions was acrobatic dolphins. They danced, jumped through hoops, tossed a ball, sang songs in their dolphin voices, and entertained us all with their skills. But, it was during the question and answer period after the show that the trainer said something that I think is very applicable to happy courtships and marriages.

The trainer gave a lesson to the audience on how to teach dolphins to perform such amazing feats on cue. He explained that each trick was divided up into smaller segments that built on one another, with the dolphin rewarded with a fish whenever it successfully completed each step. However, an alert observer pointed out that the dolphins were sometimes given a fish during the performance for doing nothing—that's right, nothing! "Doesn't that interfere with the training?" the observer asked. The trainer responded, "Giving the dolphin a fish now and then for no reason goes against the training protocol, but...*you've got to be friends!*"

Friendship is an excellent foundation for couples who plan to marry. Friends think about you, stand by you, know you well, and talk to you. On the other hand, couples who have the most problems in their relationship are not very good friends. If they give something, they feel owed. They operate on what's called a "zero-sum game mentality"—for one person to get more, the other must get less. Their relationship may be practical ("You do this, I'll do that."), but it is not devotional. They operate on rules that are rigid, self-serving, and often arbitrary ("If you loved me, you would...") and have a hard time nurturing another's dreams because they view such things as threatening.

Friends take time to understand one another—indeed, they *want* to understand one another—and find ways to nourish one another regardless of whether or not there is a personal payoff. In other words, they "toss one another a fish" for no reason except love and friendship. No strings attached. No obligations. Just "I love you—enjoy!"

Paul Coleman, Psy.D., is a Psychologist and Relationship Therapist in private practice. He is the author of a dozen books including *The Complete Idiot's Guide to Intimacy* and *We Need to Talk: Tough Conversations with Your Spouse*. He has appeared as an expert on the television shows *Oprah* and *Today*. Dr. Coleman and his wife Jody have been married for twenty-seven years, and they have three children. He can be reached at www.paul-coleman.com.

❤ ❤ ❤

What Is a Friend?
Susanne M. Alexander

One of the best foundations and indicators that a future marriage will last is a deep friendship with your spouse-to-be. Ideally, you will be closer to your spouse than to any other human being. If you have a friendship with your partner that has provided you with mutual support and understanding and you choose to marry, the foundation of your marriage will be stronger. You will already have had the practice of confiding in one another, seeing one another through difficulties, sharing joys, and turning to one another for fun and relaxation. Marriage is very much about companionship and is in many ways one long conversation with a close friend. You will appreciate being with someone you love to talk and spend time with.

Reaching out and having a deep, meaningful, intimate friendship requires you to be courageous and willing to be vulnerable. In the case of marriage, it also requires a willingness to sustain the friendship over time.

These are some of the aspects of friendship that will be valuable in your marriage:

- Ability to share honestly about both positive and difficult matters; good communication
- Acknowledgement of positive qualities in each other
- Ability to spend quiet, peaceful time together
- Play, fun, and laughter
- Acceptance; ability to be oneself rather than putting on an act to impress the other
- Responsiveness, help, assistance, and appropriate sympathy or empathy during difficulties
- Enthusiasm about individual and shared achievements
- Loving, spiritual connection
- Encouragement
- Accessibility
- Loyalty
- Trust that shared information and experiences will not be used

hurtfully against each other
- Trust that the other will not deliberately cause harm
- Reliability; trustworthiness
- Ability to suspend judgment and not jump to conclusions
- Affirmation and approval
- Common and bonding experiences and memories
- Shared goals
- Working together on projects
- Agreed boundaries and expectations
- Shared interests and activities
- Opportunities to learn together
- Ability to disagree peacefully and constructively
- Dedication to be of service to others together
- Ability to reconnect easily, even after being apart
- Motivational feedback or nudging that constructively influences the other to grow or go forward
- Attitude of forgiveness and willingness to grant another chance
- Respectfulness and equality

As you prepare for the possibility of marriage, consider these questions:

- What do you value about the friendship you have with each other?
- What can you do to strengthen friendship between you?

Having your spouse as your best friend is terrific!

Susanne M. Alexander is a Relationship and Marriage Coach and President of Marriage Transformation LLC. She was very blessed to marry a close friend and have a friendship-based marriage.

❤ ❤ ❤

Friendship—The Foundation Stone for Marriage
Lidy Seysener

There's a scene at the end of the movie *When Harry Met Sally* when several elderly couples are telling stories about how they met and fell in love and talking about how they are still together after so many years. These couples are so "in synch" with each other that they finish each other's sentences. They each know the other so well, even down to what the other is going to say, that without even talking over the top of each other, you get the whole story, as if it could have all come from one mouth.

This is my definition of true friendship, and it creates the foundation of every marriage that has lasted far longer than the soft skin, the agile body, and the great sex. These are the great relationships that exist beyond sickness, beyond the bad times, and will only be severed by the death that will one day separate the couple from each other.

These marriages are ageless: they have stood the test of time. These couples have discovered something that so many of us still struggle with, and that is that the love that comes from a true friendship survives all and any adversity that can be thrown at them. How does this happen? I think there is something happening in those long-time marriages that are often not present in many current relationships. These relationships began differently in the first place.

One of my clients was an older gentleman who had lost his wife six months before after forty years of marriage. He was grieving for her so badly that he didn't know what to do with himself. There was nothing he needed to understand or learn about this event. My role as his counselor was simply to give him a place to tell his story.

Peter described himself back before he met his wife as "a bit of a lad." He enjoyed the company of his mates, and they spent Saturday nights out on the town drinking and partying. On occasion, they would go to a dance and meet up with girls. This is how Peter met the woman who would become his wife and long-time partner.

Peter's mates had suggested there was someone new likely to be at the dance who Peter might fancy. This is when he first met Pip, and they instantly hit it off. The months that followed were spent going out with the group and getting to know each other more. He said *they became good friends*. It was from this friendship that their love grew. They married and made a life together. Before they fell in love, they first created a really great friendship.

I believe friendship must be a precursor to a truly great relationship and become the necessary foundation that will take the marriage into the future.

When I talk to couples now, I ask them what they do for fun. These are the activities that will create the opportunities for a friendship to flourish. Sometimes life becomes too serious as people get on with acquiring things in their lives instead of living their lives.

How about you? Are you and your partner friends? To ascertain the answer, ask yourself this question. "Do I really like this person?" If the answer is "Yes!" then you probably have what it takes to go the long term with each other. If the answer is "No," then you probably need to rethink whether what you have together will be enough to keep you connected 'til death do you part!

Lidy Seysener is the principal of Northern Beaches Counseling, a very successful hypnotherapy and Counseling Practice at Mona Vale in Sydney, Australia. Amongst her many skills, Lidy is a Counselor/Psychotherapist, Hypnotherapist, and a Neuro-Linguistic Programming and Time Line Therapy Master Practitioner, with memberships in a variety of associations, including the Australian Counselors Association and the Australian Society of Clinical Hypnotherapists. Lidy is also a qualified Family Dispute Resolution Practitioner and Community Mediator registered with the Australian Attorney General's Office, thereby accrediting her to issue certificates for applications before the Family Court of Australia. In her work, Lidy supports individuals, couples, and families in creating happier lives for themselves. In her personal life, Lidy has four adult children, all of whom are now living successful lives in their own right. You can reach Lidy at www.northernbeachescounselling.com.au or www.northernbeachesmediation.com.au.

♥ ♥ ♥

Have Friends of Your Marriage
Nisa Muhammad

Every marriage needs friends, especially another married couple who will be there to guide your union to success. These are not so-called "friends" who will rush the husband off to divorce court at the first hint of disrespect. This is not someone who will arbitrarily tell the wife, "Girl, you don't have to take that mess." Couples who are friends of your marriage will help you go in a better direction when you are struggling and your love seems to be sinking.

You can start in this direction now by hanging out with other couples who are considering marriage. Notice how good it feels when you are supporting each other and figuring out what works well as couples. You can talk about your fears and concerns about marriage, as well as build each other's confidence in success. If you walk away from these get-togethers and discussions questioning whether to marry, these are not good couple friends.

There is a gravitational pull to the world of singleness. It can seem like life might be easier on your own. There's no one to ask when you're coming home, no one to inquire why you're late, and no one to answer to when you want to go out by yourself or spend your money the way you want to. But the flipside of all that can be loneliness and less effective decisions. Unfortunately, when you're in the midst of a marriage meltdown, being single can sound really tempting.

If you surround your marriage with single friends who have little understanding of marriage and what it means to be a spouse, you are asking for unnecessary trouble. Does this mean you can't have single friends if you're married? Of course not! Does this mean singles are always bad for your marriage? Definitely not! What it does mean is that there must be balance. It is best to avoid spending excessive time with single friends who want you to live a single lifestyle. Married people need to be around other married people for strength and support.

Steel sharpens steel, men sharpen men, and women sharpen women. The same applies to husbands and wives: healthy marriages sharpen healthy marriages. Too many people today grow up without a good example of what husbands and wives should do in a family setting. Where do we learn appropriate behavior and conduct as a husband and wife? For lots of couples, it's on-the-job training without a job description or supervisor. Married couples need another healthy marriage in their life to give them someone to look up to, someone who can inspire them, provide guidance, and just be there when the hard times come.

A husband needs a friend to tap him on the shoulder when he's been talking to another woman too long or to tell him, "Go home" because it's late. That husband needs men of substance and courage in his life, someone who will remind him of his commitment to wife and family. That's a friend of your marriage. It's not cool, funny, or "manly" to be left alone to stray while disrespecting yourself and your family under the guise of "boys will be boys." That's not a friend of your marriage. In fact, it's not a real friend at all.

A wife needs a friend to remind her that her husband really does love her in spite of the current drama at hand. She needs another wife to tell her that the flirting she's doing with the waiter isn't cute, or the prolonged time she's spending with her Pastor every Sunday can't be all about the Lord. A person who will do those things for you is a friend of your marriage. It's someone who will help you take your sorrows to prayer and your joys to praise. Don't get caught up with women who love the single life or those who live with an irresponsible man and want you to be miserable with them.

Find friends of your marriage. Find couples who will love you enough to tell you the truth. Find couples who will nurture your marriage and work with you to achieve wedded bliss. Once you're there, return the favor and be a friend to someone else's marriage.

Nisa Muhammad is the Founder of the Wedded Bliss Foundation (www.weddedblissinc.com), a community-based organization helping teens and adults create healthy relationships and healthy marriages. One of its goals is giving more children the benefits of a two-parent family. She created Black Marriage Day for communities to celebrate marriage in very unique ways. It is held annually on the fourth Sunday in March, and it has grown from 30 participating cities participating in 2003 to close to 300 communities conducting celebrations in 2010. Mrs. Muhammad is the co-author of *Basic Training for Couples*, a marriage education curriculum. Her work as a pioneer in strengthening marriage in the Black community was featured in detail on CNN's *Black in America 2*. She knows both the joys of marriage and the sorrows of divorce. She works so her five children and more adults can enjoy wedded bliss.

Chapter Six
Knowing One Another

~ ~

In a world where people often behave as if marriage is a short-term activity, it is wise for you to recognize that knowing one another well will help to prevent unpleasant surprises after the wedding. As you go through this chapter, consider what activities you can do together to really help deepen your knowledge about character, learn your reactions under difficult circumstances, assess how you might be as parents, and more. Marriage is more than social dating, and you will be strengthened by doing a variety of activities together during courtship. Your thoroughness now will benefit you in the coming decades.

Here, we help you with understanding the importance of being honest with each other, going on fun and educational dates, focusing on what's important, knowing key aspects of one another's character, being bonded as partners, and more. Deeply knowing and appreciating each other is one of the joys of courtship and engagement. However, we also encourage you to pay careful attention and not make assumptions about each other—we want your minds involved, not just your hearts and passions. You are making a choice that you want to last, and ensuring that you really are good and wise partners together is part of this stage in your relationship.

❤ ❤ ❤

Honest Dating and Courting
Mark Gungor

Here's a familiar scenario: a woman is dating a guy (or beyond that and is involved in serious courtship). She thinks, "Okay, so he has A-B-C-D going on, and he's a bum, but I *love* him." Then, she marries him and in the not-too-distant future she becomes…well, Mrs. Miserable. She'll then come to someone like me for counseling. Often, one of the first things I ask is, "Didn't you see this before you were married?" Then she'll tell me, "Yes, but I thought I could change him."

Way too many women are dating guys thinking they can change or morph them into the man they want them to be. It would be far better to find a companion that is already more of what you want. If he's a frog, you aren't going to turn him into Prince Charming. You need to move on. I don't know what it is in the female psyche that makes women think the bum will be different when they are married. Guys don't think that way. In fact, most men don't want the woman they fall in love with to change one wit after marriage! They are perfectly content to have their brides stay just as they are.

I think a lot of people are not being totally honest during the dating and courting process. Or many feel obligated to follow through with a wedding just because they have been together for a while, even though they may have some strong reservations. But if you are struggling with any aspect of who a person is, you probably need to look at that as a red flag. Ultimately, that is what the dating and courting time is for—to decide, based on what you have learned, whether or not to marry that person.

If you don't like the fact that he isn't a devoted follower of Jesus or that he smokes or is a slob or whatever (fill in the blank), but you think by some "magical cosmic force" he'll be different once you are married, you are fooling yourself. Women will say they want a solid Christian man, someone with a good job, and someone with a wonderful mother. But, then they date a guy who stays in bed and watches TV rather than going to church, can't hold a steady job, and whose mother is a banshee. They mistakenly think these things will go away, won't matter, or that they can change him. These women are in for a ton of misery.

First, make sure your expectations are realistic. If your list includes a guy who looks like a Greek god, is a millionaire, loves cats, has TV's June Cleaver for a mother, sings like Pavarotti, and has the entire *Bible* memorized in three translations, you probably won't find him! Be realistic and then decide which ones are deal breakers. Maybe it's the future in-laws, health issues, or values like the depth and commitment of their faith. You have to decide what you can and can't live with—or live without! But don't kid yourself into thinking those things that bug you and you don't like will not matter down the matrimonial road. They will matter, and you'll end up wondering if the road took a detour through hell.

We oftentimes deliberately ignore a person's past when deciding on a mate, and while everyone makes mistakes, some mistakes have consequences and ramifications that can follow us for the rest of our lives. Granted, God doesn't hold our past mistakes against us if we come to Him in true repentance. But those mistakes can still have consequences that can negatively affect our future relationships, particularly in our marriage.

The dating process should be a time of discovery and analysis to determine whether or not a certain person would make a good lifetime mate. A person's history can be a major factor in determining how they will handle their future relationships. Don't be fooled by thinking that just because God—and even people—have forgiven a past issue that it won't occur again. The wise seeker of a mate will do well to look into the history of their potential spouse and understand the personality and character traits and weaknesses that could lead to history repeating itself. And doing so is not unfair, nor is it an unspiritual act. I counsel people all the time who struggle with issues that go back to their pasts. For example, there are situations when women feel like their husbands are using them for sex because it happened in the past. That is something her now-husband should have learned about during the dating process. Realize that these things could impact your marriage.

If you think you may not be able to deal with those issues down the road, or if you can't carry that heavy load, then let them go so they can find someone who can. There are very wonderful, compassionate, and kind people who have been gifted by God to do just that—people who can say, "I will love you, cherish you, and take care of you no matter what." God can give people great gifts of compassion or encouragement or mercy. It doesn't mean that those who don't have those gifts are bad people; it just makes you honest when you realize you aren't comfortable dealing with the baggage of someone's past.

Let's say you learn the person you are dating has a past record of shoplifting. You may wonder what values that person grew up with that allowed them to make a decision like that. Knowing the choices they've made in the past, you may not want to continue on in the relationship—and that is fair. The dating process is about finding out about someone, the choices they've made, and who they are.

You may say "But what about forgiveness?!" It's not about refusing to forgive a person's shortcomings or judging someone harshly for their mistakes. You can forgive them (God certainly does), but it doesn't mean you have to marry them. Remember, dating and courting are really about looking at the person as a whole and thinking, "Yes, I am very comfortable with who this person is" or "No, I'm not."

Let's say your girlfriend tells you she had an abortion a few years ago. If you truly believe this is something you can deal with, and you are able to love and cherish this woman and help her with the emotional and physical effects, then great! If, on the other hand, you struggle with some things in her character that allowed her to make that decision, or if you are concerned about the emotional and possible physical issues that may result, you have every right to move on. That doesn't make you a bad person; it just makes you honest. It's better to decide *now*, before you are married, than to have great difficulty with the issue afterwards. Once you say, "I do," it's a whole different ball game, and you're in for life. But it is okay to move on before you marry. Remember: That is what dating and courting are for. Besides, it would be better for her to find someone that God has gifted to be able to handle her past.

Maybe your special someone tells you they have a sexually transmitted disease, one that you, too, will get once you marry them. Now's the time to walk away if that is something you don't want to live with.

It could be simpler things like his family is gross or her father drives you crazy. You might see a problem in how her mother treats her father, which could be an indicator of how their daughter will treat you. If these things are not things you can handle, now is the time to walk away.

Some could be more difficult issues like sexual abuse, addictions to alcohol, or use of pornography. These types of issues are all fair game during the discovery process of dating and courting. Again, that's part of what they are about. You get to analyze the situation and view the person as a whole and see if you can handle all that goes with taking this person as your spouse.

It is imperative that men and women are totally honest with each other while they are thinking of and preparing for marriage. These types of issues should be revealed at the front end. It's not fair to be eighteen months, two years, or five years into a marriage and for your spouse to be struggling with issues they didn't even know existed in you. If someone does not feel they can handle certain baggage, it's best that they move on.

What they should *not* do is drag the other person along for months or even years in courtship if they have some serious reservations. It's not fair to either of you. You have to be honest and willing to let them go so they can find someone who can deal with who they are, past and all. People will say, "I really love them. How can I just walk away?" but if you have serious reservations about marrying, the most loving thing you can do is let them go. It's not fair to keep stringing another person along, wondering if you can or can't handle their past.

You can't make a man or woman into the one you *want* them to be or the idealized version you *wish* they would be. You need to find the one that most closely fits your mold…and they still won't be perfect! There will always be things in marriage that make men and women crazy. Again, make sure your expectations are realistic. If the dude doesn't make the grade, don't assume that you can do "extreme husband makeover" on him. If she doesn't measure up to what you want and need and can handle, set her free. Expecting each other to be different than you are will just bring a lot of grief to yourself and the poor person you are trying to remodel.

> **Mark Gungor** is one of the most sought-after speakers on marriage and family in the country. Each year, thousands of couples attend his "Laugh Your Way to a Better Marriage"® seminars. His take on marriage issues is refreshingly free of both churchy and psychological lingo. Mark is Pastor of Celebration Church in Green Bay, Wisconsin. He speaks for churches, civic events, business meetings, and even the U.S. Army. Mark has been featured on national broadcasts such as *Focus on the Family* and ABC News. His daily Internet radio show is heard worldwide, and his weekly television show *Love, Marriage, and Stinking Thinking* is available on TBN and Sky Angel. Learn more about Mark and his marriage seminars at www.laughyourway.com. Mark and his wife Debbie recently celebrated their 37th wedding anniversary and have two married children and four grandsons.

❤ ❤ ❤

How Do I Look?
Molly Barrow, Ph.D.

As human beings, we automatically respond to and judge people based on appearance. Initial attraction between you and your partner probably had a lot to do with how you each looked. Certainly, maintaining your appearance and health can be a factor in keeping you attracted to one another. However, too much time spent on physical appearance, hair, makeup, or grooming will not bring you any closer to your life goals and will rob you of the precious little time you have to achieve what really matters to you. As your relationship matures, what is beneath the surface for each of you is far more important.

Have you become obsessive about your appearance and more dependent on the approval of others? Such qualities can eventually kill desire in the very people the big effort is meant to attract. Sometimes we concentrate so heavily on the preparation that we miss the joy of the event entirely.

Spending your time getting to know one another deeply, learning new skills and knowledge, working out, or playing with friends and family has a higher payoff. Can you spontaneously play in a business suit or high heels and artificial nails? On the other hand, do you just watch other people have fun and live life to the fullest? Discuss the expectations you have of one another for maintaining your appearance after marriage, especially during the difficult times like pregnancy, illness, young children, or high stress.

As you examine your lives and refine your priority lists, you may find that spending time on appearance and partying with superficial friends, making cool appearances at the "right" places, wearing emotional masks, or competing with others will have notably less value. Maybe it's better to take that two-mile walk together and concentrate on getting involved in activities that make a positive difference for others, rather than getting too focused on looking "hot."

A relationship based on artificial glitter is too fragile to last. Such a relationship is a burden that enslaves you to excessive grooming and spending your paycheck on hot heels or fancy shirts. Any new face can soon steal you away from each other if you don't love each other for what rests beneath your attractive coating.

Use glitter only to attract, and then reveal the real for a relationship that lasts.

Molly Barrow holds a Ph.D. in Clinical Psychology and is the author of *Matchlines for Singles, Matchlines for Couples, How to Survive Step Parenting*, and the *Malia and Teacup* self-esteem building series for young readers. An authority on relationship and psychological topics, Dr. Barrow is a member of the American Psychological Association, Screen Actors Guild, and Authors Guild, and is a licensed mental health counselor. Dr. Barrow has appeared as an expert in the film *My Suicide*, the documentaries *Ready to Explode* and *KTLA Impact*, NBC news, PBS *In Focus*, and on WBZT talk radio. She has been quoted in *O Magazine, Psychology Today, Newsday, New York Times, CNN, The Nest*, MSN.com, Yahoo.com, Match.com, *Women's Health*, and *Women's World*. Dr. Barrow has a radio show on www.progressiveradionetwork.com and is a columnist for www.Menstuff.org. Dr. Barrow has a counseling practice in Naples, Florida, and is happily married with a wonderful family including three children, one daughter-in-law, and two precious grandsons. Her website is www.drmollybarrow.com; Blog is: http://drmollybarrow.blogspot.com/; Twitter is: www.twitter.com/drmollybarrow; Live & Archived Radio Shows are: www.progressiveradionetwork.com/the-dr-molly-barrow-show/

❤ ❤ ❤

Character and Marriage
Linda Bloom and Charlie Bloom

Marriage preparation requires the cultivation of the necessary skills to achieve an excellent marriage. While this is the work of a lifetime, fortunately you don't have to be completely accomplished to get into the game. It's mostly on-the-job training.

Some people talk a lot about doing the work of marriage or that marriage involves hard work, but what exactly is the work that marriage involves? Essentially, it has to do with growing up and becoming an emotionally intelligent, integrated human being. This process usually involves the cultivation of certain qualities, virtues, or traits such as compassion, patience, courage, commitment, responsibility, creativity, generosity, and integrity, to name but a few.

These traits are the foundation of one's character, the quality of which is the primary factor that influences the nature of not just your primary partner relationship, but all of your relationships. The development of these traits is more influential on the success of your marriage than your level of education, choice of a partner, career, income level, or family history. It is wise to know one another's character strengths and growth areas before committing to marry and to be aware whether there are character weaknesses that may be of concern.

These character strengths are the building blocks that promote the development of the skills that good relationships require. These skills include the ability to:
- Communicate effectively
- Listen well without judgment, defensiveness, or reactivity
- Practice cooperative partnership
- Manage differences well

- Make accurate distinctions and discernments
- Establish and honor personal boundaries
- Negotiate for one's own needs while being respectful to others
- Express oneself with emotional honesty

It isn't necessary—or in most cases even possible—to master these skills prior to marriage, nor is it necessary to have a partner who has already achieved a high level of mastery. What is important is that both partners embody an intention to learn, grow, and develop themselves in the relationship and address the issues that inevitably arise with openness, respect, and honesty. We generally don't come into marriage fully developed, but rather, as a work in progress. Appreciating this concept helps each partner to be more forgiving of themselves and each other during the inevitable difficult or challenging times.

Linda Bloom, L.C.S.W., and Charlie Bloom, M.S.W., are Psychotherapists and Marriage Counselors who teach communication seminars and relationship workshops throughout the world. They are co-authors of the best-selling book, *101 Things I Wish I Knew When I Got Married, Simple Lessons to Make Love Last,* and *Secrets of Great Marriages: Real Truths from Real Couples About Lasting Love,* published in 2010. They offer educational and counseling services to individuals, couples, and organizations. Their website is www.bloomwork.com, and they can be reached at 831-421-9822 or by email at lcbloom@bloomwork.com. They live and practice in Santa Cruz, California.

❤ ❤ ❤

Choosing a Partner Who Is Right for You
Margaret Paul, Ph.D.

We all know people who appear to be very confident professionally, yet when it comes to personal relationships, they appear to be very insecure. The *Encarta World English Dictionary* defines confidence as "a belief or self-assurance in your ability to succeed."

What creates personal confidence? How does one become confident in who they are—and confident in choosing a partner who is right for them?

Recognizing Your Inner Worth

If you grew up with parents who valued their own inner qualities and were role models for inner confidence, as well as valued your inner qualities and supported you in being who you are, it is likely that you feel personally confident. But most of us did not grow up that way. We had parents or other caregivers who not only lacked personal confidence much of the time, but who may have frequently blamed and shamed us as well, undermining our sense of Self.

However, no matter how much we may have been de-valued as children, it is never too late to learn to value ourselves now. The secret in gaining personal confidence is to learn to take full responsibility for your own feelings of worth by connecting with your Higher Self, getting to know your true inner Self—your soul essence—who you really are, and learning to take loving care of yourself. This is what happens when you learn and practice the Inner Bonding® process, which is outlined below.

Your true Self is comprised of your essential inner qualities that you were born with the capacity to demonstrate, such as your ability to love, to be kind and caring, to be compassionate and empathic, and to listen well. It is about your basic goodness. It is also about your creativity, your unique talents, your particular form of intelligence, your sense of humor, your smile, your laugh—all that is uniquely you.

If you were not valued for your true Self, it is likely that you are not seeing or valuing your essence qualities. In fact, you might have decided a long time ago that you are not good enough—that you are somehow inadequate as a person. It is this false belief that creates feelings of inadequacy and a lack of personal confidence. If you do not see value in yourself, you are unlikely to be able to recognize it adequately in a partner.

Learning to value yourself starts with learning to be present inside your body, connecting with your feelings. Your feelings are your inner guidance system, letting you know each moment if you are being loving or unloving to yourself. Your feelings of inadequacy, anxiety, depression, guilt, shame, anger, emptiness, neediness, and aloneness are letting you know that you are abandoning yourself. When you abandon yourself by ignoring your feelings, judging yourself, turning to addictions to numb your feelings, or making others responsible for your feelings of safety and worth, your inner guidance will let you know this with your painful feelings. Your feelings of inner peace and joy are letting you know that you are loving yourself.

Right now, imagine that you can see yourself from the eyes of your Higher

Self, the eyes of love. Visualize yourself as a very small child and look inside at who that child is. What do you see? Is there anything about you as a small child that makes you unlovable? What are the wonderful qualities that are inherent in you as a child? If this child were your actual child, how would you feel about and treat him or her? Would you abandon this child or love this child?

The Steps of the Inner Bonding® Process

Step 1: Feeling your feelings and wanting responsibility for them.

Step 2: Moving into an intent to learn about what you are telling yourself—your false beliefs—and how you are treating yourself that may be causing your pain.

Step 3: Dialoguing with your feelings—your inner child—to discover how you may be abandoning yourself.

Step 4: Opening to learning with your Higher Self to discover the truth about your false beliefs and the loving action toward yourself.

Step 5: Taking the loving action.

Step 6: Evaluating the action to see if you are now feeling peaceful and happy inside.

The more you practice this process, the more self-confidence you will gain.

Recognizing a Valuable Partner

It's common for people before or in the early stages of a serious relationship to ask, "How will I know when I meet the right person or am with the right person for me?"

There are two different reasons people have for wanting to get married:

1. To get love, validation, security, and safety.
2. To share love, and to grow emotionally and spiritually.

Relationship Neediness

People who feel insecure and alone are likely to look for someone who will fill the inner emptiness and give them the love they are seeking. They want to find someone who will complete them and make them feel adequate and worthy. The problem is that no one can do this for another person; it is something we each need to learn to do for ourselves. Since we are always attracted to people who are at our common level of woundedness or our common level of health, a person looking to get love will attract a person also looking to get love. Each person hopes to get filled from the other, not realizing that each feels empty and really has little to give. Therefore, no one is the right person when the intent of getting married is to get love and security rather than to share love and learning.

Instead of asking, "Is this the right person for me?" why not ask, "Am I being the right person? Am I being a person who comes to a relationship filled with love to share, or am I being a needy person hoping to get love and validation?"

Many relationships don't work because each person is disappointed in not getting what they expected to get from the other person. But when a person does not know how to love and validate themselves and create an inner sense of safety and security, they certainly can't do this for another person. Yet this is what each person expects of the other. It's like trying to get water from a rock. What do you have to give when you feel empty within and want to get filled through another's love?

Sharing and Growing Love

It is actually fairly easy to know if your partner is the right person for you when your intent in being in a relationship is to learn together and share love. A person who comes from a full place within finds it easy to discern when someone is empty inside and will not be attracted to the empty person. A person who is practicing Inner Bonding® and is truly open to learning about themselves, to growing emotionally and spiritually, and to taking responsibility for their own feelings of safety and security, worth, and lovability, will not be attracted to a person who is closed, controlling, and just wants to get love.

Knowing if this is the right person for you does not happen instantly. It takes months to discover whether or not a person is who they say they are. It is wise to focus on learning whether they are personally confident and whether they are operating from their strong, attractive inner qualities—such as kindness, patience, courage, and compassion—or whether they frequently operate from their wounded self and become controlling. The more you are both interacting with one another from love rather than control, the healthier and stronger your relationship will be.

Various activities will help to give you both a better level of knowledge about each other. For instance, you cannot really know who a person is until you have a disagreement and find out what this person does when you are in conflict. Some people can appear very open and loving until a conflict comes up, and then they get angry, withdraw, resist, or comply, closing down rather than staying open to learning about themselves and the other person. An important question is, "How does this person deal with conflict? Are they able to shift into a desire to learn and resolve, and how long does it take them to open up if they do close down in the face of disharmony?"

If you are both open to learning and you want a relationship for sharing love, there are three *essential ingredients* that need to be present:

1. There is a basic spark of mental, emotional, spiritual, and physical attraction between you. If you do not feel physically attracted to this person within the first six months of the relationship, it will probably not happen. It does not need to be instant, but it does need to be there at some point.

2. You are capable of caring, compassion, and empathy—to be givers rather than just takers. You are not ready for a relationship if you both always want your own way and to always be in receiving mode.

3. You are open to learning when conflict arises rather than just wanting to win and be right. This allows you to resolve issues in loving ways rather than getting into power struggles.

Other ingredients (such as common interests and values) are also important, but without the above three ingredients, you will not be able to sustain your relationship.

Confidence, valuing your inner best qualities, and being loving are all powerful tools in helping you be ready for a relationship and helping you in recognizing the best in your partner.

Margaret Paul, Ph.D., is a noted public speaker, best-selling author, workshop leader, relationship expert, and Inner Bonding® facilitator. She has counseled individuals and couples, as well as led groups, classes, and workshops since 1968. She is the author and co-author of eight books, including the internationally best-selling *Do I Have To Give Up Me To Be Loved By You?; Healing Your Aloneness; Inner Bonding; and Do I Have To Give Up Me To Be Loved By God?* She is the co-creator, along with Dr. Erika Chopich, of the Inner Bonding® healing process, recommended by actress Lindsay Wagner and singer Alanis Morissette, and featured on *Oprah,* and of the unique and popular website www.innerbonding.com. Their transformational self-healing/conflict resolution software program, SelfQuest®, at www.selfquest.com, is being donated to prisons and schools, as well as sold to the general public. Margaret has three children and three grandchildren.

❤ ❤ ❤

Know Each Other's Character Before Marrying
Susanne M. Alexander

There are many important aspects of relationships, but it is character development that offers us the greatest capacity for improvement. This is the vital focus for any individual preparing for a relationship and any couple contemplating marriage—and for good reason. Our character qualities affect virtually every word we say or action we take, and our souls have great capacity to develop strength in most of these qualities.

As our qualities strengthen, it is like turning a light on inside us that shines out to others and creates positive outcomes. Not only that, but our character qualities travel on with us to be useful in whatever spiritual adventure follows our physical life on Earth.

What Qualities to Consider

How much time have you devoted to studying character and how to practice various qualities? If you put your mind to it, you can probably come up with over 100 qualities that any person could develop over a lifetime. However, the ones listed below are those that have the most applicability to marriage and the relationships that lead up to it:

Acceptance	Encouragement	Joyfulness	Self-Discipline
Assertiveness	Enthusiasm	Justice	Service
Beauty	Excellence	Kindness	Sincerity
Caring	Faithfulness	Love	Spirituality
Chastity	Flexibility	Loyalty	Tactfulness
Commitment	Forgiveness	Mercy	Thankfulness
Compassion	Fortitude	Moderation	Thoughtfulness
Confidence	Friendliness	Patience	Thriftiness
Contentment	Generosity	Peacefulness	Trustworthiness
Cooperation	Gentleness	Perseverance	Truthfulness
Courage	Helpfulness	Purity	Unity
Courtesy	Honesty	Purposefulness	Wisdom
Creativity	Humility	Resilience	
Detachment	Idealism	Respect	
Discernment	Integrity	Responsibility	

Time and experience have proven it impossible to come up with a top-ten list of the most important qualities. What is most applicable in your lives may not be in another couple's, and what blend of qualities works best in your relationship is unique to the two of you together. "Importance" is affected by your experiences in life. For example, if you had a parent who spent money constantly and was always in debt, Thriftiness could be something you highly value in yourself and your partner. If a previous partner betrayed you with lies, Truthfulness in your relationship is likely vital. Your need for connection with one another will be best balanced with including your clear awareness of character-related behavior.

Affirming Character Qualities

It will help you to learn about each other's character when you use *Character Quality Language* to affirm specific qualities in each other. This practice also builds love, appreciation, and happiness between you, particularly when you are specific and sincere. Here are some simple examples:

- "Thank you for being (Helpful, Flexible, Truthful…)".
- "I appreciate your (Courage, Respect, Faithfulness…)"
- "I love how (Accepting, Enthusiastic, Encouraging…) you are!"

Your character affirmations become even more powerful when you include specifics about your partner's words or actions. Consider these examples:

- "Your Patience in working with my Dad on the car in the garage yesterday and how Helpful you were to him really touched my heart."
- "It was great watching you be so Enthusiastic at my son's soccer game this morning. Thank you for being so Flexible about the change in starting time."

Using Character Quality Language will help you to strengthen and keep practicing these qualities. Having someone notice your use of a quality encourages your continued use.

This practice is also a key tool for parents in helping children learn about and strengthen specific qualities. For example, you can say, "Please be Patient" instead of "Oh, just hold on a minute!" and it helps the child (and you) with learning Patience. Learning the names of the character qualities and highlighting them in your children builds their self-respect. Then you can say, "Thank you for being Caring to your little sister today when she was sad" instead of "You were nice to your sister today." If the children see you affirming these qualities in each other, this will also give them Confidence in your marriage.

Levels of Functioning

As you are observing each other's words and actions and assessing each other's character, you will see that every quality has these levels of functioning:

- Your weakness in practicing the quality results in negative outcomes
- Your ineffectiveness in practicing the quality sometimes results in negative outcomes
- Although you understand the quality and know quite well how to practice it, you often struggle to do so effectively
- You practice the quality effectively, although not consistently, usually with positive outcomes
- You consistently practice the quality effectively and with positive outcomes

An additional concept that may be useful for you to understand is "misusing a quality." You may know how to practice a quality, and it may be a clear strength, but when you use it in excess or at the wrong time or place, it causes harm. A common example of this is with the quality of Helpfulness. Stepping in to help someone without asking them when they do not welcome your attempt to help can harm a relationship.

Couple Guidelines

Here are some guidelines about character that will help you as you determine whether to marry:

1. Know your own character strengths and growth areas.

2. Know your partner's character strengths and growth areas.

3. Romance and passion can blind you to each other's character strengths and flaws; getting input from people who know you well (such as parents) can be helpful.

4. Empower yourselves in building a strong relationship by making character strengthening a priority in your life.

5. Look for where your character strengths complement each other; for example, someone living with a Creative person may need Patience and Flexibility. Someone looking for a peaceful home may want a partner skilled in Kindness.

6. Identify qualities that need to be strengths in both of you for harmonious marital living; for example, mutual Faithfulness.

7. Never attack each other's character with harsh criticisms; for example, "You are dishonest...lazy...irresponsible..." and so on. [Note: Research from John Gottman, Ph.D., shows that divorce is likely where this character attack pattern is a common occurrence.]

8. Agree on ways to help and influence each other toward strengthening character qualities; for example, being open to Gentle, Loving feedback.

9. Apply Acceptance and Encouragement as you each practice self-improvement.

10. Avoid the pitfall of thinking you should only look at a person's good qualities and not their areas of character weakness in this period before marriage. Character strengths will help you establish a healthy, happy, harmonious marriage; character flaws may destroy it.

A caution about observing character qualities in someone: It can be a pitfall if you can only describe your partner in relation *to you*. For instance, when asked to tell what the person is like, you might respond with, "He's so Courteous *to me*," or "She is always doing Helpful things *for me*." These are good but limited observations. To know that your partner's actions are a true reflection of their character, it is wise to know whether they are Generous, Friendly, or Courageous generally, with most other people—not just in the behavior that is directed toward you. Remember that any behavior directly with you may be influenced by infatuation.

Character in Marriage

Even once you have been careful in knowing your own and each other's characters and concluded that you are a good match, there are still many adjustments to make within marriage. Consider this wisdom:

> Marriage, like all our other relationships in life, is a process which, among other things, serves to grind the sharp edges off us. The grinding often hurts, the adjustment to another person's character

is difficult at first, that is why love is needed here more than in any other relationship. Love, being essentially a divine force, binds; it leaps like a spark the gaps between people's thoughts and conflicting desires, between perhaps widely different temperaments. It heals the wounds we all inflict on each other....[1]

The process of knowing and developing your own characters began long before you were in a relationship, and it is a lifelong journey. One of the key benefits of marriage can be an acceleration of character growth because of new experiences and because you are partners helping and encouraging one another. *Character growth is one of the key purposes of marriage.*

1 Rúhíyyih Rabbani, *Prescription for Living* (1978 ed.), pp. 87-88

Susanne M. Alexander is a Relationship and Marriage Coach who specializes in how character factors into successful personal growth, relationships, and marriages. www.marriagetransformation.com

© 2010 S. Alexander

❤ ❤ ❤

Bejeweled: Gemstones to Consider Before the Rock Goes on the Finger
Barbara Jenkins Spires

There are plenty of things to think about when contemplating marriage. There are the four "W" questions to address: When and where? (which address the wedding); and Who and why? (which focus on the marriage).

Below are "Gemstones" to help you with who you are and why you are marrying. These will offer some tips and guidance to prepare for your marriage—or, at the very least, to invest in a loving, healthy relationship.

Sapphire: Forgive the Flaws and Lose "The List"

Can you look beyond his flaws? Most women are known, literally, for creating a "man made" wish list of the top 100 non-negotiable qualities they want, need, and expect from their perfect mate. Making up such a love-mate list has its merits (and there may be a few men making lists as well). For some, it puts them in the mindset of not settling for just anything or anyone. However, trying to find a perfect match for that perfect list can sometimes steer you into focusing on superficial aspects of a person instead of their gem-like qualities. Finding someone to measure up can be unrealistic. It can leave you disillusioned and quite honestly, lonely. In matters of the heart, you don't need a list to remind you of what's important to you for an ideal mate. Unless the flaws or imperfections involve disrespect or abuse of any kind, accepting each other's flaws, ironically, makes you perfect for each other.

Ruby: Support—Rain or Shine

Figure out how you need to be emotionally supported and whether your partner is willing and able to be that anchor. Can you depend on him to comfort you if you are an emotional blob when you have the blues? Can she be supportive when you're achieving white hot success or encourage you to get there? Perhaps you can only support each other the best way you know how. You have to ask yourself if what your partner can offer is good enough for you.

Opal: Fight Fairly—Don't Attack Below the Belt

One issue that frustrates couples is when their mate qualifies their feelings. In other words, if you don't feel your partner is being supportive, you might say, "If you loved me, you would…" This type of comment is really being manipulative of each other. Your feelings are your own, and no one has the right to question how authentically you feel. How we express those feelings is a different matter and one that can be addressed fairly. Arguing about your love for each other takes it to a whole different level. If he's not calling enough or she's not available enough, work together on a plan to get you both the attention you need. Learn to deal with the tangible issues.

Turquoise: Share Core Values

How do you feel about marriage, raising children, and your roles as wife and husband, mother and father? How do you feel about religious practices, family ties, and money matters? How do you both want to live your lives? There should be some lifestyle compatibility. Although we are all evolving creatures, we don't usually deviate from our core values, and sharing them will keep you both centered.

Peridot: Physical Attraction—Sizzle or Fizzle?

Call it chemistry, connection, spark, energy, or vibe—whatever the reference, its presence is undeniable, and the lack of it is just as obvious. It's that unknown attraction that causes two people to turn a quick glance into a curious stare. Chemistry can exist between you and your partner from the first time you meet, or it can be a vibe that builds up over a course of time and the forming of a friendship. If you don't have it right from the start and you have a mutual fondness for each other, try to focus on friendship. Some of the best marriages begin between best friends. The sparks may come later while you both are busy being friends. Whenever or however it occurs, physical attraction is one of the key ingredients to blend into a strong relationship.

Amethyst: Communication Is the Key

You have heard it before that communication is the key to having a good relationship, but knowing how to communicate is just as important. How do you both listen and talk to each other? Do you talk over each other without really hearing what your partner is saying? Some of us are guilty of hearing our partners through "filtered" listening. In other words, taking disagreements and negative experiences from the past and applying them to process what you hear your partner or spouse saying. Paraphrasing what each other says is a good way to say, "I understand," or to clarify a misunderstanding.

Aquamarine: Gut Feeling? Trust Your Instincts

He may seem like the perfect guy. She might have all the essentials you are looking for in a mate. But what does your gut tell you? If you have an instinct that something just isn't quite right with the connection, more than likely you're right. Learn to trust yourself and know what's right for you.

Garnet: Respect—You Have to Give It to Get It

Do you like who you are and how you are behaving in your relationship? That's one sign of knowing you're in a respectful and healthy relationship.

Some other signs include:
- You can relax and be yourself around each other
- You speak highly of each other to other people, even when your partner is not around
- Your partner honors and tries to fulfill your wants and needs

These are signs of a lack of respect:
- Criticizing your partner's physical appearance
- Criticizing your partner's intelligence
- Criticizing your partner's character
- Insulting your partner's sexual performance

Emerald: Problem Solving—Do the Right Thing

It doesn't matter how compatible you are during the course of your relationship and marriage, problems between the two of you WILL occur. You both need the skills necessary to resolve those problems. Do you both have those skills? If not, you can both acquire them. Partners need to identify what the issue is when it surfaces and evaluate the best outcome to resolve it. Practice focusing on what's best without bullying, manipulation, judgment, or projection, and it will strengthen your relationship. Also monitor whom you vent your frustrations to about your partner's irritating ways. Is this person skilled and in a position to offer the best possible advice? If you and your partner find it difficult to resolve the problem on your own, it might be best to seek professional help from a relationship counselor or clergyperson.

Topaz: Sexual Compatibility—Does It Click or Clank?

If you are choosing to be sexually active before marriage, are you and your partner sexually compatible? How important is sex to you? Do you both have a similar sex drive? Having a good sexual relationship is probably not the most important part of the relationship, but it is one of the most valued. It is certainly an important part of marriage. If you both are not connecting, so to speak, dig deep and find out what's going on emotionally with the two of you. Are there any unresolved issues going on *outside* the bedroom that are affecting what's not going on inside the bedroom? Emotional and sexual compatibility go hand in hand.

If you both are just in a rut and life's demands are pushing sex way down the priority list, find creative ways to bring it back up to the level of importance it deserves. After all, the brain is the sexiest part of the body, so free your mind to explore and adore your partner.

Pearl: Trust Is a Must

Do you trust each other? Can you be completely vulnerable with her and know that she's got your back? Do you believe he's truthful in what he says and does? Through honesty and loyalty, trust is one of the simplest ways to build a strong foundation between the two of you and one of the toughest to renovate if it's compromised. Open and honest communication is one of the primary road signs on the journey toward a trusting and loving relationship. It is the secrets that become the road blocks.

Diamond: Commitment

Commitment
Barbara Jenkins Spires

If she's stuck in a rut, can you be there to pull her out?
If he's unsure of himself, can you inspire him to remove his doubt?

If she has big dreams that would take her far across the land,
will you be right there beside her to hold her by the hand?

If he becomes ill and has a job he can no longer keep,
will you provide for him and still have your love run deep?

When her beauty fades, and she becomes gray and older,
will you stroke her silver strands and whisper the sweet nothings you've always told her?

If both of your woven heartstrings can bind stronger than life's drama through and through

Then you'll know what true commitment is

And what it really means to say

"I do."

Barbara Jenkins Spires is an entrepreneur and creator of Couple Links, a patented relationship board game endorsed by Smart Marriages®. The Couple Links board game is designed to help couples understand, appreciate, and validate each other. Couple Links board games can be purchased at www.couplelinksgame.com. Barbara resides in New York with her loving husband of thirteen years and two children.

© 2010 B. Jenkins

❤ ❤ ❤

Dating Can Help You Prepare for Your Future
Claudia Arp and Dave Arp

One of our sayings is, "Fun in marriage is serious business." We have never met a couple on the way to the divorce court who were having fun together. You can learn new skills, but if you're not having a little bit of fun along the way, you're not going to use the skills as effectively. And one way to keep the fun in your relationship is to develop the dating habit now and then carry it into your marriage.

When we talk to married couples about dating, they say, "Oh, that's what we did before marriage. Now we're married. We don't have to date. We're together at the house." Actually dating is also important after marriage, because it helps you keep your relationship a priority. Plus, dating helps to build your friendship. We found in our national survey of successful long-term marriages that friendship is a key factor.

Why Structured Dates?

You may be used to having dates that are just social, and those are good, too, but we encourage couples to have what we call "great dates" focusing on specific topics. You have a meaningful conversation, and you feel good about your relationship, because you really are getting to know each other better than you normally would. Having a little structure can turn a bland dinner-and-a-movie date into a fun, purposeful, relationship-building date.

Here's a tip: Over the years we have observed that men and women relax in different ways. Men tend to relax by doing something. Women like to relax and unwind by talking. So, if you plan a date around an activity where you can also talk—like taking a walk together—you have a real winner for both.

On great dates you talk about topics that you might not normally talk about, such as your family of origin and finances or when or whether you want to have children. Or, if you're heading into a second marriage and you're bringing children into it, you can discuss how you will manage that.

On these dates, you look at your strengths as a couple, how you mesh together. Then you take a more realistic look at what your growth areas are and which points you might have conflicts at in the future. When you're dating, it's tempting to gloss over some of those areas. We have a lot of couples who say, "Well, after we're married, he's gonna change," or "She's gonna change." As Dave says, "It ain't gonna happen." Using a relationship inventory also helps this process of knowing each other well.[1]

Setting Up Your Dates

We encourage couples to agree before their dates that they are going to stay positive. It's not a time to tell the other person what he or she has done wrong or focus on past arguments or failures. It's a time to focus on the future and what you want your relationship to look like as you go forward. It is not the time to talk about your wedding details or your future in-laws, unless that's part of the topic. It's a time to plan your life together.

One caution: Some topics one of you will find more interesting than the other, but be willing to discuss the topic you agree on for each date. Sometimes, just listening and participating is a gift of love in itself. We also encourage couples not to force it. If you're on a date and you're starting to get into an argument, just stop that discussion and go get a cup of coffee or some ice cream or do whatever you need to for a break. Do something fun, because if you're not having fun on the date, you're not going to continue dating as a positive relationship habit.

We encourage couples in a serious relationship or planning marriage to experience ten dates—each focused on a particular topic that is good to talk about with each other. Below are highlights of ten dating topics to help you prepare for your future.

Date 1: Start the discussion by talking about your expectations, hopes, and dreams. Sometimes, it can be eye opening, like learning, "Oh, I didn't know that is important to you." Having this discussion can help you make sure you're on the same page for where you'd like to see your relationship go in the future. Another part of this date is dreaming together. Where would you like to live? What's your ideal home? What are your career plans and goals? What family traditions would you want to celebrate? What's your dream getaway? Choose a couple of these topics and dream together. Make this first date a mixture of reality and dreams.

Date 2: On this date, talk about the ways you are you are alike and the ways you are different. Couples don't realize how things that attract you to each other before marriage will become irritations after you're married, but they can also be grounds for a great marriage partnership.

We are very different, personality wise. Claudia's the high-energy, let's-go-get-'em, conquer-the-world-yesterday type, and Dave's the more laidback, easygoing one. When we were dating, Dave would listen to Claudia, and he never hurried. It was so relaxing for Claudia to be around him. Then we got married and guess what? The guy was so slow, Claudia couldn't get him to move! Dave was trying to slow her down, and she was trying to speed him up, and it wasn't a very pretty picture. Finally, after several years of marriage, we realized that our differences were just the way God had created us, and we weren't going to change each other's personalities. Even though we are at opposite ends of the personality spectrum, we learned that if we would let each other operate in our areas of strength, we could benefit from our differences and make a great team.

Date 3: This is a good time to focus on communicating and connecting. Couples are so in love they often feel really connected, but a lot of that is hormones and chemistry. You also need to connect on a deeper level. One practice we encourage couples to do is make a "contract" for communication practices that you will or won't do. Two that we consider important are "We will not intentionally attack each other" and "We will not defend ourselves when we feel attacked." We've found that "I" statements are much better than "You" statements, which tend to be attacking. These practices help you to move into more constructive patterns of communicating. We encourage you to learn together how to recognize and express your feelings and really listen to one another.

Date 4: With a foundation of good communication skills, you can then discuss how you will solve problems as a couple together. You need to learn to share your deeper positive and negative emotions in ways that don't violate your contract agreements.

It helps if you can identify what your usual pattern is for dealing with difficult situations and topics. It may include withdrawing, attacking, yielding, avoiding, intellectualizing, or winning at all costs. None of these will serve you well as regular patterns in your relationship and marriage. As you build your communication skills, you will notice that you are more effective at solving problems when you take them one issue at a time, share the opportunities to speak, and work to fully understand the issue before making a decision.

Date 5: This date focuses on money, something that can be a huge topic for couples who are considering marriage. You may have graduated from college, have jobs and 401Ks, and own a house. Or maybe as you begin to talk about money, you realize that one of you has a huge amount of debt. When you're thinking about marriage, the discussion is about how you are going to merge your two financial worlds together. It is also good to talk about your financial goals, a workable financial plan, and how you want to manage and monitor your money.

On this date, you can talk about how your families of origin managed money as you were growing up. Maybe your family pinched every penny, saved for a rainy day, and made wise investments. Instead, maybe they spent money like it grew on trees, invested unwisely, or borrowed money. Maybe they rarely gave money away, or they really liked to donate and give to others. Knowing their patterns will help you see what choices you may make and what choices are best for you as a couple.

Date 6: This date will help you with understanding the transition of separating from your original families and joining with one another. You have the opportunity to share about your families of origin and their expectations, the homes you grew up in, the values and habits of the family, and things like holiday traditions. You can also look at your friendships and how they will blend and relate to your marriage. What mutual friendships do you want to pursue?

So many of the issues that married couples face go back to the failure to "leave" Mom and Dad. When your first allegiance remains to your parents rather than to your spouse, trouble is just up ahead! The discussion on this date helps you say, "Okay, we are going to shift our primary allegiance from our parents to each other." It doesn't mean you ever stop loving and respecting your parents; that will never cease. But in priority relationships, your spouse has to come first—before parents and before children.

Date 7: It's now time to explore, understand, and celebrate intimacy, love, and romance. You may think, "Whoa! We've got that one covered," but after marriage, you may discover that you have different expectations, wants, likes, and dislikes. It helps to talk about these beforehand and be specific and realistic.

You can talk about the different facets of a star-studded love life. It's far more than just a physical relationship. It involves trust, feeling safe with each other, mutuality, freely choosing to love each other and how to express it, honesty, openly communicating with each other, intimacy, being spiritual soulmates, feeling close, giving joy and comfort to each other, romance, and sex. What are your expectations? What are your needs?

Date 8: It is wise to take this opportunity to discuss your roles and planning for family. Talking about roles helps you think about who's going to do what around the house and what each other's roles might be. We have, in the back of our minds, things that we expect our wife or husband to do. What do you think the male should do? What should the female do? What do we both do? This date will help you begin planning realistically for sharing household tasks.

The second part of Date 8 is planning for family. Do you want to have children? If so, when and how many? There are also situations where it's a second or a third marriage where you're bringing his or her kids into the relationship. This can bring challenges, so you need to talk about it before marriage.

Date 9: The purpose of this date is to share together where you are on your spiritual quest and look for ways to develop spiritual intimacy. We realize "spiritual intimacy" may mean different things to different people, depending on what your faith background is. We challenge couples with: What are your core values? What do you believe about life, death, marriage, God, and family? What beliefs do you have in common? How important is the spiritual dimension of life to you? What were the religious practices and spiritual beliefs in your family of origin, and what beliefs do you have in common? Will you pray together? What are your beliefs and practices about forgiveness? What are your attitudes about being of service to others?

Even if you're coming from a common faith background, you may have different ways of expressing your faith—some people are more formal and some more casual. What are your views of different types of worship? We also challenge couples to think about if there is some kind of community or religious service project that they might want to do together to see how well they work together in this arena of life.

In our marriage, we have personally found that spiritual intimacy and our faith in God make a tremendous impact and a difference in our relationship. For us, it's foundational.

Date 10: This "final" date is about choosing an intentional marriage. We set goals for our businesses and maybe our personal lives, but we don't really think about setting goals for our relationship, where we would like it to be in a year or two from now. You can talk about whether you go from seriously dating to being engaged or from being engaged to marrying.

This is also a time to explore the level of involvement in the marriage you envision. How much time will you make for your couple relationship? What does sustaining your marriage look like to both of you? Be as specific as you can.

We encourage you to make a list of older couples you know who could be mentors to you. Look at people you really admire, their relationships, and their marriages and invite them to give you input. You could check with your church, synagogue, or place of worship and see if there's a mentoring program already in place that you could participate in. If you get stuck, you can ask for help from your mentor, your clergy member, or a counselor. It's much better to get help before you're engaged or married, but always be willing to ask for help. After marriage, a Mentor Couple can continue to give you encouragement and help when needed.

Looking Back and Looking Forward

When we look back over our own marriage, what has kept us together are love, laughter, fun, dating, our faith in God, and a whole lot of work! When we look at couples today, there are so many more resources to help them prepare for marriage, but at the same time, couples today face many more challenges than we faced. Remember: Marriage is a journey, not a destination. You never arrive, but it can be a great trip!

We encourage couples to do all they can to prepare for what can be one of the greatest, most rewarding blessings in their whole life. We just can't think what our life would be like without each other! Marriage is an honor, a privilege, and a joy, but it's also hard, hard work. Dating before and after can help.

1 An inventory like PREPARE-ENRICH has been taken by millions of couples (www.prepare-enrich.com) and helps couples understand their areas of strength and areas for growth. The Internet-based Couple Checkup (powered by PREPARE/ENRICH) goes hand-in-hand with our book, *10 Great Dates Before You Say "I Do."* This book provides detailed information and dating exercises for each recommended date.

Editor's Note: Parts of this article are based on an interview that Susanne Alexander did with Dave and Claudia Arp on March 26, 2010.

Claudia Arp and **David Arp**, a husband-wife team, are marriage educators, and founders of Marriage Alive International (www.marriagealive.com). They are conference speakers and frequent contributors to national print and broadcast media. The Arps are authors of over 30 books, including the popular *10 Great Dates* series and the Gold Medallion Award-winning book, *The Second Half of Marriage*. The Arp's have a newly released DVD curriculum, *10 Great Dates Before You Say I Do*, which was co-produced with PREPARE-ENRICH. Dave and Claudia have been married for over 45 years. They have three sons and eight grandchildren and live in Northern Virginia.

♥ ♥ ♥

Follow Your Heart Without Losing Your Mind
John Van Epp, Ph.D.

I'm inviting you to rethink your entire approach to dating, courting, and approaching marriage. When you see some red flags, *please pay attention* instead of minimizing and rationalizing them. Look to your family and friends and listen. Everyone else can likely see the danger signs, while the people actually in danger (the two of you) are stuck in denial.

During my twenty-five years of counseling, I have heard many clients reflect on a previous romantic dating relationship, only to wonder why they kept underestimating the effects of specific warning signals they had noticed. Many times they knew better, but their hearts seemed to betray their judgment. While it is true that some experience the "love is blind" phenomenon because they do not *know* better, there are others who know that something needs to be addressed. Instead of dealing with it, though, they continue to remain trusting, committed, dependent, and in love. This perseverance may be necessary to help you move past a difficult and challenging time, but it is a quality you can also misuse, so it backfires when the problem area keeps repeating with no sign of improvement.

Let me suggest a basic premise about love: *Your heart needs a pacemaker.* It is true that you fall in love with your heart. It is true that you grow in love with your heart. But it is also true that your heart can mislead you if you do not pace the developing bonds of love.

Let me give you an example from when I first met my wife, Shirley. I will be the first to admit I was struck by the arrow of *love at first sight.* I had just transferred to a small, private college in Philadelphia, Pennsylvania, and during the weekend orientation, I noticed an attractive freshman I was determined to meet.

However, I was shy at that time of my life and apprehensive about approaching her, so it was not until six weeks later that I finally found the opportunity to create an "accidental" encounter. I noticed she was walking about half a block behind me as I made my way toward the other educational building. I plotted our "chance" meeting by walking slowly enough for her to catch up just before I entered the door. I examined the buildings along the way, looked at interesting trash discarded on the sidewalk, and did a little window-shopping. Just as I was about to open the door, I heard her voice exclaim, "Man, you sure do walk slowly." However, I did not actually hear her say those words. In my head, what I heard her really say to me was, "I'm in love with you!"

Now, isn't that just the way that *love at first sight works?* I don't think I was much different than others who have fallen head-over-heels in love. I heard what I wanted to hear and saw what I wanted to see. In my "heart," there was a loss of reality.

It would have been easy—even natural—to indulge in our passions. Fortunately, both Shirley and I paced our relationship over the next couple of years instead, channeling our in-love feelings into endless conversations and experiences that welded us in a bond of deeply knowing each other. It was an *intentional pacing* that set boundaries on developing our sexual relationship to focus on building a foundation of friendship, trust, and reliance that has proven strong enough to withstand the challenges encountered over our thirty-plus years of marriage and parenthood.

And this is just one of many examples of why you need to *pace* the bonds of your heart. However, the real question is not why. Rather, it is how you pace your heart's connection with one another. Relationships can be complicated, so it is no wonder most couples never even think about pacing their relationship. But it is possible. Please read on…

Balancing Your Bond—The RAM Plan

Helping couples succeed at pacing was one of the reasons I developed a model of relationship bonds in 1985 that I have since used in teaching graduate coursework, counseling, developing programs, and writing. The model is the Relationship Attachment Model (RAM), and it portrays five major relationship bonds that contribute to your overall feeling of closeness. It is a visual, interactive model that can easily depict both a balanced relationship as well as a relationship that is out of balance.

Picture a chart with five up-and-down sliders, somewhat like the audio settings you might see on your computer (see Figure 1 on the next page).

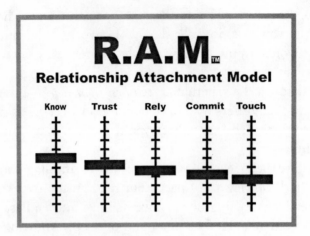

Figure 1 Relationship Attachment Model (RAM)®
© 2010 J. Van Epp

Each slider symbolizes a major bonding dynamic in your relationship. The one on the far left denotes the extent to which you KNOW someone. As you move the bar on this slider up over time, you signify a richer, fuller, and more personal knowledge of the other. The second slider represents your range of TRUST. The third portrays your ability to RELY on someone. The fourth indicates the degree of your COMMITment. The fifth represents TOUCH and the extent of your attraction, chemistry, and sexual involvement.

These dynamic connections are universal in all romantic relationships. They are also reciprocal or two-way streets. For example, you know your partner, and your partner knows you; you trust your partner, and your partner trusts you. They are distinct from each other, but they definitely interact. When one slider goes up or down, it automatically affects the others, and most importantly, there is a logic to them that helps you to know what it means to pace a relationship!

Here lies one of the most important keys to building a healthy relationship: *Keep the bonds of your relationship in balance with each other.* In other words, never go further in one bonding area than you have gone in the others. Whenever your relationship shifts out of balance, you will feel unsafe and experience feelings of hurt, betrayal, mistrust, unfairness, anger, loneliness, or some other insecure emotion. Feeling confident in your relationship is based on the logic of staying within the safe zone. For example:

- What you KNOW should set the limits of what you TRUST
- Your RELYing on your partner should never exceed the ways that your partner has proven to be TRUSTworthy
- Your COMMITment or investment in this relationship should be restricted by what you truly KNOW, TRUST, and have found dependable in your partner
- What you KNOW, TRUST, RELY on, and are COMMITted to should set the ceiling of how far you take TOUCH and your sexual relationship

Pacing your relationship means you work to get to know the most important areas of each other, while being careful to not "fill in all of the gaps" of what you don't know with fantasy or blind trust. As you work to pace your trust, you limit what you fully believe about your partner until you see evidence of their trustworthiness. As you share what you would like from each other, your relationship becomes a proving ground for what you trust and expect, increasing your feelings of reliance and confidence in each other's dependability and commitment. And your relationship will mature in more healthy ways when you develop these four areas of bonding before you go too far in your sexual relationship.

You may be thinking, "Let's see—I didn't do that right…nor that…been there, done that wrong too." If your relationship is out of balance, use the RAM to talk about where you are and what each of you needs. Setting some goals to balance any imbalances will definitely help your relationship become stronger and healthier. The RAM is a tool that provides a picture of how to pace what is happening in the invisible dynamics of your relationship so you can visualize it, talk about it, and make concrete plans to improve it. The RAM will help you to untangle the complex and mixed feelings that often occur in an intimate relationship.

Each time you take a "time out" to review where you are in the five bonding dynamics represented in the RAM, you actually practice one of the most important strategies for achieving success in marriage. Happy marriages don't just happen. Relationships won't run themselves; YOU have to *run* your relationship! The RAM provides an easy-to-use plan for staying on top of your relationship and steering you in a healthy, happy direction toward a successful marriage.

Imagine a marriage where you weekly or monthly talk through:

- Your communication and openness (KNOW)
- Your respect and appreciation of each other (TRUST)
- The ways you are there for each other, working together, and keeping active in your relationship (RELY)
- Your commitment and security with each other (COMMIT)
- Your romance and sexual intimacy (TOUCH)

Then, when you take steps to balance any imbalances, little deals do not become big deals, and small leaks do not lead to major blowouts.

Healthy marriages are not relationships where everything is always held in perfect balance. A healthy marriage involves two partners who are regularly balancing all aspects of their relationship. As you establish the habit of talking through the RAM during your dating relationship, you will not only strengthen and improve your relationship in the present, but you will also make one of the most important investments in your future.

John Van Epp, Ph.D., President/Founder of *Love Thinks, LCC* is the author of *How to Avoid Falling in Love with a Jerk* (McGraw-Hill), which blends in-depth research with humorous stories to provide a map for making healthy relationship choices. His twenty-five years of clinical experience and extensive research in premarital, marital, and family relations have paved the way for his teach-out-of-the-box courses, PICK (How to Avoid Falling for a Jerk) and Marriage LINKS to be taught in thousands of churches, singles organizations, educational settings, and social agencies in all fifty states, ten countries, and by more than 2,500 military personnel. Van Epp and his innovative Relationship Attachment Model, book, and relationship courses were awarded the Smart Marriages® Impact Award in 2008, and they have been featured in *The Wall Street Journal, Time, Psychology Today, O Magazine,* and *Cosmopolitan.* Dr. Van Epp has appeared on the *CBS Early Show, The O'Reilly Factor, Fox News,* and *Focus on the Family.* He has been happily married for over thirty years and is the proud father of two daughters. His website is www.lovethinks.com, and he can be reached at vanepp@nojerks.com.

❤ ❤ ❤

How Well Do You Get Along with Others?
Susanne M. Alexander

You aren't a couple in isolation from the rest of the world, even though at times being in love may make you feel this way. Part of ensuring you know each other well and discussing how interactions with others will go after marriage is to be involved now with others, pay attention, and be very observant of specifics.

A good place to begin is to understand more about each other's friendships. Consider these questions:

- Do you enjoy long-term, healthy friendships? How do you describe them?

- Do you stay in touch with friends or generally ignore them? Why or why not?

- How do you speak about friends when they are absent?

- What type of influence are your friends? Do they encourage wise or unwise activities?

- How do your friends benefit your lives? What benefit do you add to theirs?

- How do you speak and act in response to your friends?

Another layer of understanding each other and your individual characters is to be in a wide variety of circumstances together and observe how you each respond. How well (or poorly) do you each:

- Adapt to different social situations appropriately?

- Begin conversations and/or participate in them easily?

- Interact well with and show courtesy, confidence, and respect to:

  ◦ Both genders, all ages, friends, professional associates, and new acquaintances?

  ◦ People of a lower socio-economic level?

  ◦ People who provide service to you, such as restaurant servers, cleaning staff, bus drivers, store clerks, trash collectors, administrative clerks, or store employees?

- ○ People of a higher socio-economic level?
- ○ People from different cultures or races?
- ○ People with different spiritual or religious beliefs?
- ○ People with physical, mental, or emotional disabilities or limitations?
- ○ Anyone smaller or weaker, such as children or pets?

What is important in a mature person is that you tend to be consistent in most circumstances. You don't change temporarily and insincerely to please other people, gain something from them, or to obtain an advantage in a situation.

How well (or poorly) you treat others is likely a reflection of how you will treat each other and each other's family and friends over time.

Susanne M. Alexander is a Relationship and Marriage Coach with a specialty in character (www.marriagetransformation.com). She is a firm believer in people learning good observation and discernment skills before being in a relationship and then using those skills in relationships to ensure they are making good choices.

© 2010 S. Alexander

❤ ❤ ❤

Character in Action
Jim Hughes

When no one else is around, how do you act? Character is that quality that defines who you really are without the pretenses we usually display before others. It is the reason why we do what we do and say what we say. It is the part of our lives that God sees and judges us by. Character is our reality check.

A person of good character is one who seeks to be a responsible citizen and partner in life. A person of character tries to live rightly in relationship to others simply because it is the right thing to do. They adhere to a high standard of behavior in their daily conduct, whether it is in the privacy of their home or in public. A person of good character is one who says what they mean and means what they say. Vows are spoken and commitments are made with the full intent of keeping them—especially marriage vows.

As you plan the possibility of a future marriage together, consider how your characters prompt you to treat one another. Two people cannot build a life together on the foundation of self-centeredness. If they do, the life they share will be filled with fights, ill feelings, and emotional detachment. Marriage is more than a coexistence; it is a blending of two lives into one. It takes a lot of work to live charitably with another person on a daily basis. It does not come naturally, and sometimes it's met with resistance. However, it's well worth the effort!

There is no greater contentment and joy between two people than a marital relationship rooted in a charitable spirit. Charity includes a forgiving spirit. It does not hold grudges, nor does it seek revenge when wronged. It is sensitive to when we wrong others and motivates us to say, "I'm sorry." It seeks forgiveness for our sinful behavior that hurts another. Charity means we go the extra mile for our spouse, even when at times we don't feel like it. It is a sacrificial commitment, the type of love that draws one's spouse into one's life and lets them know they are the most important person in the world to them.

It is important that we understand the need to treat one another with a sense of dignity. It is so easy to let down our guard when someone becomes very familiar to us, to the point instead of looking up to one another, we begin to look down on one another. And no marriage can succeed where there is little appreciation for the value of the person one is married to. Being courteous to one another conveys a strong message: "I respect you. I honor you. I love you." It is going the extra mile to make one's partner or spouse feel special and important, and the wonderful thing about it is, when your partner or spouse feels special, they will return the favor and go the extra mile to make you feel special and important. Everybody wins.

Being courteous and showing good manners sends a strong message. Gentlemen open doors and allow their partners or wives to enter first (It helps to do so with a smile!). They escort them in and see them seated. They will hold their hands in public. They make an effort to let their partner and later their wife know that they are the most important person in the world to them. Ladies show their appreciation with a "Thank you," a smile, or a kiss.

Both of them know how to say "Excuse me" when they do or say something uncouth. They put forth an effort to keep their conversations out of the gutter. They know how to convey the message that "I think you deserve the best," and they are willing to give it. They understand the need to bring out the best in one's partner or spouse and not the worst. Living with good character choices is a couple's greatest insurance policy against infidelity and divorce.

God's Spirit is the source of your ability to be kind, gracious, loving, patient, in control of yourselves, and faithful toward one another. The end result is that you will live out your lives together in peace, and it will be good.

Jim Hughes is the author of *C Through Marriage, Revitalizing Your Vows*. He is an ordained Pastor, now retired, who served in churches for nearly forty years before turning to a writing ministry. Jim lives in Iowa and has been married for nearly forty years, has two adult married children and one son still at home, and one granddaughter. Jim can be reached through Facebook; at thefourj@mchsi.com; and www.cthroughmarriage.blogspot.com.

Chapter Seven
Appreciating Diversity

~ ~

In a global community that is becoming more intermingled and diverse by the day, you may very well be in an interfaith or intercultural relationship—or both. You may also be of similar faiths or the same general culture but reared differently or have made different choices as an adult. Diversity in relationships is a new area for researchers and experts to study and understand. Tools are developing that will help you maintain unity in your relationship in the face of major differences.

There are some selections in this chapter to prompt you to consider the role of spirituality and religion in your relationship, marriage, and family, and these are at the beginning. Then there are selections that share perspectives for you to consider in understanding the effect of culture on your relationship, as well as some specific guidance for Latino and African-American/Black couples. *We encourage you to read even the selections that do not, on the surface, seem to apply directly to you; there may be new insights that result.* The selections do not even come close to covering the full range of diversity and religious or cultural complexity in the world, but they will give you enough to prompt focused thought and discussion. Spiritual and religious perspectives are also included in selections located in other chapters of the book.

Even though resources and experts are more limited for this complex subject area, the other chapters will also help you with paying attention to how you respond to and work with your differences, as well as what you appreciate about what is different, and similar, in one another.

❤ ❤ ❤

Exploring the Spiritual Side of Marriage
Fiona McDonald

What interests me is how you build unity within a marriage, whether it is between two people of the same faith or two people from diverse or interfaith backgrounds. Even though unity is the foundation upon which any marriage must be built, that doesn't mean sameness. Some of the greatest challenges between couples are when beliefs and values are involved, as people often feel they can't compromise if their values and beliefs are being questioned. It is crucial for those from different faiths to discuss just where each sits with their values and beliefs before marrying. Those in the marriage field recognize that many issues or differences that arise between couples in marriage are not resolvable. Therefore, it becomes a question of managing the differences so that each feels respected and valued.

Marriage ceremonies run the gamut of religious practices, from Hindu to Buddhist to Muslim to Christian, each with their own unique vows. The Bahá'í Faith marriage vow, said by the man and woman separately, is "We will all, verily, abide by the Will of God." The marriage carries the expectation of an eternal love connection between the souls of the couple on a journey moving ever closer to God. Their focus is trying to live their life according to spiritual principles to please God rather than pleasing each other, for pleasing God will ultimately be in the best interest of their partner, even if they don't recognize it.

Having an attitude of service to each other to assist them in their spiritual development is important but shouldn't be confused with being submissive. For Bahá'ís, in a spiritual union, loyalty and truthfulness are important qualities that assist in binding the relationship together and creating trust and friendship. If each knows that when problems arise they stay within the relationship and are not discussed outside (unless perhaps together with a professional), then they build trust and create strong foundations. Praying together and creating other common spiritual practices can be unifying for a couple as they create shared meaning and strengthen the relationship.

While couples of all faiths often like to write their own promises to one another, there is a sacredness to also affirming beliefs and practices as part of a wedding commitment. Interfaith couples often choose to have two ceremonies or blend their faith practices into one. What I see happening more and more in the world is that marriages are reflecting the diversity and oneness of all humanity—religiously, culturally, and racially. As couples establish their own small bond of unity, they also contribute to the wider unity between all people.

Focus Questions

As you contemplate living together as a married couple, please ask yourselves these questions and discuss them thoroughly:

- What are our spiritual beliefs and values? (Please don't assume they are the same simply because you are of the same faith)
- What spiritual practices are important for us? Will we pray together?
- Do we wish to worship together, and if so, what would that look like?
- What spiritual beliefs and values do we want to teach our children?
- If we come from different faiths, how do we decide which faith the children will be brought up in, or will it be both? If both, how will that work?
- How much time would we each spend being of service to our religious community each month?
- What amounts of financial donations do we want to make?

Religion and spirituality are ideally a source of precious bonding between you, whatever your faith path or even if you have no formal path. You can best achieve this ideally by thoroughly exploring this important topic before you marry. And then have a wonderful, spirit-filled ceremony followed by an enduring marriage.

Fiona McDonald has been employed at Relationships Australia in Perth, Western Australia, since 2001 (www.wa.relationships.com.au). She is the Senior Manager of Education Services and Professional Training Development. Fiona is an accredited Relationship Educator, having spent more than twenty years in the field. Fiona has had extensive experience training facilitators and running many groups, covering such areas as: communication and conflict resolution, assertiveness, relationship development and education, self-esteem raising, and parenting children and adolescents. She was President of the Marriage and Relationship Educators Association of Australia for four years. Fiona is also a Bahá'í Faith Marriage celebrant (authorized by the Bahá'í institutions and the civil government to officiate Bahá'í weddings). She has served on the National Spiritual Assembly of the Bahá'ís of Australia for over eighteen years (www.bahai.org). She has been married to Keith for thirty-five years and has four grown children and two grandchildren.

❤ ❤ ❤

Marriage Readiness in the Jewish Tradition
Susan Heitler, Ph.D.

Traditional Jewish texts abound with important information about the attitudes and skills that create healthy marriage partnerships. The following gathering of ideas from the *Talmud* and other writing by Jewish sages hopefully will prove useful for both Jewish and non-Jewish couples.

Unfortunately, few Jewish couples study or are taught the collected wisdom from their tradition before, or even after, their wedding. This trend is gradually reversing. Groups that gather to study together from Jewish texts are on the rise in America. And in Israel, rabbis and therapists are launching a marriage education movement based on the model of America's Smart Marriages® coalition.[1] One of the primary goals of this movement will be to enhance the content of the marriage training required for engaged couples before their wedding.

While it has been relatively sparse overall, Jewish marriage preparation also varies by whether the officiating rabbi comes from a more reform or more orthodox perspective. Tradition-oriented rabbis tend to offer more instruction on orthodox rituals in Jewish married life, including those pertaining to the sexual dimensions of marriage partnership. Reform rabbis each decide for themselves what issues to discuss with couples before officiating under the *huppah,* the wedding canopy under which Jewish brides and grooms participate in wedding ceremonials.

Perspectives on Sex

Sexual relations are considered highly important in a Jewish marriage. The Jewish groom is expected to learn to satisfy his wife sexually, preferably before himself. He must be available to his wife for sexual interaction, both for their mutual pleasure and to produce children. "Be fruitful and multiply" is one of the first commandments of Jewish life.

Jewish brides preparing for marriage in orthodox traditions learn the Jewish customs of refraining from sexual relations during menstruation, and then submerging in a ritual bath that signifies readiness for resumption of sexual availability. Alternating between sexual and non-sexual times in a marriage encourages a monthly renewal of enthusiasm each time that sexual activity resumes. In addition, during the times of the month when sexual sharing is not an option, the couple is encouraged to focus on enhancing their friendship. Talking together and enjoying sexual interactions both are considered vital ingredients of a full and healthy marriage.

Sustaining Monogamy

The Talmud, Judaism's main gathering of wisdom from the sages, discusses what is referred to as the "Open Door Rule." According to Jewish tradition, it is good that men and women are endowed with sexual feelings. The challenge is to insure that such feelings be acted upon only in the context of marriage.

If a man and a woman are alone in a private space, the risk increases that they will become excessively intimate in their discussion, which would increase the temptation to indulge in physical contact. To prevent sexualized relationships from developing with a partner other than a spouse, the Open Door Rule says that contact between individual men and women who are not married to each other should take place only in public spaces. With the door open, anyone could enter at any time. Staying in public view decreases the risk of sexualized interactions, and therefore of violations of marriage vows.

Assessing Character

Another focus of marriage readiness is *midot* (pronounced "mee-dote"), which is the Hebrew term for character traits. When courting partners assess each other as potential mates, they may focus initially on attraction and similarities. They and their families are encouraged, however, to also assess the potential marriage partner's positive traits; such as, honesty, generosity, kindness, slowness to anger, willingness to work hard, willingness to live a life of learning, spiritual activity, community involvement, and other traits valued in the religion. Married adults are expected to continue to develop these midot throughout their lives.

During the selection and engagement periods prior to a wedding, it is vital that prospective fiancés pay attention to signs of problematic character patterns. Indications of any of the three most common deal-breakers—addictions, excessive anger, and sexual unfaithfulness—merit especially serious evaluation. If one or more of the fundamental character traits for successful marriage partnership look questionable, marriage plans can be postponed or cancelled.

Filling the Home with Peace, Not Anger or Fighting

Jewish teachings place a high value on *shalom bayit,* which is peace in the home. Anger is strongly frowned upon. The Jewish tradition teaches that Moses, in spite of his greatness as a prophet, was not allowed to enter the Promised Land. Why was that? Moses had a habit of getting angry instead of staying in the calm zone. To enter the promised land of a peaceful loving marriage, both spouses need strong skills for self-soothing when anger arises.

Anger is a vitally important emotion for alerting people to a problem. At the same time, anger is not a useful modality for solving problems. Dominating or attacking one's partner in anger generally makes problems worse. When differences provoke angry feelings, spouses need to note the problem that triggered the negative emotional response. They then are advised to allow their potentially hurtful emotions to abate. By waiting to address difficult problems until both of them feel calm enough to talk together in a mutually respectful manner, spouses significantly decrease the likelihood that they will hurt each other with angry comments. They also become more likely to succeed in finding solutions.

While couples are expected to learn to talk over their disputes and disappointments in quiet collaborative dialogue, a man and wife also are expected to have different opinions. Jewish tradition says that when Adam was given a life partner, he was told that he would receive an *ezer ka-neg-doe,* which is Hebrew for "a helper/friend who will have different perspectives from his own."

How can there be peace in households where the viewpoints of wives and husbands differ? The Hebrew term for "peace"–*shalom*—does not mean that spouses should always see things the same way. "Yes dear" is inappropriate as a standard response if it means that one partner is not sharing their alternative viewpoint. Better to share both viewpoints. Shalom refers to the collaborative process of building a consensus that incorporates both people's initial views.

Peace of the shalom variety emerges from resolving differences by:

- Treasuring differences of opinion
- Listening for what's right in both perspectives
- Building a consensus understanding based on the input from both
- Creating plans of action that are responsive to all the concerns of both spouses

The peace that comes from finding win-win resolutions to conflicts enables two mutually respectful adults to build a loving home in which both spouses, and their children, can thrive.

Healing from Upsets

Jewish couples benefit from learning to live the concept of *t'shuvah,* a Hebrew term that refers to the process of healing by learning from upsets. The tradition assumes that no one is perfect. Since humans are imperfect, couples are imperfect as well. Imperfection means that from time to time in all marriages, there are mistakes, misunderstandings, miscommunications, and the like that will lead to upsets. The important question then is not whether spouses will make mistakes but rather what they do after their errors. *The goal of recovery from errors is learning.*

To accomplish this goal, spouses are responsible for discovering and acknowledging their own mistakes in the upsetting event, and then for figuring out how to prevent similar mistakes in the future. Mistakes are not for criticizing, blaming, punishing the other, or holding onto resentments. Mistakes are for learning.

Learning to Love

Jewish texts talk about seeing with the *good eye,* not the *bad eye.* The bad eye focuses on what you don't like about your spouse. Hyper-focusing on negative attributes builds animosity and invites in the ultimate marriage-killer— contempt. The good eye by contrast focuses mainly on what is positive in a partner's behaviors and character. Focusing on what you like in what your partner says and does enhances love.

Summary

Jewish marriage readiness means that new spouses need to take very seriously the personal maturity, skills, and special requirements of marriage. They then hopefully can enjoy a partnership enriched by sexual pleasure, the enjoyment of children, trust in each other's basic character traits, freedom from angry interactions or fights, ability to see events from two differing perspectives, a healing process after upsets that leads to learning from errors so as to prevent similar problems in the future, and building an ever-better and ever-more-loving future together.

1 www.smartmarriages.com

Susan Heitler, Ph.D., a clinical psychologist based in Denver, Colorado, specializes in helping couples build strong marriages. Dr. Heitler is author of a book on marriage therapy, *From Conflict to Resolution,* and a book on the skills for marriage success called *The Power of Two.* Her online Power of Two course offers a fun way for couples to learn these skills from the comfort of home. Dr. Heitler and her husband, married almost forty years, are proud parents of four adult children and nine grandchildren. Office contact information: 303-388-4211; drheitler@therapyhelp.com; www.TherapyHelp.com; www.po2.com; www.poweroftwo.org

© 2010 S. Heitler

❤ ❤ ❤

Two Shall Become One
Nisa Muhammad

How do couples from different backgrounds, cultures, and religions achieve wedded bliss? Can it really work? While backgrounds and cultures can be difficult to mesh, it can be even more challenging being married to someone of a different religion. Can that work too? Consider Tariq Saleem Ziyad and Krsnanandini Devi Dasi from Cleveland, Ohio. He's Muslim and she's Hare Krsna. From afar, it might look like a recipe for disaster, but up close, it's an everyday smorgasbord of love. Their motto? "We believe in one God and honor and respect our friendship every day."

Bilal and Natasha are considering marriage. He's Muslim, while she's Christian. Can love and marriage work for them? They've discussed the differences and similarities. They've talked to other couples who have successfully married with various religious backgrounds.

"It's a challenge we're willing to take. We've heard the good and bad from lots of people," explains Natasha. "This isn't for everyone, but we want to make it work. We know we have to surround ourselves with family and other couples who believe and support us. We are determined to be successful."

She was surprised to learn, like many, that the *Qur'án,* the Muslim scripture, acknowledges the great works of Jesus and reverences His mother Mary as well.

For Bilal, choosing Natasha was more about who she was than her religion. "She's the woman for me. We can talk about anything and everything. We are willing to put in the work to make this work. Our faiths will guide us." They see the affirmation of similarity to *The Bible* in this quotation from the *Qu'rán:* "It is He who created you from a single person (Adam), and made his mate (Eve) of like nature, in order that he might dwell with her (in love)."[1]

Relationships with significant differences like religion require more time and attention to be successful. However, it's possible when you are interested in sharing your lives and making marriage work with different religions.

Strive to find and focus on the commonalities that bring you together instead of the differences that separate you. Regardless of their source, differences between couples who love each other should be seen as opportunities to grow closer and not obstacles that move them farther apart. To move forward, find the universal principles in your scriptures and religious practices. These could include a belief in God, practicing charity, a common moral code of conduct, and more. As you find these points of agreement, project forward to marriage and see whether you have enough common principles to guide you harmoniously with your family and child rearing. These conversations are crucial to your success.

Once you are clear on your shared beliefs, shared activities will cement your bond. This has to happen with full participation and involvement from both sides. It can't be done halfheartedly or with reservations if you are truly interested in building a life together. Consider praying together or try alternating your places of worship from week to week. Celebrate each other's traditions. As you go through each experience together, assess how it would work after marriage. It is best to know now, before marriage, that you can be spiritually harmonious.

Building a spiritually based marriage with your two faiths cooperating will teach your children honor, respect, and tolerance. They will learn that conflict can be resolved peacefully with love and respect as guiding forces. They will learn from you the value of wedded bliss.

1 *Qu'rán* 7:189 (Yúsuf 'Alí)

Nisa Muhammad is the Founder of the Wedded Bliss Foundation (www.weddedblissinc.com), a community-based organization helping teens and adults create healthy relationships and healthy marriages. One of its goals is giving more children the benefits of a two-parent family. She created Black Marriage Day for communities to celebrate marriage in very unique ways. It is held annually on the fourth Sunday in March, and it has grown from 30 participating cities participating in 2003 to close to 300 communities conducting celebrations in 2010. Mrs. Muhammad is the co-author of *Basic Training for Couples*, a marriage education curriculum. Her work as a pioneer in strengthening marriage in the Black community was featured in detail on CNN's *Black in America 2*. She knows both the joys of marriage and the sorrows of divorce. She works so her five children and more adults can enjoy wedded bliss.

© 2010 N. Muhammad

♥ ♥ ♥

Marriage Rituals in the Jewish Tradition
Gabrielle Kaplan-Mayer

In the Jewish tradition, marriage is considered a sacred commitment with origins in the very beginning of the *Torah*. In the Book of Genesis 2:24, it says, "man shall leave his father and mother and cleave unto his wife; they shall be one flesh." Throughout rabbinic literature, the importance of marriage is depicted in numerous colorful stories. Perhaps one of the most descriptive stories about marriage is when a Roman matron asks a rabbi how long it took for God to create the world. The rabbi explains that it took the Holy One six days to create the world. "And what has God been doing from that time until now?" the matron asks. "God," explains the rabbi, "has been busy making matches."

One of the ways Judaism emphasizes the sacredness of marriage has been through the creation of beautiful pre-wedding, wedding ceremony, and post-wedding rituals that allow couples preparing for marriage to explore their spiritual lives, to find strength in community, and to clarify the values that each partner will bring to their marriage. Though ancient in origin, these rituals can be infused with contemporary meaning and have great resonance for many couples who are marrying today. Non-Jewish couples may also want to consider these rituals and incorporate them into their own wedding preparations and celebrations.

Pre-Wedding Rituals

One traditional Jewish pre-wedding ritual is for the bride to immerse in a *mikvah,* a ritual bath, before her wedding day. This symbolically acknowledges her transformation from a single woman to a married woman. Many women resonate spiritually with this practice and appreciate that it helps them "wash off any stress or negative energy" that comes as part of wedding planning. It helps them prepare to be fully present in the experience of the marriage ceremony itself—free from anything that might tie them down.

Many men also appreciate immersing in the mikvah before their weddings as a ritual to acknowledge their status change. Several of the larger Jewish communities provide community-run mikvahs where couples can go, but any source of running water works well. A bride or groom might go to a quiet stream or creek and take a ritual bath to let go of the worries and constraints that have (naturally) been part of the wedding planning process. Some people like to go to the mikvah with a close gathering of friends, or it can be an intimate opportunity to connect with parents.

Another pre-wedding opportunity for couples to prepare for marriage is in considering their *ketubah.* Ketubah (which means "writing") refers to the written marriage contract that is signed and read as part of a Jewish wedding. Traditional Orthodox couples use a standard ketubah that was composed around 200 B.C.E. Many progressive Jewish couples utilize a more contemporary version with an egalitarian text. Often couples choose to write part of or all of the text themselves, using the ketubah to serve as the vows they commit to one another. Choosing or writing a text helps couples clarify their commitments to each other and to their marriage.

Historically, the ketubah is not only a legal document, but also an artistic one. *Ketubot* (plural of ketubah) have long been—and continue to be—an expression of Jewish creativity. Couples may choose a lithograph print or have an original work of art commissioned for the ketubah. The process of choosing the art to match their ketubah text is another opportunity for couples to better know each other. The ketubah is signed by witnesses—close friends who will stand up for the bride and groom—at the wedding and then is hung in the home as an ongoing reminder of the couple's commitments to each other.

The Wedding Ceremony

One of the most recognizable customs of a Jewish wedding is the couple marrying under a *huppah.* The huppah is the canopy that covers the bride and groom during the wedding ceremony, creating a sacred space that is both open for all to see, yet private and intimate for the couple beneath it. It symbolizes their new home together and is said to be open, as was the tent of Abraham and Sarah, who were always ready to receive visitors.

In planning their wedding, couples are encouraged to think about what kind of huppah would be special for them. Some are covered in flowers, and others are made of fabric squares that friends and family decorate for the couple. The huppah is attached to four poles, which can be free-standing or held by four people. It is considered a great honor to hold a huppah pole, so this job should be given to people very close to the bride or groom. This and all of the other elements of a Jewish wedding ceremony can be infused with the intentions of the couple as they prepare to stand together before their loved ones and community and make a sacred, eternal vow.

After the Wedding

While most newly married couples of today are eager to sneak away for the honeymoon time alone (and often to de-stress from their wedding planning marathons), Jewish tradition held that the bride and groom needed time with the community to help start their marriage out on the right foot. For the seven days following the wedding, the bride and groom were treated like a queen and king, invited to dine at the home of a different friend or relative each night. These festive meals were called *sheva berakhot* ("seven blessings"). Following dinner, the same seven blessings recited for the couple in the ceremony were recited again. The idea of the dinners was to have community celebrations for the couple, and parties often went into the night.

Today, the sheva berakhot festive meals are still an important custom, though they are observed more regularly in traditional circles. Some couples postpone their honeymoon trips so they can celebrate with their community first, and then celebrate their marriage together later. Other contemporary Jewish couples choose to engage in the custom for some of their first week of marriage or will even celebrate a week of sheva berakhot when they return from their honeymoons. In this way, the couple moves from the intimacy of their time together under the huppah to the richness of being part of a larger community that can help support and guide them through the beginning of their marriage.

Another important custom for the newly married couple is to find a prominent spot in the home to hang their ketubah marriage contract. Many rabbis recommend that when a couple gets into a fight, they take time to come together and read their ketubah to one another. In this way, the vows and commitments that each made under the huppah become rekindled.

In Jewish tradition, marriage is a sacred commitment of two individuals, one to be supported by a loving community. For contemporary couples, there is much wisdom and beauty to draw from these ancient ideas. With creativity and mindful intention, the planning for and experience of a wedding will set a couple on a firm foundation for their life ahead.

> **Gabrielle Kaplan-Mayer** is a writer, educator, and wedding officiant based in Philadelphia. She is the author of *The Creative Jewish Wedding Book* (www.jewishlights.com) and currently serves as Director of Spirituality for Children and Youth at Congregation Mishkan Shalom. She also creates and officiates at personalized spiritual and secular wedding ceremonies for Jewish and interfaith couples through Journeys of the Heart (www.journeysoftheheart.org). She loves working with couples and is available for long distance consultations related to wedding rituals and ceremony through phone, Skype, or email. Gabrielle has been married to Fred Kaplan-Mayer for nine years and is the proud mother of two young children. You can reach her at gabriellekm@gmail.com.

❤ ❤ ❤

Finding Your Good Thing and Being the Good Thing
Clarence Walker, Ph.D. and Ja'Ola Walker, D.D.

There are skills and preparation in *The Bible* that we need to use to select a mate. It is a Manual for Life, and it is the Word of God.

Couples who live together prior to marriage are **two times** more likely to divorce than couples who don't. Rather than testing your compatibility by living together, below are some guidelines to consider before deciding to marry:

Guideline 1: The Man Does the Looking and Finding

Sisters, you are to focus on *being* the "good thing, and God brings your man to you. Remember, "Whoso findeth a wife findeth a good thing, and obtaineth favor of the Lord."[1]

Today, when women act as pursuers, they revert the divine union process, and whatever we revert, we pervert. A woman can help a man pursue her, but she should not pursue him.

Guideline 2: Ladies, Be the Good Thing.

In the African-American community, the chance of finding an unmarried, working, drug-free, straight, Christian man who has never spent time in jail is not only difficult, but many feel divine intervention is needed. Because of this shortage of men, there is an unwise, unhealthy tendency to grab whoever walks through the church door or settle for whatever piece of man comes into view. When women pursue, men think *they* are the "good thing" themselves. They were created to be the hunter, looking for the prize. When roles are reversed, women are seen as easy conquests rather than as a precious lifetime partner.

Believe what the Word says about you and carry yourself like the prize.

Once you believe you are the "good thing," you have two things to determine: who you are giving and who you are getting.

Who Are You Giving?

Do you know who you are? Do you know your needs, goals, desires, dreams, ministry and community service, spiritual gifts, strengths, and weaknesses?

Sometimes women traditionally submerge their lives into a husband and children, disregarding their own dreams, career, and ministry. Later they feel unfulfilled, used, and unhappy; they have lost their sense of personhood and purpose.

When you know who you are, you can better achieve who you want to become.

Learn what it takes to be a good wife who honors God. "…[T]each the young women to be sober, to love their husbands, to love their children,[t]o be discreet, chaste, keepers at home, good, obedient to their own husbands, that the word of God be not blasphemed."[2]

Some of the qualities you need to possess and strive for include the following:

Sober: This word means self-discipline, to limit your own freedom. Marriage is not for selfish, immature people. There is a lot of sacrifice and self-discipline needed to be a good wife and mother.

Loving: The word love in this verse is a friendship type of love. Most women have their own concept of romance, but we must learn to develop a friendship with a man. This means learning how to talk to him, dealing with his ego, sharing, and listening to his dreams. Your ability to give and receive love is affected by your emotional health. Are you the child of an alcoholic, divorce, or abuse? Are you depressed, unstable, or in need of inner healing? If so, it's time to get some help.

Discreet: Be self-controlled with money, your mouth, and your temper.

Chaste: This quality means being innocent, clean, and pure in your thoughts, heart, and body. Being the "good thing" demands respect, holds out on sex until marriage, and makes no occasion for sin. Don't fall for "We're getting married anyway." Make him wait! There are always consequences for stepping outside of God's boundaries. No discipline before marriage means none after marriage either.

Keeper at Home: Yes, most men expect you to cook, clean, and take care of the needs of the family. Do what you can to invite him and encourage him into sharing and partnership with the home and family, but recognize this as an area of leadership for you.

Obedient: You can take the word "obey" out of your vows if you want, but it is still in the Word of God. Don't think you will transform from a rebellious woman into a submissive bride. Learn why and how to submit, as well as God's plan for submission.

As you develop the qualities above, also remember to strengthen your self-sufficiency. It is wise to know that you CAN make it by yourself. Feeling like you cannot live without a man causes you to be overly dependent. Keep on maturing spiritually, socially, emotionally, educationally, and get practical knowledge.

Who Are You Getting?

You don't have to settle for being in a terrible relationship. Put your emotions on a shelf for a moment, take your rose-colored glasses off, and take a good look at the man you are considering for marriage. What is his character? Is he honest, faithful, flirtatious, sneaky, a bad boy, a con man, or a liar? Forget romance. Do you think he'll make it through the long haul of marriage, which includes sickness, struggles, and the tragedies of life? What type of father will he make? Is he responsible, handy, willing to learn, willing to get counsel, and receptive to the Word of God?

Face the things you are trying to ignore, analyze them, and pray about them. Marriage is not some magical state that cures all your problems. If he is crazy before marriage, he will be crazy after marriage, except you'll be legally, financially, physically, emotionally, and spiritually chained to him.

If you get to the altar and change your mind, turn around and walk out. Next to your decision about salvation, marriage is the most crucial choice you make in life. It is better to have a time of embarrassment than years of pain. Don't push a man to the altar. You will hear about it later if he feels trapped, and he will eventually escape.

Ask yourself some real questions about his spiritual commitments, his work record, how he deals with anger, and his attitude toward women and children. You two have a lot to talk about. Pull your lips off of his and talk to really find out who he is, and then check out the answers by observing his behavior and learning from his family and friends.

Guideline 3: Men—Finding Your Good Thing

Your First Prerequisite for Marriage is Having a Relationship with God

If you do not have a relationship with God, you are not marriage material. Husbands are commanded to love their wives as Christ loved the church. How can you love like Christ if you do not know Him?

"Then the man and his wife heard the sound of the Lord God as he was walking in the garden…But the Lord God called to the man, 'Where are you?'"[3]

The Second Prerequisite for Marriage Is to Work

Adam had a job and a life assignment prior to Eve. If a man does not have this, he is not ready for marriage. God calls Eve Adam's helpmeet. The purpose of the helpmeet is to help him fulfill his assignment. If he does not know his assignment, then he does not need a helpmeet and is not ready for one.

"And the Lord God took the man and put him into the Garden of Eden to dress it and to keep it."[4]

The Third Prerequisite for Marriage Is to Learn What It Takes to Be a Good Husband

"And the Lord God said, it is not good that the man should be alone; I will make him an help meet for him."[5]

"Therefore shall a man leave his father and his mother, and shall cleave unto his wife: and they shall be one flesh."[6]

Here are some reflections on these words:

Moral Limitation: If a man cannot resist the forbidden (illicit sex, drugs, alcohol, or stealing other's property), he is not ready for marriage. If he engages in the unrighteous, illegal, or immoral on a regular basis, he should not be a prospect to marry.

Wife First, Parents Second: He must change his relationship with his parents, not allowing them to control, dominate, and manipulate him. If a man is a mama's boy, he is not ready for marriage. Your marriage will always have third-party interference.

Relational Closeness: When a man is a negative name-caller, his wife will be a victim of verbal abuse, and he is not a good prospect. Adam affirmed Eve's gender identity and her femininity. Cleave means to cling, stay, catch, and closely pursue. Men often have a natural propensity to distance themselves because of a fear of closeness. A man must overcome this tendency to be ready for marriage.

Brothers, look for your helpmeet. A wife is called to be a suitable helper. There is a difference between a helper and an enabler. An enabler gives a man what he wants; a helper gives a man what he needs. Look for the woman who will help you with the truth and will speak it in love.

When your spirit shouts, "…This is now bone of my bone, and flesh of my flesh," you have found your Eve.[7]

1 *The Bible,* Proverbs 18:22 (KJV)

2 Ibid, Titus 2:4, 5 (KJV)

3 Ibid, Genesis 3:8, 9 (NIV)

4 Ibid, Genesis 2:15 (KJV)

5 Ibid, Genesis 2:18 (KJV)

6 Ibid, Genesis 2:14 (KJV)

7 Ibid, Genesis 2:23 (KJV)

Clarence Walker, Ph.D., and Ja'Ola Walker, D.D., have been Family Life Educators throughout their married life. Both currently serve as Pastors, and they share Biblical principles with couples and singles with a special focus on Black families. They are co-creators of "For Christian Lovers Only,"™ a research- and faith-based curriculum. (www.marriage.urbanministries.com) Clarence Walker worked as a Marriage and Family Therapist for twelve years. He holds a post-graduate Certificate in Marriage and Family Therapy, as well as a Ph.D. in Biblical Counseling and M.S.W. He is the author of *Biblical Counseling with African Americans* and *Breaking Strongholds in the African-American Family.* His website is www.clarencewalkerministries.com. Ja'Ola Walker has her D.D., M.Ed. in Counselor Education and her B.A. in Psychology. She has authored *The Eight Powers of a Woman.* The Walkers have been married for thirty-four years and have two sons.

♥ ♥ ♥

The Adventure of Being a Cross-Cultural Couple
Dugan Romano

In the early stages of all love relationships—and cross-cultural ones are no exception—a couple sees and clings to what draws them together. When the couple comes from different cultures, they tend to celebrate the apparent similarities that are present, dismissing the differences they encounter as unimportant, secondary, or perhaps charming and exotic. Their life together is exciting, an adventure, never boring.

It is after marriage, when the couple tries to build a family and create their own "family culture" by falling back on what they know and are used to, that these "unimportant" differences can become the devils in the brew. We're not talking about the fact that one partner feels a meal is not a meal without a daily dish of pasta and the other eats sushi. The challenge arises when pasta becomes the symbol of domestic bliss, and sushi symbolizes a refusal to accommodate. The couple can run into trouble when they get hung up on the conflicting minutia of their daily life, which are not really that important in and of themselves, but are signs of unresolved value differences between them.

With couples who hail from different lands, there are many of the same issues as those faced by same-culture couples, such as sex, money, in-laws, male-female roles, and raising and educating children. However, a relationship and marriage can be more complicated for them because they are coming at the issues from different starting points. Their own country, ethnic, or family cultures have trained each of them to see certain things as universal, obvious, clear, and right, or at the least preferable. When couples have divergent views on significant aspects of their relationship, not only is there the experience of the "right and obvious" being challenged for the first time, but it's being challenged by a partner and loved one. They don't know what hit them.

When a couple runs into these early challenges, they often don't know why and play the blame game, saying, "You are selfish/rude/domineering/just plain wrong." Most of us don't even know how to define what we believe in or hold sacred until they have been threatened, and then we can feel attacked. When attacked, we react and often counter attack the wrong culprit. To move forward, the couple will need to understand that culture has come into play.

It is only by exploring—often with help from someone cross-culturally aware—that couples can begin to distinguish which conflicts are due to differences in cultural habits, expectations, and assumptions, and which are truly character-based.

Communication is key. It is essential that the couple confronts their cultural differences, talks about them, doesn't hide from them, or hopes they will just go away. While learning the nuances of their cultures is a lifelong process, the couple needs to begin their cultural exploration at the beginning of their relationship, while preparing for their marriage.

Couples from different cultural backgrounds—even more than others— need to delve into their own expectations and hopes. They need to communicate openly, verbally, and honestly about what matters to them, what hurts or angers them, and how they envision life together. They must continually question, explain, and clarify. They must never assume—NEVER. In this way, they will begin not only to open themselves to the other culture, but also to confront their own cultural prejudices and biases. Each one of them will, over time, get to know themselves as well as their partner better. In this way, their cross-cultural marriage can be a wonderful and exciting path to self-discovery and self-fulfillment, as well as the great adventure they set out on when they first met.

Dugan Romano is a cross-cultural Trainer and Consultant specializing in family adjustment to overseas moves. She is the author of *Intercultural Marriage: Promises and Pitfalls* (3rd edition, 2008) with Intercultural Press, a Nicholas Brealey Publishing Company. She has twenty years of experience in her own cross-cultural marriage with an Italian, with whom she lived in his country (Italy), hers (U.S.A.), and a third (Brazil). She also brings to her writing the knowledge she has gained from the hundreds of couples she has interviewed for each edition and revision of her book. She can be reached through her publisher at 617-523-3801 or www.interculturalpress.com.

❤ ❤ ❤

Exploring Culture, Ethnicity, and Race
Susanne M. Alexander

Population studies are showing that interracial and intercultural marriages are on the rise. Culture determines both your worldview and how you behave. If you are partners of a different race, nationality, ethnicity, social and economic class, or from a different part of the same country, you will have experienced different cultures. According to Joel Crohn, Ph.D., author of *Mixed Matches*, cultural differences between you and your partner may cause conflicting attitudes toward use of time, family relationships, sex, food, monogamy and faithfulness, how to express anger and affection, ways of disciplining and rewarding children, interactions with strangers and friends, and the roles of men and women, among other things.[1] In addition, people from various cultures or upbringing may communicate differently. For instance, some cultures use silence to express anger, while others are loud and vocal. In another culture, silence may simply indicate someone is thinking deeply about a subject.

Culture can be thought of as the glasses through which you view the world. As people who wear glasses can tell you (because they always wear them), sometimes they do not even realize they have them on. You may not actually realize the dramatic influence your culture has upon how you see the world. "Culture comprises what we feel; what we learn; what we do; who we spend our time with; memories of and preferences for smells, tastes, sounds, and feelings; images and stories we cherish. It is the resource we all draw on when we problem solve, interpret information, plan for the future, assess ourselves and others, and locate ourselves within time and space."[2] For all these reasons, you will want to understand your cultures and consider how they affect the ways you both view the world and respond to it.

Learning About Each Other's Culture

You can gain increased understanding and appreciation if you put yourself deliberately into experiences familiar to your partner. You can travel to where your partner grew up or spend time with their family and friends. You can visit an area where your partner's culture predominates, perhaps a section of a city, state, or province where people of the same culture live and gather. If your partner's family commonly speaks a different language, you may need to learn that language in order to communicate and participate with them. Reading books, taking courses in intercultural communication, watching movies, or eating at appropriate ethnic restaurants can also increase your understanding.

As you gain a deeper appreciation of your partner's culture, keep in mind that more than one culture may have influenced their life. For instance, if your partner lived in Japan for years as a young child and later moved to the United States, both cultures will have significant influence. Your partner's personal culture will be a blend of Japanese influence and the culture of the new neighborhood and friends encountered later. Explore with your partner which culture has had the most influential impact. They may need to reflect on and discuss that question with family and friends before responding. Observing each other in various circumstances will also increase your understanding.

It will be helpful to you to discuss in detail what each of you thinks, feels, and believes about the following topics, staying especially aware of how your cultures have influenced your attitudes and actions:

- Importance of family
- Relationships with parents
- Relationships with children
- Roles of women and men
- Socio-economic status
- Fundamental communication skills
- Physical hygiene/body fitness
- Your own and other people's race, ethnicity, or culture
- Role of religion
- Physical ability
- Importance of education
- Importance of employment/career
- Money/finances
- Political convictions
- Clothing/manner of dress
- People at different ages, such as teens and elders

These discussions will reveal both your differences and commonalities, and you will likely discover other matters to explore as well. Which of your commonalities encourage your hope for the future of your relationship? Which differences raise concerns? How might you address them?

If you and your partner were reared differently, you will need courtesy, flexibility, and patience to understand each other and discover what you have in common. You may need perseverance to discern whether the differences you find will divide you, or whether your commonalities will be strong enough to allow you to build a strong friendship-based marriage.

Other Factors for Success

Some of your friends and relatives may initially express discomfort about your relationship. They may or may not adjust to or accept you being together over time. If those around you express mixed reactions to you as a couple, you might remind them to focus on your love for each other and your characters as far more important factors in your relationship than your racial or cultural differences. As Dr. Crohn says, "Our differences are the source of learning and creativity in all of our important relationships, and learning to recognize, appreciate, and use these differences is the key to enriching family life."[3]

You can put the cultural differences in your relationship in perspective by discussing how you each view humanity as a whole. You can also discuss how your cultures or races fit into this global view. If you regard humanity as one family, you will see that "...the various races of humankind lend a composite harmony and beauty of color to the whole."[4] If either of you do not have this viewpoint, you are more likely to see cultural or racial differences as a significant problem. The same dynamic applies to your families, who may be accepting or prejudiced about differences between the two of you.

Understanding Prejudice

An important area for you to explore is whatever experiences either of you has had with prejudice, which can cause subtle negative actions and reactions between you. You may have picked up subtle negative attitudes from people who are prejudiced or who are angry that others have discriminated against them. You must be vigilant in eliminating these attitudes, even the momentary thoughts of prejudice or superiority that cross your mind. This is especially true if you want to sustain a successful interracial or intercultural marriage.

Honestly examine your motives to determine whether you might have chosen a partner of another race or culture just to prove that you are not prejudiced. Consider whether you respond positively to your partner because of a cultural stereotype, which may or may not be an accurate reflection of your partner. For example, you might assume all people of a certain race are hard workers, financially responsible, very sexual, or fun loving. Your relationship will have a shaky foundation if you have a bias and see your partner as a representative of a race or other group, rather than as an equal and unique human being.

It is also wise to understand the potential for prejudiced responses from others toward you and agree how you will handle them. Either you or your partner may be more sensitive than the other to prejudiced words or actions and may need help from the other to understand and accept or address them. If you and your partner are clear that you are receiving prejudiced reactions from people, agree on the character qualities you will use in responding. These can include kindness, courage, forgiveness, love, or justice, depending on the circumstances. Honest and loving discussions between you will help you deal with irrational negativity from others.

One key topic that will be a factor for you if you are in your childbearing years is having multicultural/multiracial children. Fortunately, this is now much more common. However, prejudices are still strong in enough people that your children could be targeted with verbal or physical attacks. How will you guide them to handle these? How will you both respond if your child is targeted with prejudice?

Over the last decades, laws that placed barriers between those of different races and cultures wanting to marry have largely been eliminated. With each passing decade, acceptance of these marriages is becoming more of a norm. But…there can still be issues that arise. Exploring those potential challenges and enjoying the wonderful discoveries you make along the way about one another are part of careful preparation for marriage.

1 Joel Crohn, Ph.D., *Mixed Matches*, p. 30

2 D. Osher & B. Mejia. *Overcoming barriers to intercultural relationships: A culturally competent approach*, quoted in "Reaching Today's Youth", 3(2), 48-52, 1999.

3 Joel Crohn, Ph.D., *Mixed Matches*, p. 22

4 'Abdu'l-Bahá, quoted in *The Advent of Divine Justice*, p. 31

Susanne M. Alexander is a Relationship and Marriage Coach with experience in doing workshops and coaching with intercultural couples. On the personal side, her extended family includes people of various racial and cultural backgrounds, including African-American, American, Armenian, Canadian, Chinese, Greek, Iranian, Irish, Italian, and Philipino. www.marriagetransformation.com

♥ ♥ ♥

Creating Unity Through Your Courtship and Marriage
Raymond Switzer

Marriage is for more than just our own self-benefit or the benefit of our partner, more even than for the benefit of the children who are raised within its framework. Marriage is a powerful means of helping us to grow into the new requirements of the world. Therefore, when looking for a partner, we must look beyond our own self-interests and beyond the transient thrills of falling in love.

The world is plagued by our human ego. We all have a tendency to be separate and regard others as less than us. In marriage, once the biological chemical feast of romance plays out, we are faced with living with someone who is different from us in many ways. Our egos react to this situation, using all the tools they have learned to survive throughout life. This reaction will hurt our spouses and reflect back on us in harmful ways. It also reflects our immaturity, likely our parent's immaturity, and the immaturity and divisiveness we find in the world at large. The conflict and feelings of futility that often arise in marriage are, in this sense, a call to grow in consciousness. We must find new and helpful resources in creating unified marriages and take these new skills into the world.

Cross-cultural and interracial marriages are yet another level of challenge to our egos. While it is good to recognize the extra challenge this type of relationship presents, it is not something to be avoided on this account. We have deeply engrained, largely unconscious reservations around the differences we see in people who were raised in other cultural contexts. The teachings of the Bahá'í Faith make it clear that marriage has the power to overcome these prejudices and alienating feelings and can be a primary source of healing the racial divisions in society. These teachings state that marriage between the races will "wholly destroy and eradicate the root of enmity."[1] Clearly, we have to be willing to face ourselves, our prejudices, and our fears in doing this and be ready to move far beyond whatever romantic images we may have about our partner's cultural background.

In marriage, we can learn how to transform feelings of estrangement into abiding unity, exactly the lesson the world at large is struggling to learn. The process of falling in love during courtship is not the same as learning to implement all the layers and complexities of loving another human being. Learning to love this deeply comes later and is an intense part of the work of marriage. Learning to love well will produce the spiritual fruit of your marriage, and this will contribute to the healing of humanity.

Marriage is a union of your hearts and souls, in many ways far more than your physical selves. It is from your hearts and souls that the desire comes to contribute to humanity. Marriage is a "fortress for well-being and salvation"[2] and unity the remedy the world needs today. The more you can strengthen the connections between your souls through such actions as praying together, meditating, and doing service for others, the greater your consciousness will grow.

In choosing a partner, first and foremost, you must seek out someone who is awake to the need of creating greater unity in the world through marriage—someone who is prepared to carry through with this work. Of course, this also means that you, too, will be willing to acquire an appetite for such work and develop the perseverance to make abiding reconciliation, founded on marital friendship, a reality in your life. The willingness to do this work is needed before entering into wedlock, and this is the beginning of maturity. The work of marriage itself, including rearing children together, will bring the task of growing up to completion. These are the new requirements of marriage, a perfect match for the needs of humanity today.

1 'Abdu'l-Bahá, quoted in *The Power of Unity, Beyond Prejudice and Racism*, p. 55

2 Bahá'u'lláh, *Bahá'í Prayers*, p. 118 (2002)

Raymond Switzer, author of *Conscious Courtship: Finding Someone to Love for the Rest of Your Life*, is a Canadian Psychologist living with his wife Furugh and their children, Nasim and Nabil, in Gödöllő, Hugary, to help establish the Bahá'í Faith community in that country. He has given seminars and presentations on courtship and marriage in Germany, Poland, Cyprus, Slovakia, Croatia, Austria, England, Greece, the Czech Republic, Turkey, and Italy. He is the only therapist in Hungary trained in Imago Relationship Therapy, and much of his practice involves working with couples. You may visit the Switzer's website at www.switzer.hu.

♥ ♥ ♥

Intercultural Maturity
Grete Shelling

To make an intercultural relationship work, partners need to harmonize. Harmony means unity—not unison, but unity with and despite diversity. It means taking on the adventure of differences, working through conflicts, and tackling difficult challenges.

Harmony under these circumstances is a task that requires a certain level of maturity. The more mature you are, the better chance you will have at maintaining and nurturing an intercultural relationship.

So, what does it mean to be mature? Since there is no absolute definition for maturity, let us say it differently. Partners who are more likely to make an intercultural relationship work well are the ones who:

1. Know and realize their own identity. They know what they like, value, want, and need, and they can express themselves with others at the risk of being opposed or critiqued.

2. Ask and explore their partner's core values, interests, beliefs, likes, dislikes, and customs, especially when different from their own. They have an attitude that says, "Maybe *my* way is not necessarily better or right, but simply different."

3. Function at their best together and individually, even if they do *not* share some of the same beliefs, likes, tastes, customs, and values.

4. Are willing and able to set aside or adjust some of their beliefs, likes, tastes, customs, and values for the other.

5. Can tolerate the tastes, values, and customs of their partner.

6. Explore their differences openly, honestly, and respectfully. Facing differences when in love is like driving over potholes with shock absorbers. Once the shock absorbers of new love wear out, the potholes may feel a LOT rougher! The solution? Identify the potholes earlier on and learn to drive around them!

7. Can differentiate between emotional and rational thinking and between drives and behavior.

8. Are able to separate triggers of the past with those of today; such as differentiating between a parent's tyranny in the past and a partner's demands or requests in the present.

9. Are interdependent, not overly dependent (emotionally and materially), nor too independent or detached. They are able to be loyal, near, and close, yet secure enough to be left alone at times.

10. Are willing and able to set aside their own wants and needs for the sake of other people's wants and needs. In other words, they love unselfishly. (This is not the same as helping others to perpetuate their unhealthy dependencies.)

A definition of the Greek words for sacrificial love, or *agape*, aptly describes the kind of love that would make any relationship work, especially an intercultural one:

> Love is patient, love is kind. It does not envy, it does not boast, it is not proud. It is not rude, it is not self-seeking, it is not easily angered, it keeps no record of wrongs. Love does not delight in evil but rejoices with the truth. It always protects, always trusts, always hopes, always perseveres. Love never fails.[1]

Now, how many immature people do you know who can love like that? Yet a bigger question is, "How do I learn to love like that?" It helps to have received that type of mature love at some point in one's life—if not from a human source, then consciously from a Divine source. In either case, developing this type of mature love is a process. An intercultural relationship certainly contributes to that process, along with lots of bumps and bruises along the way. We need others to mirror back to us who we are and to confront us with the truth of who we are. That is often painful in itself. Along with that, it helps if we:

1. Have an attitude of humility and willingness to acknowledge our immaturity;

2. Make apologies that communicate a willingness and resolve to change;

3. Ask our partner, "What would you like me to do differently and how?"

This may sound like the opposite of maturity, like being a child again, but this type of attitude is exactly the mark of maturity necessary to make any relationship work, especially an intercultural one.

1 *The Bible:* 1 Corinthians, 13:5-7 (NIV)

> **Grete Shelling,** Ed.S., M.S. is the author of the book *In Love But Worlds Apart— Insights, Questions and Tips for the Intercultural Couple.* She has been involved in multicultural social work for over thirty years and specializes in counseling intercultural couples. She holds both Master's and Education Specialist degrees in Professional Counseling from Georgia State University and a diploma in Pastoral Counseling from Richmont Graduate School of Counseling. Austrian-born but raised in the United States, Grete is married to a "very" American husband who, she says, is culturally very different from her. They have a grown son who now lives in Austria. She can be contacted through InLoveButWorldsApart@yahoo.com.

💜 💜 💜

Strengthening Latino Relationships and Marriages
Ana Morante

Everything that applies to everyone else for marriage preparation applies to Latinos, including the importance of knowing, strengthening, and working on ourselves. In addition to that, it is important to look at our culture and how it will play out in our relationship. Latinos in the United States need to assess how our culture of origin can merge with the dominant culture in this country. We have the responsibility to determine the elements of our culture that are going to be good and helpful in this new society.

We get gifts from our culture that are important to remember and to pass on to the next generation. Many times, in our attempt to assimilate to a new culture, we forget some of the gifts our own culture brings. On the other hand, we will also find other elements of our culture that might not be as helpful in this society. Having flexibility to keep what is helpful from our culture and to leave the rest is a key element for a successful process of acculturation.

Assimilation

When we talk about Latino couples, even if both are Latinos, sometimes even from the same country, there are always going to be differences. Latinos are very different depending on the country (even the area) where they come from. It's very important that we talk about these differences: the ways we were raised, what our values are, what our expectations are, and also where are we in terms of the level of assimilation or acculturation.

I've seen many difficulties when one member of the couple may be more assimilated than the other and their values start clashing. It's very important to discuss those issues ahead of time and see what it is going to be like when we form this couple relationship. We need to ask, "How are we going to make our lives now, based on where we both are in terms of the assimilation-acculturation spectrum?" It's good for the couple to create their own couple or family cultural statement of how they are going to live life together.

The Family

An element for Latinos to consider is the importance our culture places on family, *la familia*. Family is a tremendous gift. However, it can also be a tremendous source of conflict. In general, when families act as a source of strength and support for the couple connection, there is nothing better than having extended family close by.

The difficulty comes when we are not very clear with where our biggest commitment lies. In some couples one of the members (or sometimes both) is apparently more committed to their family of origin than to their new couple relationship. That can create a lot of struggle. To have a healthy marriage, our strongest commitment should be with our spouse. As a couple, it is important to discuss how we are going to include our families, what role they are going to play in our lives, and what boundaries we will have with them. Having clarity about these issues can empower the couple to define how their extended families can be a source of support rather than stress for their relationship.

Research shows that women in the Latino culture have a stronger sense of being mothers than wives. Our main commitment many times is to our children, even more than to our spouses. That could be very difficult, especially in this society. In most Latin American countries, because there is an extended support network and the *familia* itself is so much bigger than it is in the United States, this dynamic is not that detrimental. If they have some frustrations and difficulties, there's always someone they can get support from, but in the United States, many people do not have this extended support network. Therefore, our spouse is usually our main source of support, and it's crucial to have our strongest alliance with our spouse. When both of us are working together and are strong, we will be in a better position to provide for our children.

Gender Roles

Women need to continue being good mothers, but at the same time be very aware of the importance of our role as wives. It's also especially important to take care of ourselves. For Latino women, our children, our husbands, and everybody else come before us. When we try to care for everybody else and forget about ourselves, we end up exhausted or irritable and aren't the best we can be for everybody. When we assert ourselves and take care of our needs, this will bring better things for ourselves, our spouse, and our children.

As for men, it's important to step away from some of the stereotypes in our Latino culture about how men should be. It's emphasized that men don't cry or express emotion, so men are robbed of their opportunity to be in touch with their feelings. That is a very important skill that we need if we are going to have a close couple relationship. If I want to get close to my spouse and don't know how I feel and cannot tell her how I feel, there's not going to be much of a connection. When Latino males are more in touch with their feelings and more in touch with who they are and what they want, they can give more to their spouses and to their children.

There also has to be more flexibility in terms of gender roles than in our countries of origin. Life in the United States is more demanding of both partners. Without an extended support system, having a more traditional division of labor can create a lot of stress and conflict between the couple. It is important for Latinos to revisit the way we distribute the responsibilities in our family. The more we can help and support each other, the better the chances that we can enjoy a strong couple connection.

Some Problem Areas

There are a couple of other issues that are very common in the Latino population. One of them is substance abuse, especially the use of alcohol. It is not just openly accepted but almost promoted in our culture. A problem with alcohol addiction is one of the most destructive things for a family and a marriage. We have to be very careful and very aware of whether our use is just social or if it is getting in the way of having stronger couple and family relationships.

The other issue is domestic violence. I see a lot of violence happening in the relationships of the people that I work with. Many people raised in a different country tell me that when they were growing up, corporal punishment was used as a form of discipline. That makes us a little bit more numb and desensitized to the harm of physical violence. In addition, adjusting to a new culture can be very challenging and overwhelming. This can create a high level of stress and even a sense of powerlessness. If we have been raised in families where power and control were used as a coping mechanism, we may be more at risk of repeating that cycle. We need to carefully recognize when we may be in a relationship where power and control are used rather than having mutual respect. If that were the case, it is very important to look for help in order to be more respectful to ourselves and have a better connection with each other.

Editor's Note: The above is excerpted and edited from an interview between Susanne Alexander and Ana Morante on March 10, 2010.

Ana Morante, L.M.F.T., C.F.L.E., is a bilingual Marriage, Family, and Child Therapist, helping people in both Spanish and English. She is dedicated to strengthening couples and families and assisting in the creation of the best environment possible for children. She has a private practice in San Jose, California, and is a certified Parent and Family Life Educator and a Family Wellness Partner and Trainer. Ana has been married for sixteen years and has two daughters and a stepson. She can be reached through www.familywellness.com.

❤ ❤ ❤

A Challenge to Be More Responsible
Jamil Muhammad and Nisa Muhammad

In the Black community, marriage is the exception rather than the rule, and couples have few healthy models of married couples. What wives and husbands do is often a confusing dilemma for many couples, and they end up replicating what they see on TV or watch in the movies—not the greatest of examples by far. The cultural cues that guide young people to learn the responsibilities of spouses are missing. It's time to change these patterns, and it begins now as you prepare for marriage. What healthy patterns can you begin now and carry forward into marriage?

Keeping the FIRE Burning

FIRE is an acronym for Faithfulness, Intimacy, Responsibility, and Excitement. With these four ingredients, couples can be on their way to wedded bliss. Below is a deeper look at what the "Responsibility" part of this process involves. Of course, these are generalities and must be customized to fit the specific needs and challenges of your marriage and your spouse. Discuss together what actions you can take now and in the future to be responsible partners.

A Message to Black Men

Men are responsible for supporting women in five different ways: spiritually, intellectually, emotionally, physically, and financially:

Spiritually: Gentlemen, please bear in mind that whatever your concept of the Higher Power is, your wife must be encouraged to have her own independent relationship with that Great Force. She cannot be just a shadow of you. When she is able to walk her walk as she is guided, there can only be benefit for you, who encouraged her along the way.

Intellectually: It's simple: You're not the only smart one in the family, buddy! Your spouse has an intellectual and academic ability of her own. We must not let fear of being outshined, mindless conformity to archaic limits on women, laziness, or anything at all stop us from fostering the mental gifts of our women. If she shines, we just GLOW!

Emotionally: In short, be nice to your wife! She is not likely to give you the result you seek if all you do is shout at her, insult her, and hurt her feelings. She is not a man; therefore, you can't talk to her as if she were one of your old buddies from rodeo school or from the college football team. Try a little tenderness, will ya? Accept the differences between her femininity and your masculinity, and she'll make you glad you did.

Physically: Your physical support of your beloved doesn't just refer to the marital bedroom. That's a part of it, but it doesn't stop there. The idea here is to create a space of safety for your wife to begin making you and your family a functional group. She cannot do that if she is constantly worried over potential eviction, utilities being disconnected, or the repossession of major purchases. She can't be distracted by the fear of crime against her person or her property. As her husband, you must help her physically.

Financially: Isn't it interesting that in a materialistic society like ours has become, this category would be the last of the group? The financial wellbeing of the couple is your responsibility as the husband. It causes serious problems if the family budget falls short too often. Your wife will honor and respect you when you give your best effort and your every resource toward the upkeep of your family. This holds true even if the wife contributes income to help the family, as is all too often necessary in an economy like the one we face in these uncertain times.

When a man is hard at work for his wife and family, the natural inclination of the wife is to support the man who she sees involved in the work to maintain her and their children.

Below, we will discuss the ways a wife should support her husband in order to strengthen the bond of marriage and encourage commitment.

A Message to Black Women

When a husband is doing his job, what can he expect from his wife? Below are the ways a wife can support her husband.

Comfort: It can be exhausting for your husband to carry the weight of responsibility and obligation for supporting the family. Comforting him is a natural and very fulfilling expression that you will enjoy too. Setting his mind and body at ease is like repairing and maintaining a fine vehicle. (Gentlemen, whether you are a Ferrari, a Model T, or a 1948 Buick Roadmaster is totally up to your wife!) Properly comforted, your husband can go back out and do it all again the next day. Comfort includes things like the beautification of your home, well-prepared meals, and the comfort of your personality.

Console: You provide a vital role in soothing your husband's disappointment and defeat and encouraging him to get up and try again. No one makes it through this life without losing sometimes. The male ego resists losing, but men are socialized to feel real shame and authentic sorrow when they are not the victors in daily competition or in the advancement of their professional and community status. Your husband will turn to you for consolation. Even a simple, "Baby, it's gonna be alright," helps them feel uplifted and psychologically ready to compete again.

Challenge: This does NOT mean to go toe to toe with your hubby! Instead, be aware of what your husband could and should do better. Encourage him to act on behalf of your family by appealing to the "winner" inside of him. Say to him, "I know these problems look bad, but you're not gonna let small-time stuff like that get to YOU, are ya? After all, you're my hero!" Does that sound corny? Well, just try it. The response you get will be anything but corny. Your husband, like millions of other men, has been brought up to see his own manhood in light of how willing he is to accept a challenge and rise to any occasion. Gently and wisely, help him to be a man of consequence. Believe he can do it, and tell him so, and you might be surprised!

There are great possibilities ahead for Black families who take on new patterns of action. The more you both practice responsibility for your family, the better the future will be.

Jamil Muhammad is the Director of Programming for Wedded Bliss Foundation, www.weddedblissinc.com, a community-based organization helping teens and adults create healthy relationships and healthy marriages. One of its goals is giving more children the benefits of a two-parent family. He has worked with families for decades and has a special love for working with men. His work with Nisa Muhammad (no relation) as pioneers in strengthening marriage in the Black community was featured on CNN's *Black in America 2*. He is single and looking for wedded bliss.

Nisa Muhammad is the Founder of the Wedded Bliss Foundation (www.weddedblissinc.com), a community-based organization helping teens and adults create healthy relationships and healthy marriages. One of its goals is giving more children the benefits of a two-parent family. She created Black Marriage Day for communities to celebrate marriage in very unique ways. It is held annually on the fourth Sunday in March, and it has grown from 30 participating cities participating in 2003 to close to 300 communities conducting celebrations in 2010. Mrs. Muhammad is the co-author of *Basic Training for Couples*, a marriage education curriculum. Her work as a pioneer in strengthening marriage in the Black community was featured in detail on CNN's *Black in America 2*. She knows both the joys of marriage and the sorrows of divorce. She works so her five children and more adults can enjoy wedded bliss.

Chapter Eight
Understanding Sex

~ ~

If there is a spark of attraction between you, sex has certainly come up as a topic of discussion. You may have already had sex with each other and with previous partners. You may, instead, be choosing to wait until after you are married.

Keep an open mind as you explore our wisdom in these selections. We are guiding you through understanding and productively using infatuation, making wise choices about sexual activity, understanding the importance of marital sex, appreciating passion, and observing whether sexual addiction is potentially an issue in either of you. Sexual intimacy is a complex subject, one that will be an ongoing topic for discussion as you go forward. Fortunately, resources for this topic are plentiful.

❤ ❤ ❤

Using the Power of Your Infatuation for Good
Dave Carder

Infatuation is a drug. Like most drugs, it can create intoxication and addiction, as well as leave you disappointed, disillusioned, and angry. Yet, the search for its thrill is evident everywhere! Look at the percentages on adultery, read the research on workplace affairs, and consider the surveys in which 68 percent of women say they would have an affair if they knew they would not be caught.

On the other hand, infatuation—though potentially dangerous—is a very necessary part of the initial bonding process in a couple's attachment. Below are some guidelines to help you manage it, some cautions about how infatuation distorts sexual activity and can appeal to your emotional deficits, and finally, some warnings about resurrecting old infatuations in this new relationship.

Powerfully Using Infatuation

Infatuation causes one to distort, deny, or discount differences between the two of you. Rather than fight infatuation, use it to your benefit by:

- **Focusing on your differences and the unknowns** that exist within each of you. You will never be more accepting of each other than when you are infatuated with each other.

- **Limiting your time together.** Research is clear that the more time you spend together while infatuated, the more likely you are to become sexual with each other. Sex can be dangerous to the longevity of the relationship during the infatuation period.

- **Satisfying your need for touch** by using Sensate Focus exercises. Search the Internet for "sensate focus exercises," a series of non-sexual but very healing touching experiences. These exercises also encourage respect and trust between you as a couple.

- **Taking the Couples Checkup** in order to highlight the topics the two of you need to talk about. (See www.prepare-enrich.com.)

Dangers of Mixing Infatuation and Sex

When you hop in bed on your wedding night, you will find at least six of you in there: his mother and father, her mother and father, and the two of you! Disgusting thought, isn't it? Even if you are virgins on your wedding night, you have a family and sexual history that travels with you. It's something you need to be thoroughly cognizant of before you marry. Infatuation makes you think the two of you can create your own sexual experience apart from this history, but you have been collecting sexual attitudes, experiences, perceptions, and more since the day you were born. (See the Sexual History Survey at the end of this article.)

Sexual activity while infatuated creates an artificial sense of closeness. Infatuation, combined with great sex (and it is almost always "great" during this period of time), sets a couple up for disillusionment later in courtship or after marriage when real life and real schedules set in. Genuine closeness comes from using this sexual energy, this time of infatuation, to explore all of your differences, your values, your history, and your goals. It is always more fun to make love than conversation when you are together, but even that will end when you begin to think, after marriage, that due to your differences, you married the wrong person.

Here's an interesting truth: Your relationship is only as "old" as it is non-sexual. Sexual activity while infatuated keeps the relationship from developing. If your relationship is a year old but you have been sexual with each other since shortly after the first three months of dating, you have a three-month-old relationship. Why? Because, though it is always more fun to make love, it is the resolution of differences that will provide long-term potential for genuine intimacy. Lovemaking may seem more exciting than time spent talking and getting to know one another. When a couple sees each other less frequently (such as only on weekends, during college breaks, trips between military deployments, and so on), the thinking often goes like this: "Why rock the boat by discussing what I know could create a disagreement? We have so little time together anyway."

If sexual trauma occurred for either of you prior to this relationship, know that it cannot be healed by a spouse should you decide to marry this person. Infatuation and premature sex will make you think otherwise. You think you have found the healer of your soul, but this is not true. Infatuation will make you think childhood wounds and neglect can also be taken care of by your spouse. It will not happen. Self-disclosure helps, when embraced by an infatuated lover, but you need to bring to the marriage as clean a slate as you can create.

Using Infatuation to Fill Emotional Deficits

We all leave home about half baked. It is this unfinished business, these issues, this baggage that often enhances the infatuation. You think you have found a soulmate, someone who understands your deepest needs. Maybe it is a woman who appears to provide you the nurturing and mothering that you missed when living with your stepmom. Or it's a male mentor, the father figure that you lost forever when your Dad left the family. Maybe it's someone who accepts you just the way you are, not like the "black sheep" you have been in your family. Or it's a woman who loves your music and doesn't view you as a dreamer, but believes in your vision. Your partner is someone who is fun, impulsive, and spontaneous, while everyone in your family has always been rigid, organized, and disciplined.

It is this opposite image—this exhilarating breath of fresh air you have always been looking for—that fuels the attraction, the intrigue, and the infatuation. But beware! These differences hold great potential for future conflict if you don't use the energy from the feelings of infatuation to explore your histories and create solutions.

Infatuation Connected to "First Loves"

The feelings of infatuation are stored in the brain. This is especially true of the infatuations of adolescence. One never forgets adolescent music, sporting events, movies, cars, dating experiences, and certainly "first loves." Just look at the retro designs, reunions, popular music, and the interest in the lives of the actors and actresses of your teenage years.

Engagement is a period where you must learn to leave behind forever the boyfriends and girlfriends of adolescence. The Internet makes it possible to quickly find first loves (or they can find you!) when feelings of infatuation have faded in a marriage. When you enter a marriage, people with whom you shared an infatuation history (other than your spouse) are now off limits. Why? Because you don't need time to develop infatuation with these folks; you already have a full dose of it stored in your brain just waiting to be rekindled!

It will shock you how quickly this reconnection to an old infatuation can sweep you off your feet, confuse you, and make you question the relationship you are in now. This fast reconnection is especially true if you had a sexual relationship with and thought of marrying this first love. Internet contacts with old first loves are developing into one of the biggest threats ever to marital stability. It is important to remember that studies indicate that those who wait for marriage to have sex and are faithful within marriage report the highest level of happiness in their relationship.

Conclusion

Infatuation is a great source of energy that can be very reassuring to both partners as you continue to forge this relationship. Use it for the purpose it serves best—keeping you connected when discussions of differences could drive you apart. This successful use of infatuation will only draw you closer and confirm that just maybe, the two of you really are meant for each other!

Sexual History Survey

1. Three words Dad would have used to describe their sexual relationship in his marriage:

_____

2. Three words Mom would have used to describe their sexual relationship in her marriage:

_____

3. Sex was used in my parents' marriage as/to:

_____

4. Feelings from your first sexual experiences in childhood:

_____

5. Family attitude toward sexuality:

_____

6. What did sex mean to you in adolescence?

_____

7. Three words I would like to use to describe our sex life after marriage:

_____

8. My greatest fear about sex is:

_____

9. Sex to my fiancé/fiancée means:

_____

David M. Carder is a Marriage and Family Therapist with a specialty in adultery prevention and recovery. His website is www.TornAsunder.org. Dave has applied his specialty for the Tony Robbins Passion Project, Discovery Health Channel, *Marriage Uncensored, Focus on the Family, The Psych Journal, Family Life Today,* Smart Marriages® and Happy Families Conference, *100 Huntley Street,* Departments of the Army and Navy, the Salvation Army Leadership Training Conference, and The American Association of Christian Counselors. His articles and observations have appeared in *The Ladies Home Journal, USA Today,* and *The Counseling Connection.*

His book credits include *Close Calls: What Adulterers Want You to Know About Protecting Your Marriage, Torn Asunder: Helping Couples Recover from Infidelity*, and *Torn Asunder Workbook.* Dave currently serves as Pastor for Marriage and Lay Counseling Ministries at the First Evangelical Free Church of Fullerton, California. He also gives pastoral oversight to Caregivers of the Mentally Ill and Family to Family, the National Alliance on Mental Illness family training program. Dave also serves on the boards of The Center for Individual and Family Therapy and Marble Retreat Center, Marble, Colorado. Dave has been married to Ronnie, his jogging partner, for over 40 years, and they have four grown children, three of whom are married. They love to travel the globe when they are not playing with their five grandchildren.

❤ ❤ ❤

Choosing to Wait for Sex Until Marriage
Mark Gungor

Giving People the Full Story

Not everyone who has sex gets pregnant, and not everyone who has unprotected sex gets AIDS or other sexually transmitted diseases. Yet enough do that we take great lengths to warn people of the potential dangers. Sadly, little has been said of the danger of how premarital sex can negatively affect people for the rest of their lives.

The Potential Damage to the Man

Some years ago, while doing some videotaping of cranes in the wild from a helicopter, I learned of how these birds "imprint" when they are first born. In other words, whatever creature they first interact with after birth, they assume is their mother, even if it is a human. I immediately thought of what first-time sex does to a man. This overwhelming new experience IMPRINTS on him, and he connects the context with the experience. Those who have their first sexual experience outside of marriage imprint on the lust of illicit sex. Those who have their first sexual experience in the context of marriage imprint on the girl or woman.

Consider Scenario A:

Boy gets girl to let him fondle her in the back seat of a car. Soon, he is undressing her. His heart is pounding as it becomes clear that she will allow him to have sex with her. The windows are steamy, and he is now in a major hurry (lest she changes her mind or someone catches them). He experiences an adrenaline rush not unlike a thief experiences when he first steals or a thrill-seeker gets when jumping from an airplane. He then enters her body and experiences his first sexual experience with a woman.

This incredible experience leaves a major imprint on him. Now (possibly for the rest of his life), he is likely to view sex in the context of "lust" and "naughtiness." This is the man who will constantly be pushing his wife to try some outrageous new behavior, take sexual risks, or constantly role-play—all in an attempt to re-live that initial experience that had such a profound effect on his psyche. This is the guy who wants to "do it" in the elevator or in the backyard or in some semi-public place. This is the guy who needs his wife to pretend she is a cheerleader or a naughty nurse before he can get excited, as he tries to re-create his sexual imprinting. He is not as interested in the woman as he is interested in the sex.

Now Consider Scenario B:

A man falls in love with a woman and asks her to marry him. His family approves, his friends approve, and his coworkers approve. They all join in a concerted effort to make the wedding a success, with detailed planning and appropriate celebrations. They all come together at the wedding in one unified effort to communicate their approval of what he has chosen. They now gather in the presence of God, with the approval of his minister. They commit themselves before God, and then they are off for what will arguably be one of the biggest events of his life—the wedding night and honeymoon.

With the joyous approval of every important person in his life, he takes his bride to their honeymoon suite, and for the first time in his life—without the rush or fear of a backseat encounter—he experiences the most wonderful sensation of his life as he enters his bride's body and reaches his sexual peak.

He now ties *everything* to that one woman—all the approval of his family, friends, and coworkers, the church, the celebration, and most importantly, the incredible sensation he has just felt. All these elements join together, and he *imprints on his wife*, for it is because of her and only her that he has just experienced the most wonderful day of his life. *Nothing* impacts a man like his first sexual experience.

If a man has his first sex outside of marriage, what he *imprints on is the sex*;

indeed, it becomes as if any woman willing to have sex with him would suffice. Many of these men later turn to illicit affairs, pornography, fantasies, and masturbation in a pathetic attempt to re-visit the early imprinted first-sex experience. Women who marry such men can sense this and try desperately to get their man to focus solely on them. Sadly, it is a battle that most will lose. On the other hand, when a man has his first sexual experience in the context of marriage, he imprints on the *woman*, for she is the sole reason for his incredible experiences. Indeed, these men tend to marry once and stay married for life.

What About the Woman?

Women also receive a great deal of damage from being sexually promiscuous, and the damage is both psychological and physiological. When a woman experiences sex without commitment, she soon learns (falsely) that sex means little to nothing. Why? Because nothing happens as a result: No meaningful relationship ensues, and he may never even call her or talk to her again. She has inaccurately learned that sex and commitment are two completely separate issues, which they are not. That is why so many married woman view sex as an unimportant side issue in marriage, when it is, in fact, a vital part of a successful marriage.

Science also shows us that when a woman has sex with a man, a chemical called oxytocin is released into her system, which helps a woman bond with her lover during sex. New scientific studies, however, suggest that if a woman has multiple sexual partners, this will lower her levels of oxytocin, which in turn can inhibit her ability to bond to her husband. It is like taking a piece of strong packing tape and applying it to a box. Leave it alone, and it will hold that box together for decades and decades. Take it off and re-apply it—especially multiple times—and it just doesn't stick as well anymore.

Men Are the Biggest Losers

Even though a woman also can suffer negative consequences from promiscuity, men can have the most to lose. Why? Because a sexually promiscuous woman, despite lowered levels of oxytocin and a less than positive attitude toward sex in general, still is internally wired to *want to connect with her husband*. Indeed, that desire is so strong that it causes her to fight through many of the negative side effects of her previous sexual experiences. A man, however, has no such natural wiring. If he fails to properly imprint and bond to his wife, he may spend the rest of their marriage in a disconnected state from her—indeed, from any woman.

Sex Clouds Your Vision

There is more for you to consider. For starters, sex makes you stupid. It really does. Having sex outside of marriage clouds your vision. People can't see clearly and aren't able to make a decision about whether the two of you are wise to marry or not. The potent spell of sex causes women (and some men) to tolerate and allow the most outrageous behaviors, continue the relationship into marriage, and then come to me a year, two, or three into the deal and want me to unscramble the eggs. When I ask the obvious question, "Didn't you see this before you got married?" they almost without fail say, "Yeah, but I thought it would be different when we got married." It will be different: WORSE!

Becoming sexually involved with someone outside of marriage is a bad idea for many reasons. First and foremost, is because *God said so!* And when God says so, you would think that is good enough, since the Almighty Maker of the Universe pretty much knows what He's doing. If He says, "No," it's for good reason. God created sex, He knows the power of it, and He knows that it will make you stupid outside of marriage. But *within* the marriage covenant is another story.

Sex Within Marriage

The same phenomenon that makes men and women dumber than bricks when it comes to making the right decisions in premarital or extra-marital relationships has extreme power when the sex is according to God's plan. The very same idea that "sex clouds your vision" is *wonderful and necessary* in marriage. God has created sex to have this kind of effect to help us forget and overlook the faults and missteps, the offenses and transgressions, and forgive our spouse. It's like a drug you can get a hit of that gives you selective amnesia. It's also another reason why married people need to be having regular sex—so they can get a little clouded vision to overlook the everyday annoyances like toilet seats and toothpaste caps and sometimes even the bigger things that need to be forgiven. We should be "blind" to those types of things.

God has given us the gift of sex, one of the very things that will aid and enable us to live out His type of unselfish love. But it only works to our benefit if the sex is in the context of marriage. Consider the analogy of fire only being a good thing when it's contained in a fireplace. God made sex to be the single most powerful physical force to bring a husband and wife together and to keep them together. But it has to be in marriage, or it is the equivalent of taking the fire and putting it on the living room floor—or out in the forest to rage and destroy, having no more warmth and benefit, and just being a disastrous inferno.

Chastity

You must be very intentional about making chastity a high priority when you are dating. As the saying goes, *If you play with fire, you're going to get burned.* It doesn't matter if you are seventeen years old or forty-seven. The best way to avoid letting a relationship become physical is to steer clear of situations where you will have the opportunity. That includes things like spending a lot of time alone; snuggling and cuddling watching TV or movies (especially those with romantic or sexually charged content); or heavy touching or make-out sessions when you are doing everything but actual intercourse. Even prolonged kissing can release those same hormones and have the similar effects as intercourse.

Avoiding sex before marriage can be especially tricky for those dating later in life after a previous marriage ends through death or divorce. Relationships tend to move very quickly, and most people in this situation think it's not a big deal to wait for marriage since they were already married and have had sex before. But the same truth applies, and it will cloud your vision. You won't be able to see all vital aspects of your partner clearly, especially their character. You will then become entangled in a relationship that may not be good for you at all, but you will not be able to recognize it. Besides that, the Word of God still applies: No sex outside of marriage.

There are lots of other things you can do besides letting every date turn into a temptation zone. Find things to do together in public or in a group. Get involved in a spiritually based group or community service. Date with other couples or hang out with family. Building a premarital relationship with family is very important anyway. Protect yourselves from the temptation and be smart. You must be intentional about it and make the choice to avoid going down a path that could be detrimental to you and the relationship.

Overcoming Sexual Damage

The reality is that many people don't put up boundaries or make a conscious decision, and they end up becoming physically involved. If that is you, the first thing you need to do is *stop it*. No one can re-claim virginity, but re-claiming chastity is always possible. Make no mistake, it will be tough to do, but it will be worth the effort and work that it takes. The degree of damage people receive largely depends on the degree to which people become sexually involved before marriage, particularly if there are numerous partners. It also can vary from person to person. Some who have had just a few consensual experiences may seem to carry few residual effects. For others, even just one consensual experience can cause them to struggle later in their marriage. If a person's experiences were not consensual (as in rape or incest), it is likely that much more damage will have occurred.

The question now is: Can a person who has been damaged have a meaningful sex life? Thankfully, the answer is yes, any person can have a wonderful sex life, but it will more likely come easier to those who waited until marriage. Those who did not may find they will have to work a lot harder to establish a healthy, bonded marital sex life.

Here's an analogy I like to use: There are people who can seemingly eat anything they want and never gain any weight. Then there are those who allow themselves the slightest indulgence and gain a couple of pounds! What is the difference? One has a very different metabolism from the other.

So it is true with those who did not wait until marriage for sex. Their "sexual metabolism" may be very different from those who did wait. Evidence shows that couples who wait until marriage report more satisfying sex lives than those who do not wait. And since sex is so important to the bonding of the couple, this is why couples who marry as virgins have a much lower divorce rate than those who did not wait. A couple whose only sexual experience has been with each other is much more likely to experience a natural bonding. Those who have been promiscuous may find they will need to be much more intentional and deliberate in their approach to sex in order to bond.

Virtually anyone can still experience a wonderful sex life, but let's stop pretending that sex before marriage is "no big deal" and start telling people the truth. This is vital for two reasons: 1) so that our kids can avoid the problem in the first place, and 2) so those who have been negatively affected can learn how they can still succeed by changing the way they think about sex, and change what actions they choose to take or not take. Always remember, God is not a prude. He does not tell us to avoid sexual promiscuity because He is somehow embarrassed about sex. He just knows how we are wired and wants us to experience the very best.

Mark Gungor is one of the most sought-after speakers on marriage and family in the country. Each year, thousands of couples attend his "Laugh Your Way to a Better Marriage"® seminars. His take on marriage issues is refreshingly free of both churchy and psychological lingo. Mark is Pastor of Celebration Church in Green Bay, Wisconsin. He speaks for churches, civic events, business meetings, and even the U.S. Army. Mark has been featured on national broadcasts such as *Focus on the Family* and ABC News. His daily Internet radio show is heard worldwide, and his weekly television show *Love, Marriage, and Stinking Thinking* is available on TBN and Sky Angel. Learn more about Mark and his marriage seminars at www.laughyourway.com. Mark and his wife Debbie recently celebrated their 37th wedding anniversary and have two married children and four grandsons.

❤ ❤ ❤

Start Your Marriage with Passion and Skills
Anne Bercht

Wow, marriage! I've been married for twenty-eight years, and I'm still madly, deeply, passionately in love with my husband. I still get tingles when I see him, I'm still excited to go out on dates with him, and I even still lust after him. Don't believe those naysayers who tell you your love will die with time. Don't believe those t-shirts that picture a groom getting married wearing a ball and a chain. No doubt, there are those who have experienced marriage that way, but this does not need to be your marriage story.

When I was twenty years old, I married my husband, Brian Bercht, five weeks after the day we met. It was a whirlwind romance. With what I know now, I would advise caution about moving that fast, yet, at the same time, I'm happily married, so I have few regrets. We had no special knowledge of what to do at the time, but now that I've learned about what it takes to make a relationship work, it turns out we did a few important things right, as well as some things wrong.

Commitment First

One of the most important things for any couple considering marriage is to do things in the right order. Get to know each other first. Then establish trust, then make a commitment, and then and only then, be physically intimate. Practicing faithfulness before marriage can also go a long way in establishing monogamy throughout your marriage.

In today's world, half of marriages end in divorce, and a large number of those who do stay married are not happy. Apparently, if you want a lasting love, you will have to do something different than most.

Mutual Respect

If your goal is to enjoy a lifelong, enduring, passionate love, then mutual respect will be an essential component. That has to start now. When we cross lines into having physical intimacy before we've established a friendship, trust, and—most importantly—commitment, we cheapen ourselves, set ourselves up for possible hurt, and establish a pattern of crossing boundaries that can play out negatively in our relationship later.

When I was dating my husband, we ended up one night at the beach, parked in my car, a long distance from our homes. I was very physically attracted to him at that moment (as was he to me), but Brian took the lead at the time and was a man of honor. He told me to sleep in the back seat, while he slept in the front. He told me I was far too valuable a woman for him to take advantage of me in that way before he had made a public commitment to love me and take care of me for a lifetime. Talk about establishing your relationship with commitment first!

What are you prepared to do to establish commitment, friendship, and trust before physical intimacy?

What Went Wrong?

In spite of all the good we began marriage with, a few years later, we were faced with Brian having an affair. What went wrong?

Simply, we just didn't have the tools to prevent one. As a married couple, you are going to experience life together, and that means ups and downs. There will be good times, and there will be bad times, the proverbial "for better or worse." We didn't possess the relationship skills to prevent a marriage crisis in the bad times.

Brian lacked the skill of self-awareness. He wasn't able to be honest with himself about his feelings when his father died, we were experiencing disrespect from our teenagers, and significant job issues were pressing in on him all at the same time. Even less was Brian able to be honest with me about how the pressures of life were causing significant pain for him.

Extramarital affairs, contrary to most people's perceptions, are not about someone else being younger, better looking, sexier, more fun, or different in any way. Affairs are about pain in the unfaithful person's life. Extramarital affairs have the same effect on a person's life as drugs or alcohol: a temporary escape from reality and pain.

The affair happened in our marriage because we didn't understand what it really takes to prevent affairs. Will power, commitments, and promises are not enough. It takes understanding. My husband was not only unaware of his feelings and needs, but he also lacked the skill of being able to communicate with me openly and honestly about difficult issues. I lacked the skill to really listen to him, and although I respected Brian, I lacked the skill of making him feel respected. We've now learned those skills, recovered from the affair, and kept our marriage strong and happy. But we wish we had developed those skills before marrying.

Don't Slide into Marriage—Experience Passion First

One thing that has served us well throughout our lives together was to marry while we were still in the passion stage and to have had the passion stage in the first place. This strong foundation contributed to resiliency that gave us strength to bounce back and recover from our later marital crisis.

Today, I work as an affair-recovery expert, helping couples that face this devastating situation. I know "affair" is a word you don't even want to hear, and if you're contemplating marriage, you are most likely feeling so in love with each other that you are sure this could never happen to you. But, it's wise to be certain. So, allow me to share what will help you make sure it doesn't. You can learn from the mistakes of others.

Consider the Story of Jenny and Marc

Jenny and Marc came to see me for help to restore their marriage after Marc's extramarital affair. While working with Jenny, trying to help her rebuild connection with Marc, she was understandably full of pain. When people are in this place, they often rewrite their history together and see everything through a black, negative filter. They forget they ever had fun when they were dating or engaged.

Jenny was in such a dark place. I was working to pull her up, even just a little bit so we could begin to make progress, so I asked her to remember a time in her life when she and Marc had a good time together.

Jenny informed me that they never once had a good time together. I assumed she was just in the dark cloud (which I understood), so I patiently worked to jar her memory. I asked many questions about many situations that most people experience in married life as being positive. But, no matter how many questions I asked, Jenny continued to assure me she had never once had a positive experience with Marc—ever.

I asked her to recall meeting Marc for the first time, their courtship, and times when they were dating. She continued to assure me that they had never once had a positive experience together, even then. Finally, she began to convince me that perhaps there was truth in what she was saying, so I asked, "If you never once had a positive experience with Marc, then why did you marry him?"

She explained to me that they had a good friendship, although never any passion. She had observed him being romantic with his previous girlfriend, so she knew he could act this way with her, and that's what she wanted in her life. She started being a friend to her husband when he was on the rebound after breaking up with the other woman. She thought in due time, he would give her the romance he had given his previous partner.

You better love the one you're marrying just the way they are. Don't expect that they are going to change in fundamental ways or that you are going to change them after the wedding.

Although Marc had been a responsible husband and father for more than thirty years, the couple had never experienced passion together. After working with us for some time, Marc left his marriage and went back to his affair partner.

Don't get married just because you've been together so long that it seems like the next logical step.

I was so astounded that someone would actually marry someone after no positive experiences together. In our discussions and trying to understand why, we discovered that while growing up, Jenny had a sister whom her father blatantly favored. All throughout Jenny's childhood, she felt she was second best. She recreated this scenario with Marc, even while longing to get him to treat her as number one. Sadly, this unresolved baggage from Jenny's past sabotaged their marriage.

Deal with Baggage from Your Past

To have a healthy marriage, we need to deal with our issues with parents, family, and previous relationships. It's so important to present ourselves as emotionally whole in the relationship.

Ask yourselves about and discuss any baggage from your past that you might be bringing into this relationship that could affect the future of your relationship in a negative way. What can you do to address, resolve, and heal it?

The bottom line is that effective marriage preparation, education, and skill building can help you to ensure that an affair NEVER happens in your marriage. Monogamous, long-term, passionate, fulfilling marriages ARE possible, and many people do experience them, but they don't happen by accident or because your love is special. They happen by being prepared, educated, aware, and intentional about keeping your relationship working well for both of you.

Anne Bercht is the author of *My Husband's Affair Became the Best Thing That Ever Happened to Me*, host of the website: www.beyondaffairs.com, and Director of the Beyond Affairs Network (BAN) International. She is also a professional speaker and relationship coach. Together with her husband, Brian Bercht, she has created and delivers a series of marriage education seminars. She is most known for the Healing From Affairs Intensive weekend designed especially for couples in marital affair recovery. Anne and Brian reside in Vancouver, British Columbia, Canada. They have three grown children and two grandchildren.

❤ ❤ ❤

What's the Big Deal About Sex, Anyway?
Susanne M. Alexander

It took me a long time to begin figuring out some answers to that question—the topics of sex before and after marriage get a lot of attention. Like many other people, I thought that sex was primarily a form of physical expression. Oh, I got that it had emotional components, but really, it was mostly just about physical pleasure. I encouraged people to practice abstinence outside of marriage, but I really wasn't sure why it was important. I also thought that abstinence and chastity were close to being the same thing. You may have some of the same perplexing questions that I did.

In 2003, I found this quotation, "One speck of chastity is greater than a hundred thousand years of worship and a sea of knowledge."[1] Okay, that said to me I *really* didn't understand what chastity was if it was that powerful. Chastity (rather than the "just say no" focus of abstinence) seems to be about filling your life with positive images and actions that include respectful boundaries, and choosing to have sex only within marriage. It includes avoiding images and experiences that draw you toward sex, especially with someone other than your spouse. It means being vigilant about your thoughts and keeping them focused in non-sexual directions. One of its gifts is being able to have straightforward and non-sexual friendships with people, so that there is nothing that prompts jealousy in a partner. Chastity certainly applies before and after the vows.

Even with this expanded understanding of chastity, I was still struggling with why choosing to practice it is so powerful for couples. In one of those briefly profound airplane conversations, I shared the above quotation with a fellow passenger and asked his view on the subject. He said to stop and think about what the world would look like if through practicing chastity the male and female energy in the world was concentrated and balanced equally within happy marriages instead of dissipated through things like pornography and infidelity. He suggested that the resulting healthy marriages might be a significant contributor to peace on the planet. So, a glimpse of chastity's potential power.

But, what is the big deal about sex IN marriage? If you've chosen to practice chastity, you come to marriage without the baggage picked up from other partners and can focus on one another and learn together. And, look at sex in the context of what is spiritual about it, not just physical, and you'll begin to get a glimmer of its importance. Marriage is a union of your bodies, minds, hearts, and souls. "Out of the fusion of two souls a third subtle entity is born. Though invisible and intangible on earth it is the composite soul of true lovers. The progress of one mysteriously influences the other, they become the tutors of each other's soul. Distance or death, being physical forces, cannot cause its disintegration."[2]

There are many aspects of marriage that can help you feel unified with each other. The act of joining your bodies closely together in intense intimacy certainly is one of them, and it is one of the gifts of a good marriage. Of course, it's helped by you understanding how your bodies work and being open to learning.

Creating oneness with someone—however it's done—is a spiritual act. The character qualities, which are really the essence of our souls, all apply to making love. Think about how these qualities can affect the experience: flexibility, helpfulness, courage, gentleness, enthusiasm… Then, of course, there's conception, which guides a new soul into life in this world.

Consider what sex accomplishes when it goes well in marriage. It can increase feelings of love and connection, release tension, provide opportunities for fun and play, provide a foundation for meaningful communication, and much more. Marriage gives us a great place to engage in the natural and appropriate expression of the sexual parts of ourselves.

Sex outside of marriage is…well…sex outside of marriage. And, sex within marriage is an act of physical, mental, emotional, and spiritual union. If you want to have spiritual sex, it can only happen within marriage. Practicing chastity helps you to have a happy and successful marital life.

1 'Abdu'l-Bahá , cited in a letter dated November 26, 2003, from the Universal House of Justice

2 Rosemary Sala, *The Bahá'í World*, Vol. 7, p. 763

Susanne M. Alexander is a Relationship and Marriage Coach with a specialty in character (www.marriagetransformation.com).

© 2010 S. Alexander

❤ ❤ ❤

The Challenges of Sexual Addiction on Relationships
Mark Laaser, Ph.D.

Editor's Note: Below is an edited transcription of an interview conducted March 22, 2010, between Susanne Alexander and Dr. Laaser about his specialty of sexual addiction and his personal experience with it.

Is It an Addiction?

My own family has been through this healing, and mainly what that means is that I, myself, am a recovering sex addict. I went to treatment in 1987 and have been sober now a little over twenty-three years.

When I first got involved for myself, the whole field was just starting to be defined. And to this day, it's still somewhat controversial as to whether or not sexual addiction can, in fact, be an addiction. Certainly, there are no chemical substances involved in it, unless you're using chemical substances to enhance your sexual excitement, like cocaine or methamphetamine. But, generally, we think of several criteria. **One aspect is typical for any field of addiction, in that the addict will at least feel like they are out of control.** The Twelve Steps (originally developed by Alcoholics Anonymous) say an addict is powerless over the addictive substance, which in this case, is their sexual behavior.

So, the addict (who can be a man or a woman) has made attempts to stop and hasn't been able to. They've wanted to be free and just haven't gotten there. They've maybe made what seems like a hundred attempts to stop and have stopped for a while, but then it hasn't lasted very long. And so, we have people that get themselves into all types of trouble and consequences, despite the fact that they know their behavior is very harmful to them.

When it comes to this first criteria of addiction, your average addict is what we call "double-minded." There's a part of them that wants to be free of the addiction, and there's another part of them that likes holding on to it. This is because it's one of the ways they medicate their pain, wherever it's coming from. One of the things we have to do in treatment is help an addict get more single-focused on why, in fact, they want to give it up and where their motivation is coming from.

The second criteria for something to be an addiction according to the medical definition, is that it has to create neurochemical tolerance. The brain has to become adjusted to whatever it is you're putting into it, and it is going to demand that you put more of that same substance in to achieve the same effect. So, does sexual activity involve substances?

The truth of it is that I believe it does. If we look at the various neurochemicals involved in the pleasure center of the brain when we have a sexual response, we find that adrenalin, dopamine, and serotonin can all be involved in that response. When we touch each other, skin to skin, there's a neurochemical called oxytocin that it is involved in the contact. This is not unique to the human sexual response, but it is certainly a part of it.

And then, of course, when we do have an orgasm, there's a whole set of heroin-like neurochemicals called chatacholamines. And so on the front end, which is sexual arousal, all we have to do is think about being sexual, and that's enough to release adrenaline and dopamine and so forth, giving us an exciting anti-depressing response.

If we are engaging in sexual activity, even with ourselves in an act of masturbation, there is skin-to-touch, and that increases oxytocin. If we achieve an orgasm, that gives us a heroin-like effect. So, on the front end there is a cocaine-like effect, and on the back end a heroin-like effect. Those of us who agree with the idea that there is such a thing as sexual addiction believe there is a neurochemical addiction happening in the brain.

Neurochemical receptor sites in the brain adjust to whatever we put into it by creating more receptor sites, which create a craving for more of the same substance. In this case, it means more sexual fantasy, more acts of masturbation, and more acts of sexual activity.

If adrenaline is part of the mix, which it is, the addict may need to also do things that are more dangerous, more challenging, or more exciting.

The third indication of addiction is an escalating pattern. For some addicts, this escalation could be from their adolescence all the way up to their adult years, where we see a gradual increase in the sexual activity that a person is doing.

In the case of some Internet sex addicts, we can see a definite escalation over several months from casually searching Internet websites to the point where the person is on the Internet regularly looking at sex-oriented sites. I had a client who started looking at the Internet adult sexual partner finders sites and got so hooked on it that he was actually having three affairs within a month's time.

The fourth criteria for addiction has to involve some kind of negative consequences to the person—social, emotional, or physical. Legal consequences, sexually-transmitted diseases, and broken relationships are common.

If a person meets all of those criteria, we believe they are addicted and need help and treatment.

Signs of a Problem in Your Relationship

The main word that comes to me is *preoccupation*. Signs of struggle with addiction include if your partner:

- Seems preoccupied with sexual thoughts, sexual jokes, sexual conversation, and sexual activity
- Often scans the room checking out the opposite gender
- Turns even normal conversation in a sexual direction
- Teases or makes jokes about sexuality

- Pressures you for sexual activity
- Has phone bills, text messages, and emails making contact with other people for the purposes of being sexual, either through chats or phone or in-person contact

Does Being Abstinent as Partners Help?

Unfortunately, whether your spiritual morality believes in abstinence before marriage or not, this will have no effect on preventing the addiction. The common belief held by a sex addict going into marriage is that being married will somehow prevent them from their otherwise out-of-control behavior.

They're really hoping sexual intercourse will be the "be all, end all" in terms of controlling this pattern. They think the vows or the mystical nature of the wedding sacrament will somehow indemnify them against all inappropriate lust. Unfortunately, it doesn't. I've worked with over 3,000 men, and they were all hoping the same thing.

If you are sexually active in your relationship before marriage, you may see some of the signs of your partner's addiction. If your partner seems like they want more and more and more over a period of time, that would be a sign of possible escalation. Or if it's not just a matter of frequency, they will constantly want a certain level of variety.

Another symptom—albeit somewhat counterintuitive—is if they seem to become bored with you or tired of you. If they are not as sexually demanding or initiating, it could be because they are going to other places in their mind (looking at pornography or Internet sites) or masturbating more frequently. In the worst-case scenario, they're actually having sexual encounters with other partners.

Sexuality will become dissatisfying to them in some extreme way. There may be too much absence of it, which we oftentimes refer to as sexual anorexia, or there's too much sexual demand in it. There's too much boredom, or there's too much anger and aggression.

When you're engaged in an act of sexuality, intuitively most people can tell whether their partner is actually emotionally present in the room. If their mind is elsewhere, you know that's a good symptom that your partner is struggling with something.

Trust your own intuition, which a lot of people have tried to turn off. They say, "Oh, I love him, and I don't want to confront him." If you are somewhat co-dependent to begin with, you know you will deny your own awareness and intuition. There is a level of denial that exists for some people that they simply have to get past.

Does Discovering an Addiction Mean Not Marrying?

I wouldn't automatically say that a couple realizing they are dealing with an addiction issue should not marry. I do believe in love, romance, connection, providential meeting, and so forth. That said, however, I do think that if a partner does become aware that their fiancé or their committed partner is struggling with sexual addiction, it would be *wise to pause all relationship plans and ensure that that person participates in some program of treatment or healing.* A wedding should not occur until the addicted partner is at least six to twelve months sober and can demonstrate and testify to the fact that they haven't acted out in an inappropriate sexual way during that entire time.

The definition of sobriety somewhat depends on a couple's morality, because it can vary. For some, it might mean all the way down to the most rigid of forms: no masturbation and no sex outside of their relationship. Then there would be other people who say, "Masturbation is okay, not a big deal. Everybody does that. My main bottom-line boundary is that you don't have sex outside of our relationship. That's what I would mean by sobriety." So a couple has to negotiate that, talk about it, and be open and honest about it.

Family Addiction Patterns

In my research, every sexual addict I've ever encountered has at least one addict in the previous generation. It might not always be another sex addict; it could be an alcoholic, chemically dependent person, gambler, or overeater. These family patterns of addiction are very profound, and it's wise for a couple to understand each other's family backgrounds and some of the system dynamics in the family.

Now, again, I don't think this should prevent a couple from getting married. I think the healthy couple is one that recognizes that they do bring certain genetics, inherited patterns, and emotional baggage as part of their family system and is willing to engage in the process of healing. Each partner has to be willing to own their own baggage, story, family tradition, and family background. Hopefully, you're able to understand it, realize it's there, and be willing to go get help should some triggers for you arise. If you can do that, the relationship can proceed.

Is There a Connection to Sexual Abuse?

There's a pretty dramatic connection between abuse and addiction. The research revealed the fact that in a population of sex addicts, about 75 percent of them had been sexually abused as a child. They also tested the partners of those sex addicts and found that about 75 percent of the partners of the sex addicts were also sexually abused.

The percentages have come down somewhat because sexual activity has become so much more accessible—primarily through the Internet—but we still see it quite often. It's an ongoing issue and just really requires that a person be willing to work on it.

Being Married to a Sex Addict

One of the things we have found is that if the partners are aware of the addiction before marriage, and if the addict has been honest about the addiction, then the chances that they can survive even acts of infidelity in the marriage is a lot greater.

If an addict and partner—despite whatever level of fear, anxiety, or co-dependency they have going into the marriage—can get honest about their sexual struggles, I think it's much more likely that the two people can be each other's companions and intimate partners.

If they are struggling with this issue prior to marriage or in marriage, there are a lot of resources, healing options, and great therapists who can help. I personally believe infidelity is something that cannot only be survived, but if the couple gets the right kind of help, they can learn how to turn it into something that will allow their marriage to thrive.

Mark Laaser, Ph.D., is a Counselor and Founder of Faithful and True Ministries based in Minnesota (www.faithfulandtrueministries.com). His specialty is sexual addiction, and he is the author of *Healing the Wounds of Sexual Addiction* and *The Pornography Trap*. Dr. Laaser is a frequent speaker at the annual Smart Marriages® and Happy Families Conference, where he includes in his presentation the healing he and his family have experienced from this challenge. Mark and his wife Debbie have been married for 37 years and have three grown children.

Chapter Nine
Concerning Cohabiting

~ ~

You may be considering cohabiting or already living together. A high percentage of couples make this choice for a variety of reasons. You may fear marriage and divorce, you could be trying to save on expenses, or you may believe trying marriage out ahead of time is smart. However, there are many myths and misunderstandings about the value of cohabitation.

In this chapter, we give you some likely new perspectives on your choices, as well as ways to manage your relationship together if you are cohabiting. The relationship knowledge and skills throughout most of the book may also be useful if you are cohabiting. We encourage you to now consider whether you can successfully marry.

♥ ♥ ♥

Cohabitation Mergers
John Curtis, Ph.D.

Typically, when two companies merge, the hope is that the whole will be greater than the sum of the parts. Ideally, businesses unite to create a new organization with a fresh identity and culture. This same kind of hoped-for new identity is an idealized state that is the goal when choosing to marry. Many cohabiting couples also strive to achieve a couple identity that is beyond the two of them as individuals.

Living together before or after marriage means creating a new partnership that allows each participant to gain, grow, and benefit—in other words, to profit from the union by bringing together two people to form a more valuable and worthy partnership. In a couple merger, you may also gain a larger family system that includes each other's children and parents.

The Challenges of Merging

Sometimes I'm hired as a business consultant to help manage the changes and personnel challenges that occur during and after a merger. It often seems similar to my long-time work as a marriage counselor with couples who are remarrying. My task with both is to help successfully blend the previously separate—and sometimes quite different—cultures into a new enterprise. The goal is to achieve what both parties envisioned when they decided to join forces.

As you look at the merger you create during cohabitation, you realize that you need to integrate the structural components of what both parties bring to the relationship, such as financial resources, automobiles, furniture, and other possessions. But you also have to integrate the cultural dimensions, such as the expectations, visions, objectives, and values that each of you brings. You will also need to successfully integrate patterns of communication, negotiation styles, problem-solving skills, and stress-coping mechanisms.

This integration and negotiation process can be similar to the process that occurs with marriage, but in cohabitation, you may keep more separation between you. Finances and possessions may be clearly associated with each of you as separate owners. It is wise for you to agree on your approach and your reasons for your choices.

Whether they be business or personal, few mergers, if any, happen without challenges. Suppose for a moment that you fall in love with someone who has two sons from a previous marriage and an ailing parent. Do you run away screaming, "It can't be done!" which is certainly a viable option, or do you roll up your sleeves and accept the challenge of a very tough merger? Remember: Nothing worthwhile is ever easy.

Merging "Mindstyles"

Each of you comes to the relationship with your own beliefs, attitudes, values, and behavior, as well as your own unique life experiences. Together, these make up what I like to call your "mindstyles." One of the most common and difficult forms of merging mindstyles is when one or both of you are rearing children from a previous relationship or marriage. This is true whether you are dealing with custody or only visitation rights. As with marriage and step-parenting, you may face some unique challenges. Disciplining issues may be frequent, in part, because the roles, responsibilities, and relationships in your home may be unclear, particularly to the children.

Value conflicts—such as what type of discipline to administer—are difficult to address and are rarely resolved by compromising your standards of discipline. The key to successfully blending mindstyles is to ensure that you and your partner establish a common vision that includes the children, set clear objectives regarding how the children will be reared, and determine your parenting roles and responsibilities.

Gaining a Partner, Not Losing Yourself

No one purposely moves in with someone to lose who they are. Neither of you wants to lose your respective personal identities, beliefs, or values when you cohabitate. However, cohabitation may mean that your roles will change, priorities may shift, and your attention may be diverted from your children to each other.

The overarching goal here is to keep the best of each person's personal mindstyle.

Remember to focus on strengthening who you each are as individuals, while at the same time eliminating barriers in your relationship by discussing—not avoiding—difficult issues. Growing your relationship takes forethought and courage to focus on and resolve what is most contentious so that the love and intimacy can flourish with fewer roadblocks. As with a business, interpersonal harmony is an important goal.

Interacting with the Extended Family

Major holidays can be the source of great tension for many cohabiting couples, just as with married couples. If there are significant differences in your families and the expectations they try to impose on you, you will have adjustments to make. It can be challenging to work out how to celebrate special occasions, as well as who should host them and where they should be held. This difficulty is especially true if you both come from big families who love to gather and celebrate holidays.

Extended family dynamics may be smooth, or they may challenge you. Sometimes it can be difficult for family members to make the effort to get to know your partner or become bonded out of fear that your relationship may be short-term. If the family perceives that you are not in a committed relationship together, there may be awkwardness in relating at family events; for instance, there are not easy replacement terms for son-in-law or daughter-in-law.

Topics to Consider

Below are a few of the possible questions you may want to consider to help you better navigate the cohabitation merger process before you hit an unplanned obstacle.

1. How much, if any, contact will we likely have with our ex-spouses or partners?
2. How will we deal with disciplining our children from a previous relationship?
3. What is our plan about having (or not having) children together?
4. What is our commitment to being faithful to each other?
5. How do we feel about having friends of the opposite/same sex?
6. What are our fears about marrying? How can we address them?
7. What do we want to create in our living together that will help us be successful as marriage partners later?

Relationships of all types have their challenges and their joys. Cohabiting is a choice that many are making these days, especially as the fear of dealing with divorce rises. As you look to the future and consider marriage, remember that the more you build your knowledge and skills as partners now, the better it will be for you going forward.

John Curtis, Ph.D., is a consultant, researcher, business trainer, and author. Previously, John was a full-time marriage and family counselor, who achieved clinical membership in the American Association for Marriage and Family Therapy. His education includes a Masters in Counseling and a Ph.D. in Human Resource Development. John is married with two children and two grandchildren. John's book, *Marriage Built to Last: 9 Steps to Life-Long Love!* can be found at www.marriagebuilttolast.org. His book *Happily Un-Married: Living Together & Loving It* is at www.wecohabitate.com.

♥ ♥ ♥

Cohabitation: Good Idea, or a Marriage Killer?
Mike McManus

Cohabitation Is a Stealth Killer of Marriage

Two-thirds of couples marrying in America are living together. For most, it seems to them like a reasonable way to test the relationship for marriage. However, the marriage rate in America has plunged 51 percent since 1970 according to *The State of Our Unions 2009*.[1] And the divorce rate has risen. Why? *Cohabitation is a stealth killer of marriage.* It decreases the odds that people will marry at all, and living together greatly increases the odds a couple will divorce if they do marry.[2]

Myths About Cohabitation

There are prevalent myths about cohabitation that may be unwisely causing you to consider living together while unmarried. Carefully consider the explanations of these myths below.

Myth 1: Living together is a step toward marriage.
Actually, cohabitation is a step away from marriage. Evidence?

The number of couples cohabiting soared thirteen-fold from 523,000 in 1970 to 6.8 million in 2008. Yet the number of never-married adults tripled in those years from 21 million in 1970 to 63 million in 2008. No wonder the marriage rate plunged in half! Cohabitation has diverted tens of millions away from marriage. It seduced them with the notion that they could test the possibility of marriage without making a full commitment. But you can't practice permanence.

Couples who break up after living together experience a "premarital divorce," which can be almost as emotionally painful as a real divorce. Millions who have done so are so severely impacted that they never do marry. That's why the number of never-married adults tripled at a time the population grew only 50 percent.

A woman who has lived with a man who breaks up with her is typically shattered by the experience. She feels used and embittered, having squandered hope and time she can never recapture. She has pinned her hopes and dreams on an uncommitted man. Men often simply move on to the next woman.

Myth 2: Living together is a trial marriage.

No, it is more like a "trial divorce," in which most couples break up either before or after the wedding. Of the 6.8 million couples mentioned above who lived together, only about 1.4 million married. What happened to the other 5.4 million couples? While some continued living together, millions experienced the premarital divorce I referred to above.

Reverend Myles Munroe of the Bahamas laces his fingers together as he says, "When you live with a person of the opposite sex, you 'become one,' as Scripture says. But if you break apart, you do not just separate. You tear," he said as he slowly pulls his fingers apart, "and part of you stays with that other person, and part of that person stays with you. That's what makes it so painful."

But what of those who marry after living together? Dr. Pamela Smock, a sociologist at the University of Michigan, writes, "Common sense suggests that premarital cohabitation should provide an opportunity for couples to learn about each other, strengthen their bonds, and increase their chances for a successful marriage…. The evidence, however, suggests just the opposite. Premarital cohabitation tends to be associated with lower marital quality and to increase the risk of divorce…. The degree of consensus about this central finding is impressive."[3]

In 1989, Dr. Larry Bumpass and colleagues at the University of Wisconsin reported that, "Marriages that are preceded by living together have 50 percent higher disruption rates than marriages without premarital cohabitation.[4] Bumpass found that those entering cohabitation have a lower commitment to marriage and reduced conflict-resolution and support skills. Many are children of divorce or of non-marriage, which makes them fearful of marriage. When their marriages experience strife, these couples are less able to cope and are more likely to give up and leave.

Several years ago, Dr. Paul Amato of Pennsylvania State University wondered if Dr. Bumpass's study overstated the dangers of cohabitation. The original study measured what happened to couples in the 1980s, when relatively few couples cohabited. As larger numbers of middle-class couples lived together, presumably the success of their unions would be higher.

However, as he and his colleagues compared cohabitants who married in the 1980s with those in the late 1990s and early 2000s, they found the risk of divorce for couples who married after living together actually *increased from a 50 percent higher rate, to a 61 percent higher rate of divorce, than for couples who lived separately before marrying.*[5] Though the stigma of cohabitation has largely evaporated, the likelihood of marriage failing after cohabitation has increased. Dr. Amato asserted in 2010 that cohabiting couples who marry have less happiness, more conflict, and more problems in their marriages, as well as a higher divorce rate.

Why Doesn't Cohabitation Work?

Why is cohabitation such a destructive force for couples who marry after living together? Dr. Catherine Cohan, also of Penn State, constructed an experiment to find out. Researchers interviewed married couples, some of whom had cohabited and others who had not. They put the couples into a living room setting and asked them to discuss an issue in their relationship, such as sex, money, children, housework, or careers. Video cameras taped their conversations for later study.

"Those people who lived together were more negative and less positive when resolving a marital problem," Dr. Cohan said. Those who first cohabited, *even only for one month* before marriage, displayed poorer communication and problem-solving skills than those who had not lived together first. Husbands who had cohabited, for example, were more likely to attempt to control their wives, while their wives were more verbally aggressive.[6]

Why? My theory is that those who cohabit lose respect for themselves and their partner. Those who live separately until the wedding have more self-respect and more respect for their spouse. Christian scripture says, "Flee fornication."[7] Fornication is consensual intercourse between unmarried people. What is cohabitation but fornication raised to the 100th power?

Myth 3: What we do is nobody's business.

Couples often believe that whether or not they cohabit is a private matter that has no effect on anyone else. However, 41 percent of cohabiting couples have children—almost the same as the 46 percent of married couples who have children under age eighteen. "By 2001, the majority of nonmarital births (52 percent) occurred within cohabiting unions," according to a 2010 report by the National Center for Health Statistics (NCHS).[8]

The NCHS estimates that about two-fifths of all children will spend some time in a cohabiting household before age sixteen.[9] Children of cohabiting unions are likely to be brought up by a single mother, because most fathers drift away or are driven off. Those mothers and their children then become eligible for government aid, such as welfare, food stamps, and Medicaid. A

Heritage Foundation study estimates that the 13 million single parent families cost taxpayers $20,000 per family in Fiscal 2004, a total of $260 billion.[10] What cohabiting couples do matters to ALL taxpayers.

A Better Way to Prepare for Marriage

Paul, in his Epistle to the Thessalonians, wrote: "Test everything. Hold onto the good. Avoid every kind of evil.[11] Cohabitation is evil. That's what an 80 to 90 percent failure rate is.

There are better ways than cohabitation for couples to prepare for marriage. I've outlined them for you below.

1. **Take a test called a premarital inventory.** This is a detailed relationship questionnaire and can be taken over the Internet. The PREPARE-ENRICH inventory (www.prepare-enrich.com), for example, is composed of more than 150 statements for couples to respond to, such as these:

- I go out of my way to avoid conflict with my partner.

- When we are having a problem, my partner often refuses to talk about it.

2. **Meet with a trained Mentor Couple.** They are skilled in talking you through the relational issues that are surfaced by the inventory. One poll estimates 86 percent of weddings are performed by clergy.[12] Some congregations have trained couples in healthy marriages to serve as marriage mentors; however, most have not. You can go to www.prepare-enrich.com and type in your ZIP Code™ to identify scores of people in your community who are trained to administer the inventory. If you are not religious, you may choose from the therapists who are listed; however, they will charge a fee, while most clergy charge nothing. I recommend that you ask the church if it has Mentor Couples who go over the results with couples. Otherwise, you are likely to find that the clergy member only talks about the inventory results with you for an hour, while mentors will give you four to six sessions. My wife and I run a national organization called Marriage Savers, which has trained thousands of clergy and Mentor Couples to administer a premarital inventory and then go through the results with couples. What's the impact? Divorce and cohabitation rates for the whole city or county drop significantly, and the marriage rate rises. (PREPARE-ENRICH at 800-331-1661 can identify the religious institutions with its trained Mentor Couples in your area.)

The inventory becomes a bridge between an older generation whose marriage has worked and the next generation, eager to learn how to build a strong relationship that thrives over the decades. Mentors can also teach communication and conflict-resolution skills.

3. **Stop living together.** Cohabitation causes you and your relationship harm. In considering living together, you may attempt to justify it. You may say it saves money, for instance. However, there are likely other living arrangements possible for you or financial assistance available from family or friends. It is more likely that you are considering cohabitation because sexual activities have become part of the norm of your relationship.

4. **Stop having sex.** Bottom line, not having sex before marriage increases your odds of marital success significantly. Of the sixty couples my wife and I have mentored over the years, only ten were chaste. We provided them evidence from a study that over four decades showed the sexually active are about two-thirds more likely to divorce than those who remain chaste. I say to them, "If you want God's blessing, you need to consider playing by His rules. You can increase the odds of a lifelong marriage by becoming chaste until the wedding." We then ask them to consider signing an Optional Premarital Sexual Covenant (created by Marriage Savers).

Chastity is important not just before marriage, but afterwards as well. Adultery is a major cause of divorce. One way to get in training for lifelong chastity is to begin practicing it now, with the person you plan to marry. If you can't be chaste with each other, how will you trust each other after the wedding? The good news is that chastity before marriage actually increases your odds of a lifelong marriage. Of the fifty sexually active couples we worked with, how many do you think became chaste? Guess before looking at the endnote.[13]

Insurance for Successful Marriages

During the 1990s, our church's Mentor Couples prepared 288 couples for marriage with the type of premarital program outlined above. Of that number, fifty-eight couples decided *not* to marry, a whopping 20 percent. Studies show that such couples avoided a bad marriage before it began—essentially divorce prevention. But of the 230 couples who married, we know of only 16 divorces, for a divorce rate of only 7 percent over nearly two decades.

That is a 93 percent success rate, virtual *marriage insurance*. Compare that with the nearly 90 percent breakup rate of those who cohabit either before or after the wedding.

The answer is not cohabitation, but solid marriage preparation led by trained Mentor Couples. The more you as a couple are committed to being ready for marriage, and the more marriage officiants and clergy members of all faiths are committed to helping you prepare and succeed, the more happy, lasting marriages we will have.

1 *The State of Our Unions: Marriage In America 2009,* W. Bradford Wilson & Elizabeth Marquardt, The National Marriage Project, University of Virginia and the Institute for American Values.

2 Note: All statistics referenced in this document are about the United States and may or may not reflect the situation in other countries.

3 Pamela Smock, "Living Together: Facts, Myths about 'Living in Sin' Studied," a speech at the University of Michigan Institute for Social Research, Feb. 4, 2000.

4 Larry Bumpass, James Sweet, and Andrew Cherlin, "The Role of Cohabitation in Declining Rates of Marriage," *Journal of Marriage and the Family 53* (November 1991): 913-27.

5 Claire M. Kamp Dush, Catherine L. Cohan, and Paul R. Amato, "The Relationship Between Cohabitation and Marital Quality and Stability: Change Across Cohorts?" *Journal of Marriage and Family 65* (August 2002): 539-549.

6 Catherine Cohan and Stacey Kleinbaum, *Journal of Marriage and Family,* February 2002, quoted by Reuters Health.

7 *The Bible,* I Corinthians, 5:18 (KJV).

8 "Marriage and Cohabitation in the United States: A Statistical Portrait Based on Cycle 6 (2002) of the National Survey of Family Growth." U.S. Department of Health and Human Services, National Center for Health Statistics, February 2010, page 4.

9 Ibid, page 4

10 Robert Rector & Christine Kim, "Fiscal Distribution Analysis of Single-Parent Families in the United States, FY 2004", Nov. 10, 2007, The Heritage Foundation.

11 *The Bible,* I Thessalonians 5:21-22 (NIV).

12 Peter Hart Survey 2003.

13 Of the 50 couples, 43 signed the Optional Premarital Sexual Covenant. And only one of our couples divorced.

Mike McManus is President of Marriage Savers, a non-profit organization which has helped 10,000 clergy create Community Marriage Policies in 228 cities in the United States (www.marriagesavers.org; 301-469- 5873). These cities have since reduced their divorce and cohabitation rates and raised marriage rates. Mike and his wife Harriet co-authored *Living Together: Myths, Risks & Answers,* with a foreword by Chuck Colson. It is the definitive book on addressing the soaring problem of cohabitation. He has also written about reforming no-fault-divorce laws: *How to Cut America's Divorce Rate in Half: A Strategy Every State Should Adopt,* with a foreword by Governor Mike Huckabee. Mike also wrote *Marriage Savers: How To Help Your Family and Friends Avoid Divorce.* A former *Time* magazine correspondent, Mike has written an award-winning "Ethics & Religion" newspaper column weekly since 1981 (www.EthicsandReligion.com). He has appeared on the *700 Club, Oprah,* ABC *World News,* NBC *Nightly News,* the CBS *Early Show, 48*

Hours, Focus on the Family, and more. Articles on Mike and Marriage Savers have appeared in *TIME, Newsweek, U.S. News & World Report, The Wall Street Journal, USA Today,* and hundreds of local papers. Mike and Harriet McManus have been married forty-three years and have three married sons and seven grandchildren.

❤ ❤ ❤

Cohabitation and Commitment
Susanne M. Alexander

One of the ongoing discussions in the relationship and marriage field is whether a couple can truly experience commitment without the solemnizing of the union through marriage. What comes with marriage that enhances the commitment factor is publicly saying vows, which is making promises to each other in front of others. Generally, there are also legal supports that help the couple function well together when considering property ownership, medical care, and more.

What you may find as a cohabiting couple is that you set up living patterns that emphasize a lack of commitment. For instance, you might identify which pieces of furniture belong to each other instead of the normal joint ownership assumed with marriage. Not only will you likely maintain separate finances, but even more problematic is the potential for a pattern of making financial decisions independently rather than as partners. One key success factor in marriage is joint decision making and acting as a unit. Acting independently instead of together can be a challenge both if you are cohabiting and if you choose to marry.

If you view your relationship as temporary or potentially short-term, you may develop the habit of turning to friends to talk about and resolve difficulties instead of handling them together. This can be an unwise practice within marriage. Because you are functioning more independently and still exploring whether to be together for the long haul, it may feel safer to talk issues through with a friend or family member than with each other. Successful and happy marriages include discussing almost everything with each other, even if you choose to have some agreed independence (such as separate bank accounts).

In any relationship where you are not *fully* committed, you may slip into the mindset of thinking every time a problem comes up that you will simply leave. In contrast, with marriage, the options of separating and divorce are *last* resorts for a couple to pursue and only in extreme circumstances. Many married couples make the commitment early in their relationship that divorce will not be a proposed solution to any problem that comes up between them. This resolution decreases the likelihood of divorce being used as a threat during arguments. It allows the couple to focus their energy on resolving the issues instead.

When cohabitation is against one's spiritual teachings, living together may cause disruptions—and in some cases estrangement—between you and your religious community. Based on their religious convictions, its members cannot show support for your relationship in the same way as they can when you are married. If you pretend you are not living together, you may feel hypocritical and dishonest and suffer internal conflicts as a result. In some cases, religious leaders may simply strongly encourage you to marry if you are ready; in other cases, they may ask you to restrict your involvement in community and religious activities so you are not being an unwise example to others, particularly teens and young adults.

Over the last two decades and in most countries in the world, many couples have chosen to live together instead of marrying. As social scientists study this trend, they are increasingly finding evidence that marrying is the choice that best leads to strong, healthy relationships and to the wellbeing of children. Some specific research-identified benefits of marriage include:

- A higher level of commitment; greater confidence in the longevity of the relationship
- Better communication and problem solving
- Less conflict and violence
- Families and community members offer their wisdom, support, and experience in greater abundance
- More settled relationships and parents who are more likely to include the couple in family events and offer emotional support during difficulties
- Greater family unity
- Children are born into or live in a more stable household and relationship; better child health, wellbeing, and achievement

- Tendency to be more productive in the workforce and have higher incomes
- Greater physical and mental health and happiness; tendency to live longer
- Families tend to share more of their financial resources with the couple, including financing educations
- A higher level of satisfaction, including greater sexual satisfaction; greater motivation to please a partner
- More faithfulness and less likelihood of an affair (contributes to protecting partners from sexually transmitted diseases)[1]

No matter how long you have been together as a couple, if you are living together and transitioning toward marriage, it is still wise to take time to assess yourselves and prepare for the change in your circumstances and relationship. It is often not an easy process to go from living together to being in a marriage. One key reason is that expectations of how a wife or how a husband *should* behave arise and come into play, reinforced by any family patterns that each of you have experienced. It will be wise for you to discuss what changes might happen with marriage and not simply assume that all will stay the same or get better.

If you are struggling at any point with whether to continue cohabiting or to marry, it may be beneficial to live apart for an agreed amount of time to assess your situation with a greater degree of objectivity. Resources such as counselors, Mentor Couples, coaches, family members, and more may also assist you in making choices that are best for the two of you and any children involved.

1 Some of these benefits draw on *Why Marriage Matters,* published by the Institute for American Values www.center.americanvalues.org/

Susanne M. Alexander is a Relationship and Marriage Coach with Marriage Transformation (www.marriagetransformation.com). She has coached cohabiting couples through the process of considering marrying.

❤ ❤ ❤

Take Time to Take Space!
Robert Buchicchio

Joe and Sue have been dating for about a year, since being introduced by a mutual friend. They were immediately very attracted to each other and initially spent hours just talking and hanging out. They emailed and texted each other and spent much of their free time on the phone. Both had been in other relationships before, but not like this one. Sue was living with her parents when she met Joe, and Joe had his own apartment. Both of them had good jobs and were able to support themselves. Their relationship grew stronger, the sex was passionate and fun, and Joe and Sue became inseparable. After three months of dating, Sue moved in with Joe, and both began to talk about the possibility of a long-term relationship and marriage.

"Another Great Summer?"

Their second summer was approaching, and Sue had such fond memories of their previous summer. They had filled it with swimming, biking, taking walks, and great picnics where they would just hang out, wrapped in each other's arms until sunset. This summer, however, Joe said he was joining a softball team. Initially, Sue didn't mind, because she thought it would be great and planned on going to the games. Instead, Joe explained that although some wives and girlfriends did go, many of the guys felt it was a "boys' night out" and after the game wanted to stop and have a couple of beers before going home. Sue said she understood. However, she didn't realize that Joe's commitment was two nights a week and sometimes a practice on the weekend. Some of those after-the-game beers lasted way too long for her.

After two weeks, Sue felt angry and jealous of the other players on the team for taking away her time with Joe. She tried to hide her feelings, but every time Joe left for a game, he noticed how unhappy Sue looked. He loved playing sports and really enjoyed hanging out with friends, but he also felt very guilty and responsible for Sue's feelings. Joe noticed that when he came home, Sue tended to be withdrawn and seemed angry with him. However, when he questioned her, she denied any ill feelings. But deep inside, Sue was disappointed and felt that her relationship with Joe was changing. Sue had lost contact with her own friends months before, and she felt awkward about calling them now. Besides, she only wanted to be with Joe.

"We're Falling Out of Love!"

Things came to a head one evening when Joe tried to warm up to Sue after he came home from a night out. He once again felt snubbed and rejected. This time, he started to get openly angry and asked, "What exactly is wrong with you?"

Sue broke down and cried and said, "I think we're falling out of love with each other." Joe said this was nonsense and that his feelings for her had not changed, but Sue felt differently. She blurted out, "I remember how much time we spent together last summer and all of last year. Now you seem so focused on your work, softball, and your friends. I hardly see you!"

Sue became very upset when Joe angrily told her to find some friends and to get a life of her own. This really convinced Sue that Joe was feeling differently. She became fearful that Joe was pulling away and that he was ready to tell her "Goodbye." Sue would secretly call her Mom, crying, upset, and asking her what to do.

Are Joe and Sue Falling Out of Love with Each Other?

Stages of Relationship

1. Romance/Fantasy Stage

The very first stage of a relationship is referred to as the Romance/Fantasy Stage and is a very important part of becoming a couple. Partners usually get along great with minimal conflict, a lot of talking, affection, and strong sexual attraction. The task for couples in this stage is to form a strong "we" bond. Each partner's "me" temporarily takes a back seat to forming the "we."

2. Disillusionment/Compromise Stage

This stage is predictable and affects all relationships. After a few months— and often within a year—the second stage of relationship, Disillusionment/ Compromise, begins to occur. It is during this stage when partners begin to reclaim themselves and focus more on "me" again. It is here that we begin to see other aspects of the person with whom we fell in love. More complaints begin to emerge. "He spends so much time with his work…He loves those video games…She spends every night talking to her friends and mother…I didn't realize he was such a slob…He doesn't want to cuddle, and he hardly listens to me anymore…She used to love to have sex, now I feel like I have to beg for it!…I never knew he had such a temper!…She's so moody!"

Whereas the Romance/Fantasy Stage was filled with what's similar about partners, this second stage begins to focus on differences. This often creates more conflict between partners and some doubting whether they have made the right choice. This conflict and tension *must* be discussed and worked out so that there is a balance between "me" and "we."

Changes occur when at least one partner begins to want more time and space for themselves. With our example couple, Joe began to get in touch with how important his friends and recreational activities were. He loved Sue, but he also valued life away from her. He began to reclaim those parts of his life that had always been there and were very important to him. When he came home from work and from being out with his friends, he couldn't wait to share with Sue. Because Sue was still heavily attached to that first relationship stage, she began to see Joe's time away as a threat, which created more tension and conflict.

Much of Sue's interests involved time with Joe. She struggled to understand why his primary focus didn't center on her and their relationship. Instead of Joe's time away being fun and exciting, producing energy that could add to his relationship with Sue, he now felt guilty and responsible for Sue's unhappiness. Joe did not see his time alone or with his friends as "not loving Sue," but when her withdrawal from him started to increase, he did begin to wonder whether Sue was the right choice for him.

The skills needed to work with this naturally occurring pattern in relationships are to be able to manage conflict, talk together, and see your partner's side.

Sue must understand that Joe had a life before her, and she must now integrate their relationship with individual pursuits. Joe's taking more space, and this has now forced Sue to examine her own values. If Joe gives up his recreational pursuits and friends, he will most likely be resentful and feel controlled by Sue. If Sue feels rejected, betrayed, and replaced by Joe's other activities, she will become very unhappy and stressed about their relationship.

Couples who fight openly and aggressively must learn to time out their fights and listen and talk with each other. **Supporting what is important to your partner actually draws your partner closer to you.** Fighting about what your partner likes and loves will feel over-controlling and push them further away. Couples that don't fight openly must learn how to express how they feel about the changes that are happening in their relationship. Writing down what you think and feel so your partner can read it may open doors to productive discussion.

When Is Too Much Space a Problem?

Problems could emerge if Joe begins to spend too much time away from Sue and neglects their relationship. Compromise often means striking a balance between the time you spend with a partner and time alone, with friends, work, or other pursuits.

Sometimes partners realize they can have a great romance, but the transition to a new stage shows how different two people really are. This is a very important assessment point about the future success of a relationship. Sometimes couples who marry while in the Romance/Fantasy Stage find that soon after the marriage, conflict increases, and they feel getting married ruined their relationship. What stressed their relationship was not being able to negotiate a compromise between the "me" and "we" time in their relationship in the second stage.

Unhappy couples and partners are often that way because the "we" has fallen to the bottom of the priority list, and "me" time and activities are viewed as controlling and punishing each other. Continuing to work out the space you need for your own pursuits and also managing to nurture and support your relationship are vital skills for a happy and successful future relationship and marriage. Neither can be neglected. The skills of conflict resolution, learning to listen, and expressing your feelings and what is important to you can be learned and form the basis of any good, lasting relationship.

Learning to develop these conflict-management and communication skills early in your relationship provides the insurance for all future changes and the maintenance of a strong marriage that encourages self-development.

Author's Note: At times after marriage, couples may find that "taking space" can become an actual separation. This can be anything from sleeping in separate rooms to actually living in separate homes. The key with any period of taking space is to make a plan for reconciliation efforts. This can include scheduling time with a counselor or coach, arranging time between parents and children, agreeing on how to handle finances, and spending time together having dates. You both need to be clear about taking time to calm down angry or upset feelings, but at the same time not allowing so much distance that reconciliation becomes very difficult.

Robert Buchicchio, L.I.C.S.W., D.C.S.W., has a B.A. in Psychology from the University of Rhode Island and an M.S.W. in Clinical Social Work from Ohio State University. He holds a diplomate from the National Association of Social

Workers. He is a licensed Clinical Social Worker in Vermont, where he has had a private mental health practice for the past thirty years, working with individuals and families and specializing in couples work. Bob is the author of *Taking Space, How To Use Separation To Explore The Future Of Your Relationship* and *For Those Wanting Changes in Their Relationship*, a home-study course for couples, which is a ten-step problem-solving guide for struggling relationships, managing separations, and recovery and rebuilding after an affair. Information is at www.takingspace.com. Bob has conducted couples workshops throughout his professional career and has taught at Vermont College and Norwich University. As a professional associate with the American Humane Association (children's division) and Action for Child Protection, Inc., he has trained social workers nationally and internationally on building therapeutic relationships in the casework process for child maltreatment situations. He served as the Chief Social Worker (Captain) in the U.S. Army Hospital in Seoul, South Korea, where he worked with individuals and families stationed overseas. Bob has been married to Harriet for 40 years. They have two grown children.

Chapter Ten
Growing in Love

~ ~

It is likely if you are talking about marriage that you already believe you love each other. Feelings of love often go through changes and cycles within marriage, however, so part of the skill building for you in this chapter is learning how to sustain loving feelings and actions. You will expand your understanding and practice of love and learn how to make it last.

There are often discussions in this field about whether love is a feeling, a character quality, a choice, a noun, or a verb. Perhaps it is sufficient to say that it's an essential part of a happy marriage!

♥ ♥ ♥

Setting a Foundation of Loving for Your Future Marriage
Gary Chapman, Ph.D.

Positive, affirming relationships bring great pleasure, but poor relationships bring deep pain. Life's greatest happiness is found in good relationships, and life's deepest pain is found in bad relationships. All your relationships spring from the relationship with your parents. The nature of that relationship will have a positive—or negative—influence on all other relationships.

Many single adults have felt unloved by one or both parents, and they have been extremely unsuccessful in building positive relationships with other adults. Most have never stopped to ask, "What do I need to learn about love in order to build successful, positive relationships?" Understanding the five love languages will answer that question. Couples can often become good marital partners if they discover each other's primary love language and learn to speak it.

If we learn to express love in the other person's love language, they will feel loved. And if that person reciprocates by speaking our love language, they will meet our emotional need for love. There are five primary love languages. We can receive love through all five, but if we don't receive our primary love language, we will not feel loved even though the person is speaking the other four. However, if they speak our primary love language sufficiently, then the other four provide icing on the cake.

Five Love Languages

1. **Words of Affirmation:** verbal compliments; words of appreciation, praise, and encouragement; kind words; expressions of appreciation for the other's positive actions and qualities

2. **Gifts:** tangible objects freely offered; gifts of any size, shape, color, or price; gifts that indicate thoughtfulness; visual symbols of love with no strings attached and no attempt to cover up a failure; unexpected gifts, not just on special occasions

3. **Acts of Service:** things done willingly for the other; offers of helpfulness; timely and positive response to requests (not demands) of the other; acts of kindness; favors done with a loving attitude (not fear, guilt, or resentment); acts that reflect equality and partnership

4. **Quality Time:** being available; doing something enjoyable and interactive together; giving uninterrupted, undivided, and focused attention; participating in quality conversation in which both talk and listen; creating memorable moments; intimate revealing of self

5. **Physical Touch:** loving (never abusive) physical contact at appropriate times and places; tender hugs, touches, or pats on the arm, shoulder, or back; foot or back rubs or massages; kissing; holding hands; holding while comforting; intimate touch and sex only within the covenant of marriage with your marriage partner

How to Identify Your Love Languages

Here are some ways you can determine what your primary love language is:

- Observe your own behavior so that you notice how you typically express love and appreciation to others; 75 percent of people express what they most want to receive

- Observe what you most often request of others; your requests reveal your heart and what would make you feel loved

- Make notes of your own complaints about what you do not receive
- Ask yourself what your partner (or spouse) says and does that cause you to have a positive response

If you want to determine the love language of someone else, the method is similar:

- Observe their expressions, complaints, and requests
- Ask questions
- Experiment with offering various expressions of love and observe and listen to the responses

Note: Two categories of people typically struggle to discover their primary love language. The first consists of singles who have always felt loved and who received all five love languages from their parents; the other is composed of singles who have never felt loved.

In seeking a mate, love is the foundational motivation, which not only leads to marriage but to a successful marriage. If this is true, then learning to express love in a language your dating partner will feel becomes extremely important. When the dating partner feels loved, they are much more likely to be open to an authentic relationship in which they can each help the other.

Gary Chapman, Ph.D., is the author of the best-selling *Five Love Languages* Series, including *The Five Love Languages for Singles,* as well as many other relationship books. He is the director of Marriage and Family Life Consultants, Inc. in North Carolina. Dr. Chapman is a Senior Associate Pastor at Calvary Baptist Church in Winston-Salem, North Carolina, where he has served for thirty-six years. He and his wife Karolyn have been married for forty-five years and have two adult children and two grandchildren. His websites are www.5lovelanguages.com, where couples can also complete their love language profiles, and www.garychapman.org.

❤ ❤ ❤

Beneath the Masquerades of Love
John Buri, Ph.D.

Love requires three things: passion, intimacy, and commitment. Anything less, and we end up with an imposter masquerading as love. And an imposter will never bring us life in the way and with the vitality that love is meant to. In fact, imposters deceive, and deception will never result in genuine love.

First, there is the imposter of passion *alone*. This one is easy to achieve. In fact, achievement is an odd term to use in this context, since "to achieve" implies some degree of effort. But when most of us have fallen in love, the passion has been so spontaneous and so effortless that it is hardly an achievement. But what if we are referring to passion in a long-term love relationship? Ah, now that's an achievement, and well worth it—ongoing passion in a marriage is one of the strongest predictors of marital satisfaction.

Then there is the imposter of passion *and* intimacy (but no commitment). Some couples have managed to develop intimacy—an ongoing closeness, connection, warmth, and friendship—to go along with their passion. In brief, they have learned to communicate with each other and to enjoy one another's company, as well as to fall in love with each other.

And some would suggest that in this fast-paced world of short-term relationships, this is about as good as it gets. We have been led to believe that if you experience intimacy to go along with the passion, you are one lucky lover. But this, too, masquerades as love. It is an imposter.

What happens if (when) the mask is torn off, the relationship ends, and each goes their separate ways to search anew for lasting love? The wounds of this imposter cut deep. In fact, this may be my greatest concern for the way in which we do dating today. Men and women are encouraged to give of themselves, but there is no promise of a future together. It is in this type of situation—one in which the third component of love is lacking—that there is the greatest potential for scar tissue on the heart.

The antidote—the third component of love—is commitment.

I live in Minnesota, but I did not grow up there. When I first arrived in the state several years ago, I befriended some men who had grown up in Minnesota. They thought it would be a good idea to help me get acclimated to my new resident state by going up north in the woods to hunt.

Before heading off into the woods, one of the guys asked me if I had a compass. I did not; the closest I had ever come to a large forest growing up in Iowa were expansive cornfields. The thing about cornfields is that if you do get lost, you just start walking, and eventually you will find your way out. As this man informed me, the woods in northern Minnesota don't work that way. You could start walking and never find your way out. So, they gave me a compass.

After hours in the woods and near the end of the day, I had become separated from everyone else. No problem. I knew where the car was, and I started walking in that direction. After half an hour of walking in that direction and still nothing looked familiar, I decided to take out the compass. When I checked, the road (to my surprise) was in the exact opposite direction of where I had been walking!

Commitment is like that compass.

William Doherty, a colleague at the University of Minnesota, has suggested that most long-term relationships (and marriages) go through times something like Minnesota's winter weather. It can be cold, overcast, a little gloomy, and there are no signs of anything green, since everything is covered with snow. There are moments when many couples look at their long-term relationship (or their marriage) and it looks a lot like this season.

Commitment is what sees us through these (inevitable?) winter seasons of love. Commitment is what keeps us pointed in the right direction. Commitment is what enables us to continue to be patient with the gloomy times and continue pursuing passion and intimacy with the one we love.

Don't settle for anything short of all three components of love. Anything less is an imposter, and an imposter will never satisfy that desire for love that has brought the two of you together.

John Buri, Ph.D., is a professor of Psychology at the University of St. Thomas in St. Paul, Minnesota. He and the love of his life, Kathy, also his high school sweetheart, have been married for thirty-eight years and have six children and six grandchildren. Dr. Buri has taught a university course on the Psychology of Marriage and the Family for the past twenty-five years. He is the author of the marriage book *How To Love Your Wife*, as well as over fifty research articles and book chapters. He is a frequent speaker on topics of dating, marriage preparation, marriage enrichment, parenting, and family life. Dr. Buri can be reached at jrburi@stthomas.edu.

❤ ❤ ❤

Assessing Your Relationship Capacity
Molly Barrow, Ph.D.

Would you find it helpful to know how the two of you match up in your abilities and capacities to give and receive love? Everyone has their own unique Relationship Capacity Line, and a good fit between your lines—a Matchline—is vital. The single most important factor in finding and maintaining a quality love relationship is then balancing any differences between your loving capacities.

Determining Relationship Capacity

Someone develops a shorter Relationship Capacity Line if they do not feel loved while growing up, or experience trauma or neglect and fail to learn to give love easily to others. These shorter Lines have less capacity to show love toward a partner, frequently behave in a selfish protective way, and often feel inadequate in relationships. In contrast, a longer Line has greater capacity to give emotionally to a partner, because they clearly felt parental love growing up in a safe environment and learned to share love with others.

You may think you are a Longline in general, compared to all people, however, if your partner's Relationship Capacity Line is longer than yours, then you become the Shortline in that relationship. The power of Matchlines is to illustrate a "relative" relationship between two people—never an absolute judgment about anyone's value as a person. You will benefit from thoroughly assessing your relationships, past and present, to determine your Line Gaps, or differences.

Once you recognize your Relationship Capacity Lines, you can then determine your compatibility. Ideally, you will have Lines close to the same length. If not, challenges result. The Longline often pours out love to someone unable to adequately receive it. The Shortline feels overwhelmed. One partner seems to be doing all the right, loving things, but may unconsciously ruin the relationship. The Shortline in defense often ends up in the loving arms of a rival, who is usually a fellow-Shortline. Why does this happen? If we deliberately strive to make our interactions happy and loving, then why do they backfire? Why does one person leave a partner who brings boundless love, support, and energy to a relationship?

One's Line length does not necessarily reflect a more valuable or worthy partner than another. The difference or Line Gap between the two Lines of partners is important. You are not in competition with each other, but being successful in marriage will require you knowing how you can make each other more comfortable in the relationship. The difference between your Lines— the Line Gap—must be very slight to enjoy easy happiness in a love relationship. When Lines are mismatched, people must work harder to keep a relationship balanced.

If you are the Longline in the relationship, then the responsibility for establishing and maintaining that balance is mostly up to you. Perfect Matchlines are rare, and most relationships need balancing with new ways of interacting so you can have a satisfying and fulfilling love relationship. You can learn how to love each other as partners, so you are content and feel free to love each other without rash reactions. Matchlines can help to set rocky relationships on a more tranquil course and demonstrate how the route to a more intimate connection with the one you love follows the course of two Lines, not just one.

I Really Love You

When Longlines use the word "love," their definition of that word includes their entire experience of love since their earliest childhood. Unfortunately, Shortlines use the exact same word, "love," but their experience of love may bear no resemblance whatsoever to that of the Longline. This is where understanding the dynamics of a large Gap between the Lines in a relationship begins. Shortlines may have experienced less nurturing and affection in life, and/or possess a history of pain and neglect mixed into their very earliest memories.

When a person loves you, they are giving you the best love they know how to give and are currently capable of giving. It is wise to accept this whether you find those efforts satisfactory or unsatisfactory, fulfilling or disappointing. This is the fundamental secret in understanding the concept of finding balance between two distinctly different Lines in a relationship.

We cannot see beyond our past, our experience, our personal limits, or beyond the end of our Line. We each have a Line Ceiling. Quite often, Shortlines know very little about the type of love that is sky high and limitless, unconditional, and genuinely passionate. This type of love Longlines are more capable of giving and receiving and tend to expect in return. For the Shortline, possible past trauma or neglect can form an internal "ceiling," which inhibits them and obscures emotional heights. Shortlines have great difficulty seeing above their personal ceiling to meet the needs of the Longlines—and that is the crux of many problems in such a relationship.

Shortlines are giving as much love as they have to give, all they perceive love to be. They do not think about the qualities of love beyond the confines of their own ceiling. This limited vision inhibits their ability to love beyond the length or Capacity of their Line. Each of us is limited by our own Line Ceiling.

Love You My Way

The size of the Line Gap, not the existence of one, makes or breaks relationships. The important point to focus on is determining the extent of the Line Gap between the two of you. If the Line Gap is small, love will be easier for you both. If the Line Gap is great, finding a harmonious love will be harder. Unfortunately, Line Gaps are common, but the good news is that the better you understand them, and their effects on you as a couple, the easier the work to balance your relationship.

If you are the Longline in a relationship, then think of your Shortline partner as someone who is emotionally more numb or distant in most circumstances than you are, because they have been hurt more. Imagine a cut that even when healed may have tough scar tissue protectively remaining and lessening sensitivity. Shortlines' emotional defenses diminish their ability and openness to meeting the needs of others. They have more difficulty establishing a close, trusting, and loving relationship than a longer Line does. Shortlines have less control over the factors that influence them, and react differently than Longlines within their respective Line ceilings. Consequently, a Shortline's approach to giving and receiving emotional intimacy will differ from the approach of the longer Line in a relationship.

Longlines are more prone to share intimate feelings openly and actively seek the understanding and support of their partners. Conversely, because Shortlines' needs for close companionship and emotional intimacy are either less accessible or simply less than Longlines' needs, Shortlines can completely satisfy their own needs with less investment of time or energy.

Think of this concept in terms of a person's appetite for food and nourishment, predicated on the physical capacity of their stomach—that is, how much they can actually hold. How much do they need to eat in a given meal to feel full? When a person with a smaller appetite eats a little, they soon feel full and satisfied and do not want any more to eat. However, their partner, who may have a much larger appetite, may get their feelings hurt when halfway through a meal they see their smaller-appetite partner push away from the table and stop eating. The Longline is left wondering if it is because their cooking or company is bad—when neither was the case at all.

At first, Shortlines may not feel the existence of the Line Gap, perhaps obliviously and frustratingly so for the Longlines, but Longlines surely will feel it. Feeling content themselves, Shortlines are typically completely unaware of Line Gaps and the resulting unmet needs of their Longline partners. The inevitable result in this situation is that Shortlines unintentionally starve Longlines of intimacy, and Longlines invariably overstuff and suffocate Shortlines. Longlines eventually feel desperate, and Shortlines just want to get away.

Since Shortlines cannot see beyond the top of their own Line Ceiling, they often fail to realize that an intimacy potential may exist beyond what merely fulfills them. They cannot imagine that their partner needs more, or that "more" exists other than what they have experienced in their lifetime. Nevertheless, Shortlines' efforts are one hundred percent of their ability. The Longline must therefore always remember that the Shortline partner is doing all they can to love the Longline—even if it does not feel like enough. Lonely Longlines often need to find other outlets for their loving feelings, such as a pet, community service, and friendships.

The closer you are to being a Matchline, with similar capacities to share love with one another, the greater your marital harmony is likely to be. Matchline balancing techniques provide hope and help for relationships suffering from challenging Line Gaps. With care, knowledge, and mutual respect, your relationship can become a successful loving marriage.

Molly Barrow holds a Ph.D. in Clinical Psychology and is the author of *Matchlines for Singles, Matchlines for Couples, How to Survive Step Parenting,* and the *Malia and Teacup* self-esteem building series for young readers. An authority on relationship and psychological topics, Dr. Barrow is a member of the American Psychological Association, Screen Actors Guild, and Authors Guild, and is a licensed mental health counselor. Dr. Barrow has appeared as an expert in the film *My Suicide,* the documentaries *Ready to Explode* and *KTLA Impact,* NBC news, PBS *In Focus,* and on WBZT talk radio. She has been quoted in *O Magazine, Psychology Today, Newsday, New York Times, CNN, The Nest,* MSN.com, Yahoo.com, Match.com, *Women's Health,* and *Women's World.* Dr. Barrow has a radio show on www.progressiveradionetwork.com and is a columnist for www.Menstuff.org. Dr. Barrow has a counseling practice in Naples, Florida, and is happily married with a wonderful family including three children, one daughter-in-law, and two precious grandsons. Her website is www.drmollybarrow.com; Blog is: http://drmollybarrow.blogspot.com/; Twitter is: www.twitter.com/drmollybarrow; Live & Archived Radio Shows are: www.progressiveradionetwork.com/the-dr-molly-barrow-show/

❤ ❤ ❤

The Journey of Love and Marriage: Know the Stages and Set Your Priorities
Rita DeMaria, Ph.D.

Marriage is a journey often beginning with two people who are very much in love and who are looking forward to a shared lifetime of love and happiness. However, being in love isn't all that's needed for preparing for a journey that everyone will tell you has twists, turns, and unexpected events. These events are sometimes pleasurable, but unfortunately, many times they are also difficult, stressful, and challenging.

As a journey through life, marriage has some predictable stages for most couples. Each stage includes specific skills and tasks for you to focus on learning and accomplishing as a couple. It will help you to talk about these stages and how you will traverse them as you discuss what it will look like to be married.

The seven stages I use with couples are:

1. Passion
2. Realization
3. Rebellion
4. Cooperation
5. Reunion
6. Completion
7. Explosion

These stages tend to be linear, progressing forward throughout your time together. The one exception is the Explosion Stage, which can happen at any time.

One of the most important steps couples can take as they begin their journey together is to maintain focus on the romance and attraction that exists between them. Through every stage, couples must nurture the romance between them. In the early stages of love, couples create memories they can build on throughout their life together. Positive mutual memories are a strength to draw on throughout your marriage. When you are going through a difficult time and looking for reconnection, it may help you to remember and recreate activities that you enjoy now during your courtship or engagement. Enjoy the "now" of your new love and nurture it with knowledge and skills through the stages that will unfold before you.

Overview of the Stages of Marriage

As you go through marriage, it will be useful for you to assess the stage you are in and understand the tasks and skills that are a priority for you at that time.

STAGE 1—Passion

Your relationship is all about the two of you and the excitement, sex, and intimacy you are experiencing.

Priorities: Strengthen your sense of "us." Make time for each other. Leave work at work.

STAGE 2—Realization

You are beginning to get to know each other's real strengths and weaknesses in ways you never knew before.

Priorities: Develop the important communication habits of listening and confiding that are essential to expanding understanding and trust. Consider enrolling in a communication class for couples.

STAGE 3—Rebellion

You seek to assert your self-interests and end up having volatile (or hidden) power struggles.

Priorities: Learn how to negotiate and keep agreements, because keeping promises builds trust. Identify areas of difference and start talking about them one at a time, without changing the subject.

STAGE 4—Cooperation

Both of you seem more preoccupied with the kids, money, home, and work than with each other. You start to feel like business partners more than lovers.

Priorities: Make your marriage a priority, de-stress, and keep the passion alive. Set up a regular date night and have fun on it—not serious discussions!

STAGE 5—Reunion

You have created a life together that is working most of the time. You are beginning to have more time for yourselves and for each other to renew your friendship and passion.

Priorities: Refocus on your marriage. Get off autopilot and work through unresolved issues that will interfere with the continued growth of your marriage AND your satisfaction.

STAGE 6—Completion

Stability and security reign. You enjoy each other and the life you have created for yourselves as individuals and as a couple. Sharing a life together that has been built on deep love and deep empathy brings deep satisfaction and comfort.

Priorities: Look to create a new sense of meaning and purpose for yourselves and your marriage. Assess how you will handle changes in your health and physical abilities. Carefully ensure that your financial life and recordkeeping are in good order. Consider together how you wish to prepare for a spiritual life after you pass on.

STAGE 7—Explosion

Remember, the Explosion Stage can happen ANYTIME throughout your marriage in which you are experiencing major career, health, parenting, and family crises. The Explosion Stage can also take place during the courtship and engagement with things like unexpected illnesses, unexpected deaths, job changes, and of course, wedding planning disasters like a hotel that closes two weeks before the wedding. However, the couples who navigate and negotiate the recurring Explosion Stages with love, compassion, and support in their lives often are the strongest couples of all!

Priorities: Pay close attention to your physical, mental, emotional, and spiritual wellbeing, and make use of supports for all these aspects in yourselves and in your relationship or marriage.

Some Tips and Recommendations

For first-time engaged couples: Remember, these stages are normal! Going through changes helps you get to know each other better and form closer bonds, friendship, and commitment. Most couples will go through the first three stages within the first three to five years of marriage, so get ready to learn more about each other.

For remarrying couples: Having been married before, you already know something about the sometimes tumultuous early days of marriage. However, as a remarrying couple you often bring all the pressures, demands, and expectations that couples who have been together for at least five to seven years have had a bit of time to work out. For many remarrying couples, the challenges of bringing two different and often complicated lives together often throws you directly into the Cooperation Stage, which is all about teamwork. Frequently, though, remarrying couples are very much in love and really want to enjoy the honeymoon.

Celebrating Our Love: Our Marriage Priorities

Knowing what's ahead can help you prepare for your new marriage. Here are some specific steps you can take now to strengthen the foundation you are building on your romantic love for each other. Review them together and then create your goals and priorities for your new marriage.

Talk with each other about your thoughts, needs, and feelings on the subjects below. Some people like to create a portfolio, letterbox, or file to keep track of agreements they make, goals they set, or hopes they have for their relationship and for themselves. Pictures, notes, cards, letters, and copies of emails can be included. Review your Celebrating Love and Marriage Priorities on some periodic basis when you are both in an open and calm state.

Topics for Consideration

1. How will we maintain our sense of "We"? What is the story of our unique romance? What are our strengths as a couple?

2. How will we keep our sexual relationship passionate, interesting, and enjoyable? What type of commitment will we make to date nights, romance, and making time for our sexual relationship? What are our challenges? How might we continue strengthening this special part of our relationship?

3. How will we continue to strengthen our emotional connection and intimacy? What is our plan for sharing our feelings or beginning to learn how to share our fears, vulnerabilities, and special wishes?

4. What are our expectations for our first year of marriage? What are any potential trouble spots? (Consider household responsibilities and standards; parenting and co-parenting issues, needs, and expectations; and financial goals and plans that begin with an open accounting of each person's financial status.)

5. How will we become better friends? What mutually interesting activities

do we want to explore, try out, or share together that create a different bond from the romantic and sexual relationship? What do we see as a reasonable amount of time to spend separately with our same-sex friends? Are we interested in developing relationships with other couples? How will we do this? What shows us that our friends are supportive of our marriage?

6. What important aspects of our past relationship experiences that could affect our marriage do we still need to share? Are there unresolved questions either of us has? Are there inappropriate secrets? What boundaries do we need in place with people from previous relationships so that our marriage is protected from harm or infidelity?

Helpful Practices

1. Establish two or three healthy personal goals for yourselves as individuals that will assist you in being prepared for marriage and make sure each of you can enthusiastically support each other's goals.

2. Establish two or three relationship-strengthening goals and ways to achieve them before marriage.

3. Establish a "Kiss and Make Up" policy to use both before and after marriage. Forgiveness is an important way to keep resentments from mounting.

4. Identify any worrisome trouble spots in your relationship, find a support group, couples communication program, a couples counselor, or other resources, such as those offered through faith-based organizations and others in the community or www.smartmarriages.com. Learning and growing together is an important way for couples to keep their relationship healthy.

Rita DeMaria, Ph.D., has been a Couples and Family Therapist for over thirty-five years. She is a senior staff member and Director of Relationship Education at Council for Relationships in Philadelphia. She is the co-author, along with Sari Harrar, of *The 7 Stages of Marriage* (Readers Digest Books, 2007). She has also produced resources for couples programs that can be found on her website www.MarriageDoctor.com. Dr. DeMaria specializes in helping couples rekindle love and commitment in marriage. She has been interviewed by *The Today Show* and many other TV, radio, and media programs. She also publishes professionally and teaches in the Post-Graduate Training Program in Couples and Family Therapy at Council for Relationships. For more information about that program, visit www.CouncilforRelationships.org. Dr. DeMaria has been married for thirty-two years and has two children.

♥ ♥ ♥

Real Love Defined
Sheryl Paul

Real love is a conscious choice that often employs the rational part of our brains. Some couples enjoy a free ride in the early stages of their relationship when they experience the intense feelings characterized by romantic love—but not everyone. And these feelings certainly aren't necessary for real love to emerge as the relationship grows, as evidenced by the success rate of arranged marriages in other parts of the world. It's when the infatuation feelings diminish that the couple has to learn that "love is a choice, not a feeling," as M. Scott Peck says in *The Road Less Traveled*.

Real love accepts that your partner is a fallible, imperfect human, just as you are. Unlike romantic love, which ascends the object of desire to the realm of a god, part of the jolt down to Earth that many experience during their engagements is the realization that their partner is not perfect. Maybe they aren't as smart or witty or fun or good-looking as they thought the person they would marry would be. The romantic bubble of marrying a Prince or Princess is burst. You might be focusing on one missing area—sometimes to the point of obsession—and it's often an attribute that never bothered you before you were engaged. As time passes, the real fears are addressed, love is redefined, the obsession mellows, and you learn to accept and fully love each other as you are.

Real love ebbs and flows in terms of interest, ease, and feelings. In other words, in any healthy relationship, there will be times when things work effortlessly, where the spark is alive and the couple is interested in one another and life. And there will be times when your relationship seems quite ordinary and unexciting. Part of accepting real love is understanding that this experience is normal and not a symptom that something is wrong with the relationship or that you don't love each other enough.

Real love is based on shared values and a solid friendship. You genuinely like each other most of the time, even though you might not like everything about each other.

Real love is action. Real love asks that you give, even when you don't feel like giving (in a healthy way, not a codependent way). Real love is more concerned with how you can give to your partner than what you can get from them. And the more actions you take to express your real love, the stronger and happier your relationship will be.

Real love is a spiritual practice of self-growth. Your focus is not on how you can change your partner to alleviate your anger, pain, or annoyance, but how you can assume full responsibility for those feelings and find healthy and constructive ways to attend to them. When you change in positive ways, the relationship will positively change as well.

Real love is a lifelong practice. You're not expected to know how to give and receive real love at the onset of marriage, but you are expected to work at it. Over the course of your life together, it is this effort that allows your capacity to love to grow.

The next time you watch a romantic comedy and find yourself doubting if you love your wonderful, supportive, honest, loving partner enough, read over this description of real love and see if your anxiety lessens as you redefine what love really is.

Sheryl Paul, M.A., pioneered the field of bridal counseling in 1998. She has since counseled thousands of people worldwide through her private practice, her best-selling books, *The Conscious Bride* and *The Conscious Bride's Wedding Planner*, and her website, www.consciousweddings.com. She's regarded as the international expert on the wedding transition and has appeared several times on *The Oprah Winfrey Show*, as well as on *Good Morning America* and other top television and radio shows and in newspapers around the globe. She lives in Boulder, Colorado, with her husband and two young sons. Phone sessions are available worldwide by calling 303-474-4786. Her blog is http://myconscioustransitions.com.

❤ ❤ ❤

Create Lasting Love by Experiencing Your Experience
David Steele

When singles become couples, each partner has different hopes and dreams, wants and needs, attitudes and experiences. These differences too often result in relationship failure and disappointment when one or both partners attempts to mold the relationship and their partner to fit what they want, rather than accepting and embracing what is. While we must have a vision and requirements and choose a partner and relationship aligned with what we want, we can't be so rigid that we reject reality.

How do we let go of needing perfection without settling for less than what we really want? One strategy I recommend is to "experience your experience."

What Does It Mean to Experience Your Experience?

Your "experience" is what happens inside of you, and it happens automatically. It is the thoughts that pop into your head; the sensations you have in your body; what you see, hear, feel, touch, and taste. It is what you are feeling emotionally.

Your experience just happens. You go to a movie, and you love the movie, and you feel tingly and warm; you have a positive experience of the movie. You go to a movie and it scares you, turns you off, you hate it and it repulses you; you have a negative experience of the movie.

Your experience is involuntary. It just happens, and it always happens in the now, so you must be present in the now to experience your experience. You can't be mentally and emotionally in the past, thinking about what was, and you can't be in the future, thinking about what will be. Relationships only happen in the present. Connection can only happen in the present. To be in touch with what is real and to have a fulfilling relationship, you must be able to experience your experience. This means to be present, be in the now, experiencing what is going on for you right now, and what's real for you right now, instead of your fantasies about what will be and your associations about what happened in the past.

Full awareness of your experience is important because, too often, we bring our past baggage into a relationship. We don't see the person and the relationship for what they are, or we are absorbed in fantasy about the future—what it might be and could be and will be.

Experience Comes First, Then Meaning and Action

Your experience is what's real for you, and you get to decide what it means. If you went to a movie and it repulsed you, you might make up a story, an interpretation of your experience, that the movie was horrible and the worst movie ever made. That's because of your experience. Your experience results in your stories or your interpretations and meanings. If you didn't like the movie, you will create a story about it. Then you might tell everybody you know, "That was the worst movie. Don't see it." So your stories, which come from your experience, result in what you say and do.

Three Stages of Relationship

Stage One: Romantic Love

A relationship is a process, not an event, and there are stages you will both go through. When you fall in love, you enter a Romantic Love Stage that feels wonderful. Chemistry is high, your hormones are pumping, the world is more beautiful than it has ever looked before, and you feel alive and glowing.

In this stage, you notice your similarities with your partner, the ways in which you're alike, and you feel as if you've known this person your whole life. You are positive that all of your needs are going to be met, and everything you've ever dreamed for your life is going to come true because you've met this person.

This is an important stage, because it is bonding you with your partner. This bonding will be needed to get you through the stage that comes next, because Romantic Love—as much as many of us would like to hold onto it because it feels so good—inevitably comes to an end. The next stage, then, is the Power Struggle.

The Romantic Love Stage can last up to two years and typically wears off soon after a commitment of some type is made. When you're in the Romantic Love Stage, you want to please your partner, and even if you were your own person before you met them, you often give up parts of yourself to please them. But you don't do this for long. Eventually, your real self wants to assert itself, and when that happens, you start to notice each other's differences.

Stage Two: Power Struggle

During the Power Struggle Stage, you become acutely aware of your differences and the things you don't like about your partner and the relationship. What's really happening is that the parts of yourself that you cut off as you grew up are asserting themselves in a search for wholeness. For example, if you weren't able to express anger effectively as a child, you'll struggle with expressing it as an adult. You need to do so in your intimate relationship to heal your past and become a whole, mature, developed person. Your anger or frustration is not really about your partner. The issues and dynamics that come up in this stage are your blueprint for growth. They demand change of you—something that may be difficult for you to carry out—and you may resist doing it. But if you're willing to stretch, you will reclaim your wholeness, and your relationship will deepen and progress to the next stage.

It can be very difficult to understand what's happening in the Power Struggle Stage, and it's easy to blame your partner or the relationship for the stress and conflict that you experience. Many relationships don't survive this stage. It helps to get outside support (relationship coaching, counseling, therapy) to understand and work through what's really happening. It's much easier for relationship coaches to help while the relationship is still good, before there has been a lot of damage from the conflict occurring during the Power Struggle Stage.

Stage Three: Conscious Relationship

Once you've worked through the Power Struggle Stage, you may still experience frustration and conflict. However, you've matured and learned the skills needed to take ownership of your experience and communicate effectively with your partner. When the power struggle diminishes, you can enjoy each other's company, have more fun together, and experience more synchronicity and positive energy. Your relationship seems effortless, and you're more deeply connected with each other. You know each other's warts, and you love each other unconditionally. This is the type of relationship we yearn for, and it comes with effort and as a reward for learning how to get through the Power Struggle Stage successfully.

Evolve vs. Push vs. Twist

When you become a couple, it's important to allow a relationship to evolve and be what it is instead of pushing it to happen faster or twisting the relationship (or partner) to be what you want it to be. Take the time to get to know who your partner really is instead of focusing on your fantasies, hopes, and dreams. Experience your experience, embrace "what is," and stay in the now so you are grounded in reality about your partner and relationship.

Your Pygmalion Project

Legend has it that a long time ago, there was a brash, young sculptor named Pygmalion. He found the women of Cyprus so flawed that he resolved to carve a statue of his ideal woman, embodying every feminine grace and virtue. For months, he labored with all his prodigious skill, rounding here and smoothing there until he had fashioned the most exquisite figure ever conceived by art. So exquisite indeed was his creation that Pygmalion fell passionately in love with the statue and could be seen in the studio kissing its marble lips, fingering its marble hands, dressing and grooming the figure as if caring for a doll. But soon—and in spite of the work's incomparable loveliness—Pygmalion was desperately unhappy, for the lifeless statue could not respond to his desires. The cold stone could not return the warmth of his love. He had set out to create his perfect woman, but the result was his own frustration and despair.

A "Pygmalion Project" occurs when your agenda in a relationship is to mold a partner in your own fantasy image. This doesn't work very well, and as the Greek legend or myth of the sculptor indicates, even if you think you are succeeding, you're going to be unhappy, because it's not real or lasting. Your partner isn't real if they allow you to completely re-mold them. It's not a real relationship, and you'll be frustrated because even if you think you want them to be a certain way and to be more like your dream, it's not what you really need.

We all have this tendency inside us. It's tempting to want to mold your partner and want them to be different. To prevent this from happening, you must stay conscious in your relationship and experience your experience. This means to experience your partner for who they really are and attempt to have a real relationship with them. The period before you've made a lifetime commitment to marriage is your chance to move on if the relationship doesn't work for you based on what it really is.

Triad for Creating Lasting Love

To effectively experience your experience, it is helpful to stay conscious of three aspects of your experience:

1. **Facts:** What happens to you, usually a measureable event ("The sky is blue.")

2. **Judgments:** Your "stories" about the facts, the meaning you make of the event ("The blue sky is pretty.")

3. **Feelings:** Your emotions and sensations (warm, cold, happy, sad,…)

You make judgments about things, often very strongly, and try to make them be factual and true for everyone. While they might be your personal truth at the time, they are not facts, no matter how strongly you believe them to be true. Consider these examples:

• "You make me so angry."

• "You're a jerk."

- "I love you."
- "War is hell."
- "Ice cream is good."

These examples all start with an event or stimulus. Something happens that gives us a certain experience. Then, we react to our experience by making meaning of it and forming judgments. Then, our judgments stimulate our emotions—such as, anger, sadness, gladness, fear, shame—and this all happens in the blink of an eye.

We can then react consciously or unconsciously. If we react unconsciously, we will act out our feelings and judgments, whatever they are. If we respond consciously, we will separate the facts from our feelings and judgments and then decide what meanings to make and actions to take. A conscious response begins by reviewing the facts in your head and making sure you're not mixing in judgments.

Step One: Review the Facts

"Okay, the sky is blue, we're walking in the park together, and the temperature is about seventy-six degrees. I just said, 'It's a beautiful day,' and my friend said, 'No, it stinks.'"

Step Two: Review Your Judgments

"Hmm, I believe it's a gorgeous day, walking here is wonderful, and I judge that my friend isn't getting it at all."

Step Three: Identify Your Feelings

"I'm glad it's such a beautiful day, sad that my friend is troubled and not enjoying it, and frustrated and angry at their negativity."

Step Four: Make a Conscious Choice

Once you've separated the facts from your judgments and feelings, you are in a much better position to decide what to think, feel, and how to react. Notice in the above example that the judgments and feelings are mixed, which is common. If you are conscious, you can choose amongst the mix of judgments and feelings that you will embrace and act upon, and those you will discard or leave alone.

In the above example, you might decide to focus upon your sadness that your friend is having a bad day. This focus allows you to choose a compassionate response and to discard your judgment that they aren't "getting it."

Top Ten Attitudes Necessary for Lasting Love

An "attitude" is a system of beliefs, an interpretation or way of looking at the world. Your attitude is present before you speak and act, and it can interfere or facilitate being in the present and experiencing your experience. You have control of and can choose your attitudes. Here are vital attitudes for a conscious relationship that leads to a conscious marriage:

1. I will be happy by having goals and letting go of attachment to outcomes.
2. I strive to live and "be" in the present.
3. I love, accept, and trust myself; I love, accept, and trust my chosen partner.
4. I focus on connecting, not results; a partner is someone to love, not an object or goal.
5. I strive to be authentic; being fully honest with others and myself, aligning my words, values, and actions.
6. I strive to live my life with intentionality; making choices while staying conscious of my goals and consequences.
7. I strive to take the necessary risks, overcome my fears, and stretch my comfort level to reach my goals.
8. I assume abundance; all the opportunities and resources I need and we need together will appear.
9. I take responsibility for my words, actions, and outcomes and take initiative in my life and relationships.
10. What others judge about me is about them; I strive to let go of what others think and not take it personally.

Create Lasting Love by Experiencing Your Experience

Stay grounded in the reality of what is and make your decisions based on reality instead of trying to make the relationship match with a fantasy. It is important to have a vision and to be aware of your requirements, needs, and wants, as well as to have them met. But, to create lasting love, you must choose a partner who you can love unconditionally for who they are and work with that partner in a reality-based way. You can do this by experiencing your experience with them each and every day.

David Steele, M.A., L.M.F.T., is Founder of Relationship Coaching Institute, the first and largest international relationship coach training organization. He is author of the ground-breaking book for singles *Conscious Dating: Finding the Love of Your Life in Today's World*, now in its second edition. His website is www.RelationshipCoachingInstitute.com.

Chapter Eleven
Communicating Effectively

~ ~

Skillful communication is one of the vital support pillars for a successful marriage. During dating and courtship, you have likely gained an understanding of each other's communication styles and preferences. You have hopefully met each other's parents and family members and gained perspectives on how family communication patterns might repeat in your marriage. You may also be seeing where some skill building would benefit you. This chapter will help you with that goal.

Your actions toward each other may very well weigh more than your communications in their effect on you both over time. However, the words you use and how you use them will also have a major impact on the harmony of your relationship and your ability to make effective decisions as partners.

❤ ❤ ❤

The Nice-to-Nasty Ratio
John Buri, Ph.D.

When *dating*, it is often difficult to tell just where a particular partner is apt to fall long-term on the nice-to-nasty ratio. Obviously, most people are going to be showing their best behavior, which can unfortunately sometimes be downright deceptive behavior. The goal is to get someone to go out with them again, so they work hard to hide faults. So, how can you tell whether this person is someone who is going to eventually weigh in on the nasty side of the nice-to-nasty ratio? Try tuning up your observation skills and participate in many different experiences.

I met a man to arrange a business deal, and he was pleasant, amiable, and engaging. At the start of our meeting, he had told me he might receive a call from his partner, and he did. He turned his chair away, and the conversation was nasty as he ripped into her. As he turned in his chair back facing me, it was as if he had flipped a switch, and there in front of me once again was that amiable and engaging individual.

I was doing some casual observation one night while out with my sons. As some women were approached, they could be cold, distant, aloof, and hard (downright nasty!) toward one guy. Three seconds later, these same women were warm, affectionate, gentle, and kind toward another guy. It was like watching a faucet turning from cold to hot water (and back again), right on cue.

You need to use your powers of observation to really see the dynamic between the two of you. On many occasions, I have encouraged men to be more pleasant, engaging, and loving with a partner or at home with his wife. More than once, I have received a response along these lines: "All day long, I have to be courteous and amiable with people I hardly know at work, and now you're telling me I have to do this on my off time or at home as well?! When do I get to be myself?" My response is usually something like this: "If you are a jerk, you never get to be yourself. What is needed more than being yourself, is to change."

And when I think about the nice-to-nasty ratio with women, I ask: Does she use her emotions for controlling others? Is she warm and affectionate when she desires something from her partner but cold and distant when she doesn't? Is she tender and sensitive as long as he is doing what she wants but rigid and hard whenever he strays from her wishes? In other words, does she use her emotions as a way to get what she wants—either reinforcing him for giving in to those things she desires or punishing him when he doesn't? Again, I encourage her to change.

It is fine to have feelings of disappointment at times with each other; such feelings are natural and reasonable. But it is not fine to punish each other with those feelings. Emotions are not for controlling people. They shouldn't be used to punish, and they shouldn't be used for a reward. If you have a problem with something, state clearly what your problem is. Make your voice heard, but don't hang on to your emotions as a way to try to make someone else feel bad. And the opposite is also true: Don't use your emotions as a way to get someone to go along with what you desire. We have our emotions to help give a rich flavor to the whole range of human experience—seasonings on the experience of life—not as a way to manipulate people.

John Gottman is perhaps the foremost love and marriage expert in the world, and he has reported that couples who have a five-to-one ratio of positive to negative exchanges have a happy relationship—no small thing in today's potpourri of romantic experiences. In other words, if for every negative exchange with our partner we have at least five positive exchanges, then we will maintain the love, joy, and happiness that we had while courting. This is what most of us want. And just think, all we have to do is to be more sincerely nice than nasty with the person we love.

There is a movie called *50 First Dates,* in which Adam Sandler plays a man who has fallen in love with a young woman (Drew Barrymore), who has been in a car accident. As a result of this accident, the young woman can't remember anything from the previous day; in other words, every day her life begins anew. As a result, she can't remember Adam Sandler, much less the fact that they had been in a kind, affectionate, and loving relationship the day before. Therefore, every day, Adam Sandler once again proves to her how much he loves her. Every day when she wakes up, he once again is warm, kind, and affectionate. Every day he makes his love clear as he essentially says: "You can trust me with your love because I will not take it for granted. I won't abuse it. I will not leave you with more scar tissue on your heart."

Can you imagine how your love relationship or marriage would thrive if each day you were intent upon elevating your nice-to-nasty ratio? If every day you were determined once again to show your partner just how much you love them and just how much you value them in your life?

I encourage you to spend lots of time together in many different venues—having fun, of course, but also with family and with friends. You might try working together on a specific task as well as participating in some community service. And in each situation, be that loving person who can't help but be loved in return. Elevate your nice-to-nasty ratio!

John Buri, Ph.D., is a professor of Psychology at the University of St. Thomas in St. Paul, Minnesota. He and the love of his life, Kathy, also his high school sweetheart, have been married for thirty-eight years and have six children and six grandchildren. Dr. Buri has taught a university course on the Psychology of Marriage and the Family for the past twenty-five years. He is the author of the marriage book *How To Love Your Wife,* as well as over fifty research articles and book chapters. He is a frequent speaker on topics of dating, marriage preparation, marriage enrichment, parenting, and family life. Dr. Buri can be reached at jrburi@stthomas.edu.

♥ ♥ ♥

Strengthening Your Couple Communication Skills
Susan Heitler, Ph.D.

Life can be lonely when it's a story of just one person. With two, there's a sense of completeness.

So what does a partner in marriage bring? A partner means there's someone to share all aspects of the business of living—someone to help with earning a living, cleaning the house, cooking meals, and rearing children. Marriage partnership can bring you a perpetual playmate, a pal to do things with, a sexual partner, and a partner at social events. Creating children especially takes the two of you. During difficult times, a partner is there to help when you're ill and to talk over situations that provoke emotional distress.

It's no wonder, therefore, why statistics indicate that people who are happily married experience more of all of life's goodies. They feel more satisfied, including with their sexual life, and they earn more money, are physically healthier with fewer ailments, and even live longer. Good deal!

What enables couples to keep their relationships, before and after marriage, happy and strong? A key factor is strong communication skills.

Benefits of Communicating

When people say, "We have a great relationship," what they're talking about is how they feel when they talk with each other. They mean, "I feel positive toward that person when we interact. I send and receive positive vibes with them."

A great relationship also means good communication in the sense that when differences arise, the partners can talk through their dilemma cooperatively. Differences don't become barriers; they become opportunities to find win-win understandings and solutions.

Making decisions together in a win-win way requires strong collaborative communication skills. Both partners need to be able to talk in a way that when they say things, their partner wants to listen—and when their partner says things, they want to hear them.

Strong communication skills enable couples not only to have fun and share their love, but also to deal with the difficult issues they inevitably will face as they proceed as partners in the business of living.

Your Tone of Voice

The tone of voice you use conveys whether you feel positive or negative about something and how intense that feeling is. Positivity in tone of voice, in words, and in actions (such as hugs and smiles) encourages the flow of open communication. Positivity enables partners to feel more relaxed with each other, which helps them to feel comfortable saying what's on their minds and eager to be responsive to each other's concerns.

Successful couples convey lots of positivity. They often use phrases such as:

- I agree that…
- What a good idea!
- I like that you…
- Thanks so much for….

They smile, and their voice has a smile in it.

In addition to conveying a consistently positive attitude of "I like you," "I agree with you," or "I care about what you say to me" in their tone of voice, successful marriage partners also control the intensity of their emotions. If they do feel a negative emotion like alarm, concern, anxiety, or even irritation, they stay in a calm emotional state, explaining the feeling in words rather than expressing themselves by speaking louder or faster.

Marriage is for grownups. Children often get upset, expressing their emotions by crying, shouting, whining, or getting mad. The ability to stay in a calm and positive emotional state—even in the face of difficult situations—is a hallmark of maturity.

In sum, relationships feel positive to the extent that the couple communicates positive feelings. Every negative emotional tone is like rust on the car: corrosive and not helpful. Relationships feel positive to the extent that the partners can discuss all their differences in a calm mode without overpowering each other via emotional escalations.

Making Decisions As a Couple

Marriage partners are, in a sense, yoked together. Couples, therefore, need skills for making decisions cooperatively. If they can choose together when to turn left and when to turn right, neither of them will feel compromised, dominated, or controlled by the other. Instead, each shared decision just enhances their loving partnership.

To make shared decisions, couples notice when one of them wants one thing and the other wants another. As soon as they see themselves preferring different plans of action, they switch from launching a tug of war over their preferred solutions to exploring the concerns that underlie each of their preferences.

As they come to understand their own and their partner's underlying concerns, they can look for a solution. They can make a plan of action responsive to all the concerns of both of them.

Case in point, let's take a look at Louise and Chad, recently engaged. They are discussing where they want to live after marrying. Louise wants to move to Montana; Chad likes living in Arkansas, where they both live now. Chad, realizing they are beginning to argue over the issue, switches into win-win mode and asks Louise what about Montana appeals to her. This question changes the discussion from a struggle over who will get their way to an exploration of both of their underlying concerns.

Louise explains that she loves the wide open spaces of Montana and wants to someday live on a small ranch. Chad's concern is whether he will be able to find work outside of the state where he has always lived. Their solution is to agree that Chad will explore job openings in Montana. If a job there looks possible, then he'll be glad to move. A month of monitoring job postings in his field, and there it is—a perfect job for Chad and a move to the state Louise loves.

The Benefits of Cooperative Dialogue Skills

Let's unpack the words *cooperative* and *dialogue*.

Cooperative means partners are interacting as friends. They feel and act like they are on the same team, not playing against each other.

Dialogue is information-sharing, with the partners taking turns talking and listening.

In effective cooperative dialogue, no one gives long monologues. Partners alternate talking and listening, each of them building on what the other has just said. They have a similar amount of air time, and each speaking time is short.

When cooperative dialogue partners are on the listening end, they listen for what makes sense, for what they can learn from what they are hearing. Their frequent use of words like "yes" and "and" indicate that they are registering their partner's views into a shared information pool.

By contrast, antagonistic dialogue partners push away what they hear. They listen for what's "wrong" with what their partner says. The word that indicates rejection of what they are hearing is "but." But works like the backspace or delete key on a computer, negating and erasing what was just said.

With strong cooperative dialogue skills, couples can sustain their love throughout whatever challenges arise on their shared life pathway.

Responding When There Are Differences

All couples sometimes have different viewpoints. All couples, especially in the early years of marriage, discover areas where *his way* and *her way* differ. The challenge of becoming fully successful marriage partners is to be able to talk over each of those differences toward the goal of creating an *our way*—a plan of action that truly works well for both partners. Differing viewpoints are especially likely to arise in the courtship, engagement, wedding planning, and first-year stages of a relationship, when couples are first making decisions together. These decision points offer excellent opportunities to practice building *our way* solutions.

Let's take a simple example. In Louise's family, birthdays were a big deal, so her expectation is that there will be a whole lot of fuss and specialness about her birthday celebration. In Chad's family, by contrast, people at most offered a pleasant "Happy birthday!" When Louise's birthday comes along, she's at risk for feeling disappointed if Chad handles her birthday the way his family of origin would have—with words only. The initial irritation or hurt Louise would feel signals that she and Chad have a *his way/her way* conflict they need to talk over. Their challenge is to create an *our way* responsive to both of their concerns.

Louise and Chad's solution? Louise will become the choreographer of all their birthday celebrations, hers and her husband's. Chad will be glad to join in on shopping trips to pick out presents and also offers to take out his banjo to enhance their celebrations with music. This new *our way* to celebrate birthdays delights them both!

Understanding Indirect and Direct Communications

Indirect communication means hinting or acting out. For instance, if a partner or spouse feels disappointed, and says "Hmmm" with a frown on their face, this would be hinting. Slamming a car door and pouting would be acting out feelings instead of saying them.

One difficulty with indirect communications is that the data they give is insufficient. There is not enough information for the partner or spouse to be able to address the problem and prevent it from happening again. With indirect communication, whatever was a problem today is likely to be a problem tomorrow, the next week, and still in five years.

Saying directly one's concerns, by contrast, leads to solutions.

Here's an example. Louise says, "I'm feeling overwhelmed by cooking and also cleaning the kitchen after we eat. How would you feel about taking over kitchen cleanup?" Chad might then answer, "If it's okay with you that I nap right after dinner, when I always feel so sleepy, I'd be glad to clean the kitchen after I wake up."

Direct communication—putting into words one's feelings and explaining one's concerns—leads to mutual understanding. With understanding plus goodwill, problems get solved!

Provocative Words

The more that couples use the words *you, never, always, not, should,* or *shouldn't,* the more likely their communication will sound negative, critical, controlling, or otherwise off-putting. *"You never* ask what I want when... *You* are *not* paying attention to...*You should...*" all put a negative pall on the conversation and invite defensive responses.

"I don't like..." sneaks the *not* word in via *n't.* Beware! It's far better to say what you *would like* than to talk about *don't likes.* "I *don't like* when you come home late" is far less inviting than "I *would like* so much to be able to count on your coming home on time."

Complaints, criticism, disparagement, and blame all focus on the partner. They start with "you." In addition, the negativity of *not* and the guilt-induction of *shoulds* and *shouldn'ts* make them all the more likely to invite defensive responses and hurt feelings.

The basic rule for keeping dialogue flowing smoothly is: *I can talk about myself, sharing my own thoughts and feelings, or ask about my partner's thoughts and feelings. It's not for me to say what I think my partner thinks, feels, or should do. To discuss my partner's perspectives, I need to ask good questions beginning with "How" or "What."*

Remember, instead of talking about what a partner or spouse is doing, ask good questions. *"What* happened that you were so late tonight?" or *"How* can you be sure this won't happen as a regular pattern? " *Why* is best to avoid; too often, it conveys a sense of blame.

254 Susanne M. Alexander

The basic rule of communication is like the basic rule of driving: I have to drive always in my lane. If I cross over the center line and start driving in the other lane, especially on a two-way road, I'm going to crash into you. That's how accidents happen.

What is the difference between the phrases, "I would like to …," and "I would like *you* to…"? The second version crosses the center line, telling the other person what to do. Crash ahead!

Being an Excellent Listener

Good listeners listen to learn, not to show what's wrong with what they are hearing. In addition, in their response, they begin by mentioning a word, phrase, or idea that they heard and explain what they are doing with this information.

For instance, if Louise says, "Look, there are a lot of clouds in the sky today," she would hope that Chad is going to respond with some kind of comment on what she has told him.

If Chad says, "Yes, that type of cloud probably means rain. I'll bring my raincoat," Louise feels fine. She knows Chad has heard what she said and is taking her comment seriously.

Good dialogue depends on these two core good listening skills: listening to learn rather than to negate, reject, or point out what was wrong in what was said; and responding by digesting aloud.

Good listeners catch the information balls tossed to them. If a receiver holds onto the ball forever, though, that's a monologue, which interferes with the flow of good dialogue. Likewise, if receivers ignore the balls that have been tossed their way, that's frustrating for their partner.

Good listeners avoid negating responses. If they listen in a negative way, focused on pointing out what's wrong with what a partner has said, they are likely to create a bumpy dialogue with a growing sense of frustration and irritation.

For example, if when Louise says, "There are a lot of clouds out there today," Chad replies, "No, there aren't really that many clouds," in response to this negating response, Louise is likely to feel nixed and irritated. Beware of negating!

If he really didn't see the clouds, Chad would be better off asking Louise what she means by "a lot of clouds." She could then explain, "We've had nothing but blue skies for weeks, so those little white puffs on the horizon look like a lot of clouds to me!"

When couples really do disagree with each other, how can they communicate effectively? There's an art to disagreeing. Instead of saying, "No, that's not right," find something in what was said that is possible to genuinely agree with. After expressing what makes sense in what was said, use the connecting words *and* or *and at the same time* to then add an alternative perspective. So if Louise says, "There are quite a few clouds up there today, and it's a gorgeous, sunny day," Chad's at risk for negating if he says, "No, there's actually a lot of sunshine." Instead of disagreeing, Chad would be better off agreeing and then adding his alternative view. "Yes, I can see a few clouds from my window, *and at the same time,* in the part of the world where I grew up, this would be considered a glorious day. So for me, it's bright sunshine."

What did Chad do that worked so well? He first agreed, and then he used the connective word *and*—or even better, *and at the same time*. If Chad had used *but*, he would have erased his earlier comment that had indicated agreement. In contrast, by agreeing, saying *and*, and then adding his alternative perspective, Chad could share quite contradictory information and yet kept the dialogue collaborative.

Building Couple Understanding

The good news is that couples do not have to be mind-readers. They also don't need to be feelings-readers. They just need to ask good questions.

When Chad sees Louise's brow quiver, tears begin to form in her eyes, or a special sparkle in her eyes, he assumes there's an emotional thought that's come up for her. He reads these signs as invitations to ask Louise what she's thinking or feeling. "Louise, what are those tears about?" And if Louise says, "I'm feeling kind of sad," Chad expresses his interest by asking simply, "What about?" That kind of intimate dialogue, based on genuine interest and concern, builds mutual understanding.

Remember, good questions use the words *what* or *how*: "Sad about what?" or "How come?" By contrast, questions that begin with *Are you* or *Do you,* such as "Are you mad?" or "Do you feel mad at me?" are far less helpful.

Preventing Fights

When a pot begins to boil over on the stove, what is the logical thing to do? Take it off the stove. Similarly, when irritated or other hot feelings begin to bubble up to excessive levels of intensity, loving partners remove themselves from the situation so they can cool down.

It's generally most helpful for a couple to create a shared exit/reentry choreography during a time when they are talking together cooperatively rather than to wait to invent these routines after a problem has emerged. If one of them removes themselves from a situation that's getting too emotional without having first co-designed a shared exit/re-entry plan with their partner or spouse, the one who is left will be at risk for feeling walked out on or abandoned. However, once a couple has an agreed-upon plan for removing themselves from overheating situations; they have an insurance policy for preventing fights. This agreement could be as simple as: "When either of us begins to show signs of getting too hot, let's both simultaneously get up and walk in different directions, quiet ourselves down, and then return to finish our conversation once we can talk calmly and cooperatively again."

Heated conversations rarely lead to productive understanding or creative solutions. As people overheat, they can't think. Overheated minds are unable to take up new information. In addition, high intensity emotions prevent flexible thinking and problem solving. So, if a couple is aiming to find solutions to problems—not just to criticize, blame, or punish—when either of them begins to get irritated, it's time to disengage, calm down, and then come back when they both can talk calmly.

Supporting One Another Through Difficulties

There's a full skill set for being helpful when a partner or spouse has a problem. Compassion—having feelings of concern and a desire to help—is a nice starting point. The difficulty comes because men and women often have different ideas about what would really be helpful.

Men, when they're upset, generally want to be left alone. Women, when they're upset, more often want to be able to talk the problem over with someone. Men typically think they are being asked to figure out what to do about the problem. They're immediately solution oriented. Women, on the other hand, seek first to be heard and understood.

When Louise is feeling troubled by something at work, she is likely to want to talk with Chad, but she is not looking for Chad to give her a solution to her dilemma. She's looking for Chad to help her out by taking the role of sounding-board, not of solution-giver.

In Summary

Couples nowadays are very fortunate in that there are all types of opportunities available for learning marriage communication skills. Before heading out to a baseball field, it would be helpful to know how to bat, throw, catch, where to run, and how to score. Someone about to build a house would first learn how to use a hammer and nails.

Marriage is a particularly high-skills activity. People who enter marriage without the requisite skill sets put themselves and their partner at risk for emotional injuries. With the necessary communication skills, by contrast, marriage offers a pathway to a life filled with blessings. Learn and enjoy!

Susan Heitler, Ph.D., a Clinical Psychologist based in Denver, Colorado, specializes in helping couples build strong marriages. Dr. Heitler is author of a book on marriage therapy, *From Conflict to Resolution,* and a book on the skills for marriage success called *The Power of Two.* Her online Power of Two course offers a fun way for couples to learn these skills from the comfort of home. Dr. Heitler and her husband, married almost forty years, are proud parents of four adult children and nine grandchildren. Office contact information: 303-388-4211; drheitler@therapyhelp.com; www.TherapyHelp.com; www.po2.com; www.poweroftwo.org

❤ ❤ ❤

Communicating About
What Doesn't Work and What Does
Susanne M. Alexander

One very helpful communication tool is the phrase, "It doesn't work for me…." It helps me to share what I'm upset about with a minimum of fuss and without prompting much in the way of defensiveness in return. Following this with a courteous and direct request can work wonders, as in these examples:

- "It doesn't work for me to spend an hour cleaning the kitchen floor and then have muddy footprints all over it. Please take your shoes off at the door the next time."
- "It doesn't work for me to have to unroll all your socks from tight little balls every time I do the laundry. Please unroll them before you put them with the dirty clothes."

It's often easier to spot and communicate the negative. I learned from my positive-focused husband to also say things like:

- "It really works well for me to have you make herbal tea for me every morning. I appreciate how thoughtful you are."
- "It really works well for me that you help me take breaks from working so hard. I need time to relax."

And then, of course, there are the broader perspectives in life, and you ask yourself, "How important is this anyway?" Sometimes you just decide to be tolerant, accepting, or patient and let slide what doesn't seem to quite work for you that day. Some days, I wish my husband were still around to get all excited about a new yard project and tramp across my clean kitchen floor.

Susanne M. Alexander is a Relationship and Marriage Coach. Her husband Craig loved to do yard projects every spring and summer. His two-year journey with brain cancer ended July 1, 2009, when his soul flew to the Kingdom of God. (See Introduction). (www.marriagetransformation.com)

© 2010 S. Alexander

♥ ♥ ♥

Learn How to Disagree As If the Windows Were Open
Carol Ummel Lindquist, Ph.D.

Do you know there are two major research projects that can predict whether you will be happily married twenty-five years from now?[1] In each of these projects, researchers followed people for more than twenty-five years of marriage. They learned to predict happiness within 93 to 95 percent accuracy based not on religion, common values, similarities, or anything like that, but on *how the couple disagreed*. Every happy couple needs to be able to disagree effectively.

Conduct a little test right now with your partner and figure out for yourselves if your chances for success are good or whether you need some practice and skill development:

- Set up a video camera and focus it on the two of you.
- While videotaping yourselves, discuss something you disagree about.

- Then watch the video together, counting positives (touching, mention of shared values, smiles, positive words…) and negatives (sarcasm, mean or hurtful words, calling each other names, criticizing character…).

If you have five positives to every one negative, you will very likely be happily married twenty-five years from now. If your discussions are more slanted to negative interactions, your marriage will likely be a non-starter. If you have nothing to disagree about, you are probably conflict avoiders and are likely to end up in a dead-feeling marriage where one or both of you drifts away or has an affair.

If this test bodes poorly for your relationship, don't despair. Meeting and dating someone you are attracted to, falling blissfully in love, getting married, and living happily ever after isn't something that just happens. The current divorce rate certainly attests to that! The good news is that you can build your skills together.

Like anything worth achieving, building a successful relationship for a lifetime takes time and experience. However, there are relationship skills that, with practice, can help build a strong foundation and greatly increase your chances of having a great marriage. Recent research suggests that even very unhappy married couples who do not divorce are much happier five years later when compared to equally unhappy couples who do divorce.[2] I have even had several couples survive and thrive after what seemed like unforgivable affairs: one with a father-in-law, one with a neighbor, and one that led to an abortion. When the couples learned to disagree and talk with each other, the marriages survived. They learned how to be different or disagree in a way that allowed each to have their own feelings, to feel heard, and to feel closer. It seems that it pays to hang in there and work out how to disagree, whenever possible. That is good news. However, it is more fun not to have an affair at all. Learning good disagreement skills will protect you from such dramatic bad times and help you through inevitable rough times in a normal marriage.

Yes, all couples do need to disagree—effectively—to be happy. One research study actually correlated a husband's ability to effectively express dissatisfaction with greater long-term marital happiness.[3] Happy couples need to learn to disagree in a way that not only does *no harm to their relationship*, but can also be fun and a little playful.

When couples fight instead of having a constructive discussion of their differences, most partners will say things to the other they wouldn't dream of saying to anyone else—even to someone they do not like. In the heat of battle, many people feel they are fighting for their survival and feel compelled to defend themselves aggressively. Some people go along politely for months and then explode, like one fellow who canceled an elaborate wedding just a week before the scheduled date; the wedding had been planned almost entirely by his mother-in-law. The couple went to counseling separately and together and eventually married in a small wedding and had a long, happy marriage. You need to learn to speak your point of view effectively without hurting your partner, provoking a vicious counterattack, or avoiding issues completely.

One of the happiest married women I know advises young couples getting married to "fight like the windows are open." In other words, disagree like the neighbors can hear you. Get your point across without being mean, blaming, shaming, or embarrassing yourself or your partner.

Almost by definition, when you are fighting—as opposed to having a healthy discussion of different points of view—you have lost your minds somewhere along the way. In private, couples break all sorts of communication rules that they wouldn't consider breaking elsewhere.

Here's how one man described a common fight with his partner: "She is always trying to perfect our relationship and especially me. She says things like: 'I can't believe you spend money on junk like that!' Sometimes," he said, "I answer sarcastically, 'Oh, I am not paying you to be my accountant, so lay off.' It's lame, I know. We end up in a pointless argument, but she is nuts about saving money and would never have any fun if it weren't for me. We can't really talk about money, and I worry how we will handle money together if we get married."

Almost everyone recognizes a bad fight. It is one where the woman assumes the problem is her partner's fault. He recognizes the problem but doesn't want to talk about it. He responds with something mean to deflect her away from the problem. They manage to break several rules in just a few sentences, both end up feeling bad, and the discussion and problem solving go nowhere. Good disagreements and problem-solving discussions should strengthen both of you and your relationship.

Tips for Handling Disagreements Well

- Sincerely compliment your partner on several wonderful and amazing attributes before you try to bring up a problem.
- Highlight (exaggerate) your major shared values before addressing the problem, including affirming the importance of the relationship to both of you.
- Admit to your own part in the problem first.
- Make fun of yourself, but not your partner.
- Find something humorous in the problem together, when you can.
- Commiserate about the problem together, if you can.
- When your partner makes a blooper and looks remorseful, be gracious and say nothing, or accept their regrets with a smile. Often, this prevents a fight and may keep the door open for the discussion to continue.
- Choose wisely what problem you will discuss. Handle no more than one major issue a week if you can. Write the others down for another week.
- Keep it light. Come up with as many silly solutions as serious solutions.
- Talk about how great it will be to do it differently next time.
- Talk through some preventative solutions when you foresee a problem coming up again.

Bad fight scripts are like Greek tragedies where the relationship dies at the end. Good disagreements are more like improvisational theater: One person is upset and initiates the dialogue; the other listens and helps the skit along, taking their cue from their partner until they reach a thorough understanding of each other's feelings, as well as a workable solution.

Sometimes I ask people to role-play their partner with me so they can feel what that person is feeling. I play the upset partner's role in a reasonable, non-blaming way. The upset person feels soothed because I articulate their feelings.

The listening partner responds differently during the role-play because I am presenting the partner's story (and feelings) in a way that doesn't attack them. They usually turn and say to their partner, "Is that how you really feel?" The partner nods an emphatic yes, relieved to hear what they are feeling presented in a way that seems reasonable and clear and doesn't upset the listening partner. Then I take the other partner's role and demonstrate that it is reasonable from their point of view too. Now, it is the listening partner's opportunity to feel understood and the first partner's chance to see the disagreement in a new light.

With that exercise, I demonstrate that **no matter who changes the interaction of their usual script or argument, the other partner responds differently,** and the conversation takes a better turn. In other words, if you change your moves, your partner will change the play, and the ending will be different and usually better. If you don't have a counselor or coach to do this exercise with you, a mutual friend may be willing to help with the role-play.

Specific Strategies for Success

Learn to apologize. When you break the rules, apologize quickly and take a break or move on, saying it in a better way. When she wants to start over, one clever woman says, "I apologize for *my* 5 percent of the problem." This makes her husband laugh. Learn to laugh at yourself and lighten up. Say what you genuinely wish you had done better.

Make full eye contact or other caring gestures. Do actions that say, "I am here, and I am paying attention to you. I care, and you matter to me." Sitting close for talking works best for women. Men are often happier discussing a problem side by side on a walk or a drive or talking while working together on a hands-on project. Do it the way that works best for your partner when you bring something up.

Avoid your partner's "hot buttons." One couple was struggling with bitter fights early in their marriage when their therapist asked them to each make a list of their partner's vulnerabilities and "hot buttons." Then, they agreed never to use them again. Now they are very happy and rarely fight. It is helpful to know what each other's significant triggers and issues are before marriage to help you create a marriage that is more peaceful.

Focus on the problem, not the person. Don't try to change your partner or tell them what they should or should not do. Invite them to work together to solve the problem.

Use a soft start-up, not a harsh one. Think before you speak—and then think again. Then begin gently. By simply watching the start-up, researchers can predict in the first three minutes of a disagreement whether a couple will have a good resolution.[4] A harsh start-up includes either critical or condemning words or tone of voice. If you aren't ready to talk nicely, wait, or write it in a letter and revise the content until you sound nice and like a real partner rather than a punitive parent. Consider how differently it sounds when you say, "Our relationship makes me feel so protected and connected. I wish we could spend more time together," instead of "Why can't you schedule more time with me? Don't you care?"

Leave out all the examples about how your partner did it wrong. It is human nature to want to be right, but in doing so, you make your partner wrong. This will cause your partner to feel shame, which results in them no longer hearing you. Instead, they will be busy working on their defense.

Avoid flooding. Most men become upset with emotion well before most women. When faced with potential or actual criticism, their hearts pound, they are flooded with adrenaline, and they can no longer think clearly. They will either want to flee or fight to make a point. Useful problem solving is over almost before the discussion starts. The woman often continues her discussion well past the point where a man is emotionally present and able to comprehend or remember what she is saying. A soft start-up, slowing the conversation down to a few sentences at a time, using soft voices, or putting a problem in writing dramatically improves understanding and reduces flooding.

Skip the Greek chorus. Don't say you know "several other people" who agree with your assessment of your partner's poor behavior. Your partner will be upset that you discussed the issue with many people first, and having a group think badly of them won't increase the chance of a good outcome from the discussion. Even saying, "Everyone knows that you don't..." is a bad strategy.

Give gifts and recognize good intentions. Leading with, "I know you love me and didn't mean to hurt me," (if you believe that) helps smooth the way. A soft start-up like, "I know you don't mean to hurt my feelings when you tell me you don't like my parents, but they are my parents. If you say, 'Could we cut the time short with your parents so we can spend more time just the two of us?', it would mean a lot to me, and I would jump at the chance."

Use truce triggers. Find a key word or action that signals to the other that you are in danger of fighting and you can skip it. Some people use a hug, a wink, a word, a phrase, or a funny face. One of my favorites is to be asked, "Do you need a hug?" when I am starting to wind up about something. Other times a funny face or comic line busts me up laughing, and I can start over with a smile.

Ask for what you want instead of describing what you don't want. Saying what you don't want is whining, negative, and saps the other person's energy and motivation to talk to you. Ask as nicely as you would a friend or coworker for exactly what you want your partner to do that would make you feel better.

Compromise on unsolvable problems and personal quirks. Researchers have found that most couples have a few problems that don't seem to have any real solutions. Agreeing to stop arguing about them can help the relationship. Of course, before marriage, it helps to pay attention to what types of things you cannot resolve. If you completely disagree or do not or cannot even discuss whether to have children, how much time to spend with family and friends, major priorities for spending money, or when to have sex, you will want to assess whether marriage makes sense for the two of you.

As most people go through courtship, marry, and then live together, they learn that they react very differently to some issues. Learn to work together in ways that protect each person's vulnerabilities. Ask yourselves if the solution takes both peoples' quirks and personalities into account.

Quite often, couples are better at resolving issues at work than they are at home. Why? At work, they are following the guideline of disagreeing as if the windows were open. I have asked couples who come to therapy to fight politely in front of me and then to audiotape and listen to their fights when in private. I want them to see that if they can be civil at work or out in public, they can be civil when they are alone, too—and they will be if they think someone's listening. Pretending the windows are open works, regardless of how you learn to do it.

1 Markman, Howard J., Scott M. Stanley, and Susan L. Blumberg. *Fighting for Your Marriage: A Deluxe Revised Edition of the Classic Best-seller for Enhancing Marriage and Preventing Divorce 3rd Edition,* Paperback. Jossey-Bass, 2010. Gottman, John M. and Nan Silver. *The Seven Principles for Making Marriage Work: A Practical Guide from the Country's Foremost Relationship Expert.* Three Rivers Press, 2000.

2 Gardner, Dr. Jonathan and Professor Andrew J. Oswald. "Do Divorcing Couples Become Happier By Breaking Up?" Watson Wyatt Worldwide and Department of Economics, University of Warwick, UK. Journal of the Royal Statistical Society. 2005.

3 Gottman, John M., University of Washington, Seattle and Lowell J. Krokoff, Department of Clinical and Family Studies, University of Wisconsin-Madison. "Marital Interaction and Satisfaction: A Longitudinal View, Journal of Consulting and Clinical Psychology," 1989, Vol. 57, No. 1, 47-52.

4 Gottman, John M. and Nan Silver. *The Seven Principles for Making Marriage Work: A Practical Guide from the Country's Foremost Relationship Expert.* Three Rivers Press, 2000.

Carol Ummel Lindquist, Ph.D., is a Board-Certified, licensed Clinical Psychologist specializing in high-conflict couples and trauma therapy for individuals. With her husband Neil, she raised two sons in Laguna Beach, California, while maintaining a private practice for more than thirty years. Dr. Lindquist has trained numerous therapists and published articles on assertiveness, domestic violence, and social skills. Her well-received first book *Happily Married With Kids* (Penguin, 2004) is soon to be followed by a second edition. A highly ranked professor who retired as Professor Emerita from California State Fullerton after twenty-eight years, she is as comfortable at the podium as in her private clinic. Her websites are www.drcarol4couples.com, www.cullagunabeach.com, and www.happilymarriedwithkids.com.

❤ ❤ ❤

Does One of Us Have a Problem with Anger?
Michael J. Beck, Ph.D.

The most common reason why marriages break up is because of fighting between couples, whatever the topic. It's a bit of an oversimplification, but what happens eventually is that people become so afraid that they are going to hurt the other person or be hurt themselves that they decide to retreat from the relationship. As a matter of fact, Dr. John Gottman, a marriage researcher, has determined from studying couples that how they interact with each other when there is a serious conflict often determines whether their marriages will last.[1] There are aspects of your interactions as a couple that you can consider before getting married, and these will help you assess whether you're going to make it to marriage and beyond.

Understanding Patterns from the Past

One of the key topics to discuss is how your parents got along. We know that children who are products of marriages ending in divorce tend to follow in this pattern. If your parents divorced, they were probably high conflict, and you should give serious thought as to how you, as a couple, deal with disagreements and how often they escalate into conflicts between you. You can look into your own collective backgrounds to get some indications about this.

One of the areas for you to inquire about with each other is what happened in your academic settings. People who have had academic suspensions, a really hard time with the curriculum, did not do homework, failed tests, or just scraped by through high school or college are probably more at risk for marital conflict. Why is this? Because teachers represent an extension of the home, as far as their ability to impose various sanctions and to invoke their authority. They tend to represent the parent to the child. If the child has seen examples of the parents not getting along, he's very likely to have trouble getting along with the school authority figures. Each parent represents an authority to the other one, and if the parents are defiant with each other, it's likely that the child will reenact this defiance in the academic setting. Of course, people can have an exemplary academic career and still have difficulties in interpersonal relationships. Therefore, this is just one of the things you should discuss as a couple.

Another thing a couple should explore with each other is whether either person has actually gotten into physical fights. Look at whether this was a pattern or whether they had trouble with authorities in the community; such as, running afoul with the law, drug use, or excessive alcohol use. These are all ways that people express defiance, and they tend to bring these problems into the relationship, where it often shows up as a lack of cooperation and partnership.

Strategies for Improvement

If you do have a problem with cooperation, what can you do about it? If you find that before or after getting married you are not getting along well, and one or both of you are doing things to bring negative attention to yourself, there are a number of actions you can take to increase the likelihood of sustaining your relationship. Some are simple, and some require more effort and investment.

At a very basic level, people can try to strengthen their ability to be patient. One way to do this is to stand in long lines at banks or supermarkets and pay attention. People who are impatient tend to be intolerant of waiting and think they should be served immediately. Developing more patience is certainly going to help you get along with other people, particularly partners or spouses. Another way is to observe and change your attitude when driving. It's not important that you be the first one to get to your destination. Desiring this may involve exceeding the speed limit, cutting in and out of lanes, gesturing at other drivers, and other behaviors that we associate with road rage. Usually, if your partner brings concerns about this type of behavior to your attention, it means there's a problem.

Think about what can assist you with strengthening your ability to be patient. If you know you are going somewhere that is likely to require a significant wait, consider taking a book or MP3 player with headphones to keep you occupied. If you have difficulty being patient behind the wheel, perhaps there is calming (not sleep-producing!) music that you can play to help you. Overall in your life, you might benefit from taking a meditation class. If you are spiritually oriented, saying a prayer before entering a difficult situation can assist you.

As you consider how to have a harmonious and peaceful relationship together, it will be important to equally consider each other's needs. For instance, my wife and I have different tastes in types of musical entertainment, so we take turns going with each other's preferences. Neither of you should dominate or dictate that choices always go your own way.

Another thing you can do if you have a problem with your anger is to think of ways you can make an experience very positive for your partner. As an example, I became interested in bird watching as the relationship with my now-wife developed. I didn't want to go birding by myself, so I thought about what would make coming with me a tremendous experience for her. Of course, I had to go to the Galapagos Islands. The birds there bring out women's maternal instincts. You get about as close to the birds as you can get to your dog or favorite pet animal. They have very little fear of people, so this is an awe-inspiring experience for people, and my wife was happy with the fabulous island experience.

This notion of easing things for people is something I learned from one of my landlords. When we married and moved in together, our landlord sent a stamped, self-addressed envelope with a rent receipt every month to make it less painful to send him the rent check. We couldn't say that we lost his address, didn't have a stamp, or didn't have an envelope. If you want somebody to do something for you or with you, make it as easy as possible for them to do it.

If some of these techniques don't help you effectively manage your anger, and you find that there's still constant conflict between the two of you, you can move to more dramatic measures. Self-help books, classes, and therapists are all resources to deal with anger management. Psychotherapy can help you spend time figuring out the sources of your anger, teach you not to act impulsively, and help you learn to think before acting. Many psychologists have tools such as personality and behavior tests that help the process of gaining insights on how you can deal with your own negative impulses.

Also, in psychotherapy, you learn how to sustain yourself in a relationship. All relationships have times when they are not as gratifying. For example, after a child is born, when the mother's attention is taken up to a much greater extent with somebody other than you, anger may arise from feeling neglected and frustrated. Being able to deal with frustration and meet your needs in some other way is a big key to marital success. Of course, this does not mean being unfaithful to your spouse and seeking inappropriate companionship outside of your marriage. Perhaps you can engage in a sport or exercise program or spend time with family members or friends. Keep in mind, as well, that you may also need to be more involved with childcare and rearing, so your spouse is not so exhausted. Remember that even though there are times when sexual intimacy is difficult, you can both enjoy just holding each other.

Managing your anger is not easy, especially if it has been a lifelong pattern. However, if you wish to be a good relationship and marriage partner and have a happy family life, addressing this issue and finding solutions is vital.

1 John Gottman and Nan Silver, *The Seven Principles for Making Marriage Work*

Editor's Note: You may find the following book to be a useful resource: *You Don't Have to Take It Anymore: Turn Your Resentful, Angry, or Emotionally Abusive Relationship into a Compassionate, Loving One*, by Steven Stosny. Dr. Stosny also offers courses for people experiencing anger issues (www.compassionpower.com).

Michael J. Beck, Ph.D., received his post-doctoral training at the Center for Modern Psychoanalytic Studies in New York, where he published a number of his most important articles. He went on to found the Institute for Psychotherapeutic Studies, where he taught, wrote, and supervised mental health professionals for a number of years. He is published in the area of child and family dynamics in the *Long Island Clinician* and *Family Therapy and Psychoanalytic Review*. He edited the book *The Narcissistic Family Member*. He is co-author with his wife and daughter of *365 Questions for Couples*. Dr. Beck has led workshops on Family and Marital Therapy and Modern Treatment of Depression and Anxiety for Western Suffolk Personnel & Guidance Association, Suffolk County Psychological Association, and the American Association of Sex Educators, Counselors & Therapists (AASECT). He is a Fellow in Family Therapy of AASECT, and he has been cited as a "Supervisor of Excellence" by the California Psychological Association. Michael Beck has been married since 1967. He and Stanis Beck live in New York and have two adult daughters. Dr. Beck can be reached at mjbeck3391@att.blackberry.net.

❤ ❤ ❤

Consultative Couple Decision Making
Susanne M. Alexander

"Consultative decision making" or "consultation" is a form of full and equal discussion between two (or more) people and arriving at a decision about something. You focus on a common goal—what is best to do. Consultation helps you with exploring thoughts, feelings, and goals, as well as sharing and processing new information. It assists with clarifying situations, resolving disagreements, and making decisions about actions to take. It includes sharing points of view and finding solutions that work without blaming, arguing, or telling each other what to do. Well-developed consultation skills help you avoid negative patterns, such as destructive conflict.

Consultation is also aimed at finding out the truth "…[C]onsultation must have for its object the investigation of truth. He who expresses an opinion should not voice it as correct and right but set it forth as a contribution to the consensus of opinion, for the light of reality becomes apparent when two opinions coincide."[1]

Consultation is a useful skill for you as a premarital couple. There are many decisions to make together about whether to marry (instead of one deciding and proposing to the other), how to plan the wedding, where you will live, how to set up a household, and much more. Your effectiveness at making decisions as partners now will inform you about what decision making as a married couple will be like. Skillful decision making will benefit you throughout your marital life.

Functional Principles of Consultation

Maintaining Harmony

Harmony in music allows for different notes and melodies, but the overall outcome is unified and easy to listen to. In relationships, maintaining harmony requires that each of you has a voice, but the unity between you as a couple remains the overall goal. With harmony as a fundamental principle, each can remember to speak with respect, compassion, and courtesy. Each remembers to be conscious of choosing words that are helpful and not harmful.

Engaging in Full Expression

Both of you have equal voices in consultation, and it is vital to freely express what is on your minds and in your hearts. You must not hide issues or avoid talking about them to create a false sense of peace.

If one of you tends to be more dominant in speaking, it will take self-discipline to give your partner opportunities to speak. If one of you is withdrawn, you may need to practice assertiveness. Free expression happens when you are BOTH willing to listen patiently to one another without interrupting. Being both frank and respectful and guarding your bonds of love will help your effectiveness. If either of you gives or takes offense with what the other says, the consultation will become sidetracked into negative emotions, and you will stop focusing on the goal.

Encouraging and Listening

As you consult, using phrases such as the following ones will encourage each other:

- "That is a good idea!"
- "I see what you mean."
- "That is an interesting way of looking at it."
- "Please, help me to understand."
- "That was helpful to me!"

As you listen to one another and respond to each other's concerns, remember to be kind and loving.

Holding Pure Motives

If either of you has a hidden agenda—an unspoken intention or goal—or wants to manipulate the other, the consultation is on a weak foundation from the very start. Also, be very aware if you have developed the habit of manipulation toward those of the opposite gender. Consultation is not a method to get your own way; it is designed to find the best solution for the problem at hand.

Detaching

One distinguishing feature of consultation is that once someone has expressed their thoughts or ideas, they no longer own them. This prevents you from holding onto opinions even when you start to see new perspectives from the input of your partner. You can detach and let go of your original viewpoint and move forward with the flow of discussion. As a couple, you can then build on what is emerging as a great idea. It is as if there is a central pot where all the input goes, and the pot belongs to both of you. *The consultation will not work well if you are fixed ahead of time on what the decision has to be.* Detachment also assists each of you in accepting and supporting an outcome that might not be exactly what each wanted initially.

Taking a Time-Out/Pausing

When you are communicating about challenging issues, it might be necessary to pause and reflect or calm down for a few minutes, hours, or days. Pausing allows you to assess the character qualities you are using—or not using—with each other, such as respect, courtesy, patience, or honesty. You can also think through how best to proceed with the discussion. Taking a break often prevents you from saying hurtful words that you will later regret.

If there is a pause, agree when to start up again and who has the responsibility for initiating it. If one or both of you leaves, be courteous and respectful and provide the necessary information about destination, contact information, and expected time of return. When consulting resumes, you may wish to try a different approach. You may consider inviting someone else to facilitate.

Avoiding Disruptive Behaviors and Maintaining Boundaries

The following behaviors can disrupt your consultation:

- Interrupting or engaging in communications with others
- Deliberately bringing up each other's hurtful "hot button" issues
- Implying or stating that one person is right and the other is wrong
- Having a competitive win-lose attitude
- Belittling, minimizing, or invalidating other's points of view or feelings
- Insulting or blaming each other or using sarcasm to wound
- Concealing key information
- Using forceful or dominating words, gestures, or tone of voice
- Walking away (unless there is danger of violence)
- Threatening each other verbally, emotionally, physically, or sexually

If any of these are occurring regularly, it is best to suspend the consultation and assess the situation. Do you need to set new boundaries? Learn better methods of problem solving? If you have reached an impasse in coming together reasonably, it is wise to get some outside assistance with resolving the matter. Consultations are not opportunities for griping and complaining, rehashing a problem, magnifying hurts, and focusing on the negative. The intent is to reduce any upset you are each feeling and to peacefully arrive at solutions.

Deferring

Even when you both handle the consultation process well, there may be times when you cannot find a solution on which you both agree. In a couple relationship, there is no such thing as a majority vote! Alternatively, perhaps one person feels strongly about a choice, and the other has no strong opinions. In these cases, in order to move forward, it is possible to defer to the person who feels strongly and agree to try out their solution. *Deferring* in this context means to give precedence to one person's opinion, not to postpone a decision. Avoid frequently deferring. This could be a signal that you are not allowing adequate time for consultations. There could also be a need for more respect and equality in your relationship.

The choice to defer is not effective if it becomes "giving in" resentfully and then undermining your partner's actions. If there is a choice to defer (this may be the case after repeated attempts at reaching a decision that you both agree on), it will need to be sincere for the outcome to work. With deferral, you both still "own" the decision. It is a mutual commitment that each must support wholeheartedly.

Supporting Unified Decisions

Even when it's difficult, the goal is to come to a unified decision whenever possible. This may require multiple consultation sessions on the same topic, especially if the matter is very important. Once you have made a decision together, both must fully support it in attitude, action, and words, or it will be impossible to know whether it was an effective decision. If you come to an agreement, but one person is not sincere, and they mentally or physically work against the decision, it will be difficult to ever know whether the decision was good or poor or why it really failed. The outcome could have been due to the poor quality of the decision or to the disunity between the two of you.

Consultation Methods

There is no set structure for consultation. Below are descriptions of both casual and formal possible approaches.

Casual Process

You may often have short discussions and make quick decisions about where to go or what to do. These can occur via texting or email, on a phone call, or over a meal. The key is whether the important information was shared and the decision made with mutual agreement.

For less formal discussions, some gender preferences may occur. Women may be more comfortable with consultations that involve sitting and dynamically sharing thoughts and feelings. They may choose to build consensus in a setting that has you sitting close together and maintaining direct eye contact. Men may be more comfortable with activity and less eye contact. These methods may include:

- Talking and walking at the same time
- Allowing thinking and processing time without everything having to be answered in one discussion
- Working with their hands at the same time as talking
- Being willing to sit together in silence for a while

Experiment with settings and methods to determine what works best for you.

Formal Process

If you have a serious, complex issue to address, a more formal method may be useful. You may also need to meet more than once to reach a decision. Below is a potential structure to consider for effective formal consultation:

At the Beginning:

1. Pray for the consultation to be effective and for the decision to be wise and unified. Alternatively, consider sitting quietly for a moment holding hands.

2. Identify and state the problem or issue precisely.

3. Agree on the amount of time you will spend on the consultation and whether there may need to be multiple conversations.

4. Identify and agree upon any principles, character qualities, or external guidance that is relevant to the matter. (External guidance could be such things as a book or article, religious instructions, or input from family.)

5. Gather and review any applicable facts.

Throughout the Consultation:

1. Turn to God by praying and meditating for guidance.

2. Listen carefully to one another.

3. Exchange information, perspectives, thoughts, and feelings.

4. Gather any additional facts or external guidance as needed.

5. Discuss frankly and lovingly many possible solutions, strategies, and plans.

6. As appropriate, include in the discussion anyone else who is affected by the decision.

Making a Decision:

1. Evaluate proposed solutions. Consider important aspects of each, such as costs, time, and energy requirements, as well as likely outcomes.

2. Eliminate unacceptable solutions.

3. Come to a unified decision based on the principles you agreed to, the guidance that applies, and all other relevant input.

4. Write down the chosen solution, what is expected of each person involved in carrying it out, and the agreed times when these actions will occur.

5. Pray together.

Carrying Out the Plan:

1. Carry out the chosen solution(s) wholeheartedly in unity, trusting in a positive outcome.

2. Pray for assistance.

3. Reflect upon and evaluate the plan at agreed-upon stages or when circumstances change.

4. Modify the plan and change direction as needed.

5. Re-assess the progress and the outcome.

When a matter is very serious, you may also make a decision but agree to wait for a while before taking any action. This allows you to reflect, pray, and then re-visit the decision to confirm whether it is still the right choice.

Consultation is not an easy skill to learn, but it is a rewarding one. As your relationship matures, you will find that making decisions together is a key factor in your connection and unity as a couple.

1 'Abdu'l-Bahá, *The Promulgation of Universal Peace*, p. 72

Susanne M. Alexander is a Relationship and Marriage Coach who loves excellent consultation sessions. She and her husband Craig discovered in their marriage that consistently using this skill virtually eliminated all fights, helped them slow down and not rush into unwise choices, and created wonderful, synergistic decisions. www.marriagetransformation.com

Chapter Twelve
Building Relationship Strengths

~ ~

This chapter takes you deep into the heart of maintaining and sustaining your partnership and marriage. We help you with understanding your values and the rituals, practices, and tools that help connect you together. We assist you with seeing the value in being a team and showing goodwill actions toward one another that bring you together instead of pushing you away from each other.

Submissions in this chapter will help you identify and strategize how to meet each other's needs in a marriage together, as well as understand how unmet childhood needs may still be affecting you. You will explore being soulmates and how to deal with situations that require acceptance and connection in order for you to stay together. You will also share a brief Mentor Couple experience to expand your view of having one yourselves.

♥ ♥ ♥

Wedded Bliss Can Be Yours
Nisa Muhammad

Love is calling your name, and you want to get it right the first time while avoiding the pain and heartache of a failed union. As you answer love's call with hope, you sincerely want to increase the benefits of marriage, while decreasing the drama. However, most couples are clueless about how to achieve and sustain wedded bliss. Some know more than others. That may be you too. However, heading into marriage often becomes an exercise in hit or miss, with more misses than hits.

Below are five suggestions for success. I also recommend going to a class, workshop, retreat, or seminar to really work on your relationship and learn how to be successful in marriage.

1. **People gravitate toward the applause in life.** Be your partner's biggest cheerleader, the president of their fan club, and their greatest supporter. Get even better at it during marriage. Many times, people get more affirmation from their jobs, children, hobbies, or religious communities than they do from the person closest to them. Be that affirmation, be that applause, and you'll be the one they hurry to now; after marriage, they'll come running home to you every day. Each spouse wants to know when it's all said and done that there is at least one person on their side, one person who loves them unconditionally. That person should be YOU.

2. **Be what you want to see.** If you want better communication, be the best communicator in the relationship. Become a model for what you want now before marriage. Be an example that helps your partner (and later your spouse) learn how it's done. If you want more romance, be the romantic in your relationship. If you want more tenderness, show the most tenderness. Asking for what you are unwilling to give doesn't work. Strive to be first in everything good in your relationship and last in everything bad. Don't wait for your partner or spouse to do what you want; lead the way. Be what you want to see, and you will see incredible results.

3. **Advance your point and build your relationship with understanding.** In your communications with your partner or spouse, have two points in mind: "How can I advance my point in the best manner with the best words and gestures?" and "How can I build my relationship by understanding my partner or spouse?" These are sometimes easier said than done. Your partner or spouse deserves the best you have to offer, your best care, your best concern, your best consideration, and your best conversation. Usually, we reserve the best we have for strangers and give the worst we have to those closest to us. Think carefully before you speak and think carefully as you understand. Give your partner or spouse what's right and everyone else what's left.

4. **How can I make this better?** Don't fight fire with fire because it only makes a bigger fire. Fight fire with water instead. In the heat of an argument, in a soft, loving voice, just say, "Honey, how can I make this better?" It is a disarming way to focus the discussion on solutions rather than problems. Listen to what's said, move forward, and keep it loving. Show you are interested in changing the

tone and tenor of the relationship and making things better.

In discussions, it's important to advance your point and build the relationship with understanding. This prevents conflict. Don't continue arguing and fussing just to make a point, when just asking how you can make it better can add lots of love to a difficult situation. According to researchers, what separates those that get divorced from those that don't are not their problems. For every couple that divorces because of money, another one solves the problems and stays together. For every couple that divorces because of infidelity, another couple works it out and stays together. The difference is each couple's ability to manage the problem when it comes. Either you manage it, or it will manage you.

5. **Make the decision to love the one you're with.** Staying focused on the partner you have and your spouse after you marry is holding a mindset about commitment. Decide that you are going to love your spouse throughout your marriage, and take your vows seriously. We are often with people that we say we love, but we go about it halfheartedly, waiting for some upset to happen so we can end it. We have one foot in the relationship and one foot out the door. We're saying, "I Do," but thinking "I don't," and it will never work that way.

Enter the room of holy matrimony and lock the door: no exits, no windows, just you and your spouse. Whatever happens, work it out and "keep it loving." You do yourself and your spouse a disservice when you operate with a Plan B in mind. When you enter with your eye on the exit, your marriage is doomed for failure from the start. Give it your all and then give it some more. Love and marriage are not a 50/50 proposition; they are 100/100. No one wants just 50 percent of the one they love. Everyone wants 100 percent and more if they can get it. Of course, this does not mean to stay in a marriage that is fraught with abuse, but most of the time that's not the problem.

There you have it! Five of the many ways to achieve wedded bliss. A great marriage is never guaranteed. What is guaranteed is that if you work at it, it will work for you. Wedded bliss can be yours.

Nisa Muhammad is the Founder of the Wedded Bliss Foundation (www.weddedblissinc.com), a community-based organization helping teens and adults create healthy relationships and healthy marriages. One of its goals is giving more children the benefits of a two-parent family. She created Black Marriage Day for communities to celebrate marriage in very unique ways. It is held annually on the fourth Sunday in March, and it has grown from 30 participating cities participating in 2003 to close to 300 communities conducting celebrations in 2010.

Mrs. Muhammad is the co-author of *Basic Training for Couples,* a marriage education curriculum. Her work as a pioneer in strengthening marriage in the Black community was featured in detail on CNN's *Black in America 2.* She knows both the joys of marriage and the sorrows of divorce. She works so her five children and more adults can enjoy wedded bliss.

❤ ❤ ❤

The Values and Rituals of Authentic Relationships: What the Relationship Enhancement Model Teaches Us About Marriage
Robert F. Scuka, Ph.D.

Successful, satisfying marriages involve a set of core values that enable partners to experience a foundation of security and safety and a set of relationship rituals or practices that promote deeper connection and intimacy.

The Relationship Enhancement (RE) model (developed by Bernard Guerney, Jr., Ph.D.) helps illuminate the core values of authentic relationships, while also recommending specific relationship rituals and practices that nurture and strengthen the emotional bond between two people. Identifying the core values you hold as a couple, and beginning to incorporate actions that bond you more closely together, are part of the important work you will want to do to prepare for a lifelong marriage of love.

Core Values

The core values of the RE model are as follows:
- Commitment to the Relationship as a Good in Itself
- Respect for Your Partner/Spouse and Relationship
- Non-Judgmental Acceptance
- Openness and Honesty Balanced by Caring and Compassion
- Equity

Commitment to the Relationship As a Good in Itself

This value of commitment is rooted in the recognition that marriage is an entity independent of either spouse, and it has needs that transcend the desires of either person. This does not mean that the feelings, concerns, and desires of either person are unimportant. Instead, it means that each spouse having a spirit of commitment to the good of the marriage will affect the quality of the marriage and the confidence that each person has in it.

When this commitment is present, couples experience a deeper level of connection and have a more satisfying relationship. When this commitment is absent, the marriage runs a high risk of degenerating into a type of competition to ensure the satisfaction of one's own desires regardless of the feelings, concerns, and desires of the other person. The practical application of this value is evident when both spouses exhibit a spirit of mutual accommodation. This choice recognizes that the satisfaction of one person's desires must also encompass the satisfaction of the other person's desires if both people are going to experience a genuinely satisfying marriage.

One important implication of this value for pre-married couples is that you will benefit from talking openly about what each of you envision for your potential future marriage. The development of a shared vision for your marriage is crucial for developing a mutual commitment to pursuing and promoting goals that enhance your marriage over time. It also is important that each of you, individually and as a couple, periodically revisits your vision and goals for the relationship as each of you grows and as the relationship evolves over time. To be successful, this process of re-evaluation and change requires you both to be flexible about considering what can enrich your relationship and marriage.

Respect for Your Partner/Spouse and Relationship

A second value embodied in and promoted by the RE model is respect: respect for your partner before marriage and your spouse after marriage, as well as respect for the relationship itself. In a sense, this value dovetails with the preceding value of commitment and reinforces it, but the value of respect also translates into very concrete behavior choices. For example, it includes not indulging verbally in harsh criticism or personal attacks.

The value of respect also translates into doing certain things for the good of the relationship or marriage, even though the choice might not match your own personal preference. An example is agreeing to take a time-out during a difficult interaction, even though one of you may prefer to keep talking about the issue. Foregoing personal preference for the good of the relationship establishes a secure foundation for you as a couple, which in turn creates a more satisfying and fulfilling marriage.

Non-Judgmental Acceptance

A third value central to the RE model is non-judgmental acceptance of each other and your thoughts, feelings, concerns, and desires, even when they differ.

Personal judgments and rejecting each other's perspectives prevent you from genuinely connecting with one another. Non-judgmental acceptance, on the other hand, helps you to empathize with one another, which, in turn, opens up communication between you. Together, empathy and non-judgmental acceptance help foster a deepened sense of security, connection, and mutual commitment to the good of the relationship.

Openness and Honesty Balanced by Caring and Compassion

Two additional sets of values function in a complementary way within the RE model: openness and honesty, and caring and compassion. The qualities of openness and honesty are essential to a healthy, thriving relationship that includes emotional intimacy. If you are feeling a strong emotion, are concerned about something, or experiencing a desire for something, it is important to communicate that to each other. This is a vital communication practice for relationships and marriage. Otherwise, you cheat yourselves of an opportunity to address an issue constructively and arrive at a mutually satisfying solution. When couples do not address key issues, the relationship suffers.

However, the RE model recognizes that openness and honesty must be balanced by the values of caring and compassion. These qualities help you as a couple to stay aware of the effect on each other of what you say and how you say it. The qualities of caring and compassion help you to avoid personal attacks on each other's character. These attacks destroy your relationship by prompting the recipient to feel defensive, shut down emotionally, and either withdraw from the relationship or reciprocate in equally destructive verbal attacks.

Combining all four of these qualities helps you communicate your feelings, concerns, and desires in a respectful manner that creates a positive atmosphere in all your interactions. You will say what you need to say caringly and compassionately, or else you won't say it at all.

Equity

Finally, the RE model also embodies and promotes the value of equity in relationships and marriage. It encourages balance between sharing your own perspectives and listening to and acknowledging your partner's or spouse's perspective. This is best accomplished through a structured dialogue process that permits the safe and equitable expression of your respective points of view. (See below for recommended guidelines.) In this way, the values of openness and honesty are further promoted and reinforced, and your relationship is strengthened.

Relationship Rituals and Practices

The core relationship values explained above are given concrete expression through three relationship rituals or practices recommended by the RE model:

1. Daily Time Talking Together
2. In-Depth Dialogue
3. Having Fun

Relationship Ritual 1: Daily Time Talking Together

Commit to spending a minimum of fifteen to twenty minutes each day where you connect with each other—in person, if possible. A wonderful way to begin this daily check-in time is to share a "partner appreciation" with each other. This means sharing something you like or admire about your partner as a person or something that you appreciate that they did. Then you can each share how your day went, how you're feeling at the moment, or small points you'd like to catch up on. You can also use this time to suggest a fun activity for the future. However, this is not a time for complaints or big issues. Keep it positive.

Relationship Ritual 2: In-Depth Dialogue

Structure into your schedule a weekly dialogue time where you sit down together for an extended conversation lasting at least thirty to sixty minutes. At this time, focus on a significant issue, a potential or real problem area, or ways to enhance your relationship. The key to a successful dialogue is to follow a few simple guidelines:

- Only one person talks at a time, and the listener does not interrupt.
- The person who is talking shares their feelings, concerns, and desires regarding the issue at hand.
- The other person tunes in empathetically, listens intently, and then verbally acknowledges what the speaker has shared. This should be done without adding any commentary from the listener's point of view. However, careful listening with a "third ear," and noting facial

expressions and tone of voice will help you to "hear" beyond the words to the emotions and needs the speaker is experiencing.

- Repeat the above steps—perhaps several times, including encouragement of full expression—until the first person completes what they wish to share.

- Change roles so that the person who was the listener has a chance to share their feelings, concerns, and desires about the issue at hand. It is helpful for the new speaker to begin by expressing what makes good sense to you about what your partner has shared.

- The partner's job now is to tune in empathetically, listen intently, and verbally acknowledge the new speaker's sharing.

- Repeat, going back and forth as long as necessary, until both of you feel well understood.

- When appropriate, reach a concrete decision or agreement about actions to take that leave both of you feeling that your concerns and desires have been taken into account, creating a win-win solution. The "secret" here is to commit yourselves to meeting your partner's or spouse's needs as much as your own.

Relationship Ritual 3: Having Fun

Do something fun with each other at least once a week. It is all too easy to allow the external pressures of work and the demands of day-to-day life to take over and push nurturing your relationship into the background. Be proactive and commit to keeping your relationship vibrant and alive through fun activities.

Help from Others

One final recommendation: If you have not already done so, attend a skills-based marriage preparation seminar in order to learn how to communicate and dialogue more effectively. Couples of all ages and levels of relationship experience are increasingly turning to marriage education to help increase the odds of having a loving marriage that endures. Careful skill building will help you to deal effectively with the inevitable issues that come up in any relationship or marriage, minimizing hurt feelings and disappointment and maximizing the satisfaction of being able to deal with issues in a constructive, respectful manner. Learning how to have a successful marriage will also reinforce the five core values that make for an authentic—and fulfilling—relationship.

Robert F. Scuka, Ph.D., M.S.W., LCSW-C, is Executive Director of the National Institute of Relationship Enhancement® (www.nire.org) in Bethesda, Maryland, and a lead member of its training faculty. Dr. Scuka specializes in marriage education and couple therapy and is the author of *Relationship Enhancement Therapy: Healing Through Deep Empathy and Intimate Dialogue* (Routledge, 2005). Rob and his wife Mary live in Kensington, Maryland, and they have two adult children. He can be reached at robscuka@earthlink.net.

♥ ♥ ♥

Creating a Goodwill Partnership
Susan Page

What is the most important key to happy marriage and to a loving, successful relationship?

Most people will answer "great communication" or "mutual respect." I agree those are important, but I have found that the real key lies elsewhere.

What Thriving Couples Have in Common

In an attempt to find any single feature they all shared, I interviewed thirty-five couples who described themselves as "thriving." I thought I might find that they all came from happy, functional families, or that they had unusual degrees of compatibility, or that their problems were relatively minor compared with other couples—none of that was true. Some of them had rotten childhoods and enormous challenges. But there was a quality I found in all of these thriving couples that I find is usually missing in more troubled relationships. I now believe that quality is a deeper key to happiness than even good communication or mutual respect.

It's a quality I call a *spirit of goodwill*. Successful couples are on each other's side. They view themselves as allies, not adversaries. They *want* to be happy together, and together they make this happen. In a spirit of goodwill, they accept the traits in their partner that they wish were different. They have given up trying to change each other. When they argue, they understand that a different point of view may be valid. Because they want to experience their love all the time, they would rather work toward a solution than hang on stubbornly to their own "right" point of view.

The most widespread belief about marriage is that it is hard work—that true happiness in marriage is a myth, a bill of goods, and that 50 percent of all marriages end in divorce and the other half are just barely escaping it. But what you *believe* has a great deal to do with what you *experience*, because you view all of life through your beliefs! This pervasive negativity about love in our culture is extremely damaging.

Happy couples simply don't buy it! They *believe* they can be happy together, and their happiness is a priority for them. They keep a sense of adventure and excitement in their lives. As one couple told me, "There's achievement and aliveness, and achievement is overrated!"

Learning the Goodwill Skill

After I identified this spirit of goodwill in couples who thrive, I had to ask myself, "Is there a way I can teach goodwill to couples who don't already have it?" The answer is "Yes!" It is possible for you to learn the practice of goodwill, and it requires a departure from some of the most commonly accepted wisdom about relationship work.

My first realization was that the excessive emphasis on communication as the primary—perhaps even the only—tool available to couples for working through problems and trying to achieve greater closeness is seriously misguided, or at least very limited. Communication techniques for couples are largely about the adversarial aspects of their relationship, so that they spend a lot of time working on their problems rather than nurturing the positive parts of their partnership. Also, communication requires skills that elude many people. And the giant problem here is that so-called communication is usually about trying to change your partner. "If you could just do things my way, if you would just change a little, this relationship would be better." Using communication to change your partner is a fundamentally flawed approach to making a relationship better.

I began to focus instead on developing specific "Loving Actions" that I found had far more power and more immediate results than, "What I hear you saying is…" or "Honey, we need to talk." All of these Loving Actions are unilateral—done by only one of the partners—and yet they have a powerful positive effect on the relationship. They are a gift to a partner, in a spirit of goodwill, often with extraordinary results.

For example, try this Loving Action experiment: Make a pact with yourself that for one week, you will refrain from saying anything negative, critical, or demanding to your partner. The first thing you may notice is how often you make negative or critical comments, often without intending to or realizing it. You may believe that your partner is the problem, because they are always late or do not phone you often enough or criticize you too much, or yada, yada, yada. But what you may learn is that you are the person who is creating the upset in the relationship by harping about the problem all the time. Once you are aware of your tendency to make negative comments, begin looking for and taking opportunities to say positive, affirming comments to your partner instead. Watch the level of love and connection go up between you.

Couples, Try It Out!

Next, work on creative ways of acting on your own to meet your own needs without expecting your partner to change. For example, Carlos thinks Gabriela is far too lenient and helpful to her teenage daughter, who is doing nothing to begin to help herself or become more independent. When Carlos sees that his comments about how Gabriela is being co-dependent with her daughter are falling on deaf ears and are creating upset between them, he resolves to stop discussing this subject altogether.

When Gabriela breaks a date with Carlos so she can drive her daughter to a sports event, even though he is angry, he simply says, "Okay," and makes plans with a friend. He does not feel a need to discuss his strategy with Gabriela. His goal is not to make her think better of him, teach her how to manage her daughter, or to change her. His goal is to end unpleasant, useless fights, and in this, he is instantly successful!

It is still hard for Carlos to watch Gabriela indulge her daughter, but he saw that his attempts to "help" (control) not only were futile, but also caused unpleasant conflict. As a spiritual discipline, he surrendered. He let it go. He gave up his desire to prove he was right about this matter. He never mentioned the topic again. His private, unilateral decision was a gift to the whole family.

Consider how a Loving Action practice can also work after marriage. Sarah thinks her husband Jim is too controlling about money. Years of explaining to Jim how unfair this is has gotten Sarah nowhere. Instead, Sarah shows her spirit of goodwill by showing Jim she is on his side. She buys shoes for the children on sale and proudly shows Jim her little victory. When she decides not to attend an expensive professional meeting, she shares this with Jim, agreeing with him that this is a good financial move for them. Now, Jim begins to feel that Sarah is his ally, not his adversary. All by herself, Sarah has created a happier, more loving atmosphere in her home. And together with a friend, she set up a small, simple business and keeps this money separate, so she does not have to negotiate every expenditure with Jim.

Partners who use Loving Actions do not solve problems. Instead, they outgrow them by developing a higher consciousness, and the problems simply fade away. There are not problems in most relationships, but rather facts of life. Don't look for a solution; look for a way to live happily with a situation that you don't like but that is minor compared with the love and benefits you receive from your relationship or marriage.

A Final Caution and Encouragement

And don't think that using Loving Actions means you are giving in! Quite the contrary! There is a world of difference between using Loving Actions compared to letting your partner become overly dominant with you. Even though your actions may look similar on the surface, they come from very different motivations. If you feel you are being dominated, you will act resentful or depressed—and usually find a way to let your partner know it. On the other hand, taking a Loving Action gives you enormous control and personal power. You are acknowledging, with compassion, that your partner does not have to change for you, and that you can take care of yourself. As the well-known Serenity Prayer suggests, you "accept the things you cannot change"—and then you act with courage to take care of yourself around those things.

Cultivating a spirit of goodwill by becoming the Loving Leader in your relationship through employing unilateral Loving Actions is a magical formula that goes far beyond communication when it comes to outgrowing what you now view as problems in your relationship.

Repeat *Oprah* guest **Susan Page** conducted workshops for couples from 1980 until 2003. Her international speaking and media career has taken her to twenty-six states, Canada, Korea, Australia, and Mexico. She is the author of five relationship books including her first international bestseller: *If I'm So Wonderful, Why Am I Still Single?*, which was translated into twenty-two languages, *The Eight Essential Traits of Couples Who Thrive*, and her latest book, *Why Talking Is Not Enough: Eight Loving Actions That Will Transform Your Marriage*. Susan offers telephone coaching to individuals and couples. Visit her website at www.susanpage.com. Susan is a graduate of Oberlin College and holds a Master of Divinity degree from San Francisco Theological Seminary. She began her career as Campus Minister at Washington University in St. Louis and at Columbia University in New York. Later, she served as Director of Women's Programs at the University of California,

Berkeley, where she helped found the nation's first university-based human sexuality program. She lives in San Miguel de Allende, Mexico, with her husband of thirty years. They have one son and three grandchildren.

❤ ❤ ❤

Meeting Your Relationship Needs
Susanne M. Alexander

"But I expected you to…!" You each have a variety of needs—some more important to you than others—and honestly, it's certainly reasonable to expect that a spouse will meet some of them. As you look ahead to the possibility of marrying, consider together:

- What primary needs do you each have?
- Are you *willing* to meet those needs for each other? *Can* you meet those needs for each other?
- What other ways of meeting specific needs are acceptable to you both?

Some of the needs you may wish to consider are listed below (in no particular order of priority). Consider the level of importance for you of having each need met. Your highest three- to five-priority needs are ones that a spouse must be able to meet effectively most of the time for a happy, satisfying marriage.

- Affection, Connection, and Love
- Sexual Fulfillment
- Financial Support
- Conversation
- Recreational Companionship
- Spiritual Companionship
- Partnership
- Openness
- Attractiveness
- Domestic Support

- Marriage Commitment
- Family Commitment
- Admiration and Significance
- Certainty and Security
- Spontaneity and Variety
- Personal Growth
- Laughter and Humor
- Being of Service to Others
- Resolution of Issues (solving problems; forgiveness; making amends)

Remember that your needs will likely change as your relationship, family, and lives change. Revisiting your priorities and how well you are meeting them for each other will be helpful throughout your marriage. However, there will be times when illness and difficulties interfere with meeting each other's needs. Practicing patience and flexibility will also be required.

Your needs also relate to what you believe about the purpose of your lives and the purpose of marriage. For example, if you believe that a primary purpose of marriage is to provide a secure and loving environment for children to grow, "Family Commitment" might be higher on your list. If you believe in being outward-focused as a couple, "Being of Service to Others" would be a vital need. What do you see as your purposes in life? In marriage?

An expert on meeting needs is Dr. Willard Harley of Marriage Builders (www.marriagebuilders.com). One of the key points he makes in his books is that marriage includes with it a promise to care about and to meet a spouse's primary needs. This means speaking and acting in ways that bring happiness and enhance the quality of each other's life and your marriage. When spouses meet one another's needs, their marital happiness and harmony increase. *Because people will often violate even their own most fundamental values to meet their perceived needs,* recognizing and meeting one another's needs is an essential way to prevent the unhappiness, resentment, relationship breakdown, and infidelity that can result from unmet needs.

As you look at your relationship together now, practice assessing your needs before marriage. Are you clear what they are? Are you able to meet them in each other? Are there needs that you have agreed to wait to fulfill within marriage?

You may feel very vulnerable sharing your needs with a partner. The discussion can be intimate and sensitive. Ensure that your relationship is at a stage that this discussion is appropriate and helpful. However, don't postpone the sharing too long, because meeting one another's needs is also a key decision-making point for whether you can marry successfully.

> **Susanne M. Alexander** is a Relationship and Marriage Coach. She and her husband found that assessing needs and meeting them was a valuable and fun part of their marriage. (www.marriagetransformation.com)

❤ ❤ ❤

Identifying and Addressing Unmet Childhood Needs
Paul Coleman, Psy.D.

Even when you are madly in love, there are times when you let each other down, disappoint each other, or worse. The good news is that by accepting yourselves as imperfect and by giving up on the belief that your partner can complete you, you can come to terms with those hurts and disappointments. The key is understanding what unmet needs you each have from childhood that are causing you challenges in your couple relationship now. Addressing these will give you the greatest opportunity to experience delight, joy, gratitude, and harmony in your courtship and marriage.

The Fundamental Question

Ask yourself honestly, "What need did not get met—even a little bit—in my childhood that I wish had been met?" In other words, "What do I wish I could have received in childhood that I didn't get enough of?"

If you are struggling now in your relationship, chances are quite high that the same thing you missed out on growing up is something you are missing out on now. Even if you had loving and devoted parents, you may still have experienced losses, hurts, or disappointments growing up that affect you still. For example, Danielle was raised by warm, responsible, hardworking parents. When her father lost his job and the family floundered financially for over a year, Danielle responded by helping to care for her younger siblings while her mother worked a part-time job. Danielle stopped asking her parents to buy her the latest product that all her friends had and instead quietly put aside her personal desires so she could help her family.

Now, in a serious relationship with Louis, they begin to have difficulties. She avoids discussing issues and automatically accommodates his wishes for the sake of harmony. However, after a while, she begins to feel resentful, unhappy, unappreciated, and unfulfilled. "When can I get what I want?" she laments. Of course, someone else with a similar background might respond just the opposite to Danielle and insist they get their way in a relationship to make up for the sacrifices that were made in childhood. In either case, it results in personal and relationship disharmony.

Identifying Unmet Needs

It is common for people to identify the following unmet needs:

- Acceptance
- Achievement
- Affection
- Approval
- Attention
- Being listened to
- Comfort and soothing/reassurances when afraid
- Empathy
- Encouragement
- Forgiveness
- Freedom from too many responsibilities
- Guidance
- Influence
- Love
- Not enough responsibility
- Nurturance
- Safety and security; freedom from harm
- Stable and predictable home life
- Trust of others/being trusted

The more a need goes unmet, the more you will either under- or overreact in your current relationship when there is a triggering reminder that you have an unmet need. For example, if you wanted affection as a child but did not get enough, you might crave affection as an adult and never feel satisfied with what your partner offers. Or, you might withdraw from affection to avoid getting hurt, in case the affection you desire is not forthcoming on a consistent basis.

A different dynamic can occur when one or both parents were physically or emotionally unavailable to you as a child. Maybe one parent was always working, there was a divorce, or both parents were around but at least one was critical or rejecting. In this case, many children learn to fend for themselves emotionally when they face typical childhood problems such as school difficulties, feelings of incompetence, issues getting along with friends, and so forth. They learn that talking about their problems at home gets them nowhere, so they learn to act independently and make their own decisions. Such children grow up to be less adept at communicating, tend to mull things over without sharing their thoughts, and dislike being told what to do. This lack of skill in connecting and sharing with others can result in relationship conflict, because negotiation, empathy, and give-and-take are required.

What to Do Differently

Once you both identify how lingering unmet needs are playing out in your relationship, there are steps you can take to reduce the times when this dynamic negatively affects your interactions. For instance, Jim and Sally both felt oppressed growing up. They had little choice over what happened to them as children, and when they complained, they were usually ignored. So now, when they disagree about where to live after they marry, each feels oppressed by the other and reacts by being stubborn and demanding—which only makes each of them feel more oppressed.

When you identify that unmet childhood needs are being triggered in one or both of you, stop and carry out the steps below:

Step 1: Identify—aloud and in a non-blaming tone—to your partner when a current divisive issue has its root in your childhood. For example, "When we're out on a date having dinner, and you're on your phone checking emails and texting your friends, it makes me really mad, because it reminds me of my father ignoring me all the time."

Step 2: Inquire what need your partner has that you aren't meeting. In the scenario above, you might ask, "What would help you not feel ignored?" Explore both of your perspectives about why the issue at hand is important. For example, you might say, "I guess I could ignore my phone messages, but sometimes it's work related and I have to respond" or "You're right. That probably is a bit rude, but to be honest, I sometimes feel a little smothered—that unless I give you my full attention every minute I'm doing something wrong."

Step 3: Try to come up with a plan of action that takes into consideration both sets of needs without making it a win-lose competition. She could start the conversation this way: "What can we do so that you don't feel so smothered or guilty for taking work-related calls but I won't feel ignored or overlooked?" With goodwill and creative ideas, most couples can find ways to get mutual needs met without feeling resentful.

Your past will play out in your present relationship—for good or ill. Knowing your unmet needs and strategically meeting them both as individuals and as a couple will help with preventing conflict. Remember that you can only meet *some* of each other's needs, so include in your plans actions others can take as well. For example, friends can be great listeners.

You may also benefit from relationship skill-building courses, coaching, or counseling to learn new ways of interacting. Conscious awareness, understanding, compassion for each other's childhood difficulties, and a willingness to move maturely forward without being dominated by leftover childhood needs will help you establish your marriage on a strong foundation. You can meet your challenges successfully.

Paul Coleman, Psy.D., is a Psychologist and Relationship Therapist in private practice. He is the author of a dozen books including *The Complete Idiot's Guide to Intimacy* and *We Need to Talk: Tough Conversations with Your Spouse*. He has appeared as an expert on the television shows *Oprah* and *Today*. Dr. Coleman and his wife Jody have been married for twenty-seven years, and they have three children. He can be reached at www.paul-coleman.com.

♥ ♥ ♥

Soulmate Skills for a Blissful Marriage
Kathryn Elliott, Ph.D., and James Elliott, Ph.D.

You may have found the love of your life; you just knew from the moment you met one another that this was the one you had long awaited. Or, maybe you're matched up with someone who may not be ideal, but your need and longing has brought you together. Either way, our message to you is this: You can craft your soulmate relationship. It's not a matter of luck or providence–it's a matter of skill!

The Anthetic Listening Skill[1]

This simple communication skill will help you improve your interactions:

- Your partner tells you a feeling they are having.
- All you have to say is, "Can you tell me more about that?"

It's that simple! All it takes is a genuine interest in your partner.

To help you understand how powerful this simple tool is, here's a story of how Jim taught Kathryn to use it before we married:

Kathryn had asked Jim to teach her how to write books, and we had arranged to meet in his room at a conference center for that discussion. Here's what happened:

Jim: "I feel scared."

Kathryn: "Oh, don't feel scared."

Jim: "No, I don't want you to say that. I want you to say, 'Can you tell me more about that?'"

Kathryn: "I can learn that."

And she did. It was the fundamental skill for creating closeness, And so, we began to move into more emotional depth—just as you will when you use this skill.

Here are other examples of how the skill works:

Example 1:

Partner 1: "I feel hurt that our friends didn't invite us to their party."

Partner 2: "Can you tell me more about that?"

Example 2:
Partner 1: "I'm not sure I'm in love with you anymore."
Partner 2: "Can you tell me more about that?"
We know it seems too easy to create amazing results by responding this way, but it's the path to connecting with your partner and creating closeness.

Some Surprising Benefits

A wonderful outcome from this simple skill of Anthetic Listening is that it can so quickly turn things around in unhappy relationships and marriages. The turnaround creates benefits for both the speaker and the listener. If you're the speaker, being heard helps to improve your self-respect. It produces the feeling that you are valued and that what you say really matters to your partner. If you're the listener, it helps to overcome self-centeredness, with the surprising pleasure of getting to know your partner. For both partners, listening in this way creates connection—and that is a warm feeling we all thrive on.

1 *Anthetic* comes from the Greek *anthein*, meaning "the blossoming of a flower." Jim created this term, as well as "Anthetic Therapy," which helps people clear away blocks so they can blossom as an individual or as a couple.

Kathryn Elliott, Ph.D. and **James Elliott**, Ph.D., are therapists and soulmates. Since childhood, they had each longed for closeness and spent much of their adult lives searching for it in a partner. In 1989, at the start of their doctoral program, they found each other. They've enjoyed the great gift of spending the last twenty years married, working as therapists and creating and practicing Anthetic Therapy, their unique approach to individual and couples therapy, as well as learning how to be soulmates. They share their love story, love letters, and unique skills on their website, www.soulmateskills.org. You can gain more ideas for creating your own soulmate relationship in the Elliotts' book, *Disarming Your Inner Critic*, and they are currently authoring *Soulmate Skills*.

♥ ♥ ♥

The Skill of Connecting
Ana Morante

Throughout your relationship, there are going to be many situations in which both of you—sometimes willingly and many times unintentionally—are going to do things that hurt each other. When that happens, it is helpful to not take things personally and especially to have the capacity to forgive each other. It's very important to be able to forgive yourself when you make mistakes and forgive the other person when they do something that hurts you. When we get hurt, we may want to withdraw and start putting up some shields. Then, slowly but surely, we start disconnecting from each other. One of the most dangerous things in a couple relationship is disconnection. If you are able to forgive and move on, you'll be able to keep your relationship strong.

It is vital for couples to maintain the strength of their connection through the challenges of life. The strength and health of a relationship is not measured by how much you fight or not, because you will definitely fight. You need to actually go through many disagreements and solve them together. Sometimes they will be solved, and many times they won't be solved, but at least agree that you don't have to solve every disagreement. Dr. Sue Johnson is a therapist who has done a lot of research about the importance of having a strong connection between the couple. She has found that when that happens, the individual's ability to deal with life, with conflict, or even with physical health problems increases. The immune system of the body increases when we have a strong, secure bond between the two of us.

It is very important to keep your couple connection alive and healthy. When we are just starting to date a person, we are looking for who this person is and what is going in their lives, and we want to know them. After marriage, when we've been together for ten or twenty years, we assume we know them already, but we all change on a daily basis. Going out together—ideally at least once a week and just the two of them—can keep the couple's connection alive. Being aware of the inevitable challenges of marriage and parenthood helps the couple plan for how are they going to first take care of themselves with all the stress and the demands on their shoulders and then keep taking care of their couple relationship. Once we have children, we tend to forget that the two of us are also a couple. Suddenly, our lives start revolving around the kids. When it's date night, forget about the children. Forget about being parents and talk about yourselves, your dreams, what is going on, and your challenges.

Another important practical thing is the ability to have fun together. We know couples do much better when they can have fun together. It's very helpful if they can find similar interests or find something that might be a new shared interest for both of them.

It also increases the strength of your connection when you trust and open yourself up to each other. It's very difficult to get close to someone when you are holding back. Many times, people hold back when they've been hurt. If you've been hurt in life, you're naturally going to keep yourself very guarded. It's very important for a strong couple relationship to be able to slowly start opening up and letting your partner see you for who you are. A healthy couple relationship is one where both of you can risk being who you are, and where you can accept and embrace yourself and your partner exactly for who they are. That is what intimacy is all about.

Editor's Notes: The above is excerpted and edited from an interview between Susanne Alexander and Ana Morante on March 10, 2010. Dr. Sue Johnson, mentioned above, is the developer of Emotionally Focused Couple Therapy and author of *Hold Me Tight, Seven Conversations for a Lifetime of Love.* (www.holdmetight.net)

Ana Morante, L.M.F.T., C.F.L.E., is a bilingual Marriage, Family, and Child Therapist, helping people in both Spanish and English. She is dedicated to strengthening couples and families and assisting in the creation of the best environment possible for children. She has a private practice in San Jose, California, and is a certified Parent and Family Life Educator and a Family Wellness Partner and Trainer. Ana has been married for sixteen years and has two daughters and a stepson. She can be reached through www.familywellness.com.

❤ ❤ ❤

Essential Tools for Keeping Your Relationship in Good Repair
Stanis Marusak Beck

There are often many ways in which each person has the power to help or hurt their growing relationship, especially when communicating. However, most of us are never really taught how to communicate well with a partner, and we wind up having to wing it for better or worse (mostly for worse, unfortunately). You can change this trend by learning excellent communication skills before you marry and carrying them with you into the marriage. What follows are a few of the basic tools for fostering successful partner communication.

Constructive Conversations

Every relationship has its troubles, but it's how we traverse them that matters most. If, for example, a person feels upset by the behavior of their partner and it doesn't go away fairly quickly, it's important to have a constructive conversation about the incident. This prevents it from festering and accumulating enough steam for a delayed explosion. A constructive conversation about a straightforward issue can simply be a one-way communication that follows Haim Ginott's ABC formula:

- A) Speaking from the "I" perspective, identify the problem without using the word "you" at all.
- B) State how the situation makes you feel.
- C) State what you prefer instead.

When you follow this ABC formula, your partner is likely to perceive the communication as very non-threatening. They can usually actually hear what is being said, and they are not prompted to be defensive or critical in response. In fact, no response is quite all right, as it is basically one person just sharing their concern, feelings, and preference and another just receiving the information. Sometimes, this is all that is required to help a couple overcome a small hurdle, since they are fostering understanding.

Active Listening

For more difficult issues that need to be explored more fully, successful couples learn how to become experts at "active listening." This skill involves a specific process:

- The speaker asks the listener when they can talk (sometime that day is best).

- When the couple begins the discussion, the speaker begins to identify the issue in one or two sentences at a time, which the listener then mirrors. Mirroring is simply repeating (or paraphrasing) what the speaker has said without adding anything extra.

- The speaker continues to share (without using the word "you" at all) until the incident is fully identified, including feelings and what would be preferred.

- The listener continues to mirror whatever the speaker says, even if the listener disagrees completely, until the speaker has described the situation fully. The listener adds nothing of their own thoughts to the dialogue but only mirrors what the speaker is saying, until the next step.

- The listener then comes up with one or two feelings they have heard or that they sense the speaker has felt as a result of this conflict and asks if this is correct. The speaker then affirms or denies the feelings and adds to it if necessary. The listener then mirrors any additional feelings identified by the speaker.

- When the speaker is finished, the listener summarizes the one or two main points and then asks if they identified the main points correctly. If so, the listener goes on to make a validating statement, such as, "I hear what you're saying" or "I get what you're saying" or "I understand where you're coming from." The statement does not require agreement with the speaker's perspective, only validation.

- If the listener has not identified the one or two main points correctly, the speaker identifies them and the listener mirrors them before going on to make the validating statement.

- No further discussion is recommended at this time, and there should be only one speaker for a day, not two speakers. The entire process should take no more than forty-five minutes, and if that is not enough time, the active listening should be postponed to the next day, at a time the listener prefers, for a final forty-five minutes. It is not recommended to continue the same discussion beyond two days.

One can see that active listening does not immediately resolve a problem, but it sets the stage for the couple to resolve it. Listening carefully to one another helps to change the climate in your relationship from negative to positive, gives the speaker a chance to get something off their mind and share emotions in a constructive way, gives the listener an opportunity to see the situation from the speaker's point of view, and fosters understanding and empathy. This understanding and empathy, along with an improved climate, makes it much easier to resolve the problem later. Though it takes a bit of practice to get it right and often feels somewhat mechanical at first, active listening can be one of the most powerful tools to ultimately resolve conflict constructively.

Deepening Your Connection

Nourishing a relationship is important, and spending quality time together regularly is essential for keeping the emotional bank account healthy and happy. Too many withdrawals from the account—like arguing, criticizing, and complaining—drain the emotional bank account instead, leading the relationship to bankruptcy. Filling your life up with non-relationship activities also often leads to an overdrawn account. If either of you already have children, they can become such a focus that your relationship may suffer, so remember to stay balanced.

Love maps are a constructive way to get to know one another well as partners and keep you connected. This is a tool recommended in marriage researcher John Gottman's book, *The 7 Principles for Making Marriage Work* (written with Nan Silver). Couples are asked to write down (or draw) a map of everything they know about their partner and then have a discussion sharing the results and filling in the blanks. You can consider such aspects as:

- Everyday life
- Wounds in the middle of healing
- Upcoming events
- Who they are striving to be

- Favorite activities and high priorities
- Best friends
- Current fears, stresses, and worries
- Irritants
- Life dreams
- Religious beliefs and ideas
- Basic philosophy of life
- Favorite music, movies, TV shows
- Most special times in life
- Childhood traumas/stresses
- Major aspirations and hopes
- What they would do with a major sum of money

Learning as much as we can about our partner, what they like, how they think, and all the little details of their preferences and dislikes keeps the communication lively and interesting. Once married, though, other things can take priority. Creating new love maps when you realize you are not as connected as you wish to be can help you be as sensitive and understanding as you initially were with each other. Love maps are a tool that can help you to keep your relationship humming along smoothly.

Understanding and Meeting Needs

Finally, it will help you prepare for marriage to have some knowledge about Abraham Maslow's Hierarchy of Needs and how that knowledge helps you with having constructive communication. We all have basic human needs that have to be met if we are to be content in our primary relationship. Maslow identifies them as: physical needs (food, clothing, shelter); safety and security; respect and recognition; belonging; and self-actualization. Usually, based on our family history, one of these categories of need is more dominant than others for each of us. It can lead to an escalation of problems in your relationship when your primary needs are not addressed well.

During a conflict or a time of being upset, you will notice that you are angry at your partner. However, anger is often a secondary emotion. If you think about what made you feel angry in the first place, you can usually trace it back fairly easily to an unmet need. Then, if you speak to your partner about your unhappiness at the needs level instead of the anger level, you will make constructive progress in resolving the issue.

Sometimes, unfortunately, one's past history will have a tremendous negative impact on one's present relationship (as Harville Hendricks's Imago Theory makes clear; www.gettingtheloveyouwant.com). In that case, you may be wise to seek the services of a professional before you marry. Whether you need counseling or not, however, becoming very familiar with these five essential tools will help you to enhance your relationship or mend your communication and relationship problems and prevent expensive repairs after you marry.

Author's Note: Columbia University's Teachers College Conflict Resolution Program put together Maslow and active listening.

Stanis Marusak Beck, M.S.W., A.C.S.W.-R, M.A., a Clinical Social Worker since 1973, has received post-graduate training through Manhattan Center for Advanced Psychoanalytic Studies in New York City. She co-founded the Long Island Institute for Psychotherapeutic Studies and is experienced in a number of mental health settings, where she has functioned as both advocate and supervisor. She has supervised graduate social work students in the field placement services for Adelphi, Fordham, and Yeshiva Graduate Schools of Social Work and for graduate counseling students from C. W. Post. She has been approved as a Feminist Therapist by the South Shore Chapter of N.O.W. and has published in the field of psychotherapy. She is a Diplomate with ACSW, Diplomate with NASW, and was a Board-certified Diplomate with the American Board of Examiners in Clinical Social Work. She completed a post-graduate M.A. program at Columbia University (Graduate Studies in Conflict Resolution and Organizational Psychology) and is a New York State Mediator through International Center for Cooperation and Conflict Resolution. She is currently on the faculty of the Long Island Center for Modern Psychoanalysis. Stanis co-authored *365 Questions for Couples* with Dr. Michael Beck and Seanna Beck. She and Michael Beck have been married since 1967. They live in New York and have two adult daughters. She can be reached at 631-587-1924.

❤ ❤ ❤

Mentoring a Couple Toward Praying Together
Cynthia Sarles and Bill Sarles

This is really two different stories about prayer. First, it is about the two of us building a prayer life together, and then it is the story of the engaged couple we mentored, James and Amy, building their prayer life.

We had been married for twenty-six years when we were invited to become a Mentor Couple at our church. We attended our first training to use *For Better and For Ever*, a program authored and directed by Father Rob Ruhnke. We had not ever prayed together at that point, nor discussed it. Father Rob talked during our training about the value of praying together for our engaged couples, and we weren't even doing that ourselves! We both saved a handout he gave us on praying as a couple and tucked it away, knowing we would have to face it at some point, but kind of dreading it too.

It wasn't until we were doing our mentoring preparation work in *For Better and For Ever* that we faced the challenge. We talked for the first time about how we were going to have to begin praying together if we were going to be able to teach it to other couples. We were very glad to have the steps provided by an article on prayer written by Pat and June Kennedy.[1]

The most helpful part of that article for us was the outline for praying as a couple:

- Facing each other
- Holding hands
- Beginning by praising God for the incredible God that He is
- Asking His forgiveness for the hurts we've inflicted on anyone, but most especially each other
- Petitioning God for what we need
- Finally, thanking God for all the great things He's put in our way

Even with the help, we knew it was going to be uncomfortable and awkward, and it was, but it was also incredibly intimate, joyful, and wonderful! We found that remembering to pray together helped us so much to be honest with each other and brought us so much closer to God and each other.

A few weeks later, we began working with our first engaged couple, James and Amy. He was raised Protestant but didn't really believe in organized religion or go to church. She was raised Catholic, but she didn't attend Mass often.

At our third meeting, we gently introduced the idea of prayer to them and told them that at our next meeting, we would be looking at the chapter on prayer. We said we would like to show them how we pray as a couple and help them to begin that, if they'd like. Immediately, Amy said, "He won't do that." James agreed, saying that he didn't consider himself "religious," and he didn't pray by himself, much less with anyone else. We backed off, telling them not to worry about it, and we wouldn't cram anything down their throats or make them feel too uncomfortable.

So, we panicked and wrote an email to Father Rob asking him how we should handle the problem. We were blessed by this couple in our lives, and we did not want to chase them off or make them dread meeting with us. On the other hand, we didn't want to ignore this wonderful piece of a Christian marriage. Father wrote back to say that this topic could be treated like family of origin, financial, or parenting concerns—something to be put on the table, talked about, and handled with them as it seemed fit. He told us to tell them about our own journey toward prayer and invite them to be open to it as a positive contributor toward their Christian marriage.

We read over all that Father Rob wrote to us many times and talked about it over and over in the days between those two meetings. When James and Amy came back to talk about prayer, we were amazed! James started out by saying he'd had no idea what prayer really was before he read the chapter in Father Rob's book (*For Better and For Ever*). He thought it had to be like what he'd seen on TV. He acknowledged that he did, in fact, do a lot of praying on his own. He just hadn't realized it was prayer that he was doing as he sat at his desk at work, drove home from work, or spent any other time alone in his head.

Before that night, we had been afraid James would refuse to be part of the conversation. Instead, he drove the conversation. He wanted to know how we brought God into our heads as we prayed by ourselves, what we prayed about, how we knew it was prayer and not just thinking, when we had started praying together as a couple, what we said in our prayers, how often we prayed together, if it would be okay to pray silently while he prayed with Amy, and on and on and on. We were so surprised and delighted that he was open to inviting God into his head when he prayed. When we asked if we could give them the Kennedys' article on praying as a couple, they both said "yes," and it was James who reached out to take it from us!

Of the five nights we spent with that dear couple, that was without a doubt the most productive, and they agreed. For them, it was the meeting that brought them closer together and closer to what they wanted for their marriage. In that meeting, all four of us grew closer to God and each other than we had in any of the others.

We asked James and Amy to spend the next few weeks and months developing their prayer lives as individuals, being open to praying together. We asked them to keep the handout, read it, and when they thought they might be ready, to talk about it with each other. We told them we would like to discuss it at our meeting after they'd been married for three months, and we'd be happy to show them how we prayed together at that time, if they were ready.

1 www.marriagepreparation.com/Prayer_by_Pat&June.htm

Cynthia Sarles and **William Sarles** have been married almost thirty years. They are a Mentor Couple with the Galveston-Houston, Texas, Catholic diocese. They smilingly, lovingly, and proudly say they have two perfect children and a perfect grandchild due soon. Bill works for a NASA contractor, and Cynthia teaches math at a community college.

Chapter Thirteen
Creating a Partnership

~ ~

As your relationship grows, you will increasingly find yourself in experiences where the quality of your partnership will be a factor in how well you handle situations. The concept of equality in marriage is evolving, and experts as well as couples are still exploring and learning how it works. Your marriage will be stronger when you can reach agreement on a mutual team approach to key areas such as housework, earning a living, and parenting. As you will see, mutual respect is a vital piece of the puzzle.

It will take conscious effort for you to avoid assumptions and roles based solely on gender and the practices of previous generations. You will also discover that you are in an ongoing learning-in-action experiment, because models of equality in marriage are in the early stages of emerging. You are part of a cultural change, and as such, you will have many opportunities to simply say, "Well, let's try it this way, and if it doesn't work, let's try something new."

♥ ♥ ♥

Let's Face It: Men and Women Communicate Differently
Noelle Nelson, Ph.D.

Are there differences between men and women? Yes, there are! One of the biggest is the way we communicate. Understanding these communication differences will go a long way in helping a marriage get and stay on solid ground.

For women, a common question is, "Why is getting men to talk about anything such a big deal?" The simple answer is: Because it is—for a lot of guys anyway. You see, women are generally great talkers; they express themselves freely to most anybody, anytime, on just about any subject. Gals will start a deep conversation while having their nails done or during a commercial in response to something prompted by the TV show they're watching.

Men are quite different. For starters, men usually prefer to attend to one thing at a time. If they're watching TV, they're watching TV. (Don't be fooled by the channel surfing, ladies; they're still watching TV!) If they're cooking, they're cooking. If they're changing a tire, they're changing a tire. Few men are comfortable doing any of the above *and* having a conversation about something else.

These differences between men and women aren't just anecdotal, they're biologically based. Research has shown that male and female brains are composed of different amounts of gray and white matter. Women's brains contain about 15 to 20 percent more gray matter than men's, which gives women more processing power. This power facilitates their multi-tasking abilities that are so often envied by male friends and spouses. The white matter in female brains is found primarily in that area of the brain which links the brain's two hemispheres, making it easier for women's brains to respond to verbal tasks, which is one of the reasons why women are usually better at talking than their partners are.

Men have more white matter than women do in their brains overall, giving them the uncanny ability to parallel park in two swift, accurate maneuvers, as opposed to women's three or more stabs at it. They can also glance in the trunk of the car and say, "Oh, sure, that'll fit," while the woman in their life is saying, "No way." And, yes, indeed it fits. The white matter is also what allows men's single-mindedness, the ease with which they can focus all their attention on one task, even if that does drive women nuts when they want his attention on several things at once.

The key is respecting each other's biology. As a gal, when you want to talk with your partner or spouse about a matter of consequence, make sure nothing else is going on so he doesn't feel torn between two (or more) points of attention. And then, be attentive and just wait. Many men don't have thoughts just ready to pop out on cue; they have to dig deep and rummage around in their minds so that their next thought will be considered genuine. His thought process deserves your respect, not your impatience.

For men, if your wife wants to talk about something when you're on the computer, say, "Just a moment, Honey," hit pause or save, turn to her, and engage in the conversation. Don't just say "Uh-huh," if you can't think of anything to say. Offer an acknowledgement like, "So, what you're saying is you'd like us to spend more time at the gym together?" Increasing your verbal response to your partner or spouse will go a long way toward her feeling loved and appreciated.

With just a little attention to each other's different brain power, you'll find communicating will become better than you ever thought possible. And that's vital for a good and happy marriage.

> **Noelle C. Nelson**, Ph.D., is a relationship expert and popular speaker in the U.S. and abroad. She is the author of nine best-selling books, including her most recent, *Your Man is Wonderful: How to Appreciate Your Partner, Romance Your Differences, and Love the One You've Got* (www.yourmaniswonderful.com) and *Dangerous Relationships: The Seven Warning Signs of a Troubled Relationship*. Dr. Nelson focuses on how we can all enjoy happy, fulfilling lives while accomplishing great things in love, at home, and at work. Visit www.drnoellenelson.com for more information.

♥ ♥ ♥

In Pursuit of a Mate
Raymond Switzer

Humans, much more than any other creatures, have long-term needs for nurturance and education before being ready to go out into the world. We possess an instinct for mating, but to ensure the best interests and long-term needs for our children, a higher commitment to move into an enduring marital relationship is required. Mere instinct is not enough, and with high divorce rates eroding the very basis of our civilization, it is time to look at some traps we have fallen into in the ways we go about finding and committing to a mate.

Examining Our Patterns of Courtship

An aspect of courtship to examine is one that is happening under the mistaken guise of gender equality. Just as the sexual revolution was in many ways antithetical to the interests of feminism, so is the belief that women—in the name of equality—can simply fall into the role of pursuers of men in finding a mate. As men and women meet each other and get to know one another in their quest for a mate, there is a biological and psychological imperative for men to be involved in the pursuit.

Now that society has given women the go-ahead to go after men, the usually superior female insights and skills in relating will allow them to quickly take the lead. Just as quickly, enjoying the attention and freed from the desperate fear of rejection, men can fall into passivity. Men and women are not behaving as equal partners in this situation. With the man in passive mode, the interests—not only of the man and woman, but also of the future generation of their children—are largely compromised.

The needs women feel in the course of finding a mate are different than for most men. A woman does not need or seek a mate at all costs; she needs a man who will actively commit himself to being and staying married. This allows the woman to feel secure that she will have a caring, supportive partner throughout the very long period that it takes to bring children into maturity. (Cohabiting couples with children are ten times more likely to break up than married couples with children). Even where the roles of financial support and domestic nurturing are shared, if the relationship or marriage breaks up after children are born, in the majority of cases, the woman will bear the brunt of looking after them, even when they are all too often left with meager financial resources.

Further, while there are many great examples of exemplary single parenting (and certainly at times inferior parenting comes from couples who remain together), the overall picture of single parenthood is one that causes challenging consequences throughout the children's lives. There is no substitute for what children receive from happily married parents who grow in their love for each other through the challenges of rearing children and providing for a family.

Even if the laws of society firmly reinforce the need for fathers to stay around to help rear the children, this alone cannot ensure the father's involvement. Nature seems to have left the father's participation to be somehow voluntary, in spite of the fact that spiritually and psychologically his parenting is crucial for the wellbeing of the children. The mother's involvement, on the other hand, is more biologically and emotionally determined. This vital role of men in the family calls for women to take care that the man they are interested in is serious about getting married and being a father if the courtship proceeds well (and carefully).

Research suggests that commitment, for males, is generally different from commitment in the female experience.[1] Women feel committed when they are close to a man, loving and feeling loved. Men love the attention of a woman and appreciate them being around, but they still keep their options open and don't feel committed until they make a decision. In the present dating scene, a woman will often use her feminine wiles to pursue men in the interest of "landing" one. However, even after she feels she has one, she comes to realize this is far from the case. Wanting real commitment, what she is left with in so many cases is the conundrum of dragging her so-called partner toward marriage. Feeling pressured, he resists decision making, finds resistance kicking in, and experiences less and less psychological space to actually make a commitment. From this all-too-common scenario, three possibilities develop for the couple. They will:

- Stay together in extended limbo without marrying;
- Break up before marrying; or
- Marry with the man in a state of ambivalence, putting the marriage on a shaky foundation from the start, with a greater likelihood of ending in divorce.

The imbalance in these familiar scenarios is felt deeply by the woman, who by now has lost precious years of possible child rearing, and her biological clock is ticking. Far from having a biological clock—or even realizing or considering that women have one—men see the couples scene growing more and more in their apparent favor. Older men often look good to younger women and, of course, vice versa. While men also lose big in this process (research indicates that men become generally better and more satisfied human beings when they are married), their egos tempt them with, "What's the hurry?"—especially when they don't have to do the work of pursuing because women have made themselves so available.

What is more, the singles scene as it presently stands enables both men and women to avoid developing some critical, largely gender-related aspects of their respective psyches. For men, this is the need to become decisive, step out, reveal themselves, and risk failure in something that is authentically crucial to them. Women need to connect with their nobility and their worth as women and mothers. Marriage will call forth much more than these basic archetypal gender qualities, but it is almost bound to flounder if these basics aren't in place from the beginning and if the couple has not developed consciousness about their future role in mutually rearing their children.

In many ways, courtship is a rite of passage for the development of these somewhat gender-specific qualities. A woman who has not developed and experienced her worthiness tends to make a poor partner and parent. A man who does not connect inwardly with what he really wants, and doesn't experience the vulnerability inherent in the chase, may never be there fully and confidently as a partner and a father. He may also never feel truly successful in maintaining a loving connection with his wife (something much more than being able to get a female into bed). And, of course, the man who feels dragged into marriage after an already long-term cohabitation will still usually not feel the measure of commitment needed.

A man who has taken the risk, made the decision, and worked hard to overcome his male ego, while pursuing a woman who was not ready to immediately fall into his arms, or who was not willing to pander to his emotional and physical yearnings while waiting for him to get serious about the question of marriage, is more likely to stay present and willing to do the work when the going gets tough.

Commitment and Equality

"…[T]he world of humanity possesses two wings: man and woman. If one wing remains incapable and defective, it will restrict the power of the other, and full flight will be impossible. Therefore, the completeness and perfection of the human world are dependent upon the equal development of these two wings."[2]

Equality between the genders, as stated in the above quotation from the Bahá'í Faith, is crucial for humanity's movement forward into maturity, and that includes in courtship and marriage. However, the challenges of understanding and practicing equality are adding pressure to the age-old institution of marriage. Since we lack working models of equality (and often marriage) in our upbringing, we may enter courtship and marriage limping from this crucial lack in our socialization. Faced with the difficulties this lack entails in the intimate and sensitive domain of couplehood, we tend to want to avoid or escape. High rates of cohabitation and divorce are among the signs that couples are unskilled with equality-related behaviors and orientations.

One orientation crucial to marriage is the need to understand that one's spouse lives—at least to some degree—in a different world, one aspect of which is gender-related. This skill of understanding your partner is needed throughout marriage and presents many challenges. In practice, equality is not a relationship between two who are the same, but a relationship across ego boundaries that recognizes and seeks to understand the reality of the other and honor it. Realizing that this equality is vital motivates the couple to use their capacity to stretch into new behaviors, helping them both to grow in new and positive directions. These are some of the important ingredients for a happy marriage and wholesome family life. They are also important tools for creating unity in the wider circles of diversity beyond the family.

Commitment is vital for successful relationships and marriages, and this includes commitment to practicing equality. Also required is determination to go through the process of learning how to make equality work in marriage. In this, the somewhat gender-specific internal decision-making process of the male needs to be honored and given the space it deserves in making the crucial decisions to move forward in the process of mating.

Similarly, the female needs to connect with her nobility and move out of the reflex of trying to overly please in order to secure a man's attention or keep him near at all costs. The new requirements of marriage make it all the more important to reflect on and change the process we use to get into it. Let's let men show their seriousness (and cultivate it if it's lacking) early in the dating and courtship process, and let's encourage women to connect with their self-respect rather than wear their sense of dignity thin trying to make the men they have set their hopes on become serious. Proceeding in these ways will be better for all concerned.

1 Scott M. Stanley, "What is it with Men and Commitment, Anyway?" Keynote address to the 6th Annual Smart Marriages® Conference, Washington, D. C., July 2002

2 'Abdu'l-Bahá, *The Promulgation of Universal Peace*, p. 317

Editor's Note: For a personal story about the effect of feminism on her search for a mate, consider reading *Marry Him, The Case for Settling for Mr. Good Enough,* by Lori Gottlieb. (Dutton 2010)

Raymond Switzer, author of *Conscious Courtship: Finding Someone to Love for the Rest of Your Life,* is a Canadian Psychologist living with his wife Furugh and their children, Nasim and Nabil, in Gödöllő, Hungary, to help establish the Bahá'í Faith community in that country. He has given seminars and presentations on courtship and marriage in Germany, Poland, Cyprus, Slovakia, Croatia, Austria, England, Greece, the Czech Republic, Turkey, and Italy. He is the only therapist in Hungary trained in Imago Relationship Therapy, and much of his practice involves working with couples. You may visit the Switzer's website at www.switzer.hu.

❤ ❤ ❤

Creating a Flexible Team Marriage
Patty Howell, Ed.M.

Who you are when you meet and first fall in love does not necessarily resemble who each of you might be at various points down what I hope will be a long and happy road together. What you are doing years from now might also change significantly. The high-earning husband I married thirty years ago, who I figured would take care of me, has turned out to be a wonderful husband. I would not trade him for the world, but guess what: I currently earn more than he does. He LOVES that I'm now playing an important role in the financial aspect of our lives, and I'm proud and happy that I can!

This is not the only major shift we've experienced over the course of our relationship. From time to time, each of us has been sick and needed nursing from the other—ranging from chicken soup for the common cold to needing much greater assistance. This includes the time he helped me rehab after knee surgery, wherein he alternately hooked my leg up to a perpetual motion machine, then set up a thermostat-controlled icing machine, a nearly twenty-four/seven nursing regimen that lasted several weeks.

Over the years, our domestic responsibilities have shifted considerably, and on the professional front, sometimes Ralph is the lead player, and sometimes it has been me. Either way, we move easily back and forth across a variety of roles, and we both enjoy the continual variation.

My point is that to have a highly successful relationship, you need to function as a well-oiled team, which includes the capacity to shift roles as times and circumstances change. Premarital conversations are perfect opportunities for you to explore together how flexible each of you is willing to be as a member of this newly forming team. A team's success increases as it can put its best player into the position they are best suited for at any given time, and believe me, who that person is will change over time.

Discuss together possible shifts that might occur during a potential marriage between the two of you and some responses you might have to those changes. Having this discussion in advance will help you shake off any preconceived stereotypes about who should do what, as well as assist you to look at the value of operating with a more flexible approach. Keep in mind that there is much in the future that you cannot anticipate. Anything can happen! You may someday be teaching a month-long workshop in Budapest, as I was a few years ago, and have your husband volunteer to join you there and be your *haus frau*. I then saw him revel in the simple joys of shopping for food and preparing a wonderful dinner when I returned to our little Hungarian apartment after a long day of training. Believe me, role flexibility can bring you lovely and unexpected rewards!

> **Patty Howell**, Ed.M., A.G.C., is Vice President of Operations & Media Relations, California Healthy Marriages Coalition. Patty is the author of the *Healthy Marriage* series of booklets (available at www.CaMarriage.com), for which she was a 2010 recipient of the Smart Marriages® Impact Award. Patty and her husband, Ralph Jones, have taught relationship skills in fourteen countries around the world and are co-authors of *World Class Marriage* (available at Amazon.com and barnesandnoble.com) and the Sixteen-Hour World Class Marriage Workshop for couples (www.WorldClassMarriage.com). Email: Patty@CaMarriage.com.

❤ ❤ ❤

Gender Equality in Marriage
Susanne M. Alexander

The topic of equality is complex and filled with various emotions and attitudes on the part of both men and women. It has an effect on your relationship now, and it certainly will affect your marriage. Just stop and think about any discussions you've had about who pays for what, who holds the door open for the other, and who (if either of you) will stay home with the kids, and you know how true this is. Consider, too, are you waiting for the man to propose to the woman, or does equality include making a mutual decision or the woman initiating the possibility of marriage?

What Is Equality?

We can define equality as respecting the balanced partnership between two people who work together and honor each other as worthy team members. Practicing equal partnership means that neither of you unilaterally takes control or dictates to the other. You must pay attention to the principle of justice when making decisions together about who does what in your marriage and family and why. For instance, in some marriages, it is a common pattern for couples to begin on an equal footing with education, career, and financial earning ability. However, when children come, sometimes unjust patterns may begin. Often, the wife makes a greater sacrifice of her leisure time, professional accomplishments, and personal fulfillment. And being a mother is not a lesser role; rather, it is a vital one.

Creating Equality

To achieve gender balance, men must be willing to try new actions and ways of treating and interacting with women that do not oppress their minds, hearts, and spirits. They must become champions of equality with women, encouraging and praising their roles, abilities, and qualities. Men have attitudes and habits to change so that they can help create climates that are welcoming to women. Women must also behave with assertiveness and self-respect in claiming their rightful place as full participants in family and society. Each of you can choose to speak with respect, avoiding demeaning, belittling, or insulting the other. Men who truly respect women and think of them as equals actually gain the most. Women who feel respected are more likely to help men achieve their highest potential.

One of the vital purposes of equality of the sexes in marriage is to create a balance of mutual thoughtfulness and shared power in the division of rights and work within your household. If you want to achieve equality in your marriage, it means that the man must try new tasks and responsibilities. Women, in return, learn to respect and accept his efforts as valid, even when he performs actions differently than she might expect. Both of you may need to learn new ways of interacting and accomplishing the tasks required in your home and family. You must both speak up when either of you feels you are not receiving equitable treatment and request new actions and attitudes instead. The key is to mutually discuss and create a plan together for how you will approach what needs to be done rather than making assumptions or dictating to each other.

Equality does not mean sameness; men and women are complements of each other. The most obvious differences are physical, and these will lead to some gender-specific roles, such as carrying and giving birth to a child. However, gender differences can also affect how men and women process and express thoughts and emotions. The different ways they approach issues, communicate, experience emotions, and interpret eye contact are complex subjects that have been the objects of many scientific and psychological studies.

As one example, sometimes the woman may assume the man is lying or avoiding an issue when he looks away during conversation. In fact, it might be that he is trying to calm and de-escalate the discussion. Many women feel intimacy from direct eye contact, whereas men often see it as an aggressive stance. (See *Why Men Won't Talk to Women and What To Do About It* by Paul McWilliams as a resource on this topic.) In exploring this and other differences, the key is to see those differences as areas to understand and accommodate, not necessarily that you are showing disrespect to each other.

Checking for Effectiveness

Below is a brief checklist to help you recognize when you are being *effective* at practicing equality:

- Communicates thoughts and feelings and encourages others to do the same
- Listens carefully to others and respects their point of view
- Honors the participation of others
- Regards both others and themselves as valuable human beings with diverse, valuable contributions to make
- Determines with others in a fair and equitable manner their roles and how they will handle joint responsibilities
- Discusses issues and makes decisions in partnership with others as appropriate and whenever possible
- Learns new skills to increase balance between others and themselves

This next list gives you some warning indications of when you are being *less effective* at practicing equality:

- Gives orders to, makes demands of, or tries to dominate or control others
- Acts as if they are superior or inferior to another or bases interactions on bias, prejudice, or stereotypes
- Expects others to do their fair share of tasks for them
- Insists that everyone's roles and responsibilities be identical or divided along unexamined traditional roles

- Holds back important information, thoughts, or feelings related to a discussion or decision, perhaps devaluing them and thinking they are not really valuable or legitimate or that others are not capable of understanding

Relationship Coaching

1. It is easy to become overly sensitive to the issue of equality and to verbally react or to become defensive and upset when you perceive someone has behaved toward you in an unfair, unequal manner. Take a deep breath, reflect, and discuss the situation together. Remember, you are both learning, and neither of you is likely to be 100 percent right—or 100 percent wrong. Search for the truth as a team together.

2. One way to explore equality in a relationship and marriage is to observe and better understand the relationship your parents had/have. Parents are the first teachers of attitudes and behavior toward the opposite gender.

3. Reflect on your pasts to explore how your behavior and attitudes about equality (both positive and negative) formed through experiences with parents, siblings, friends, and previous romantic relationships/marriage(s). Consider how you treat other people (possibly inequitably) based on such factors as physical appearance, intelligence, culture, race, and monetary factors, as well as gender.

4. You may find it useful to involve family, friends, and peers in discussing what roles and responsibilities you will each have in your future home. These discussions may challenge you to consider new perspectives and choices. They may also assist you in understanding where you are struggling in practicing equality-related behavior. For instance, it may take time for a man to accept that sharing housework does not diminish his masculinity, and doing housework is not a "favor" he is doing for his wife. A woman may also take time to understand that repairing an appliance does not make her less feminine, nor is it a "favor" she is doing for her husband. You are both simply doing the acts of service that move your family forward.

5. If you marry, the household tasks you will each perform will likely shift and change depending on your family's needs, service commitments, work schedules, health, and more. The balance of sharing between you may become unfair without your realizing it. It will help you to prevent this if you ask yourselves at the end of each day, "Was today a partnership?" or "Were we

equitable today?" and "What will we do differently tomorrow to create a balance of equality?"

Susanne M. Alexander is a Relationship and Marriage Coach. She thinks marriages are still in the early stages of practicing equality and hopes her grandchildren will be much better at it than her great grandparents were! (www.marriagetransformation.com)

❤ ❤ ❤

Six Keys to an Outrageously Happy Marriage
Joel Davisson and Kathy Davisson

So, you're thinking of getting married? Congratulations!

We were married in 1984, and our marriage has been what we call "outrageously happy" for the past sixteen years. We've now written two books to help troubled married couples, and today we help couples with troubled marriages on a full-time basis.

But it wasn't always this way.

A Troubled Beginning for Our Marriage

As is the case with many couples, we found ourselves in a mess in about a year.

The mess lasted nine years, as Joel abused Kathy spiritually, emotionally, mentally, and verbally. Kathy often reacted with desperation. She yelled, cried, and threw things. This reaction fueled Joel's fire, as he was able to expertly shift the blame for problems over onto Kathy's shoulders. Joel thought, "After all, I am a great husband! Look at all that I do!" In the seventh year, Joel committed adultery. The next three years were worse than the first! It was "all Kathy's fault," according to Joel—at the time.

Why did Kathy stay in the marriage? Simple: Joel treated Kathy great about half the time (although it was all on Joel's schedule and in the way that Joel dictated), giving her flowers, compliments, dinner, and other dates on a regular basis. We were in ministry, serving as Pastors of a small church. We had a youth ministry and did street evangelism, and we both loved the Lord.

There was one big, huge, gaping problem in the foundation of our marriage though. What we had learned before and after marriage about being married totally misled us.

Marriage Misinformation

We were taught in Bible School, in marriage seminars, and at church that husbands are the leaders of the home and that a good wife will "submit to her husband and follow his leadership." We were taught that a wife is to "respect" her husband, even if he is treating her poorly. We were taught that a good wife will not "nag" her husband and will accept him as he is. This same principle is referred to today as "servant leadership." However you define it, the bottom line is still the same: The husband is the boss. In a good marriage, he is a benevolent dictator, assuming that his wife does not ask or demand much from him. In the worst of homes, the wife is simply a subject in the home of a tyrannical leader.

If we had been taught differently before marriage, Kathy could have been saved from years of intermittent misery, and Joel could have become a mature and healthy husband.

Our hope for you is that you will begin a journey of understanding that will form the basis of what will prove to be an outrageously happy marriage forever! Real success does not include living in turmoil with the one you promised to love, honor, and cherish.

Creating an Outrageously Happy Marriage

If we had understood the following basic concepts before getting married, then we could have enjoyed twenty-six years of happiness instead of enduring ten years of misery and only sixteen great years! These concepts begin in courtship as you establish the foundation of your relationship, and they carry forward into marriage.

1. The husband is the initiator of the good or bad in the marriage. If a husband continues to treat his wife with the same love, attention, and care after they say "I do," then the marriage will stay in a positive place of love and care. Sadly, the idea is often expressed that a woman cannot expect to be her husband's first priority forever. She is told that it is unrealistic to expect that he will treat her forever like he did when he won her heart before the wedding. If you nurture your wife with love, she will overflow with vitality, peace, and joy. She will be well balanced and wise. If you poison her with death, she will be off balance, angry, resentful, or teary-eyed. She might be close to certifiable insanity. Either way, you are *the key*.

2. A great marriage is one of mutual submission and mutual change. A husband is to lay his life down for his wife in submission first—and yes, a wife is then to flow in harmony with him in the same way. Many young married men will say, "My wife needs to accept me the way I am." Don't ever say that! If your wife accepts you the way you are, then you are doomed to stay at the level of maturity you are at before marriage. Most men do not realize how immature they are until after they marry.

3. Spouses must show mutual respect. Sadly, we were taught that a wife is to respect her husband and that this is his greatest need! Misusing this teaching was probably the number one killer of our relationship. When Kathy would tell Joel that she did not like something he was doing or not doing, Joel would accuse her of "not respecting" him. Kathy was not disrespecting him when she expressed to Joel that he was hurting her and must stop. The truth is that Joel was supposed to offer respect to Kathy first, acknowledging her value to him and making her happiness his first priority. Happy wife = happy life!

4. Both are on the Leadership Team. We were taught that a loving husband would listen to his wife's opinion and carefully consider her thoughts and feelings. We were taught that he would then make the decisions, relying heavily upon her opinion. We discovered that this is not scriptural. Instead, a husband and wife are to be "one flesh," making decisions together, with a husband putting his wife's desires, hopes, and concerns as being more important than his own. Why? A husband is called to give his life for his wife as Christ gave his life for the Church, not vice versa. Every woman is born with a gift—the deep desire for a bonded, one-flesh relationship with her husband. If a husband works with that desire after you are married by making his wife the priority, listening to her heart, and meeting her needs, they can eliminate the common relationship difficulties that plague so many marriages.

5. The marriage is the number one priority. If Joel had been taught that his most important priority on Planet Earth was Kathy, then many of our problems would have been eliminated. After we got married, work, ministry, and other people became more important to Joel. Kathy was a distant second, third, fourth, or fifth place in his priorities.

Consider how you feel as you are courting your future wife. Do you feel insecure at times? Do you think about her all the time? When she is distant, does your heart drop? Do you want her to love you so badly it hurts? On the wedding day, your wife's heart will turn more intensely toward you. Your heart will be tempted to slowly turn away. You will be tempted to refocus on your next goal—perhaps a hobby, television, or something else. If you are not alert, your wife will slowly lose her position of first place in your heart. If you are not careful and watchful, you may begin to view her as just a tagalong who is to support you in all of your so-called manly activities of life.

6. **You can fulfill high expectations.** Kathy was told that her "high expectations" were not realistic. She was told she could not expect Joel to maintain the romantic pursuit that had hallmarked the couple's courtship. Sadly, that was bad information. The truth is that God puts a picture or dream of a great marriage in the heart of every woman. A husband's job is to participate in bringing that picture of a great marriage into existence. He can only help to bring it to pass if a wife is allowed the freedom to share her dream with him regularly, and if he grants her the permission to mold or influence him into being the man that she dreams he can become.

These are just a few of the keys we teach couples today. Unfortunately, we are doing "marriage repair" most of the time! If couples would learn these concepts BEFORE getting married, then they could avoid needing our help in the future! If we had understood these concepts ourselves, and if we had regular support of these principles at church and from counselors, then our entire marriage could have been one of happiness and joy.

Marriage is God's best idea for our happiness. Yes, a husband will have to sacrifice a lot of selfishness and self-centeredness in order to make his life all about her happiness. When he does this and maintains this approach, he will experience the happy life that he enjoyed in the days of courtship.

The bottom line of our approach is common sense: If a woman is happy when her partner is pursuing her in courtship, then she will stay happy if he continues that pursuit after the wedding. If she basks in the sunshine of him making her his number one priority in courtship, she will continue to enjoy the limelight after they say their wedding vows.

Good premarital counsel could have saved us from the years of misery that resulted from the wrong teachings we were exposed to. Today, after seeing the Church ravaged by a 50 percent divorce rate, many people are realizing that the old paradigms of marriage simply do not produce happiness and joy.

We are here to tell you that you can live a "happily ever after" marriage! Your hope for joy and happiness is attainable.

Joel Davisson and **Kathy Davisson** identify themselves as husband and wife, parents, friends, pastors, and authors. They have been married for twenty-six years (sixteen of them happy years) and have four children: Chris, Jenifer, Josiah, and Shekinah Glory (who went to Heaven in September 2008). Joel and Kathy have written two life-changing books that teach many new paradigms of marriage, *The Man of Her Dreams/The Woman of His!* and *Livin' It and Lovin' It!* Miracles happen everywhere they are read. Many marriages have also been touched by their live seminars and personal appearances. You can contact Joel and Kathy at joelandkathy4@aol.com or by calling 386-206-3128. You can order the books, DVDs, and CD sets of these teachings at www.bestmarriage.com or www.godsavemymarriage.com.

❤ ❤ ❤

Do You Respect One Another?
Scott Haltzman, M.D.

Remember that line? You know, the one you've seen in movies about a million times? It's a scene where the guy and gal throw themselves onto the bed, and, in the midst of ripping off all their clothes and struggling to get under the covers, the woman turns to the man and asks, "Will you respect me in the morning?"

On one level, the meaning of this question is quite obvious. Traditional social mores suggest that women who go to bed with a man on the first date are less reputable than those who hold back until marriage, or least, "until we've gotten to know each other better." The movies and novels that return to this theme are demonstrating that schism between what we ought to do as upright members of society and what our passions push us to do, particularly when there is a strong sense of romantic attraction. Invariably, as theatrics would have it, this discourse concludes with solid reassurances on the part of the man that, indeed, he will fully respect his lady in the morning. And so the story goes.

But there is another level in which the question of respect—whether posed in the throes of a cinematic one-night stand or never verbalized at all during the course of a long courtship—is of vital importance in the evolution of a relationship. It is this deeper nature of respect and how individuals can sustain mutual positive regard for their partners that are so very important to the long-term success of a relationship.

Respect isn't the first thing you think of when you begin your search for that special someone. In fact, the first order of business is simply trying to figure out whether the person you have your eye on has any interest in even talking to you! I can remember back when I was in my teens and early twenties, that gut-wrenching feeling when I anticipated approaching an attractive girl to try to talk to her. Today I can say that I was experiencing a heightened level of anxiety, but I didn't know those medical terms back then. It was simply a sick feeling in my stomach, a sense of dread, and a playing and replaying of a thousand different scenarios in my head. Many of those scenarios included an escape plan to be instituted at the first moment of rejection, but often I never had a chance to bail out because I aborted my mission even before I spoke to her. Just finding out whether somebody liked you was as difficult as winning the Nobel Prize in physics.

With all the emotional turmoil that goes into asking for a first date, you would think humans would never find romance at all. Yet evolution and the Higher Power that directs human behavior have somehow devised a way for men and women to get together in spite of the odds. But, as a new relationship emerges, another task befalls the two interested parties: Are they a good fit?

These two heretofore romantic strangers must figure out whether they are compatible. This complicated task is trickier than it seems, because when two individuals like each other, their immediate assumption is that they are, in fact, very compatible, and they find much incontrovertible evidence that this is true. He likes movies; she likes movies! A match made in heaven! Forget, for the moment, that 85 percent of all young adults state that they like going to the movies (I made that statistic up, but it *could* be true). They both like pizza, and they both hate chopped liver! Be still my beating heart! Could this be the real thing? When two individuals want to find commonalities, they will find them, and they're convinced that the special connection is proof that they should be together.

Of course, similar interests are important. But as the relationship evolves past the first meeting, and two individuals hone in on each other's positive attributes, it's natural to wish to spend more time with each other, to heighten the level of attraction, and to develop more shared interests simply through hanging out together. Thus, attraction, compatibility, and spending time together are the foundations of every relationship, and it's not a bad start. But many couples believe these elements are all they need, and they rest easy thinking they'll be happy ever after.

However, differences between two individuals who care deeply for each other will naturally arise. In moments of intense discord, it's common for couples to reflect back on the heady romantic days—the days when they were convinced they were meant for each other and only each other—and think, "We were blind!" You may be inclined to wonder how you could have ever thought you were destined to share a life together.

These types of disagreements could be about whether you should live in the city or in the suburbs, whether your partner should be allowed to read copies of the *Sports Illustrated* Swimsuit Edition, or how much money each partner should budget for shoes. Here's the hard truth: When you first met and decided there was an attraction, your focus was on those things you have in common. Now, after spending more time with each other, you're beginning to notice those things that make you different from each other.

So, what strategies can you use to move forward in the relationship and not get mired down in resentment, anger, or frustration? What's the best road to take when you are disagreeing about living quarters, appropriate reading material, or whether your girlfriend has the right shoes to match her dress?

The key to overcoming obstacles as the relationship moves forward is that very same factor that movie studios interweave into those ecstatic one-night stands: respect. It is essential for finding a way to tolerate the differences and disagreements between the two of you. Without respect, you can have a lot of fun. You can have wild nights and blockbuster sex. You can see Broadway plays and opening days of Red Sox baseball games. But, without respect, you cannot have a meaningful and long-lasting relationship.

Respect is one of those phenomena that everyone knows when they see it, but they have a hard time pinning a definition to it. When a Cardinal kisses the ring of the Pope, that's respect. When a young man gets up to offer his seat to an elderly person on a bus, that's respect. Likewise, just about everyone has an easy time defining what respect isn't. For instance, when a teenager cuts in line for concert tickets and then proceeds to make a rude gesture when you confront him about it, that's disrespect!

Dictionaries define respect as "doing acts with particular attention, as in *consideration*, and giving a high amount or special regard to others, which would be like *esteem*." These two descriptions of respect are enlightening—and very applicable—when it comes to cementing a powerful and lifelong marital attachment to that person you love so much.

Respect is vital, because when difficult issues confront the two of you, you might not always agree on how to approach them. When your partner or spouse starts to rattle off all the justifications for their point of view, what approach are you going to take? Here's the way long-married couples handle it peacefully: They tell themselves, "Well, that's sure not the way I would look at it, but I think a heck of a lot of that spouse of mine, so I'll do my best to try to demonstrate my respect for their point of view." In effect, what happy couples learn to do is to make an effort to hear what the other is saying without negative judgments. In fact, if anything, their listening is infused with many positive judgments, such as "This person's smart, so maybe there's something I should hear in what they're saying," or "You know, I chose this person, at least in part, for their different way of thinking about things, so maybe I could learn something if I listen carefully."

To allow someone to hold different ideas from yours and still see that person in a positive light is the cornerstone of respect. And it's often during the most trying of times that the ability to respect another person is called into question. A patient of mine described how the husband had forgotten to pick up their child at school and left her stranded for two hours! Another patient told me how his wife had begun to smoke cigarettes again after being told by her doctor that she could die if she continued. It's hard to hold someone in high esteem when they let you down so profoundly.

But what are the options if your partner or spouse disappoints you? If you remove respect from the equation, then all you are left with is resentment and contempt, and the foundation of the relationship crumbles under the influence of these destructive emotions. When we stop and see our partners as complete human beings, with many flaws, and who won't always meet our expectations—shock!—we give them the message that we love them despite the errors of their ways. In effect, you can see beyond their bad actions and inside to the part of them that made you want to be a part of their life. Cultivating respect, then, is cultivating a lasting connection.

The heady days of dating and courting are amazing, but they don't last forever. At some point, like the characters in the picture shows and soap operas, you have to ask whether you respect your partner enough to go forward into marriage. Take your time. Think about it. And if you decide that respect is truly there, then proceed full throttle into the relationship of your life! But hold on for dear life to that respect. Because without it, you'll never reach your destination.

Scott Haltzman, M.D., is Board-certified in Psychiatry and a Distinguished Fellow of the American Psychiatric Association. He is a Clinical Assistant Professor at Brown University Department of Psychiatry and Human Behavior and the Medical Director of NRI Community Services in Woonsocket, Rhode Island. Dr. Haltzman is a member of the "Love Network" of *Redbook* magazine. He co-authored the chapter, "Men, Marriage, and Divorce" in the American Psychiatric Press book, *Men and Mental Health.* He is an internationally recognized speaker, presenting at the annual Smart Marriages® and Happy Families Conference and at the annual meeting of the American Psychiatric Association. Scott Haltzman is the Founder and Editor of www.DrScott.com and www.365Reasons.com and author of *The Secrets of Happily Married Men, The Secrets of Happily Married Women,* and *The Secrets of Happy Families.* Dr. Haltzman has gained international recognition for his work in support of marriage and committed relationships. He has appeared on *The Today Show, 20/20, Good Morning America,* and in publications such as *Time, Glamour, Redbook, Parent's, Cosmopolitan, Men's Health, The New York Times, The Washington Post, The Los Angeles Times, The Chicago Tribune,* and local and national radio, TV, and print. He resides in Rhode Island with his wife of twenty-two years and two children.

Chapter Fourteen
Interacting with Family
~ ~

Family relationships these days often seem to be fractured and distant, and what counts as a "family" seems to be constantly redefined. One of the opportunities in your being together is finding ways to mend relationships and come closer together. Marriages are often more sustainable where there is excellent family support and unity. Parental approval of your relationship and marriage can be a strength as you go forward.

You can learn much from understanding each other's family relationships and seeing how you each interact with your parents. We share how to succeed at marriage, even if your parents divorced. Marriage often brings together two very different families, and your commitment to building harmony will help you as you go through marriage and your family expands with children and/or stepchildren and in-laws.

♥ ♥ ♥

Your Relationship with Your Parents
Molly Barrow, Ph.D.

As you date someone, or as the two of you as a couple begin to talk about marriage, many emotions and stories about your parents are likely to arise. Listen to your tone of voice and attitude about your parents as you talk and share. Resolve to heal any negative emotions that are present.

Be grateful to your parents for your life and your ability to think, move, and reason. The decisions and sacrifices they made in their lives made it possible for you to know life. Perhaps that is all your parents could give to you. Without that, you would not be alive at this point considering marriage.

As an adult, isn't it time to lose the grudges and bitterness for people who failed you in the past? A large majority of the people in your future will also disappoint you, betray you, or hurt you. That comes with life. If you keep your mind on the failures of the past, then your world becomes about failure. Shine a dazzling smile into your life and let the negative go.

An excellent way to approach life is to start believing that you are lucky and that your life is bountiful. Be thankful for the opportunities you have and the people who are coming into your life to love you. Maybe they are already here. You may find there is a short road to happiness when you choose to feel grateful. See what looking forward with hope and an attitude of gratitude can do to change your world.

As you focus on gratitude, is there anything you would like to express to your parents? What role do you want them to play in your wedding and marriage? It's time to determine what will work.

Molly Barrow holds a Ph.D. in Clinical Psychology and is the author of *Matchlines for Singles, Matchlines for Couples, How to Survive Step Parenting*, and the *Malia and Teacup* self-esteem building series for young readers. An authority on relationship and psychological topics, Dr. Barrow is a member of the American Psychological Association, Screen Actors Guild, and Authors Guild, and is a licensed mental health counselor. Dr. Barrow has appeared as an expert in the film *My Suicide*, the documentaries *Ready to Explode* and *KTLA Impact*, NBC news, PBS *In Focus*, and on WBZT talk radio. She has been quoted in *O Magazine, Psychology Today, Newsday, New York Times, CNN, The Nest*, MSN.com, Yahoo.com, Match.com, *Women's Health*, and *Women's World*. Dr. Barrow has a radio show on www.progressiveradionetwork.com and is a columnist for www.Menstuff.org. Dr. Barrow has a counseling practice in Naples, Florida, and is happily married with a wonderful family including three children, one daughter-in-law, and two precious grandsons. Her website is www.drmollybarrow.com; Blog is: http://drmollybarrow.blogspot.com/; Twitter is: www.twitter.com/drmollybarrow; Live & Archived Radio Shows are: www.progressiveradionetwork.com/the-dr-molly-barrow-show/

❤ ❤ ❤

Check Out the Family
John Van Epp, Ph.D.

Childhood experiences are some of the strongest predictors of what someone will be like as a spouse and parent. The *imprints* from your families and growing-up experiences are a crucial, but often overlooked area to get to know when considering marrying. When you meet members of each other's family and hear the stories of your growing-up years, it's vital to consider the relevancy it all has to your relationship and the ways you will treat each other and your children in the future.

A Couple's Experience

Carla was attracted to George's easygoing nature. His parents were divorced, and George lived with his Mom and two sisters most of the time. He only lived with his father for two weekends a month. He never created many waves with his Mom, although she was fairly dominant and bossy. Carla just blamed George's mother's angry and controlling ways on the challenges of being a single parent. Many times, Carla and George had talked about his Mom—from an off-hand grumble to extensive gripe sessions. But never had Carla considered the effect that George's relationship with his mother would have on his attitude toward her as his wife in a future marriage.

After they were married, Carla noticed that George was less attentive and more aloof. She tried to talk with him about it, but he became defensive, accusing her of being critical. She backed off, but in a short amount of time, a pattern developed where she found herself practically chasing George for attention, help around the house, and even time together. His relaxed temperament that had originally seemed so appealing now appeared to be lazy and unloving. In the heat of an argument, she had a key insight as she mumbled under her breath, "I feel more like his mother than his wife." For the first time, Carla realized that George's relationship with her was following the same script as George's relationship with his mother.

Carla's insight was meaningful to her but certainly not original. She must have never heard or taken to heart the age-old wisdom, "Before you marry a man, check out the way he treats his mother, because you can be sure that is how he will treat you." Although this saying does hold true, it does not go far enough! First, this saying should be modified to apply to both genders. George should have been checking out Carla's family background just as seriously as Carla should have been looking at the implications of George's upbringing. In addition, there are definitely more family issues that both should have considered than just his relationship with his mother.

So, should Carla have dumped George and simply found a man with the perfect family? Good luck with that! Obviously not—but there are a number of relationship "scripts and templates" that you learn from your family that can be explored, examined, and revised before you create a marriage and family of your own. These changes are much more easily accomplished before marriage than afterwards.

Carla and George could have avoided many of the conflicts that eroded their positive relationship if they had taken the time in their dating relationship to seriously address some of their family patterns.

Remember: Patterns from childhood often recur in adult relationships unless concerted efforts are made to change. You can discover these dormant seeds during your dating and courting time, as well as during your engagement, with open and honest reflection, observation, and communication.

Take a Practical Approach

It is hard to find the right answers when you are not asking the right questions. Consider asking each other the following ones:

- What was your relationship like with your parent or caregiver of the same gender?
- How did your relationship with your same-gender parent affect what you learned about the role of being a husband? A wife? A mother? A father?
- How did you learn to handle differences or conflicts in a marriage and family setting?
- What was your relationship with your parent or caregiver of the opposite gender?
- How has your relationship with your opposite-gender parent affected your view and expectations of a spouse in marriage?
- What behaviors and practices would you want to repeat, revise, or discard from your family experiences growing up?

Cultivate many conversations about the experiences and effects of your family backgrounds. Define the roles you would like to have in your marriage, and then compare how these roles are similar or different to what was practiced in your families. Ask yourself and your partner: "How have we changed the areas that we do not want to repeat from our families so that we can have the relationship we desire?" The time and energy you take to unearth many of the seeds that were planted from your family experiences will empower you to more accurately see and direct your future.

In addition to talking with one another, it is also very important whenever possible to spend time in person with each other's families. This includes time with parents and siblings individually (as well as any key influential others, such as grandparents), as well as time with the whole family together. You will observe and learn different aspects about each other in all of these circumstances.

Exploring your family backgrounds is prudent and wise. You can remove the blinders of love and look at your partner *and* your future with confidence when you know the questions to ask and the areas of your relationship to explore and change.

John Van Epp, Ph.D., President/Founder of *Love Thinks, LCC* is the author of *How to Avoid Falling in Love with a Jerk* (McGraw-Hill), which blends in-depth research with humorous stories to provide a map for making healthy relationship choices. His twenty-five years of clinical experience and extensive research in premarital, marital, and family relations have paved the way for his teach-out-of-the-box courses, PICK (How to Avoid Falling for a Jerk) and Marriage LINKS to be taught in thousands of churches, singles organizations, educational settings, and social agencies in all fifty states, ten countries, and by more than 2,500 military personnel. Van Epp and his innovative Relationship Attachment Model, book, and relationship courses were awarded the Smart Marriages® Impact Award in 2008, and they have been featured in *The Wall Street Journal, Time, Psychology Today, O Magazine,* and *Cosmopolitan.* Dr. Van Epp has appeared on the CBS *Early Show, The O'Reilly Factor, Fox News,* and *Focus on the Family.* He has been happily married for over thirty years and is the proud father of two daughters. His website is www.lovethinks.com, and he can be reached at vanepp@nojerks.com.

❤ ❤ ❤

"If Our Parents Divorced, Can Our Marriage Succeed?": Striving for Unity in an Era of High Family Fragmentation

Elizabeth Marquardt

As any clergy member or wedding planner can affirm, nothing is simple in planning today's weddings. The bride's or groom's parents are often divorced. There might be stepparents, Mom's boyfriend, Dad's new wife, and a slew of siblings, including biological, halfs, and steps. All the different relationships might add in new cultures and faiths. Where do you put everybody? Whom do you honor, and how do you do it? How do you plan one coherent wedding out of all of these pieces?

It turns out that the wedding day is only the beginning. With high rates of family fragmentation, today's couples quite often bring a potent mixture of high hopes, uncertainty, and loss into their marriages. Even if their own parents did not divorce, they have seen it all around them. If so many people can't make it, they ask themselves, "How can we? Can our hope for a unified, lasting family become a reality?"

My colleagues and I have heard this theme of having high hopes but few models time and again. In a study of college women, those from divorced families generally told us they were eager to marry, yet they were more likely to be uncertain that their marriages would endure. We asked, "If you marry, do you expect your marriage to last for a lifetime?" Those whose parents had divorced said things like, "Hopefully. From what I've seen, it looks doubtful" or "Well, I would hope so. I know [many marriages] fail, but I hope I'm going to be one of the [lasting marriage] statistics" or "I hope so. I really do. I saw what happened to my mom." [1]

Divorce not only affects the marriage dreams of young people, but it also significantly changes their relationships with their parents. In a national study of young adults in the United States from divorced and intact families, those from divorced families more often felt the need to protect their parents emotionally, especially their mothers. They were more likely to report that when they were growing up, they felt too responsible for taking care of their mothers and fathers. While most of these children do love and respect their parents, they were substantially less likely than their peers from intact families to agree strongly that they share similar moral values with their mothers and fathers, that their parents taught them clearly the difference between right and wrong, and that they consider their mothers and fathers to be good people. They were more likely to agree that they had struggled with forgiving their mothers and fathers. A surprising number even said they doubt the sincerity of their parents' religious beliefs.[2]

For at least some of these young people, it might be tempting as they contemplate their wedding day to leave all that behind. "Let's forge a new path, just the two of us," they might think. While that desire is understandable, it is perhaps not the wisest choice.

Marriage does many things. Among them, it constructs a narrative that connects a couple back to the families from which they came and forward to the families their own children will someday form. Marriage has the potential to be a powerful force that satisfies longings for unity, family love, and wholeness deep in the human heart. Given this potential, a couple's courtship, wedding planning, and early marriage can and should be about much more than just the couple themselves. The process of developing a relationship with a partner can also be a time to grow in one's relationship with one's own parents, to establish a new maturity, and to set the tone for positive family interactions for the future.

Religious communities of all types generally see a role for mothers and fathers in the courtship, marriage, and family formation of their own children. One example of the role parents can play is found in the Bahá'í Faith, which has marital and family unity among its key teachings.

In the Bahá'í Faith, grown children have the choice of their marriage partner without interference from their parents. Parents can give general input, especially if asked, but they don't choose the partner, arrange the marriage, or discourage a choice of partner before the couple makes a marriage decision. But, somewhat uniquely, the laws of the faith require that all living, natural parents (no matter their own faith tradition) give consent before the marriage can take place. As parents make this decision, they are encouraged especially to consider the character qualities of their child's potential husband or wife—the virtues that person seeks to live out in their life—and to take their own child's happiness into account. Once the parents give their consent and the marriage takes place, they are to wholeheartedly support and love the new couple and the family they form.

The central theme of the consent process is unity. The process is intended to help the grown children grow in love and respect for their parents; to engender closeness among the family members; and, ultimately, to strengthen the family as the core building block of society. More than anything, the process of consent encourages and requires an openness and building of trust too often lacking in many families (and not just divorced families). In the rush and tumble of fractured daily lives, young people swept up in passionate emotion, high aspirations, and sometimes deep uncertainties are encouraged to bring these thoughts and feelings to the people whose physical union is responsible for their Earthly lives: their parents. It is hard to imagine a more productive way to start a new family than the kind of earnest, back-and-forth discussion this process encourages.

There is much that can be learned from this model. If you and your beloved are thinking about marriage, talk to one another about your families of origin. What did you learn about marriage—good, bad, or otherwise—in your families? How do you imagine your own marriage being alike or different? What role would you like your parents to have in the family that you form? What role do you think they should have? How do you envision their involvement as grandparents?

Once you have begun a productive discussion with your future spouse—even if it's been years since you lived at home and even if you've already been divorced before—consider bringing the conversation to your parents. If they live far away or if you've lost touch with one or both of them, seek them out. As much as possible, help them get to know your partner (and you!). Have a discussion about the character traits you think you would each bring to the marriage. Ask your parents for their insights and wisdom. Consider seeking their blessing.

All around us, we see much brokenness in families. Our grief over that brokenness affirms the timeless longings of the soul for wholeness. Planning a wedding and starting a marriage can be a time of many productive and affirming new beginnings. One of those new beginnings can be a renewal and healing of your relationship with your own parents. If with grace you can achieve it, you, your children, and society will be stronger for it.

1 Norval Glenn and Elizabeth Marquardt, *Hooking Up, Hanging Out, and Hoping for Mr. Right: College Women on Dating and Mating Today* (New York: Institute for American Values, 2001), 52.

2 Reported in Elizabeth Marquardt, *Between Two Worlds: The Inner Lives of Children of Divorce* (New York: Crown Publishers, 2005). See Appendix B in the book for the data summarized in this paragraph.

Elizabeth Marquardt, M.Div., M.A. (international relations), is Vice President for Family Studies at the Institute for American Values (www.americanvalues.org). She is also Editor of the Family Scholars Blog (www.familyscholars.org) and can be contacted through that site. Elizabeth is the author of *Between Two Worlds: The Inner Lives of Children of Divorce* and many research studies. She lives near Chicago, Illinois, with her husband and two children.

♥ ♥ ♥

Unity Supports Family Happiness
Susanne M. Alexander

You are assessing your relationships with your families and creating your vision of what forming a new family will look like for the two of you. In this process, consider the principle of *unity*.

Think about how you feel when you are not getting along with someone, especially with each other. Your stomach hurts, your head aches, and you might be angry. Disagreements, arguments, contention, strife, or fights—whatever the reason—are signs of disunity. The very survival of your relationship depends upon maintaining a high level of unity. When you think of unity, think of words like affinity, attraction, unison, harmony, affection, togetherness, reconciliation, and oneness. What would a relationship be like if those were your primary focus?

When you are practicing unity, you find points of harmony with each other. This does not mean you do not have different opinions, viewpoints, or aspects of your personalities or lives. Think of a garden of flowers: Each one can be different in color or fragrance, but they blend into a harmonious whole. Consider a choir of different voices working together to achieve a beautiful song. The goal is for you to share your thoughts and feelings in a respectful way that does not harm your partner and for the two of you to work together to come to a peaceful agreement. You are friends, and your bond is vital to both of you. Sharp words and cutting actions can fray and sever that bond over time.

Biologically, union between two entities creates life and growth. Unified married couples are the foundation for unified families, communities, and a global society. For this reason, disharmony among family members or arguments about your family are very harmful. When there is unity, families instead experience prosperity, emotional comfort, security, tranquility, and happiness. Unity has enormous power. It calls on you to reconcile your differences, not magnify them.

Part of what will maintain unity between you in marriage is fairness, an aspect of justice. If either of you regularly feels a sense of injustice with what is happening in your relationship, resentment will begin to simmer. You are both partners in the relationship. Losing that feeling is a clear indication that you have some re-balancing to do to maintain unity. Remember, when you discuss situations, part of what helps you to build unity is involving all those affected by a decision in the discussion leading up to it. This may include your extended family members.

Unity occurs when diverse people—each with their individual talents, abilities, and strengths—come together and build something greater than what can happen separately. Unity flourishes when there is encouragement, support, togetherness, and courtesy. It includes both of you striving to create situations in your marriage where you are both successful.

Unity does not mean you cannot take individual initiative. Yet, acting on your own must not cause problems for each other. This means the two of you must agree on when it is appropriate to act on your own judgment and when it is best to work cooperatively. When you are successful at this cooperative effort, the result is comfort, security, tranquility, and joy.

As your relationship and marriage develop, ask yourselves, "Are the words I'm speaking and the actions I'm taking increasing or decreasing the unity in our marriage and family? What am I doing today to increase the level of unity in our home? In our extended family?" The more consciously you practice unity, the greater the happiness in your marriage, your home, and your family.

Susanne M. Alexander is a Relationship and Marriage Coach. She wants to see "unity" become more of a household word. (www.marriagetransformation.com)

Chapter Fifteen
Forming a Stepfamily

~ ~

Stepfamilies are common these days, so you may be approaching this situation. We skillfully guide you through understanding some of the challenges and pitfalls and how to create a thriving stepfamily. There are many success tips to learn and skills to gain before marriage to reduce challenges after remarrying. We give you a "trail map" for success, help with parenting challenges, and provide you with an excellent example of a couple who prepared well.

♥ ♥ ♥

Coping with Stepfamily Stress and Creating a Thriving Stepfamily
Nancy Landrum

When divorce ends a first marriage, as happens about 50 percent of the time, reasons given are often, "I was immature" or "My spouse turned out to be wrong for me." Second and subsequent marriages have an even higher failure rate however. Researchers agree that the over 65 percent divorce statistic for subsequent marriages is due to the added complexity of issues that need to be successfully resolved in a stepfamily. Lack of good communication and problem-solving skills that may have contributed to the failure of the first marriage become even more problematic in the next marriage. In addition, without realistic expectations and guidelines regarding stepfamily life, there is little hope for a happy marriage or well-adjusted children the second (or third) time around.

In spite of the challenges, it is possible for a stepfamily to thrive. A successful stepfamily is one in which the husband and wife are committed to

learning and using respectful communication skills with each other, their children, and their stepchildren. They hold realistic expectations regarding stepfamily relationships and challenges. The marriage is strong and loving. Appropriate respect is given to the other living or deceased biological parents and extended families. The children feel safe, cared for, and respected by the adults in their lives and their stepbrothers and stepsisters.

On the path to thriving as a stepfamily, couples have challenges to handle and new behaviors to learn. In addition to the normal stresses of adjusting to a new marriage, researchers have identified other potential stressors for those who re-marry with children. Some of these are cultural and will, hopefully, change over time. As for others, however, each couple has the power to reduce or eliminate them with new skills to learn and choose. Investing the time and commitment to change what you can has a huge impact on whether or not your marriage and stepfamily will thrive.

Stressors over Which You Have Little or No Control

1. **Negative Stereotypes of Stepparents.** We all know the stories about wicked stepmothers. Some of us heard them from early childhood—the story of Cinderella being the most well known. The stories in the news or from friends about abusive stepfathers permeate our consciousness. Forming a stepfamily with the determination to "not be one of those" makes the adjustments even harder.

2. **Lack of Societal Support.** The structures rarely exist to help separated and remarried parents stay connected to the child and in communication with each other. For example, few school systems are set up to deliver duplicate messages and report cards to a child's parents who live at separate addresses, and especially are not set up to include any stepparents. Maintaining open communication with a former partner or spouse while attempting to co-parent a child is even harder.

3. **The Complexity of Relationships.** With a nuclear or "first" family, the family unit is under one roof, and the interactions are straightforward and relatively simple, although, granted, sometimes dysfunctional. For *most* stepfamilies, co-parenting (acting as though you are the biological parents) of all the children—yours, mine, and ours—doesn't work very well. Consequently, the researchers have recommended that the bio-parent act to parent their own bio-children. This means administering all the discipline

and making all major decisions about your own child. This separation sets up a tricky duality in the home that has to be handled with patience and maturity.

4. The Age of the Children at the Time of the Marriage/Stepfamily Formation. In most cases, the younger the children, the easier the adjustments, and the older the children, the more challenging the situation is for everyone. And please don't think that if the children are grown and on their own that it will automatically be any easier! Questions of support, time spent, inheritances, and more color even those step-relationships.

5. Length of Time Since the Death or Divorce. This, of course, is largely within your control, although when you meet a potential new partner usually is not. But, often, the blinders are on when the heart is smitten, and you may push forward faster as a result. In reality, this issue straddles the line between "beyond control" and "within your control." It is listed here primarily because so many couples don't realize the size of the challenge they've embarked on until *after* they're married.

Most divorced or widowed people remarry within two years. The research validates that it takes between three and five years to recover from the trauma of a death or divorce. Take the time to do the math, because post-adjustment issues will complicate the new marriage.

Stressors over Which You Have Full Control— and New Behavior Choices

1. Recognizing Poor Communication Skills and Learning New Ones. Difficulty in communicating is listed as one of the major causes of second and subsequent marriage failures. Learning new, better communication skills requires very little money or time. It does, however, require strong commitment and perseverance. It isn't easy to change the communication habits you've developed over a lifetime. The rewards, however, are spectacular: deeper intimacy, greater trust, the healing of old wounds, as well as producing the soulmate relationship that meets your deepest emotional needs. Look for a Relationship Enhancement, Mastering the Mysteries of Love, or Couple Communication class near you.

2. Experiencing Conflicts and Learning Problem-Solving Skills. A high proportion of first marriages that fail are the result of a combination of poor communication skills and poor conflict management. Much pain is the result of these two stressors. Couples who avoid conflict end up as strangers. When one faces conflict and the other hides, no one wins. When both face conflict head-on but without skills, a volatile and sometimes dangerous relationship is the result. Without good problem-solving skills, there is usually a winner and a loser. Good problem-solving skills help you find solutions to issues that are a win-win, and that's a recipe for a happy marriage! *The truth is that conflict, when handled with good skills, is the gateway to greater closeness.* The above recommended classes will teach you how to use conflict resolution to build a stronger, more loving marriage.

3. **Unrealistic Expectations and Learning to Be Realistic.** We live in a world where the marriage paradigm is built around a nuclear or "first" marriage. Stepfamilies have totally different dynamics and require different solutions and practices than first families. Most—if not all—of the problems that break up step-couples are due to unrealistic expectations. They *want* to create a nuclear family out of a diverse mix of wounded adults and children. It can't and won't happen. However, with appropriate skills and a realistic view of stepfamily life, it is possible to succeed.

4. **Lack of Empathy and Learning Empathic Listening.** There is magic when couples step into each other's shoes and see or feel the issue from their partner's point of view. It's amazing what happens when a parent looks at the world through the eyes of their child. We are all more willing to do things differently once we feel the other's pain. Empathic listening is perhaps the most potent and most neglected skill that, when practiced consistently, could lessen the negative effect of all the other stressors. Most of us, however, need coaching in practicing and using this skill. Most of us do not have empathy modeled for us as children. Although we may be touched by the plight of starving children around the world (empathy), we find it much harder to empathically see our partner's point of view in regard to an issue that disturbs or angers us. This skill is essential, not just nice to have.

Author's Note: If either of you has a child from a previous relationship, educate yourselves about the unique dynamics of stepfamilies and align your expectations and actions with the recommendations made. It's much easier to start out with this information than it is to search for it in desperation after a few years of agony. Some additional authors of programs and books that can help you are: Gordon and Carrie Taylor, Ron Deal, Elizabeth Einstein, and Francesca Adler-Baeder. An excellent communications skills program is Mastering the Mysteries of Love, co-authored by Dr. Bernard Guerney, Jr. and Mary Ortwein, M.S. Mastering the Mysteries of Stepfamilies is also an excellent resource, co-authored by Nancy Landrum, Mary Ortwein, and Dr. Bernard Guerney, Jr. Search the Internet for these names or "stepfamily programs" for a wealth of choices. Re-marriage preparation is an essential investment!

Nancy Landrum, M.Psy., lived through the stepfamily experience with her husband Jim and their children. She helps couples in which at least one spouse has a child from a previous relationship to learn the skills and guidelines that enable them to build a strong and loving stepfamily marriage. She is the author of *How to Stay Married & Love It! Solving the Puzzle of a SoulMate Marriage*, co-author of the program Mastering the Mysteries of Stepfamilies, and producer of the DVD *Marriage Skits for Laughter and Learning*. Her website is www.nancylandrum.com, and she can be reached at nancy@nancylandrum.com.

❤ ❤ ❤

The Stepfamily Journey: Not for Wimps
Elizabeth Einstein

Smart hikers prepare well for their adventures. With a good trail map and sturdy equipment, they are ready for most mishaps that might occur. Hard hiking is not for wimps. Likewise, adults moving toward remarriage need the wisdom to prepare well for one of the toughest journeys they may ever take. Such an advance commitment will pay great rewards once you have solid skills and information to build a successful stepfamily in which children and adults can continue to heal and grow.

Like viewing a gorgeous mountain range from afar with high hopes of scaling the peaks, living in a stepfamily might appear at first look to be an interesting and exciting journey. Uninformed and unhealed divorced adults may delude themselves into thinking that with merely a new partner, marriage will be much easier this time. That delusion gets many new stepfamilies in trouble fast—as evidenced by the nearly 60 percent remarriage divorce rate. While not all remarriages include children who can bring great challenges, most do.

Adults who plan to succeed in their stepfamily journey should prepare just as rigorously as experienced mountain hikers who study the terrain, carry proper equipment, and prepare a backup plan to ensure success. Dreams, high hopes, and crossed fingers alone won't create successful stepfamily living. Thankfully, you now have resources that weren't available to me as I dealt with stepfamily issues personally through two marriages and divorces. A second divorce had a huge negative impact on all of our children as they tried to move into adulthood with serious loyalty conflicts and their own emotional baggage. Today, there are books, workshops, and educational programs to provide the guidance and tools stepfamilies need to succeed. To not use all that's available today is like attempting to climb a serious mountain wearing a daypack and sneakers. It's foolhardy—and dangerous!

Stepfamilies differ in so many ways—mainly in structure and development. A simple "trail map" outlines the five stages of the stepfamily journey.

Stage 1: The Fantasy Stage

Like hikers with overweight backpacks, many adults enter the remarriage trailhead in the Fantasy Stage. They are overloaded with unrealistic expectations, unresolved grief, and a lack of knowledge of what's ahead, believing the romantic and Hollywood notion that love can conquer all. When adults join up too soon or before they have cleared up relationships with their former spouses and resolved their own guilt and grief about how death or divorce has changed their children's lives forever, they deny the challenges ahead. On the way to our stepfamily wedding with our five children, my bridegroom wrote me a romantic poem about building sandcastles and dreams as a metaphor for what lay ahead—an unrealistic expectation. Of course, as our marriage eventually did, sand castles wash away with the tides of stress. It will help you to be realistic while preparing for marriage.

Stage 2: The Confusion Stage

Once the wedding happens, the second stage quickly occurs. There is confusion about rules, roles, and disciplining children. The couple often avoids discussions about what to do about absentee parents, and denial deepens. Communication that focuses on compromise and negotiation becomes essential, and it is vital to begin this process before serious wedding planning begins. Children who try to move between two households while their parents and stepparents continue to hash out their problems often struggle with loyalty conflicts.

Stage 3: The Crisis Stage

It doesn't take long for many stepfamilies to fall into the third stage, the Crisis Stage, which is when many remarriages end. It is important to understand, instead, that crisis is part of normal stepfamily development rather than a signal for quitting time. Instead of fearing it, you can use the crisis time as an opportunity to examine what's wrong and fix it. Before marriage, if you are actively engaged in planning ahead and holding family discussions, you will probably have opportunities to experience and resolve major issues. This will help to prevent at least some of the crises from happening after the wedding.

Stage 4: The Stability Stage

After getting support, guidance, and new tools, stepfamilies and potential stepfamilies can use the lessons they learned from the crisis to make the necessary changes to move into the Stability Stage. This is the time in the process of the stepfamily journey when the family finally comes together with a new understanding and a determined game plan to succeed. Even when obstacles pop up or setbacks occur, fear of failure no longer reigns, and adults come to know they can make it to the summit. The stability gained during this part of stepfamily development strengthens everyone's sense of security. While it is unrealistic that you will fully reach the stage of stability prior to marriage, your goal is to establish it as much as possible.

Stage 5: The Commitment Stage

When you reach the Commitment Stage in your development, this signals that the journey has been a healing one; the stepfamily is truly committed to success. Think about what a difference it would make to your marriage if you reach some level of commitment with all parties before the wedding about making the family work well together.

To move through these stages after marriage takes a long time—anywhere from four to seven years, as research indicates—and it is a lot longer than people realize or want to believe. So, if you use a trail map and the right tools and understand how to do it safely and successfully before marriage, the timeframe for these stages after marriage should shorten, at least somewhat. Have the wisdom to reach out for help—a strength of a strong family.

My wish is for people to open their eyes wide to prevent stepping unconsciously onto the challenging path of remarriage. Treat the journey as though you were to climb the Inca Trail to Machu Picchu in Peru—a great and challenging adventure. With a good guide who knows the way and the pitfalls, the trip can be more than safe—it can be spectacular. Prepare well for the stepfamily journey by healing your former relationships and improving skills where you're weak—especially couple and family communication and parenting. Take time to examine your part in an ended marriage, because if you can identify what mistakes you made, you'll avoid repeating them again.

The stepfamily journey can be an exciting and fulfilling adventure. Indeed, many strengths come from a solid remarriage. Research shows that a new, happy family life can even ameliorate some of the negative effects of divorce on children. A healthy couple relationship provides a positive marriage model for children, and family members provide new role models for each other about skills, expertise, values, or a philosophy of life.

To achieve these benefits, however, stepfamily living requires a carefully planned route made with wise decisions each step along the way. Just as experienced hikers prepare well and use an accurate trail map before setting out on an unknown wilderness trail, seek out the guidance you'll need and take the actions that are required. This journey is best traveled by strong, healthy adults who also are prepared and are committed to an ongoing process of working the tasks the trail map provides. Stepfamily living can be rewarding and successful, but it is definitely not for wimps!

Trail Map Tips for Stepfamily Success

1. **Understand two critical realities.** Making a stepfamily that works well is a process, and it takes time.

2. **Take time to live alone as a single person after divorce or the death of a partner.** Develop and maintain a solid network of family and friends. Start school, move into a new job, or do whatever it takes to move toward a long-awaited dream you've always held. Take risks that lead to restoring your ability to trust others. Beware of that first intense "rebound" relationship and realize that it is quite likely this person is merely your transition person and not necessarily the one you'll end up marrying. However, it can be a vital relationship for rebuilding self-confidence and self-respect, as well as learning how to be with someone again.

3. **Take time before you commit to the stepfamily journey and prepare wisely.** Resolve and heal former relationships. Learn information about stepfamily living. Help your children grieve their changed family situation

with family discussions and therapy so they can better adjust to stepfamily living.

4. **Redefine and clarify your relationship with your former spouse.** Peaceful relationships help your children move between two households. Effective co-parenting and minimizing loyalty conflicts for children only works when this original relationship is reasonably healthy.

5. **Know in advance that dealing with discipline will be your greatest challenge.** The first hurdle is dealing with discipline, so present a united front to the children as soon as possible. Examine your parenting styles. Take parenting classes during courtship. Seek out skills and communication classes. Agree on approaches that respect everyone.

6. **Examine and clarify boundary issues early.** Time, space, chores, and authority are issues to sort out early in the stepfamily journey so everyone is on the same page.

7. **Disclose and discuss finances.** These discussions are best done before remarriage, because issues surrounding money and other economic considerations are the second greatest challenge in the stepfamily.

8. **Reduce children's anxiety.** Kids worry about their roles in the new family and may be confused. Many are angry about all the changes. Reduce their concerns by talking openly with them. Can they still have a good relationship with their other parent without it upsetting you or your new partner? Will they lose touch with their grandparents? Can they still see their old friends? Clear answers to these questions and others provide the reassurance youngsters need during this important transition in their young lives. New stepparents can assure children their intent is neither to replace their biological parent nor interfere in those relationships. Ask them how they view your role in their lives, listen well for guidelines, and watch for opportunities to build good relationships with them.

9. **Participate in stepfamily education and/or focused counseling.** Because stepfamilies differ from other families in so many ways, the more you learn in advance, the fewer struggles you'll face later. Attend a stepfamily education class. Visit a therapist who's savvy about stepfamilies and is trained in family systems to help guide you—especially before marriage and in the early stages. A healthy family is one that seeks help to strengthen its family life.

10. **Celebrate with a creative ceremony that includes the children.** At the

cutting edge of tradition, stepfamily weddings can help create a storehouse of memories that provide a strong foundation for your stepfamily. Everyone who wants to take part in a meaningful way can be encouraged to do so. A child might want to play the piano, sing a song, read a poem, or manage the guest book. No one should be forced to take part. If there's resistance by a certain child, talk about it calmly to get to the bottom of what the child is feeling—usually unresolved divorce issues. A creative, joyful ceremony heralds your new beginning to friends and family and provides a positive start to what lies ahead.

> **Elizabeth Einstein**, a Marriage & Family Therapist in Ithaca, New York, is one of America's leaders in the field of stepfamily education. She has been an expert in this field for over thirty years and has also lived through two challenging stepfamily experiences. She is available for workshops and professional training. See www.stepfamilyliving.com to obtain her newest books, *Strengthening Your Stepfamily* and *Active Parenting for Stepfamilies,* for the best guidance for success. Her website includes her current workshop schedule.

❦ ❦ ❦

Parenting Challenges in Stepfamilies
Nancy Landrum

Surprise! Love is NOT always better the second time around! Second and subsequent marriages have significantly higher divorce rates than first marriages. The belief is, "I made a mistake the first time. This time I'll get the family of my dreams." Most often, one or both spouses bring one or more children from previous relationships into the marriage. The expectation is that the people being joined in this family will act and interact as though they really are a "first" family. It's a recipe for disillusionment and often disaster.

Our culture conditions us to think in a first family paradigm: Mom and Dad, a first and only marriage for each of them, children conceived and reared by them, enjoying the eventual grandchildren, partners together for life. Stepfamilies don't fit in that belief system. They are an entirely different configuration with added needs and dynamics. In addition to the normal adjustments needed in any marriage, multiple research studies confirm that stepfamilies have many added stresses that contribute to their failure rate.

Perhaps the most damaging, yet easiest-to-prevent stressor involves unrealistic expectations. Interpret that as ignorance about how stepfamilies thrive versus how "first" families thrive. Consider the experience of Gavin and Pamela and the stepfamily they created:

Gavin and Pamela were high school sweethearts who parted, married other partners, had two children each, and then divorced. They found each other again and, with first family expectations, married and joined their lives and children. There was trouble almost immediately. Problems included difficulties with Gavin's ex-wife, financial pressures, disagreements about parenting decisions, distrust between their children, and fights that escalated into bigger fights. After four years, the dream was morphing into a nightmare. Although they enrolled in Mastering the Mysteries of Stepfamilies as soon as they heard about it, the start date was a month away. I met with them because they were so desperate for relief.

With tears and frustration, Gavin and Pamela related typical results of having unrealistic expectations. Pamela's first husband had deserted her and their two children. Her second husband was an alcoholic, emotionally unavailable to them. When they divorced, Pamela's first husband gave up his two children for adoption because he didn't want to pay child support. Years later, he has decided he wants shared custody and is trying to regain his rights as a parent. Pamela believes her children have every right to know and experience a relationship with their father, but it's a challenge to be at peace with the emotional price the history has cost both Pamela and her children. She wanted a man—a father—to love her children, and she went into the marriage hoping Gavin would be that person.

The mother of Gavin's son was out of the picture. The mother of his daughter was emotionally unstable. He hung on as long as he could and finally divorced her. After a long and expensive legal battle, he was given shared custody of the girl they brought into the world, meaning the mother of his daughter is very involved with her. That relationship requires Gavin (and Pamela) to manage the split living arrangements, incorporating this daughter into the home and then letting her go over and over again. Gavin also struggles to establish appropriate boundaries and functional communication with his ex-wife. When he and Pamela married, Gavin wanted a stable, loving influence for his children.

The couple has had significant challenges with parenting, in spite of their desires to co-parent their children. Gavin's more controlling discipline style sparked Pamela's natural inclination to be protective of her children. Gavin found frequent fault with Pamela's more intuitive, relaxed parenting decisions, adding to her hurt and defensiveness. They didn't understand why they couldn't succeed at parenting together.

I was clear with them: "In order to have more peace, you must align yourselves with the guidelines suggested by multiple research outcomes for stepfamilies. It's too late to have a nuclear or first family. Let that fantasy go." I suggested that they each focus on parenting their own bio-children and refrain from criticizing each other's discipline styles. It shocked them, but they were willing to try anything.

Pamela later told me that she cried for two weeks, grieving the loss of her first family dream. But they immediately shifted their attitudes and actions so that they were each free to parent their own bio-children as they saw fit. They were able to do this without fear of criticism or conflict with each other over their respective decisions. The result was an immediate and dramatic reduction in the tension between them. All they told the children was, "We are learning some new ways of doing things. It's going to be better from now on." Without knowing the specifics, the children were soon more relaxed too.

After skating so close to the brink of disaster, Gavin and Pamela gave themselves whole-heartedly to learning the communication skills, problem-solving methods, and conflict-resolution strategies taught in the class. They also gained from learning the realistic, research-proven guidelines for a successful stepfamily. They report that it's as though a magic wand has been waved over their home. It is so much more peaceful. The fighting has stopped, and they are more in love than ever before.

Moving from a first family paradigm to a stepfamily paradigm is not easy. It requires grieving of the loss of our family fantasies. The new paradigm means different ways of being in a family that are not easy or comfortable. There are huge payoffs, however, for choosing to embrace new guidelines and skills: You can restore your own confidence in forever love; mend the shattered belief in your children that love is not lasting; and, model the skills and guidelines for a loving, lasting marriage that will serve as a solid foundation for generations to come. It's worth the effort!

Nancy Landrum, M.Psy., lived through the stepfamily experience with her husband Jim and their children. She helps couples in which at least one spouse has a child from a previous relationship to learn the skills and guidelines that enable them to build a strong and loving stepfamily marriage. She is the author of *How to Stay Married & Love It! Solving the Puzzle of a SoulMate Marriage,* co-author of the program Mastering the Mysteries of Stepfamilies, and producer of the DVD *Marriage Skits for Laughter and Learning.* Her website is www.nancylandrum.com, and she can be reached at nancy@nancylandrum.com.

❤ ❤ ❤

A Stepfamily Success Story
Nancy Landrum

Kip and Wendy were wise and fortunate.[1] They attended a church that offers a remarriage program, and they joined the class because of their determination to avoid repeating the failures of their past marriages. Their original wedding date was postponed by a year while they prepared themselves for the challenges of stepfamily living. Kip has four boys; Wendy has two girls and a boy. They have been happily married for four years. They live in Fullerton, California, and they are now active leaders in their church's remarriage program.

Did you really postpone your wedding? Kip and Wendy took Gordon and Carrie Taylor's remarriage program while preparing to marry.[2] They realized they had issues—areas of conflict—that needed addressing, but they weren't sure how to do it. They also participated in a communication skills class and counseling to make sure they were ready for the challenges of being a stepfamily. When they realized they weren't ready, the couple postponed their wedding. Kip says, "It was a hard year—one of the hardest we've had. We wondered if we were going to make it to the altar! We really pushed hard to work through the issues that had been exposed by the classes and counseling."

Wendy adds, "We learned why certain things we did with each other triggered old junk. Once I understood, I didn't get upset quite so easily. It was a combination of learning to communicate better and understanding our differences through the personality assessments we took."

Where did you learn better communication skills? Kip and Wendy attended a Couple Communication course.[3] Kip says, "It gave us the tools we needed to work through issues. In the beginning, we followed the directions very deliberately, but after a while it became more ordinary to speak and listen with caring and respect. When we recently took Mastering the Mysteries of Stepfamilies,[4] it helped us go even deeper by putting ourselves in the other's shoes—imagining what it is like to be the other. The biggest benefit to me is that now I know without a shadow of a doubt that whatever comes up, we can work it through. I used to run to an emotional corner and hide! Now I have no fear or turmoil about addressing an issue, I know that we are both committed to working anything out, AND we have the tools to do so. We both wish we had these skills before our previous marriages failed."

What has been your biggest challenge? Wendy states emphatically, "Parenting! We've raised our children differently. We have different personality types and temperaments. To try to blend our kids and our styles at their ages was not practical. We came to the conclusion through counseling and communication classes that we both have to be okay doing it the way we've done it and not trying to blend it or have a one-system program for everyone. We had to make sure the kids knew it wasn't going to be equal for all. Although we've tried to make some things uniform, discipline and the way we handle conflict is definitely different for each of us."[5]

What are those parenting differences? Kip admits to being a lot more easygoing with his kids. Wendy is more straightforward—a "This is the way it's going to be" parent. Initially, Wendy would tell Kip what she thought he should do with his son, who has lived with them the most. Because Kip wanted to please Wendy, he'd go to his son and say, "It's going to be this way." His son would be shocked because it was so different than how his father would normally have handled it. Eventually, he got so he'd say, "Dad, I know you only said that because you're trying to please Wendy." Kip learned to relax and follow his own path with his kids.

Wendy admits that Kip's strength is grace. She says, "He's able to look past things that I would find offensive. I'm more structured, disciplined. I expect them to follow the rules and be obedient. You might even say I'm more militant. Part of it was survival. My kids' dad was not as involved as I wished he was. When Kip and I got together, he was very passive about discipline. I came on strong in the beginning to try to compensate. Over time, I observed that there's strength in his grace, and he's seen that there are areas where he needs to step up and be more firm on certain issues. We've worked out a balance. But most importantly, we each discipline our own children. When we need to agree because it's a whole-family issue or it affects other family members, understanding our differences helps us to reach an agreement that suits us both."

Wendy adds, "One way to handle discipline can be that there are two ways under the same roof. We make it work because we don't judge each other's methods of handling our respective children, and we work together on the issues that affect everyone. Our kids—even the ones with the same biology—have different personalities and require different things. It's okay to have different systems."

Were finances an issue? Kip and Wendy each brought their own "stuff" about finances to the marriage as well. Wendy was burned by the way her former husband had handled money. She was also the youngest of five and had to wear hand-me-down clothes growing up. She didn't make a lot of money but wanted to spend it however she chose. Wendy says, "We adopted a full disclosure policy—no financial secrets. We agreed that we would each clean up any bad credit or debt before we got married so that we could get married debt-free. We agreed to *not* go into debt for a wedding. We started off with very little income and no home—no major assets. There were definitely some things we had to overcome. They weren't major. Along the way, we came together on the way things are handled."

Kip adds, "A year ago, we bought our first home together and recently had a huge housewarming party. It was quite a celebration of how far we've come together! Full disclosure was very important to Wendy but also for me." Over time, Kip and Wendy each did what they said they would do, and that has built trust between them. They eliminated a huge potential source of conflict by getting out of debt and saving money for their wedding.

What about the exes? Kip and Wendy are clear that the needs of the kids come first. Wendy, in particular, has had to put aside her personal "stuff" in order to facilitate what is best for Kip's kids. She says, "I'm able to be in the same room and interact with Kip's ex—to coordinate events with her for the boys. Two of the boys have expressed their appreciation for my ability to cooperate with their mother. They don't have to choose between parents. It's more important for the boys to *not* have a loyalty conflict than for me to indulge feelings of jealousy or resentment. It's huge. My relationship with Kip's boys is so much better because of it. It's not about jealousy in relationship to Kip. I'm certain I have his love and loyalty. It might be more jealousy about the relationship she has with her sons. I want to be accepted and loved by his boys too. I must move past my personal emotions and accept that for the next four hours or for this event, I put aside whatever fears or anxieties I have to help the kids feel more comfortable."

Kip says, "For me, it's been a little bit different—a difference in personality, I guess. I just tried to go out of my way to say to Wendy's ex, 'Hi! How's it going?' I've encouraged Wendy to invite him to their children's birthday parties, etc. He has a lot of things he hasn't worked through, so he's uncomfortable. I've taken the active role of trying to help him feel more comfortable when we're all together."

In Summary: Kip and Wendy believe that if they hadn't gone through the process they did *before* the wedding—if they were still trying to handle things the way they were before all the classes and counseling—they would already be divorced, or at the least, miserable! Wendy concludes, "Because we worked so hard in the beginning, our relationship is rich. We love each other deeply and have a great relationship not only with each other, but also with the kids. Even our relationships with our exes are better because of the work we've done!"

1 The complete interview of Kip and Wendy was first published by California Healthy Marriages Coalition (CHMC). This is an abbreviated summary of their experience. Used with permission of CHMC and Nancy Landrum.

2 "Designing Dynamic Stepfamilies: Bringing the Pieces to Peace" is a video-based, teach-out-of-the-box series. www.restoredandremarried.com

3 "Couple Communication" is a curriculum developed by Drs. Sherod and Phyllis Miller. www.couplecommunication.com

4 "Mastering the Mysteries of Stepfamilies" was co-authored by Nancy Landrum, Mary Ortwein, and Dr. Bernard Guerney, Jr. It combines the communication skills of Relationship Enhancement with research-tested guidelines to help stepfamilies be successful. www.skillswork.org

5 Conflict over parenting issues is the number one reason given for second and subsequent marriage failures.

Nancy Landrum, M.Psy., lived through the stepfamily experience with her husband Jim and their children. She helps couples in which at least one spouse has a child from a previous relationship to learn the skills and guidelines that enable them to build a strong and loving stepfamily marriage. She is the author of *How to Stay Married & Love It! Solving the Puzzle of a SoulMate Marriage*, co-author of the program Mastering the Mysteries of Stepfamilies, and producer of the DVD *Marriage Skits for Laughter and Learning*. Her website is www.nancylandrum.com, and she can be reached at nancy@nancylandrum.com.

❤ ❤ ❤

Preparing for Stepfamily Life
Ana Morante

If there are children involved from a prior relationship, time is very important for them. When it comes to stepfamilies, it can take a few years for everyone involved to have a sense of being a family again. There will be split loyalties to contend with, and it is important for parents on both sides to be able to allow the children to express themselves. Children can benefit greatly from the opportunity to express what it is like to miss one of their biological parents and to have another authority figure coming into their life. As a parent or stepparent, we may not like what we hear, but we need to remember that listening doesn't mean agreeing. The more we can listen to the children and the more they can talk, the more they can process the experience. This will allow them to hopefully come to an acceptance of the new family from a better position.

As parents, we are so used to telling children what to do, and we think the best thing is to talk to them about what we believe is good for them. Talking to our children is important, but it's just as important to listen to them and really hear what they have to say. If the relationship between the parents failed, that is a tremendous source of stress and pain for the children. The more they can talk about that pain and how that is affecting them, the more they are going to be able to also understand it, process it, accept it, and move on.

The problem is that many times, the parents carry so much hurt, pain, and resentment after divorce that it is difficult to shoulder their children's pain as well. If you see the pain and the sadness in your children and you cannot provide some support for them, it is advisable to seek help. Whether it is to a therapist or a trusted family member, children need someone to talk to about the pain and feelings they have resulting from a failed relationship between their parents.

Let's face it, for children, no matter how old they are, most of the time they want Mom and Dad together. They have the fantasy, even when the parents separate, that one day they will go back together. When one of the parents chooses to be in a new relationship, it is a very difficult reality for the children to accept because it gets in the way of this fantasy.

Editor's Note: The above is excerpted and edited from an interview between Susanne Alexander and Ana Morante on March 10, 2010.

Ana Morante, L.M.F.T., C.F.L.E., is a bilingual Marriage, Family, and Child Therapist, helping people in both Spanish and English. She is dedicated to strengthening couples and families and assisting in the creation of the best environment possible for children. She has a private practice in San Jose, California, and is a certified Parent and Family Life Educator and a Family Wellness Partner and Trainer. Ana has been married for sixteen years and has two daughters and a stepson. She can be reached through www.familywellness.com.

Chapter Sixteen
Becoming Parents and Rearing Children

~ ~

Sometimes couples marry and then discover that they made assumptions about whether to be parents, when to have children, and how many children to have. When they realize that they are on very different pages, it can be very traumatic for the marriage. We have provided helpful material for you to have this discussion now before marrying.

It is likely you will be parents or stepparents together within your marriage, so understanding your parenting values and styles and addressing any differing approaches will be beneficial. However, this is not a comprehensive guide to parenting. If you are already parents, or when you are parents, you will access the wide range of materials available on this topic.

♥ ♥ ♥

Why Now Is the Best Time to Talk About Parenting
Rodney Grubbs and Karen Grubbs

We know what you are thinking: "We are just so happy right now. We can't even think about having kids yet. Why would we even want to talk about it now?"

So, when do you think you should talk about parenting? Our quick answer is, talk about it WAY BEFORE you become a parent.

In our many years of counseling and preparing young engaged couples, we have always helped them discuss three main topics: Money, Communication, and Parenting.

One of the keys to happiness as a couple is to know what each other is thinking when it comes to these three main topics and come to a common understanding about them. After many years of following up with these happy couples, we have found that if you spend a little time discussing and planning around these three areas before marriage, there seems to be much less stress in the relationship later on.

If you listen to the news, you hear over and over again that the major cause of divorce is either a dispute over money or a lack of communication. Actually, we believe the primary reason is probably a lack of communication, because they probably just didn't share their concerns over the lack of money, but that is for another chapter. What does not get shared in the news is the all-important third pressure point on a marriage: Parenting.

What happens when a couple decides to start a family? What happens in the weeks and months leading up to birth? What changes will occur during pregnancy, and how will you handle even more changes after the blessed event?

Remember, life as a couple is filled with fun and happiness because you are totally focused on each other. You spend time thinking about how to make each other happy. You eagerly look forward to each day so you can spend more time together. Life is tremendous—right now.

So, what happens when a tiny tot comes into the mix? Well, like it or not, the environment in your home changes.

Babies need to be fed—often!

Babies need diapers changed—even more often!

Babies need to be held and nurtured and pampered and…well, they need almost constant attention for a while.

Parenting causes couples to have a shift in focus. The focus moves away from each other and onto the new bundle of joy. So how are you going to handle this major change? Long before you decide to become parents is the best time to talk about these important changes that will inevitably happen. If you have discussions now about how these changes will make you feel, you can lay the groundwork for how you, as a couple, are going to help each other cope with them.

If you know what is coming, and you are on the same page as far as how you are going to raise your children, the stress will be greatly reduced, and you will magically find the time to still have that special time and focus on each other. Don't ever lose that special focus on each other. It is what makes your time together—both before and after marriage—so much fun.

Remember that the greatest gift you give your children is a strong and happy marriage. And, when the time comes, you'll also notice how happy it makes your baby when they see Mom and Dad being affectionate with one another.

Remember, big stuff IS going to happen: money stuff, communication stuff, and baby stuff. Talk about the big stuff now, and then it will only be small stuff as you travel down the road of married happiness.

May your relationship with your partner always be blessed, and may you enjoy a never-ending honeymoon!

> Ecstatically happily married for over thirty years, authors and speakers, **Rodney Grubbs** and **Karen Grubbs** are Founders of www.NeverEndingHoneymoon.com. They are the creators of the "52 Weekly Marriage Boosters" series of weekly email tips and strategies to keep that Never Ending Honeymoon marriage alive and thriving. Sign up for free at www.MyMarriageBoosters.com. Their upcoming book, *The Perfect First Year,* (www.theperfectfirstyear.com), will bless your life with actionable tips and strategies to build your marriage into a Never Ending Honeymoon. Rodney and Karen have two happily married sons and one grandson.

❤ ❤ ❤

Should We Have Children?
Sue Atkins

Congratulations! You are getting married, but have you thought about children? Remember: Positive parents = confident kids.

Would you get in your car and set off from London, England, to Edinburgh, Scotland, without a map or turning on your GPS or SatNav? Probably not!

So, why it is that most couples don't ever think of what they are trying to achieve in marriage? Why don't they discuss their aspirations, dreams, hopes, and expectations about marriage and having a family?

Did you know that sex, money, and children, are usually the most commonly argued issues within marriage? So that's why it makes sense to have that chat before you tie the knot. Most people I meet feel this discussion is all a bit unromantic, but finding out whether your partner wants children and how many really are major issues to settle before the wedding. Discovering that your partner really doesn't want children or doesn't feel ready for children after you have married can cause tragic disharmony in your relationship.

Naturally, people get married for all sorts of reasons: They have fallen madly in love; they want to have children and start a family; they want to celebrate and acknowledge their love for each other publically; or they want to settle down and be more stable. Others get married because they want to feel secure, they fear being alone, they feel they are "getting on a bit," or they want the big dream wedding. Some say they are getting married for the sake of their children, and others even admit they want to get married to help them recover from a divorce.

You may have many more reasons why you want to marry, but the most important thing is that you and your partner have fully discussed your reasons. It's important that you're both fully confident you share the same values, beliefs, motivation, intentions, and common goals and direction. It's also important to share the same sense of humor: A smile is a curve that puts a lot of things straight in a relationship and marriage!

Whatever discussions you have, however, remember to include the subject of children. I coached an engaged couple who came to explore work-life balance issues and then discovered that one of the partners didn't want children. It came as a huge surprise to the fiancé, who had to take the next week really pondering the implications of what his partner had said, and wondering about whether to marry.

I also worked with a couple who came to me for divorce coaching. They both went into the marriage knowing that one of them didn't want children, but the other partner secretly believed she would change her mind over time. She didn't.

As small children, we learn about relationships by watching our parents. These messages often sink deep into our subconscious mind, waiting to pop up when we become wives or husbands ourselves. It's perfectly natural to have doubts and fears, as well as dreams and high expectations about getting married. It is, after all, one of the biggest decisions we make in our lives. But as long as you and your partner can openly share your feelings, support and reassure each other, and openly communicate and agree about all sorts of things, chances are you're on the right track.

Sue Atkins is a Parent and Relationship Coach based in Lingfield, Surry, England. She is the author of *Raising Happy Children for Dummies,* and she is the Judge for National Family Week "Family of the Year." Sue also appears regularly on *BBC Breakfast TV* and

The Jeremy Vine Show on BBC Radio 2, which has over 6,000,000 daily listeners. To receive her free newsletter bursting with practical tips and helpful advice, go to www.positive-parents.com or buy her *Parental Journey* audio CD and ideas book at www.positive-parentsclub.com/The_parental_journey_audio_CD_and_ideas_book.htm.

❤ ❤ ❤

Find and Discuss Your Hidden Parenting Beliefs
Sandra Dye

Congratulations! By reading this book, you have identified yourself as someone who wants to go beyond the romantic stage of marriage preparation to the next level. Having the more difficult but powerful conversations about your parenting values and beliefs before marriage can increase your odds of success.

Before you begin your life together, you want to make sure you address what may seem a million miles away: the discussion of your parenting approaches and beliefs about children. You have most likely already identified many issues that can lead to conflict and struggles because of different feelings, opinions, and values when it comes to things like money, intimacy, professional life, and your extended family. Before marriage is also the time to understand and address any significantly different opinions you both hold about whether to have children, when, how many, and especially your views of day-to-day parenting.

Uncovering Hidden Parenting Beliefs

One of the most important preparatory steps you can take is uncovering any *hidden* parenting beliefs you may be carrying. I identify them as hidden because you may not have identified your biases or beliefs simply because you are *already comfortable* with them. While exploring parenting together, you will realize that many of your beliefs reflect what you learned from your parents. This will include sharing with each other what your parents did and did not do.

You may find that your current parenting beliefs are a polar opposite reaction to how you were parented. Alternatively, you may find your beliefs tend to closely match your parents' style of parenting. How do the ways you were each reared compare and contrast? You may question if what worked decades ago will work now. After all, your children will live in a different world than you grew up in—one in which parenting is often more complex. How will you parent in this new world?

Previously Unquestioned Beliefs You Carry

Now is the time to look closely at some previously unquestioned beliefs you carry. I encourage you to also continue examining and discussing your parenting beliefs over time, because new life experiences and new stressors tend to open up your belief systems, making room for meaningful changes. With two people both changing, and an increasing number of constantly changing parenting resources available, you may find that your beliefs change quite rapidly, and you want to make sure you both are discussing those changes. As a couple, when your values do not match up, either from the very beginning or as life experiences create change, there can be heightened conflict and disconnect. *Stay in the conversation with each other as potential or actual co-parents!*

We know different parenting strategies are potentially *beneficial*, rather than problematic. Different beliefs and behaviors are a part of life, and mothers and fathers often take varying approaches simply because women and men are different. Children can benefit from learning to deal with differences. As long as the differences are not too great, your child may develop wonderful problem-solving and conflict-resolution skills from observing you both in action.

Take the Survey: What's Your Parenting Style?

Let's begin by looking at your current thinking and beliefs. Take the survey below, which is provocative by design. The idea is to push some buttons, reveal your beliefs, and get you into the conversation with each other. When you read each statement, don't labor over whether you agree or disagree. Just go with your initial instinct.

The survey covers four areas: Parenting Beliefs, Discipline, Parental Communication, and Bedtime for Parents (don't get too excited and skip to this section first!). Each of you should take a separate sheet of paper and write down the headings and the numbers that represent the statements. For examples, Parenting Beliefs has statements 1 through 17. Independently take the survey by writing **A** for Agree or **D** for Disagree next to the corresponding number of each statement. Next, compare your results by referencing back to the statements in the book.

Parenting Beliefs

1. It is okay for one parent to work six days a week to support the family.
2. It is important to discuss how many children you want before marriage.
3. All children need one parent to be home full-time to care for them.
4. It is better to have children when you are really young and have more energy.
5. The person with the higher paying job and greatest earning potential should be the one to maintain their job, while the other parent becomes the stay-at-home parent.
6. If both of us die, my parents should raise the children.
7. Parents should take parenting classes before marriage.
8. It is desirable to have grandparents living in the house or neighborhood when we have children.
9. All parenting decisions should be made by us alone without our parents' input.
10. The stay-at-home parent should rely on their spouse to take full responsibility for the care of their child(ren) one full day of the weekend.
11. When a child cries for the other parent, it means they are more attached to that parent.
12. Parents should buy their children their first car.
13. It is impossible to spoil a child.
14. Parents need to watch young children constantly to prevent them from hurting themselves.
15. Teens need to be kept on a short leash, so that they don't make the mistakes their parents made.
16. Children should be trusted until they prove they cannot be trusted.
17. Once bottle feeding has started, parents should alternate doing the nighttime feedings.

Disipline

1. Children shouldn't have chores.
2. It is better to let a child cry for hours than to pick them up just because they are crying.

3. A child should be punished if they say, "You can't make me."

4. When your child isn't listening or doing what they are told, harsher consequences are needed to bring them around.

5. Children should be punished for having a poor attitude, even though they did what you asked.

6. Raising your voice to your children is acceptable because you are setting the limit to your tolerance.

7. Parents should strive to make everything equal between their children.

Parental Communication

1. It is important for one parent to be the clear disciplinarian.

2. If one parent sets a limit you believe is unfair, it is important to let your child know the other parent has overreacted.

3. Parents should admit to children when they make a mistake.

4. Children should never hear their parents argue.

5. When you are angry with your child, you should let the other parent deal with the situation.

6. A little time is just as good as a lot of time with your child.

7. Praise builds self-esteem.

8. If your child doesn't do something well, instead of praising them, you should encourage them to do something else.

Bedtime for Parents

1. The woman should be the one responsible for handling the prevention of pregnancy.

2. Children should be allowed to sleep with their parents until they feel ready to sleep alone.

3. A woman should be the one to decide when she is ready to have sex again after childbirth.

4. Newborns should be moved out of your bedroom as soon as the mother stops breastfeeding.

5. It is okay to have sex while your children are in the house.

6. When it comes to biology and sex, fathers should be the ones to educate

their sons, and mothers should be the ones to educate their daughters.

7. When you are done having children, the husband should have a vasectomy to prevent pregnancy.

8. Even after children, romance and foreplay are a necessary part of having sex.

9. How often a couple has sex should be decided by the man.

10. Both husband and wife should be understanding if the other isn't in the mood for sex, even after one, two, four, or six weeks.

11. It is inappropriate to kiss in front of your children.

12. When one parent is sleep deprived, the other parent needs to take over feeding, changing, and bathing the children.

Processing the Survey Results

Now, look at each category to see how many of your answers match. This will help you determine how close you are in parenting beliefs. Next, take the differences you have identified and negotiate with each other, moving one step at a time closer to your partner's belief until you reach *a solution that will work for both of you.* If needed, consult books about parenting to learn more about various options. The solution that both of you are able to live with will become your starting point.

Challenge each other to go beyond this short survey. Come up with provocative statements designed to further the discussion. Exploring your beliefs will help you expose differences in your thinking and then work toward solutions.

Where to Turn If You Have Significant Differences

If you have significant differences about parenting, it would be easy to seek out others to fortify your position, but this could further drive you apart. What is better for your relationship is listening to each other and asking questions until you truly understand and appreciate your differing perspectives. The key here, once you both feel understood, is to *find and create solutions* that work for *both* of you.

If you find yourselves judging, harassing, or not considering your partner's opinions about parenting (or anything else), you might need some help. You could seek counseling or help from a child or relationship specialist to move you through the more difficult discussions.

John Gottman, one of the foremost marriage researchers in the country, conducted a long-term study on newlyweds and found that 67 percent of couples become discontent with each other during the first three years of their child's life. These couples were also twice as likely to divorce. This study points to how important it is to be exploring your beliefs about parenting before, during, and after having children. Dr. Gottman's book, *And Baby Makes Three,* provides a plan for preserving the marital connection in his Bringing Baby Home program. This is a great resource for couples to read in preparation for having children. You can learn more at www.gottman.com/parenting/baby/.

Putting It All Together

The first step to effective parenting is to recognize that your unique life experiences shape your beliefs about parenting. The second step is to raise your awareness of differences in your beliefs and identify potential pitfalls. The third step is to listen, understand these differences, and discuss creating solutions that work for both of you. If you find you are stuck and unable to reach a solution, you can seek out resources or assistance.

Differences that are identified, understood, and worked through make you stronger as a couple because you learn much about each other as you work toward common solutions. This helps you build trust in each other. You will know that when challenges are tough, you will be listened to, understood, and appreciated, so differences will lead to win-win rather than win-lose resolutions.

Sandra Dye is a child, teen, and parenting expert who completed her doctoral coursework at the Professional School of Psychology in San Francisco, California. Sandra is married with an eighteen-year-old son and fifteen-year-old daughter. She has extensive experience over her twenty-six years in private practice, helping parents and their children use the positive power of connecting to support and influence each other. From her education and clinical work, Sandra has developed a five-step system she uses to guide families to understand one another and resolve conflicts. Her website, www.One-Step-Ahead-Parenting.com, is a problem-solving, interactive site designed for parents, preteens, and teens to connect with, learn from, and communicate with each other. You can also connect with Sandra at www.facebook.com/OneStepAheadParenting.

Chapter Seventeen
Handling Money

~ ~

Experts and researchers widely agree that money issues are often the most challenging for married couples to handle. Since it's known that money matters can often be divisive, it is wise to spend time before marriage sorting through your histories and approaches with money, what your debts and spending habits are, and how you might approach various financial scenarios.

You likely each have strong opinions and beliefs about money. People often have layers of emotional significance that they attach to it. We will guide you with tools and humor through some of the ups and downs of this topic.

♥ ♥ ♥

Managing Your Money
Jim Hughes

As you prepare for marriage as a couple, it will be useful for you to have a thorough discussion of your current finances and how you plan to manage your money within marriage. You may find it useful to draft a preliminary monthly budget for after marriage as an aid to discussing the topic.

As you discuss the topic of money, please remember this wisdom: *Money— or the things it can buy—cannot make you happy.* If you are not content in your soul when you have little or nothing, you will never be content when you have much.

Establishing a Budget

Every couple needs to find a budgetary plan that works for them. If you don't have some sense of what you are doing with what you have, you soon won't have it. Within every budget, there should be allowances for the unexpected. A sample budget you could follow would be something like this:

- Charitable Giving (10 percent). If you are a Christian couple, this would be your tithe. Every couple must learn the joy of giving to others.
- Savings (10 percent). You will never be prepared for the future if you don't work on it today! There will always be reasons why you can't save.
- Entertainment (10 percent). This would include vacations, eating out, sporting events, movies, date nights, and more.
- Emergency Fund (10 percent).
- Normal Living Expenses (60 percent).

This is just a suggested place to start. Take into consideration your income and your goals for the future. If you establish a budget and commit yourselves to staying within it, you have a much greater chance of avoiding the pitfalls of financial ruin. Every couple must work together to keep within the budget they establish. Consistent and continued communication is a must so you can both remain responsible for the general spending within the budget. Never let the outgo exceed the inflow.

Expenditure Guidelines

Let me suggest some guidelines for you to follow:

1. Do not set your sights on whatever the world offers you. Do you really need it, or do you just want it? How would having it improve the quality of your life? Would having it create more problems than it solves?

2. Only spend within your means to pay. More, bigger, and nicer are not good criteria to use when contemplating a purchase.

3. Be responsible with your resources. Gambling is a very addictive behavior (playing the lottery included). It can and does destroy marriages! Make provision for the future of your family. Consider what you regularly spend your money on and ask yourself, "Can I live without this?" If you can, then don't buy it!

4. When you set aside money for your future, *do not spend it!* Regard it as an untouchable item. Discipline yourselves to set aside something on a regular basis, no matter how small it may seem.

5. Do not spend for the sake of spending money. Just because you have it doesn't mean you have to spend it.

6. Use the money you don't need for the betterment of others. Charitable giving instills within us the sense that we, as human beings, are all part of a larger community. No one benefits from money in the bank except the banker!

7. Do not rob God of his tithes and offerings. Recognize that it is because of God's blessings and enablement that you have what you have.

8. Be fair. Don't let your finances control you, and don't use your finances to control your spouse. Be clear about how you will generate income, and be responsible for how you spend it. Determine together what spending money you will each have, to what extent you are accountable to each other for spending, and what is personal choice. As with everything else in life, our attitude toward money is the key to whether it will be our servant or our master. You must be the master and not the slave to your finances. Learn to live within your means, and you will succeed. God honors and blesses those who do.

Discussing Debt

Debt occurs when we spend more than we make, when we foolishly use credit as a means of purchasing items. Don't believe the lie that credit card purchases are the same as cash purchases. Whenever you purchase something on credit, you also are paying interest charges on top of your purchase. It inflates the cost of your purchase and can easily drive you into a debt situation that you will find hard to get out of, particularly in trying economic times. Staying out of debt and debt reduction require much discipline.

Even debit cards can too easily be used to drain your checking account. It is easy to spend money that you don't have in your pocket when a debit card is in hand. It is good when used properly, but many people abuse it and spend what they otherwise wouldn't.

Consider the following questions in establishing your money philosophies for your future marriage:

- What items are acceptable to go into debt for?
- What items are unacceptable to go into debt for?
- When is it not acceptable to go into debt, even if the items are acceptable?

- What are some things you could do to reduce any debt you have coming into the marriage?
- How many credit/debit cards do you really need?
- What do you need and use them for?
- How much of a balance (collectively and individually) is acceptable to carry on your credit card(s)?
- How much of a debt load is appropriate and acceptable for your income level?
- Unmanageable debt is indicative of a heart that is not right with God. In order to become a good steward of the money you have, you must first be right with God:
  - Ask the Lord to forgive you for being irresponsible with what He has entrusted to you.
  - Ask the Lord to help you develop a plan of responsibility.
  - Accept the help He gives you.

It is wise to make financial plans so that money is not a source of disharmony between you in your relationship. Assess how your financial discussions before marriage are going, and determine whether you need outside help to assist you with resolving any issues.

Jim Hughes is the author of *C Through Marriage, Revitalizing Your Vows*. He is an ordained Pastor, now retired, who served in churches for nearly forty years before turning to a writing ministry. Jim lives in Iowa and has been married for nearly forty years, has two adult married children and one son still at home, and one granddaughter. Jim can be reached at thefourj@mchsi.com; www.cthroughmarriage.blogspot.com; or through Facebook.

❤ ❤ ❤

Love, Honor, and Pay for Stuff
(or Why I Wanted to Marry an Investment Banker)
Kerri Pomarolli

We went for our first premarital counseling session, and the pastor gave us a budget sheet. We started laughing. I said, "Look, Pastor, if I have two dollars and he has two dollars, that equals four dollars, and we don't need a whole sheet to figure that out! We went to college." Ron chimed in with, "Yeah, and we also play the lottery, so I think we're good!" So, I have to admit, on the way home from the counseling session, I was sulking a bit, because I really thought I'd end up with someone who was way more financially stable than myself. At least that way, I could still keep being that "starving comic."

God just put it in my heart one day: "Kerri," He said in a voice that only I could hear, "if I gave you that rich investment banker husband, why would you need to depend on Me?" I said, "God, I see your point, but I was willing to try. Try me now! Give Ron a bunch of money, and see if I don't pray to You first!"

They tell me married couples fight about two things: sex and money. Well, since I'm not married yet, I can't speak on the first topic, but I think we're proving that the money topic is a hard subject for sure. It's hard because I keep thinking I'm supposed to be on some scale compared to everyone else. Most of my college friends are married with houses and living these lives of fancy supper clubs and overseas vacations.

I just got back from a weekend with my dear sorority friends. Our conversations have changed from, "Which frat guy do you want to take to the formal dance?" to "Which color scheme is best for my dining room?" These girls are using phrases like "cappuccino mocha" and "deep sage." Last time I checked, mocha was a drink, not a color, and isn't sage some herb from South America? I don't know, and I don't care. When did my crazy sorority girls turn into the "grown-up ladies" I sat with over this past weekend? Rhinestones and sequins have been replaced with pearls and black couture dresses. Hemlines are lower, and necklines are higher. What is becoming of us? We're one step away from shopping at Chicos and wearing tankinis!

It's not like I'm immune to it. I want to play, too, but the only thing I could contribute to their conversation was that Ron and I were applying for low-income housing, and we were hoping California would bring back food stamps. (By the way, in Los Angeles, they define "low-income" as anyone who makes under $100,000 a year!) We put ourselves on the list for this new condo complex, and if you qualify, you get to buy a condo for "low-income prices," which start at $300,000. I'm not kidding! Even if we got one, what bank are we going to rob to get the down payment? The weekend with my college gals was fun, albeit a bit depressing. I'm almost the last one to get married, and they are not only hitched, but are already well on their way to real estate and mutual funds.

And once again my competitive nature rears its ugly head, and I feel like I am way behind on the grownup timeline. I'm newly engaged, still renting, living paycheck to paycheck, and can't even keep my plants alive. My fiancé lives in a commune with three other comics, sleeping on a futon under a desk, with one guy who lives in the kitchen. Just because we got engaged doesn't change who we are or where we are in life. People don't ask me the horrid "Are you seeing anyone?" question these days. They've moved on to "So, where will you be buying a house?" The cycle continues. I always thought I'd need certain things to make me completely happy. That is what the media taught me growing up: True happiness in L.A. means a beach house and two and a half kids with a full-time nanny.

My four-bedroom beach house may come in time, but it won't bring me happiness. True happiness is having a guy who loves that I shop at the ninety-nine-cent store, thinks I look totally appropriate in my pink velour jogging suit (I don't even jog), and will never make me feel stupid that I don't like to sweat or physically exert myself in any way. He embraces me for it. He supports my efforts when I step outside my comfort zone. I took up yoga, but the class was for seniors, so we just laid there for an hour. Ron said, "That's great, Kerri. Now, let's go get some half-price sushi and discount chocolate chip ice cream. You're perfect just the way you are." Now, what investment banker could top that?!

An entertainment veteran, **Kerri Pomarolli** has performed on the same stage as some of the biggest names in comedy. She has been on television many times, including *The Tonight Show* with Jay Leno, Comedy Central, ABC Family, Lifetime, Hallmark Channel, and NBC. Kerri has written three published books, including *Guys Like Girls Named Jennie,* which is being considered as a romantic comedy. Her books are well known to both secular and Christian readers, and her award-winning articles appear in newspapers and national magazines. Kerri tours extensively throughout the United States and Canada to churches, corporate events, and today's top comedy clubs. Look for Kerri in the documentary *Hollywood on Fire,* which includes some of today's and yesterday's well-known celebrities. Her husband Ron McGehee is also a standup comedian. For bookings and more information, please see www.kerripom.com.

❤ ❤ ❤

Ten Tips for Talking to Your Honey About Money
Syble Solomon

The big day is coming up! As you seriously consider marriage and as you prepare for your wedding, take the time to do something that will help you prepare for your future life together. It may not sound romantic, but sit down and have a good talk about money. Couples who communicate effectively about money can usually communicate about anything!

Did you know that money issues in a marriage are inevitable? Money has consistently been named the number one cause of conflict in marriages, whether couples said they were happy and satisfied with their marriages or not, and whether they stayed married or got divorced. Since money problems are predictable and unavoidable, be proactive and get talking before you marry. The more you understand each other's habits and attitudes about money, the clearer you will be about your compatibility, and the fewer misunderstandings you will have in the future. In fact, your ability to talk harmoniously about money and manage it well is an excellent predictor of a solid marriage!

Remember to pause in your discussion if it starts to become heated. Some conversations need to happen over time rather than all at once. Below are ten tips to help you have a productive discussion:

1. **Just do it!** If you are uncomfortable or suspect your honey may not want to talk about money, acknowledge that it feels awkward and that you are both in new territory. Sharing information about money and understanding each other's priorities builds trust to lay a strong foundation for your future, so it is worth the effort to have the conversation. To get started, find a relaxing time and place to talk.

2. **Reminisce.** An easy way to begin is to simply share your memories. What you will notice in your relationship is that your histories sometimes affect your money choices as adults, so knowing details can help you make good adult choices in the present. Here are some ideas of stories you can share:

- What was the first time you bought something with your own money? What did you buy? How did you get the money?

- What was your first job and the ones that followed? What did you do with your money?

- How did you get money as a child and a teen? What did you do with it?

- When you were a kid, did you think you were richer or poorer than your friends or others in your family? Who did you know that you thought was really wealthy or really poor? What did you and your family members think of them? How did everyone treat each other?

- Were you expected to contribute to or pay for class trips or projects when you were in school? What about going to a special dance or on a date to the movies? What else were you expected to use your own money to pay for?

3. **Consider family.** Growing up, how was money talked about in your home? Do you know who paid the bills and how big financial decisions were made, such as buying a car or house? Did the family make investments or save for the future? If there were arguments about money, what usually caused them, and how were you involved? How could you tell when your parents disagreed about money? Were you encouraged to live simply, be thrifty, and be content, or was there a sense of competition to keep up with or outdo others?

4. **Look around.** How did the lifestyle and values of your immediate family compare to those of your extended family or other people in your neighborhood or community? Did your parents encourage you to fit in or to get more education, have more, or be different? Are your lifestyle and values now similar to those of your parents, siblings, and long-time friends, or in what ways are they different?

5. **Enjoy life.** How have you spent your money for fun in the past? Has anything changed? What have you done for fun and pure enjoyment that doesn't cost a penny? In the future as a couple, how do you see spending money on entertainment, fun, and recreational activities?

6. **Face your fears.** What are your biggest fears about money? If you can, share the stories of what caused them.

7. **Share the past.** How would you describe your financial experiences (spending, saving, investing, or going into debt)? Have you ever declared

bankruptcy or had major debt? Did you save up for big expenses, or did you buy them and pay them off over time? Are you used to buying the best and newest clothes, electronics, cars, and other items, and how have you paid for them? Have you significantly changed anything about the way you manage money now from how you did in the past? What caused the change?

8. **Clarify expectations.** What financial situation would be required for each of you to feel financially secure? How much money does it take for each of you to feel independent and meet your needs? How do you both feel about giving to religious entities, charities, or helping friends and family members, and what dollar amounts are reasonable? Would you expect friends and family to repay you? How much debt are each of you comfortable having month to month? How do you each use credit cards? What lifestyle do both of you project having in five years? Would it be reasonable to set up a pre-nuptial agreement if either or both of you have assets, financial concerns, children from previous marriages, businesses, or other financial responsibilities? How can you avoid making a pre-nuptial agreement mean that you are planning to divorce?

9. **Talk money.** How much do each of you earn? How much is deducted from your income for retirement, taxes, and other obligations? If either of you are self-employed, how will you manage income fluctuating each month? What investments, bank accounts, bonds, and other financial assets do you have? What do each of you own and owe? Is there child or spousal support to consider? Student loans? What other financial obligations do you each have? When you answer these questions, be as specific as possible.

10. **Have a system.** How will you manage money as a couple? Who will take responsibility to pay bills, stay knowledgeable about investments, and monitor the general flow of money? What methods will you use to both stay informed about your ongoing finances? Will you merge all your money and have everything in joint accounts, keep everything separate, or do a combination of both? Will expenses be split 50/50 or by the percent of what each person earns? What if one person is not working—will that person have their own discretionary money? How much will you spend without talking to each other first?

Did you notice that only Item Nine actually talks about numbers and personal finances? Communicating about money really means communicating about life experiences and values. When you have productive discussions, you build trust, openness, and honesty between you—a great foundation for a long, successful marriage!

Syble Solomon is an expert on the psychology of money and is a popular speaker for groups as diverse as couples, the National Football League, the YWCA, and bankers. She created Money Habitudes™, a unique deck of cards that has helped thousands talk about money and discover their own habits and attitudes ("habitudes") about spending, saving, and giving away money in a fun, non-judgmental, non-threatening game format. Users learn how those habitudes silently influence their relationship, financial wellbeing, and life goals and make new choices. Syble was named Educator of the Year in 2006 by the Association of Financial Counseling and Planning Education. Money Habitudes™ cards won the Smart Marriages® 2009 Impact Award and are endorsed by the Institute of Consumer Financial Education. The company website is www.moneyhabitudes.com. You can reach Syble at syble@lifewise.us or 888-833-4331. Syble has been married for 37 years and has two sons.

❤ ❤ ❤

With Money, What's Really Going On?
Syble Solomon

Wouldn't it be great if we could all wear a sign that lets our partners know when they are crossing the line and hitting a sensitive emotional spot? Money is a complex topic and pushes more hot buttons than any other issue in a relationship. When money seems to be the cause of conflict, it's a good time to step back, take a deep breath, and give yourselves some space. This time-out will help you to discover what's really going on.

It's Not About Money!

It's really about what money means to you. Money represents power, control, freedom, success, security, acceptance, status, love, and many other strong emotional needs. These needs may be associated with memories that can be pleasant, hurtful, exciting, or scary. These needs and memories often cause you to react strongly to what seems to be a money issue in your relationship.

Consider this example: When growing up, Larry often heard his family didn't have enough money, and he was frequently frightened by his parents' fights about it. Now he is considering marrying, but he won't talk with his fiancée Kathy about money, because he wants to avoid a potential argument. He plans to take a hands-off approach to their finances after marriage to distance him from any potential conflict. On the other hand, Kathy associates money with making good things happen, as long as there is a plan and money is managed well. She considers Larry's behavior irresponsible and resents the expectation that she will take care of everything. The more she pressures Larry to participate in assessing their financial situation and making money decisions, the more he distances himself. If only Larry wore a warning sign saying, "Conflicts over money scare me, so I avoid everything related to it," at least that would give them a place to start talking.

While it would be great if everyone could identify his or her personal issues related to money, it's not always easy to determine those silent but strong needs and emotions that influence each person's reactions. Having a conversation to get past the money disagreements and understand the substance of those disagreements can make a huge difference in how a problem can be resolved and is definitely worth the effort.

Here are examples of experiences after marriage that can help you identify issues to talk about before marrying:

- Li and Mai both dreaded the tension at the end of the month when Li paid bills. Li was very intentional and methodical, always tracking their money and meticulously recording every expense on a spreadsheet. Mai got angry every time he asked about a charge on their credit card, resenting the fact that she had to account for every cent. When they finally were able to have a good, constructive talk about money, Mai realized that Li was actually okay with her spending. Li realized his need to know every detail came across as being judgmental and controlling. The outcome was that they set up a checking account with an automatic monthly deposit that she could use as she pleased without reporting back to him.

- Trish was adamantly against Grant giving up his corporate job and going back to school to become a teacher. She argued they couldn't afford it and that it wasn't a good financial decision. However, he had done the math and knew they could manage financially. As they explored what was really behind Trish's objection, it became clear she had concerns about status and being accepted. Her parents defined success by the title of one's job and the lifestyle that went along with being affluent. Trish was afraid her parents would consider Grant a failure if he became a teacher, and they would then also consider her a failure for making a bad choice of husband. She feared losing her parents' approval and love. This conversation led to Trish getting some help to become more assertive. She then talked to her parents about Grant's choice, loyally supporting him. To her surprise, Trish's relationship with her parents improved, and she felt better about herself as well.

It would have been so much easier if Mai wore a sign that said, "I need freedom to spend without justifying myself," and Trish had a sign that warned "I want my family's love and approval and will be opposed to anything that risks that." Think about your pattern of reacting when there is tension or arguments in your relationship due to money-related issues. What would you write on a sign to warn your partner about your hot button? Consider these signs:

- "Warning! I go a bit crazy when I feel my freedom is threatened."
- "Watch out! I become withdrawn when you interfere with my plans."
- "Back off! I'm afraid I'll let you down, so I won't commit to your plan."
- "Pay attention! Threatening my security makes me hold on to money more tightly."
- "Sorry! I can't seem to stop myself when I see a good deal."
- "Let me be! Giving to others makes me happy."

Those are a good start, but a sign doesn't necessarily tell the whole story. Because we're all human, most of us are also inconsistent, which can be confusing to ourselves as well as to our partners. That can make it even more of a challenge to identify hot buttons. For example:

- Jesse likes control and values being practical. When things are going well and there are no unexpected expenses, Jesse may be able to tolerate a partner's frivolous spending more so than after receiving a big medical bill that's not covered by insurance.
- Michael is normally very practical and cautious with his money, so his partner is shocked at how much he wants to spend on a new house. She didn't realize that, for him, a house represents a very concrete way of proving his success to his parents and others who had doubted him when he started his business.

Finding Out the Facts

So, how can you tell what's really going on? When money is the cause of arguments, avoidance, or reactions that aren't helpful for building a healthy relationship, it's a signal to have an in-depth, fact-finding discussion. Try these six steps with your partner:

1. Wait to talk at a time when emotions are calm, and there is no urgent issue that must be addressed.

2. Think about the past six months, so you each can identify your own hot buttons. When were you each angry, unhappy, or frustrated with an issue related to money? Do you recognize a pattern (like what the problem was, who was involved, where and when did it happen, and how did that issue develop or get resolved)? It may help to do this separately and write it down.

3. Share your own hot buttons, and if possible, their history and origin. Listen attentively without interrupting when you each share what is behind your strong emotional needs.

4. Share your warning signs and what might cause either of you to react differently or inconsistently. How might a particular person, place, time, or situation influence your reactions?

5. Revisit the money issues you have both identified as a source of conflict or tension to see if this conversation about hot buttons and signs has given both of you some clues about how to approach them differently for more success and less stress in the future.

6. If you identify that one or both of you need improved skills to manage money, negotiate, be assertive, manage anger, or communicate, check out the resources in your community that can help you be more effective.

Taking the time to figure out what's really going on when there are money conflicts will make your relationship richer, more compassionate, and more successful.

Syble Solomon is an expert on the psychology of money and is a popular speaker for groups as diverse as couples, the National Football League, the YWCA, and bankers. She created Money Habitudes™, a unique deck of cards that has helped thousands talk about money and discover their own habits and attitudes ("habitudes") about spending, saving, and giving away money in a fun, non-judgmental, non-threatening game format. Users learn how those habitudes silently influence their relationship, financial wellbeing, and life goals and make new choices. Syble was named Educator of the Year in 2006 by the Association of Financial Counseling and Planning Education. Money Habitudes™ cards won the Smart Marriages® 2009 Impact Award and are endorsed by the Institute of Consumer Financial Education. The company website is www.moneyhabitudes.com. You can reach Syble at syble@lifewise.us or 888-833-4331. Syble has been married for 37 years and has two sons.

Chapter Eighteen
Responding to Difficulties

~ ~

Difficulties, problems, challenges, tests, adventures—whatever you call them—are an integral part of everyone's lives. No couple is protected from them, and life is not a fairy tale with a magic wand to make it all better. There will be illness, failures, employment issues, children's misbehavior, losses, and much more. You are in the marriage together, and a high-quality friendship and partnership will serve you well.

Delving into this chapter together will help you with exploring how you have handled difficulties in the past and how you might handle future ones. You will specifically look at whether issues with alcohol use or violence are among the difficulties you are experiencing or are likely to experience. And, you will learn how to spot pitfalls before you react to each other and find ways to maintain your relationship instead.

💜 💜 💜

Prepare for "Mile Eighteen" in Your Future Marriage
Amy Spencer

You may not want to hear this advice, but like the exercise you should be doing three times a week and the broccoli you wouldn't eat as a kid, it's good for you: When you get married, your partner is going to disappoint you at some point—and you're going to disappoint your partner. You're both better off knowing this now.

I'm not saying you'll fall out of love when you get married; in fact, with the right person, you'll fall much deeper in love. Just be prepared for the rose-colored glasses you wear when you first start dating to clear up some. By all means, enjoy every second of that magical, wonderful time when the days seem longer and brighter, food tastes better, exercise is easier, work comes more naturally, and you can't help but put your partner on a pedestal. "You're perfect," you might say, "absolutely perfect." And the truth is, they may be more perfect for you than any other person has ever been. Just make sure of two things: 1) that you can see the true qualities in your partner and your partnership through that lovey-dovey haze (Are they a good, kind person? Do they treat you well? Do you share the same values?); and 2) that you're prepared for the fact that after you get married, you will both face some disappointments. *It's normal and natural.*

Here's one way to look at it: Most twenty-five-mile marathon runners will tell you that the hardest mile is somewhere between eighteen and twenty-one, when they're long past those early adrenaline-filled miles, yet still far from the end. Now, if you were doing your first marathon, wouldn't you want to know that now? Then, when you got to Mile Eighteen and felt like you were in it too deep and wanted to give up, you'd know that you weren't alone—that every single runner beside you was feeling that very same thing, right? Well, marriage is exactly the same way. You will reach points where you wonder whether you should quit, but the goal of a happy marriage is ahead if you persevere. And don't think for a moment that it takes eighteen years to go eighteen miles in your marriage! This plateau usually occurs far earlier. Some couples start huffing and puffing around years three to five; others really hit a wall somewhere from seven to ten.

I'm telling you this disappointment will happen, because I've seen couples scare so quickly from the surprise of it that they panic. They wake up one morning, realize their partner isn't doing or being what they'd hoped for, and they wonder if they've made a big mistake. I want to save you some of the unpleasant surprise by telling you now that however perfect your partner seemed when you first met, *every* marriage comes with disappointment. Again, it's normal and natural.

Think about it this way: Knowing that there is a hard part ahead—the equivalent of the dreaded Mile Eighteen in a marathon—is a gift in your relationship. Look at it as the inevitable hump that it will be. You can commit together now that you won't let your marriage fall apart when it happens and agree to work with confidence, love, and help as needed from others to get through it together.

Amy Spencer is the author of *Meeting Your Half-Orange: An Utterly Upbeat Guide to Using Dating Optimism to Find Your Perfect Match* (Running Press, 2010, www.meetingyourhalforange.com). She created the website The Dating Optimist (www.thedatingoptimist.com) and the iPhone application "Half-Orange Optimisms." Amy writes for *Glamour, New York,* CNN.com, *Cosmopolitan, In Style, Real Simple, Harper's Bazaar,* and Match.com. She was previously the host of a Sirius satellite radio relationship call-in show called Sex Files on the Maxim channel and has appeared on Fox, E!, CBS, NBC, VH-1, and others. Amy has also been featured as a Relationship Expert on Howard Stern's Sirius channel Howard 100 News. Amy is married and lives with her "half-orange"—her husband—in Venice, California.

♥ ♥ ♥

Can You Handle Difficulties Together?
Susanne M. Alexander

Difficulties are a normal part of life, so it comes as no surprise that they are a normal part of relationships and marriage. You will come to know your strengths and weaknesses as a couple as you respond together to difficult situations. These will give you opportunities to get to know one another and to develop shared approaches, which may be a new partnership skill for you.

Possible Responses

Everyone responds to difficulties differently. Some people respond poorly: brooding, swearing, retreating into substance abuse, striking out, becoming overwhelmed with fear and anxiety, running away, crying, whining, complaining, becoming immobile or apathetic, or trying to change things back to the way they were. Many go through stages that include denial, anger, and resistance before arriving at acceptance and the ability to respond constructively. Others have the skills and strengths needed and are able to pray, turn to others for help, and swiftly step into constructive action. Are you able to stay connected and respectful with one another even when you are upset or angry?

Some constructive responses for you to try out when facing difficulties include:
- Reading the scripture of your faith for guidance
- Praying and meditating
- Turning toward one another, not away from each other
- Looking for solutions

- Waiting until everyone is calmer
- Seeking professional counseling or coaching
- Obtaining spiritual counsel from an appropriate individual
- Turning to friends or family for support
- Increasing your loving actions
- Joining a support group
- Getting medical help
- Seeking financial counseling
- Getting input from respected others
- Drawing on character qualities such as acceptance, compassion, confidence, courage, creativity, detachment, encouragement, flexibility, forgiveness, fortitude, helpfulness, patience, perseverance, purposefulness, self-discipline, spirituality, resilience…
- Staying active in community life and being of service to others
- Becoming advocates for change and taking assertive action

Discuss which of these is useful for you and which you find difficult and why. Perhaps you can identify when one strategy might work better than another.

Exploring Previous Difficulties

Share with one another what difficulties you have encountered and how you have responded to them in the past. Did you use any of the strategies listed above? By understanding previous experiences, you will gain valuable insights about how each of you will probably behave after marriage when difficulties occur. This sharing will also introduce you to each other's general attitudes and beliefs about difficulties in life. Remember to be compassionate and loving as you learn about one another's challenges.

When you share your past difficulties with one another, being self-reflective and honest will be important. This focus includes seeing:

- What you were responsible for in various situations
- What was out of your control
- What actions you took and did not take
- How quickly you responded

For instance, your initial response to a problem may have been blame, anger, or resistance. Perhaps you then prayed or got help, and you began to work on solutions. Your goal is to understand how you have responded to difficult situations or problems and how you can continue to resolve any issues that arise over time.

You will also discover how resilient and creative each of you is, whether you cope with and bounce back from adversity and stressful experiences and find solutions that work, or whether the problems weigh on you and trouble you in the long-term.

Learning from Difficulties

When you accept the reality of difficulties, you can see that they help you grow and develop. As you talk about your histories, assess what you have learned about yourselves and others from these difficulties. Were you able to reach out easily for help, or was it difficult? Why? When a difficulty occurs, do you ask, "What can I learn from this? How do I need to change? How can I be better prepared to handle a situation like this in the future?" Determine whether each of you generally responds to problems with a willingness to change, learn, and grow. You may also be able to share with each other your own perspectives about how to change.

You may not easily find opportunities to observe how each other handles problems, but this is a vital piece of the process of getting acquainted. Such opportunities can be particularly scarce if you go out on social dates only or if you are in a long-distance relationship. Usually this type of observation occurs only when you spend a significant amount of time together in real-life situations.

Of course, you should not devise difficulties intentionally to see how the other reacts, but if your relationship is becoming serious, you will want to know how your partner responds when in a bad mood, short-tempered, tired, or frustrated. What character qualities do they draw on to stay calm and respond appropriately? You also want to see how you respond to each other's anger or upset feelings. How do the two of you resolve any hurt feelings or misunderstandings that come up between you? Can you be forgiving?

If the opportunity to observe how each other handles challenges does not arise naturally, you can ask key questions to learn how you react when tired or short of temper, after a long day, or when disappointed about how things turn out. You can also find challenging activities to participate in that will give you deeper experiences together. By helping with disaster clean up, traveling to and working in another country, or teaching and/or taking care of children, you can learn how you handle problems together and how effectively you can function as a team.

You can spot good character clues from how you each handle disagreements, illness, conflict, or other difficulties. What do you observe when things are not going smoothly? Do challenges bring out character strengths such as compassion, courage, or flexibility; or is there retreat into destructive anger, frustration, depression, or denial? How do you both behave when feeling sad or disappointed?

Character growth also often results from responding well to difficulties. Improving your character or changing longstanding habits takes perseverance. Sometimes you slip backward into old behaviors, and a difficulty reminds you to focus. When you do slip, are you able to forgive yourself, restate your goals, and keep going forward? If a problem occurs repeatedly, you may need to pause and assess what lesson you are failing to learn. Do you see any repeating patterns of difficulties in each other's lives?

Previous Experiences

As you share with each other, you may discover that some difficulties that can arise in marriage are similar to those you have already experienced, individually or together. You will likely know whether you have the strength to handle these types of tests smoothly in your marriage, or whether you will have difficulty in responding well to them instead. For instance, you may have regularly looked after an ill sibling, so it will be easier for you to cope with illness in your own children or each other. Alternatively, you may want to avoid anything similar to a family experience you have had. For example, if one of you had a father who lost his job and became depressed, and you remember the fears from that time, you may struggle if the same experience were to happen within your marriage.

All families and individuals experience some degree of problems. A difficult, painful background or previous unwise choices are not necessarily a barrier to a successful marriage. Again, the key is understanding whether you have effectively learned and grown from your past challenges. Everyone has frailties, but human beings are always capable of transformation; they can and do change. Regaining wholeness, reclaiming chastity, finding a healthy balance, and developing skills to deal with anger are all possible choices and responses to difficulties. A new marriage can also be one of many healing steps. Mistakes and poor choices can be sacred learning experiences.

On the other hand, a dreadful background or great or repeated mistakes from the past must be given due weight. You must both recognize that your pasts will likely affect your marriage, because they have affected who you are as individuals. It is important to avoid wishful thinking that someone (including yourselves) will change. Instead, use a rational process to determine whether, in fact, you have changed appropriately, developed new skills, and are ready and able to create a healthy marriage.

Difficulties That May Arise

Many types of difficulties can affect you individually, thereby affecting you as a couple. Below is a list of many of the types of difficulties that may arise in marriage (or life!). As you look at this list and at your lives, develop strategies together for how to handle each of these issues. Assess which ones are preventable and what preventive actions to take. Evaluate what other problems might arise, how you can prevent them, and how you could respond to them. When looking at each of them, consider what changes you would make in your responses to the difficulties if you have children, such as protecting them and helping them learn new skills that will help them respond effectively to future hardships.

How could you or will you handle these?:

- Loss or change of spiritual faith
- Getting upset, losing control, behaving or speaking in a disorderly or disrespectful way
- Treating others poorly or embarrassing them
- Compromising confidentiality
- Gossiping or backbiting
- Unreasonably complaining
- Infidelity or other unchaste choices
- Emotional or physical over-dependence on each other, such that you need each other to always be present and you avoid relationships with others
- Lack of responsibility for self
- Verbal, mental, emotional, spiritual, physical, or sexual manipulation, threats, or abuse

- Mental or emotional illness/conditions (depression, bi-polarism, anxiety, borderline personality disorder, eating disorder, suicide threats or attempts, seasonal affected disorder, et. al.)
- Addictions or substance abuse (alcohol, illegal and prescription drugs, food, sex, gambling, et. al.)
- Illnesses and allergies (preventable, non-preventable, minor, and chronic)
- Infertility
- Sexually transmitted diseases/infections
- Sexual impairment
- Discipline of children and stepchildren
- Illnesses in children
- Unruly teenagers
- Assisting aging or ill parents or other relatives
- Accidents (preventable and non-preventable)
- Restricted physical activity or permanent physical disability
- Smoking or chewing tobacco
- Financial issues (irresponsible bill paying, mismanagement, breaking trust, credit problems, bankruptcy, impulsive shopping, et. al.)
- Uncontrollable external forces (weather, fire, animals, theft, difficult neighbors, disasters, et. al.)
- Death of a child, parent, each other, close family member, or friend
- Illegal actions and/or imprisonment
- Legal problems and lawsuits

Of course, if any of these problems currently exist in your relationship, you would be wise to address them now and assess whether or not now is the time for marriage. As you acknowledge that the difficulties are occurring, accept them, and take actions in response, you will then be empowered to resolve them or make other choices. Unfortunately, it can be a common pattern—especially in romantic relationships—to resist or deny problems. This is likely counterproductive. Overcoming denial helps you to seek out and accept assistance or decide that marriage is unwise or untimely. *Problems will not just magically go away with marriage.* In fact, they often become worse, particularly if you are hiding behavior or not addressing it during courtship.

To discern how serious a problem is and how well you are responding to it, consider these questions:

- What are the facts of the situation?
- What are your thoughts and feelings?
- What spiritual principles apply to the situation?
- What character qualities will assist you to respond to it successfully?
- Are you responding by turning to God or by swearing at your bad luck?
- How important is the issue?
- Can you accept the problem so you can become free to detach from it or resolve it?
- What can be changed or resolved?
- What is each of you willing to do? Are these actions respectful and healthy for both of you now and over time?
- At what point do you need to seek help?
- To whom can you turn for help?
- What is your history of overcoming challenges and proving that you can thrive in the face of them?
- Will it be helpful to wait and re-examine the situation after some time has passed?

Helping Each Other

As you talk about assisting each other with problems, remember that what you may initially perceive as helpful may not actually be beneficial. For instance, your natural tendency might be to try to solve or eliminate your partner's pain or difficulties. This may make it impossible for them to grow, change, and make new choices on their own. An example is in responding to addiction. A partner or spouse may hide the problem or even obtain substances for the addict in order to try to keep them happy and calm. However, this type of enabling can cause the problem to worsen or remain unaddressed longer than if the person accepted personal responsibility and sought a solution. As another example, one of you may be mistreated by the other, and based on what you consider "compassion" for the abuser, you may not address and stop the abuse or seek help.

Although you cannot plan for every difficulty that may arise, you will gain significant insights through your assessment of handling difficulties from the past, current discussions, and responses to difficulties that you are having now. You can get a sense of one another's character and responses to difficult circumstances. You can use facts, prayer, and intuition to discern whether you each have the necessary strengths to handle whatever arises. You can also understand which current problems are unlikely to change for the better. You then have a choice about whether to marry each other or to part as friends.

Relationship Coaching

1. Know your own and your families' complete medical histories and the implications of these histories (including any history of psychological problems, abuse, or mental illnesses). You may be wise to speak directly with each other's family members, where appropriate.

2. Listen to your intuition for warning signs. Avoid thinking, "It will all be better after we get married." Marriage does not make problems go away! In fact, sometimes living in close personal space together often makes problems more visible and crises more likely. What are you observing now that concerns you? What would you advise someone else to do who had the same concerns as you?

3. Find support groups, counselors, books, and literature that can give you facts about whatever situation you are facing. Definitely do not use information from each other as the only source of information.

4. Know that marriage is not a cure-all, a rescue mission, or a social development project. Many problems will naturally arise in any marriage. Do not try to use marriage as a tool to save someone. That rarely works, often because there is an unbalanced relationship—not a partnership—between the rescuer and the other person. You do not need to make life more difficult by choosing to be in a relationship weighed down by behavior and character problems. *If you have to struggle to maintain harmony, you will spend all of your energy trying to keep the relationship going, with little left to focus on anything else.* This may cause you to neglect your family, friends, work, and community service.

5. Bonding happens over time and through shared experiences. However, it is unwise to rely solely on bonding that has happened primarily during a crisis or tragedy. A resulting marriage may be based on a feeling of gratitude toward someone because they helped and supported you during a specific crisis. This gratitude is unlikely to sustain a long-term marriage.

Susanne M. Alexander is a Relationship and Marriage Coach with a specialty in character (www.marriagetransformation.com). She has experienced and helped people through more of the above difficulties than she likes to remember—and she has learned much along the way!

© 2010 S. Alexander

♥ ♥ ♥

Is Alcohol a Possible Problem in Our Relationship?
Michael J. Beck, Ph.D.

These days, there is much more hope and help for people with alcohol problems than there used to be, and more awareness of the whole idea of substance abuse. Celebrities in the media and Hollywood have gone public with all types of addictions, so there is a greater visibility of the effect of them on people's lives. I think people are more willing to accept that they might have a problem or that they do have an addiction. Nevertheless, there are still many people who have denial about their addiction problems, and so do the people closest to them. Below are some ideas you can raise with each other as a couple that might put someone on the right path to getting help, and to help you with thinking about what you're involved with as a couple.

Drinkers tend to fall into three basic categories: social drinkers, teetotalers, and problem drinkers. Putting it roughly, if you regularly drink more than three drinks at a sitting, or if you are working hard to hide your drinking from others, you should start to worry about whether you have a problem. If there is a problem, you will also see negative consequences from the drinking such as car incidents, financial issues, relationship disruptions, or key tasks undone. When you do actions like these on a regular basis, or begin to see serious negative effects, you're probably drinking for some other reason than to just be friendly and sociable.

The most prevalent reason why people drink is to cover up painful experiences from their childhood or past. There is a lot of debate and opinion about whether alcoholism is a disease and what exactly that means. The disease concept is very prevalent in Alcoholic Anonymous (AA; www.aa.org). AA helps many people, so I am not going to get into a debate about whether alcoholism is a disease, but people who counsel alcoholics can certainly help them without subscribing to any one particular point of view on that topic. Friends and family members may also find it helpful to seek help through Al-Anon Family Groups (www.al-anon.alateen.org) or a counselor.

There are well-known factors that contribute to alcohol abuse. One of them is early loss of a parent. If you are quite young and lose a parent to divorce or death, this predisposes you to be depressed. If the remaining parent doesn't remarry, that parent often experiences feelings of loss and resentment. It's probably a very unpleasant environment to grow up in if you have one parent straining to do everything, and you are unlikely to experience a positive childhood. I'm not applying this outcome to everybody, but in my experience, there seems to be a disproportionate number of people who develop problems with alcohol later on who were raised in a single-parent household. Ask each other carefully about what your childhood environments were like as far as alcohol use, and about the emotional climate in the home.

An even stronger predisposing factor is having an alcoholic parent or other members of the family who have had problems with alcohol. This is a big burden for somebody to overcome. People point to this factor as indicating that there is a genetic or constitutional factor in alcoholism, and there may well be. Some people hold the theory that alcoholics have a genetic problem metabolizing sugars. Again, that's a factor.

There are also cultural factors. Certain ethnic groups have a reputation for consuming vast amounts of alcohol. Drinking alcohol is also acceptable in the broad culture of society. However, if you have alcoholic parents, your risk is much higher. I once knew a woman who had married five times, each time to an alcoholic. She was clearly comfortable around people who drank heavily! Surely, there must have been at least one alcoholic relative in her family of origin. Sometimes children grow up so traumatized by the alcohol use in their homes that they won't go near the stuff, but that is not always the case.

If either of you have any concerns about whether you have a problem with alcohol, you should consult an alcoholism professional. They can evaluate you and make treatment recommendations or try to help you overcome this problem.

Obviously, if you have an active problem with alcohol and you do get married, somebody is going to be unhappy. A woman or a man who stays in a relationship with an alcoholic is often poorly treated. I'm not necessarily recommending divorce, but it can be a pretty horrendous situation for all concerned, particularly the spouse and children of the alcoholic. There is a lot of resentment, and both spouses have unmet needs; there could be physical or sexual violence, suicide threats and attempts, and all types of financial and social problems. Any children born into the marriage are often traumatized. Therefore, if you're contemplating marriage and you think you might have a problem with alcohol or other people have said you do, or if you have had incidents driving while impaired or arrests after driving while intoxicated, take a good look at yourself and your circumstances.

If the material in this chapter has raised some concerns about either of you, start asking questions and carefully observing what is happening. If your intended spouse is hanging around with people who drink heavily, you've got social pressure reinforcing their denial. When you love someone, you could also be denying that there is anything wrong, or you could be assuming that marriage will stop the behavior and cure everything that's wrong. It won't. Look before you leap!

Michael J. Beck, Ph.D., received his post-doctoral training at the Center for Modern Psychoanalytic Studies in New York, where he published a number of his most important articles. He went on to found the Institute for Psychotherapeutic Studies, where he taught, wrote, and supervised mental health professionals for a number of years. He is published in the area of child and family dynamics in the *Long Island Clinician and Family Therapy and Psychoanalytic Review*. He edited the book *The Narcissistic Family Member*. He is co-author with his wife and daughter of *365 Questions for Couples*. Dr. Beck has led workshops on Family and Marital Therapy and Modern Treatment of Depression and Anxiety for Western Suffolk Personnel & Guidance Association, Suffolk County Psychological Association, and the American Association of Sex Educators, Counselors & Therapists (AASECT). He is a Fellow in Family Therapy of AASECT, and he has been cited as a "Supervisor of Excellence" by the California Psychological Association. Michael Beck has been married since 1967. He and Stanis Beck live in New York and have two adult daughters. Dr. Beck can be reached at mjbeck3391@att.blackberry.net.

❤ ❤ ❤

Relationship Recovery—Path to the Promised Land
Kat Knecht and Curtis Knecht

Right here at relationship recovery is where most of the work of relationships lies. All the rest is fine and well, but if you don't know how to recover when you plummet into that hot vortex of reactivity, then you will actually do damage to the heart of your relationship. And over time, those little and seemingly innocuous wounds will wear away at the love and trust between you.

The good news is that if you master this part, you can have all the rest in your marriage—good sex, lots of fun, financial success, intimate conversations, and a deep connection—oh, and let's not forget lasting love! And you can begin to practice this skill now, before you marry.

Yes, we are making a big promise to you, and it's one not made lightly. Here is why mastery of recovery will deliver the goods: When we are afraid we will be revealed in some low light, we feel small and go into a knee-jerk, protective reaction, right? When we are masters of something, we are no longer afraid. When we are no longer afraid, we are fully engaged in our relationships and operating from our true essence.

In our work with couples, we continue to find that it doesn't matter what the problem is or how much the partners love each other. It doesn't matter how good of friends they are or how much money they have. When it comes to determining the fulfillment AND the longevity of a relationship, the one thing needed is skill in processing all the crap that naturally arises in any relationship—to come clean and tell each other the truth! Any hiding or avoiding or sidestepping the truth or lying will erode a relationship. It may not kill it off completely, but it will eat into the joy and trust and sap your energy.

When Trouble Shows Up

So, how do we tell each other the truth when we are angry? When we are afraid? When we know the truth might hurt? Bottom-line: How do we tell each other the truth without getting into trouble?

As Relationship Coaches, we know that this is often difficult to do, so we have created an exercise that helps our clients face all types of tricky situations: those moments when you lose your cool or when your lovely partner or spouse has sprouted horns; moments when you are inches away from screaming, "Buzz off! And the hell with practicing all this relationship stuff!"; moments when you feel so small and alone; and moments when all you want to do is to run and hide.

It's in those exact moments when it's possible to DO something that brings about relationship mastery, even when you don't feel like it. With enough practice, you will reach the Promised Land—a rich, meaningful, positive, creative, and fun relationship heaven. You will be a relationship master, and that is a promise.

Among the numerous tools available, one of the most powerful ways to create harmony is to learn how to PAUSE. Yes, stop and pause instead of succumbing to a triggered feeling and following that murky and destructive path. The magic of this simple (but not always easy) step is that it gives you breathing room. And with this much-needed space, you have access to higher wisdom for your higher good. Practice this step on a regular basis, and you will see what we mean. After that, there are many choices.

Practice Makes…Perfect?

"Oh, Kat and Curtis, you must have a perfect marriage with all you know. You are relationship experts, right? You've studied and taught this stuff for years and devote your whole lives to the art and science of relationships. But does it really work in your marriage all the time?"

People express this sentiment to us often. The answer is, yes, we have a great marriage—*and* we have that because we are willing to do the work. We have practiced and practiced until we now naturally know how to recover *most of the time* when our emotions run high, when one of us is cranky, when we are facing stressful circumstances, or when we drift apart because we get caught up in our work. We also have practiced long enough that those moments don't come up often. But it was not always so. Let us tell you a little of our story.

Falling and Failing

Once upon a time, we fell deeply in love. We wanted to spend every single moment together. Deep down inside, we knew we were right for each other. We were soulmates, destined to be together forever. We liked doing the same things, and we complemented each other's personalities. We were not only in love; we were best friends—a match made in heaven.

And then the business we had started together failed. And then we had trouble agreeing on discipline for his son. And then Kat was lost in Curtis's city and wanted to go home. And then we showed each other our true colors.

And then the work of learning the recovery process began.

We were forced to either give up our vision of having a loving and honest relationship or to do the necessary work. We had to learn how to face difficult circumstances—the tangible, real-world situations, as well as the even more challenging enterprise of revealing sides of ourselves that were not so pretty.

So what did we do? Well, we were pulled forward by that vision of the Promised Land, of a consciously loving and romantic relationship that we KNEW was ours to have. And we committed to learning how to recover from the unavoidable messiness of relationships. We chose to eliminate our old limited and destructive behavior, once and for all.

Here's some more good news: Once you know how to recover, you can't "un-know" it. Of course, there will be moments when you forget momentarily, but just like riding a bike, it will come back to you quickly. You will choose to stay upright and peddling rather than crashing and biting the dust.

To Tell the Truth

This brings us back to learning how to tell the truth even when it looks bad—an essential element of relationship recovery. It used to be in our marriage that Kat would find herself very hurt by some conceived insensitivity that Curtis had done. The next logical step would be for her to tear up and sniffle a little and begin wondering how she could have married such a jerk—even though just minutes earlier she thought he was a prince!

What Kat has learned since then is that truthfully in those circumstances, she was angry. She was just plain mad. Instead of telling the truth about it, though, she would disguise her anger with hurt, what she thought to be a much prettier emotion. Unfortunately, this turned into a real victim stance on her part.

When Kat first started with some baby steps of telling Curtis that she was angry, she found her worst fears realized. He didn't like it a bit. He responded pretty much as he had when she expressed that she was feeling hurt. Wait a minute! She was being honest with him. Shouldn't that count for something?

To make the shift, it took many months of Kat staying true to herself. Why is that? Well, in any relationship there is always an agreed-upon (often unconscious or unspoken) give-and-take about how we're going to be when we don't like something—even if it is highly dysfunctional and a negative experience for all involved. When one person changes, it means the other person has to change. And let's face it, none of us enjoy change when it feels out of our control.

During those months when Kat was taking more and more steps toward being real about her anger, we had to work out just how we really wanted to handle conflict in our marriage. If Kat was going to express her anger, that meant Curtis had to change too. He had to learn how to not take what she was saying personally. We both had to be willing to go through a messy time of discomfort. Kat learned that she had to take responsibility for her own thinking and feelings. Just because she was angry didn't mean anything, except that she was angry. It was simply the emotion showing up to let her know something was happening in her inner world.

Again, pausing came into play. Kat found if she could do some reporting to herself about her anger, then she could allow it to be fully felt and therefore contained. She could find out what was at the heart of it before it took over and landed her in trouble at the deep end of the pool. Sometimes she needed to say it out loud, too, because it was so apparent to Curtis. He never really liked hearing it, but he, too, learned to pause and notice his own thinking.

The Promised Land Exercise

One of the easiest ways to find ourselves in hot water is to just blurt out our frustration or anger. We all know it is important not to stuff our feelings inside, right? But there is a huge difference between stuffing and doing a full expression that creates a negative impact. This exercise below is excellent at setting up a boundary that creates order rather than chaos.

When we speak directly to another person in a way that points the finger of blame, the natural consequence is for that person to shoot back, defend themselves, or shut down. None of those reactions ever does them or us any good. Nothing worthwhile gets communicated, and often we get dumped into a downward cycle of negativity and despair.

So, what do we do? Here are some new tools to help you in the exercise that follows:

- **Pause:** Breathing and taking your own personal time out. Pausing is a habit that gives us the ability to be in the present moment and access our internal wisdom instead of reacting thoughtlessly.

- **Report:** Communicating in a neutral way what you are feeling, thinking, and experiencing. Reporting is a structure for taking ownership of whatever you are considering saying. This is especially powerful when both people are aware of the term, but it can work regardless.
- **Release:** Letting go of knowing or searching for what to do next. Releasing is helpful when you are in a situation where you just know that talking or reporting is not going to work.
- All three of the above tools help you with lightening up and being grounded in yourself.

Now, let's move on to the exercise. When an incident happens, your access to handling it well, protecting your relationship, and recovering promptly depends upon taking the following steps:

1. **Pause:**

   a. Take a time out. Just plain stop the flow of negative thinking and put yourself in neutral.

2. **Report:** *You can do this silently or out loud to yourself or to your honey.*

   a. Use these phrases to start your sentence: "I need to report that..." or "I'm noticing that...." When you say these words, you are taking full responsibility for your own feelings or thoughts. When you hear them, you honor them as a loving boundary. As you'll see in the examples provided below, this is a powerful and positive tool of communication, as long as you take ownership and don't turn your report into a sneaky type of blaming.

   b. You can do these silently or out loud to yourself or your partner. Some examples might be (to yourself) "I need to report that I hate it when he does that and that I could go crazy right now" or (to your partner) "I'm noticing that I'm feeling angry. I'm noticing that my stomach is all knotted up. I'm noticing that I am thinking negative thoughts, so I am going to pause and take a bath now."

3. **Release:**

   a. This is an internal action. It might sound like, "Oh well. That didn't work. I don't know what is really going on, so I will trust that we will find our way eventually" or "I don't know what to do, so I will simply let this go for now and see what happens" or "I'm going to give this some space. I'll talk about it later when I'm calmer."

4. Hand it Back Over:

    a. This is an external action, and it is where teamwork comes in. It might sound like, "I hear what you are saying. What do you think is needed? How would that look? What are the results you want to achieve? What would it take to make this right?"

Helpful Hints:

- **Pause** and **Report** are the steps to use when you know you have stepped over a line and want to lead the two of you back to solid ground.
- **Hand it Back Over** is a brilliant way to stay grounded in situations when the other person is upset.

Marriage Case Study: Grow or Go

To give you a sense of what's ahead for you in marriage, consider the experience of Tamika and Randall:

Tamika and Randall had just passed the three-year point in a very happy marriage, working out the bumps that most couples encounter in the early years. They were past Stage One, the Glowing Stage, when everything seems perfectly magical, and you love everything about each other. They had also had passed through Stage Two, the Knowing Stage, when you get to *really* know each other, warts and all.

It's after this second stage that people often see a choice for themselves. We call this Stage Three, the Grow or Go Stage. Either do the work of accepting each other exactly as you are, learn how to navigate the waters of marriage, and learn how to grow as individuals and as a couple OR cut your losses. It's not surprising to learn that most marriages begin or end somewhere in this stage. They either grow or go.

Tamika and Randall were solidly in this Grow or Go Stage. They were now committed for the long haul in a way they hadn't been when they walked down the aisle. Tamika wanted to go the distance, but she also knew that when things got sticky in the relationship, she reverted to habits that were doing some serious damage. After learning about the PAUSE exercise, she found herself innocently entering her bathroom and noticed her immediate triggered reaction, which went something like, "Again? Can't he for once clean up those little hairs on the sink after he shaves? Of course I will have to clean it up. If I don't clean it up, nobody else will. I'm the only one who even notices or cares. My mother was right. Women have to do everything."

It was right about here that she caught herself in the act, shut the bathroom door behind her, and paused. Using the second part of the exercise, she started to REPORT to herself: "I am noticing that I just hate that Randall doesn't help clean the house. I am noticing that I suddenly feel exhausted. I am noticing that I'm about to freak out about little hairs."

Tamika continued until she got herself out of the triggered "I think I will give him a piece of my mind" state and actually began laughing hysterically. She considered all of Randall's exceptional qualities and the truth about all that he contributes to their couplehood. It was at this point that she knew she could open the door and resume her day with Randall. Tamika and Randall then went on to have a wonderful and loving day together, creating more of a bond than ever could have been built by laboring over the tidiness of the bathroom.

What happened next was even more delightful for Tamika. The next day, she noticed that Randall took out the trash and walked the dog. Then he asked if there was anything she needed while he was out at the gym. This was the payoff of taking the time to pause. **When you pause and choose your relationship over being right, magical things often happen.**

Whether you do this process internally or out loud, when you pause and allow yourself to really see what you are thinking, you can make a choice about what action to take or not to take. Then, the payoff comes when you really get to notice how your partner responds. We so often think that communication needs to be verbal. How and what we say is important, but more important is what we are thinking and feeling. That is what others actually pick up most clearly from us. If we are feeling resentment or thinking negatively about our partner, believe me, it will be responded to no matter how sweet our words.

Play around with the Promised Land Exercise. Use the steps that come most naturally. Stretch a little and allow yourself to feel stiff for a while too. Use the steps together, use them alone, or make up phrases of your own. And remember what paves the road to the Promised Land: practice, practice, practice! When you master this relationship skill, we guarantee your marriage will be strengthened, and you will grow closer together through the years.

Kat Kehres Knecht, C.P.C.C., P.C.C., and Curtis Knecht, M.F.T., P.C.C., are co-Founders of The Relationship Coaching Company (www.RelationshipCoaching.com). They developed a program that uses the 7 Keys to Relationship Success to teach and coach individuals and couples how to create extraordinary relationships. They are the creators of the Staying Engaged cards, a combination of playing cards and discussion-prompting relationship questions. Kat specializes in helping women entrepreneurs who are looking for a fulfilling love life, has her own weekly radio show, and makes regular contributions to the media. She is the author of *It's Not Just Your Wedding, It's Your Life!* Curtis uses an integration of coaching and psychotherapy, along with humor, to bring creativity, life, and light into a healing process that turns even the deepest of troubles into a rich opportunity for learning and growing. Kat and Curtis teach what they live and love what they do. They are married and live in Ventura, California. They have a blended family of four remarkable adult children. Kat and Curtis have each experienced divorce, so they know firsthand the importance of beginning any relationship with very clear intentions and a commitment to staying connected all along the way. Contact at: Connect@RelationshipCoaching.com or 805-641-3281.

❤ ❤ ❤

Violence in Relationships
Ana Morante

Violence is one of the most damaging things that can be done to a person's sense of self. Violence is a learned behavior. More than difficulties with handling our anger, domestic violence is a pattern of behaviors used to gain or maintain power and control of an intimate partner or family member. There are several forms in which the violent person may exert that power and control. These may include emotional, psychological, physical, sexual, spiritual, or financial. The danger with domestic violence is that unless a couple gets help to stop the cycle, it can escalate to the point that it may end up in the death of one of the partners.

If one of you has been raised in an environment where there was violence, you have definitely been impacted by that, and you may end up repeating the cycle unless you get help to heal. The problem with violence is that many times we get numb, and we have a tendency to minimize or deny that it's happening. Then we allow things that shouldn't be happening in our relationship.

Sometimes, when children see violence, they may identify with the more powerful one, whether it's the man or the woman being violent. They may seek to solve their own difficulties by using their power and control over another person, because that is what has been modeled for them. If the child does not learn ways of exerting their own power in a more positive way, they end up becoming violent toward another person.

On the other hand, some of the children may identify with the victim and may have difficulties asserting themselves. They may get used to being in relationships where the other person is abusing them at many different levels. Many times, people who have been raised in a violent environment tend to get into relationships either as perpetrators or as victims of violence as well.

I see perpetrators as those little children who saw violence but never got help and were never shown a better way of finding their own self and their own strength. One of the most effective ways to help perpetrators is by using a compassionate approach. It is important to teach these people that they do have a lot of good things inside and that they do not have to gain power and control over someone else. It's definitely a process they need to experience, and it's not an easy one. It takes time.

In most cases, overcoming violent tendencies does require professional assistance, because having violent experiences very young does not allow the person to develop other more adaptive skills in life. They were raised in an environment where they needed to be alert all the time and hyper-vigilant over where the violence was going to come from. In attempting to be so vigilant, they miss the opportunities to learn other skills that are going to be more socially adaptive. It does require a lot of help, but violence does not get better by itself. It's a cycle that repeats and actually intensifies with time. It's very dangerous, and we need to be very aware that we need help for it.

One of the keys to healing is strengthening who we are, enhancing our sense of self, and learning how to respect ourselves. People must learn to put some boundaries in place with other people, but when people are raised in violent situations, those boundaries are very blurred and very confused, and that creates difficulties in other relationships as well.

If you are experiencing violence in your couple relationship, especially if there is a regular pattern of it, then it would be wise to get help. There are a lot of resources available. Unless you get help and healing for this issue, you will likely pass it on to the next generation. There is a lot of hope if both of you are serious about engaging in your own healing process. A healthy marriage involves respect between both of you. Creating respect and safety within your relationship is a crucial component for a strong and long-lasting marriage.

Editor's Notes: The above is excerpted and edited from an interview between Susanne Alexander and Ana Morante on March 10, 2010. You may find the following book to be a useful resource: *You Don't Have to Take It Anymore: Turn Your Resentful, Angry, or Emotionally Abusive Relationship into a*

Compassionate, Loving One, by Steven Stosny. Dr. Stosny also offers courses for people experiencing anger issues (www.compassionpower.com).

Ana Morante, L.M.F.T., C.F.L.E., is a bilingual Marriage, Family, and Child Therapist, helping people in both Spanish and English. She is dedicated to strengthening couples and families and assisting in the creation of the best environment possible for children. She has a private practice in San Jose, California, and is a certified Parent and Family Life Educator and a Family Wellness Partner and Trainer. Ana has been married for sixteen years and has two daughters and a stepson. She can be reached through www.familywellness.com.

Chapter Nineteen
Planning for Marriage

~ ~

Now it's time to envision and write down what you want your marriage to look like. There are excellent tools and practices in this chapter that help you check out your assumptions and expectations of what being married will look like. If you are cohabiting, you may be tempted to skip this step and believe you are already living what marriage will look like, but don't be fooled! Your relationship will change with your commitment and as you begin acting out your long-held and sometimes unconscious beliefs about how husbands and wives behave.

Whatever your situation, it will be helpful to you long-term if you create your goals now. You'll continue to discuss and adjust them over time as needed, but the fundamental map that you develop now will guide your course throughout your marriage. You will also learn more in this chapter about tools and resources for engaging in a more formal relationship assessment process, something we have also mentioned in other chapters.

❤ ❤ ❤

Creating a Vision for Your Marriage
John Curtis, Ph.D.

Creating Your Ideal Marriage

Historically, few couples did any planning on how to achieve a lifelong marriage. While some vision may have been assumed and even stated as part of the wedding vows, it is unlikely that newlyweds sat down together to develop an actual written plan. It may seem somewhat unromantic, but the key to actually creating a lasting marriage that includes romance is by applying the business practice of sound, long-range vision planning.

Just like enlightened executives and entrepreneurs who create and continually refine a long-range strategic plan for their business, you can develop and continually update your own plan for how your relationship will develop and sustain itself for life. Your vision should have a lifelong time horizon.

The mental process of creating the vision statement forces you each to stop and wonder, "What is my view of our relationship in the future? I never thought about that before. I'm simply in love and want to spend the rest of my life with this person." Well, that's all fine and good, but is it enough to make a relationship last? Love alone is rarely enough to make the relationship last—at least happily!

It is important to create this vision together. If one of you does not want to participate then, at a minimum, agree to think about it and be prepared to discuss it. Tell your partner how important it is to you to jointly develop a shared vision to help plan for and ensure an excellent marriage. As is often said in business, "Those who fail to plan, plan to fail," so don't let this be the case with your intimate relationship.

Developing this vision will help the two of you determine whether you are unified enough in your outlook to marry. If you are united and choose to go forward into engagement and marriage, the vision then provides you with a guideline for making important decisions. You will be able to regularly assess: "Is this choice in alignment with our vision?"

Writing Your Vision Statement

A vision statement for your relationship is simply a few words that are poetic, elegant, and idealistic to define its future ideal state. A simple example is America's Pledge of Allegiance to the Flag. Another is: "One nation, under God, indivisible, with liberty and justice for all." On a grander scale, another vision statement is: "A world without hunger!" On a more intimate level, as is so often stated in wedding vows, there is this one: "For richer or for poorer, in good times and in bad, until death us do part!" As you can see, a vision statement can be basic and easy to understand, but it should motivate, inspire, and stimulate you to action.

Now, it is your turn to write your own vision statement!

Getting Started—Warm-up Exercises

Exercise 1: Identify some of your core values to incorporate into your vision statement. One way to spot these is to look for tangible items in your life that represent what you value most. It may be a piece of jewelry you're wearing, an emblem on your key chain, a picture on your computer desktop, or a cherished symbol on the wall. Typically, these items represent or remind you of such things as significant people and life accomplishments. A vision statement for your relationship can incorporate these core values.

Exercise 2: Search the Internet for examples of vision statements. Go to websites of organizations that you know and trust, such as your employer, your place of worship, a community hospital, your favorite electronics brand, your college or university, or even a branch of government. Many examples are readily available, and viewing how others have written vision statements may help you develop a better vision statement for your marriage.

Initial Work—As Individuals

Step 1: Work on the first draft of your vision statements individually. This way, you don't influence each other, avoid this challenging task, or unwisely give in to the other's perspective.

Step 2: This is where the hard work comes in. Initially, you may think of a vision for yourself rather than for you and your partner. That's okay! It is simply part of the process of moving from a single view of the future to one of a couple working in a unified partnership. Imagine your ideal relationship twenty, thirty, forty, or more years into the future. Envision where you would like your relationship and family to be, what you and your partner will be doing, what achievements you will have made, what your sense of purpose will be, and so forth.

Step 3: Based on this mental image, begin to write first drafts of a vision statement for your relationship that describes—in about fifty words or less—your vision for your future marriage relationship. Keep in mind that it is very unlikely that you will write the ideal statement at first. It is okay to use phases, change the wording, and do lots of editing, just get started. Be sure to use a pencil with a good eraser, or be prepared to make many changes in the statement on your computer.

Step 4: Decide on a time and place to discuss your individual vision statements together where you will work on combining them into a unified vision for the marriage. Plan for the needed time to truly explore your thoughts and emotions about the future. Remember that you may find out your vision statements appear to be quite different. You may have some major issues to discuss!

Having a Smooth, Productive Couple Discussion

When trying to combine your visions for the future of your relationship into a shared vision, you may run into disagreements. It is often at this point—when you start to dig deeper into who you each are and what you value in the relationship—that you discover new dimensions of your personalities. This process of discovery can help you reach new levels of openness and intimacy. At the same time, you may find that you appear to be far apart on the values that each of you has for your marriage vision, and this is where the hard work of negotiating begins.

No matter how long it takes, keep talking, discovering, and working toward a common vision, even if at first there seems to be irreconcilable differences. These discussions may evoke strong emotions and require a concerted effort to stay open and accepting of each other.

In addition, while doing this process, your worst fear may seem to come true—the fear that you do not appear to be compatible. Because of poor judgment, you may have entered into a relationship that was doomed from the start, and you will need to be honest with each other if it's clear that is the case. However, *don't jump to conclusions now!* The doubt you might be feeling may simply be the result of entering a new level of honesty and intimacy together, so it is only natural to feel somewhat anxious and afraid.

Just remember not to give in to anxiety or fear by compromising your values. This could lead to long-term anger and resentment. Giving up more and more of who you are and what you believe to keep the peace, will undermine your relationship and marriage over time. The result of negotiation must be a win-win outcome.

Combining Your Vision Statements

What you are looking for in this part of the activity can be compared to the lighting of a unity candle at a wedding ceremony. As you may know, the ritual begins with each partner lighting an individual candle. Together, the couple then lights the single unity candle with their individual candles. They then extinguish their separate candles, thereby taking two separate flames and making them one. This is a symbol of joining your individual visions into one common vision for the marriage.

Look at the examples below of two seemingly different vision statements from the same couple. Each partner created a statement separately:

Hers:

"In our ideal marriage, we will express our individuality through our intelligence and creativity. We are equal partners in our relationship but value each other's different approach to life. We are close to God and active in our church. We do all this with the intention of being truthful with ourselves and each other and by enriching our lives and leaving the world a better place. We will travel, expand our horizons, deepen family relationships, and live life to the fullest, free of materialistic burdens."

His:

"My vision for the future ideal state of our relationship is one based on integrity and full of rich and deep meaning that comes from ever increasing exploration of who we are and how we show our love. We each will be devoted to helping the other reach our full potential. We will give our children roots and wings and always laugh and learn with them. We will achieve financial security and maintain balance in all areas of life together."

You can see that the couple has different perspectives, but once the visions are shared and integrated, they may be closer in meaning than they seem. As you look at your own individual visions together, look for the commonalities in concepts and values, regardless of the words. Are you using terms that sound different on the surface but are really saying the same basic thing? For instance, one of you may be talking about the value of "integrity," while the other emphasizes "truth." Can you see how they are similar and resolvable when examined side by side? When you identify core concepts and values within each vision statement, you might find that you are closer to each other than you thought.

Also, don't be concerned if your vision statements sound completely different than these examples. There is no one right way to do this and no pre-determined outcome. The key is to be bold, honest, creative, and future-focused, with an emphasis on the ideal state you desire for your lifelong marriage.

Here's an example of combining the separate vision statements from above into a **unified statement:**

"Our vision for our relationship is one where we will have complete trust and honesty, free of fears or anxieties, and full of acceptance and support. We each will be devoted to helping one another reach our full potential through the ever-increasing exploration of who we are as partners and parents and by expressing our individuality. We will be close to God, Who will bless us with lives full of deep meaning. We will continue to explore our world and include our family members whenever possible. We will be free of material burdens while living a rich and full life."

Now, it's time for you to start the first draft of *your* vision statement! Remember, the words you use will ultimately form the basis of your marital vision statement. Take time to genuinely reflect on what you see as the future ideal state of your marriage. Then put your intentions into writing. This carefully crafted statement should become the foundation for all your thoughts, feelings, words and actions—as long as you both shall live.

John Curtis, Ph.D., is a consultant, researcher, business trainer, and author. Previously, John was a full-time marriage and family counselor, who achieved clinical membership in the American Association for Marriage and Family Therapy. His education includes a Masters in Counseling and a Ph.D. in Human Resource Development. John is married with two children and two grandchildren. John's book, *Marriage Built to Last: 9 Steps to Life-Long Love!* can be found at www.marriagebuilttolast.org. His book *Happily Un-Married: Living Together & Loving It* is at www.wecohabitate.com.

© 2010 J. Curtis

❤ ❤ ❤

Creating Your Marriage Commitments
Susanne M. Alexander

Craig and I were fairly certain we could have a happy marriage. However, we were coming out of unhappy marriages and divorces and clear we wanted to take a marriage together in a new direction. We also wanted to be sure we were in agreement about what this potential new marriage would look like. Over a few weeks, we wrote down and discussed what we were committed to doing if we married.

As we discussed what was important to both of us, we confirmed that we were a good match. We then shared the list with our parents and asked for their input. My mother added one item at the end to remind us that we wouldn't be perfect at all the rest of the commitments on the list.

As part of our wedding ceremony, we publicly read our marriage commitments out loud to our family and friends. Each year on our anniversary, we re-read them and assessed our progress. Where we fell short, we set goals for the coming year.

Over the years, we modified our original commitments list to create a lengthier and more general list for other couples to choose from or get ideas from. When you make your own list, please feel free to borrow from the ones below.

United in mind, heart, and soul, we affirm that the intent of our marriage is to create an extraordinary family. Our commitment is to:

- Be friends with each other and united in body, mind, heart, and soul.
- Treat others—and especially each other, family, and friends—with love, honor, respect, courtesy, and integrity.
- Help and encourage one another's personal growth and transformation and the spiritual transformation of others.
- Regularly, lovingly, and tactfully share any hurts or annoyances we are feeling using "I feel…" terms rather than "You do not…" language. Set up a regular time to share openly and honestly.
- Honor and respect our own and each other's physical, mental, emotional, and spiritual needs and assist each other in meeting those needs in whatever way possible.
- Engage in physical and recreational activities together, particularly those that contribute to our physical, emotional, and spiritual wellbeing. Create an environment that encourages each of us to maintain a healthy physical lifestyle.
- Fully express and share all aspects of our selves and our lives at appropriate times.
- Nurture a spirit of community with others.
- Ensure that the marriage bond is our primary one, and we are faithful to it. Commit to addressing actively and wholeheartedly any attractions or feelings that arise for someone else, working to rekindle love for each other and our marriage commitment.
- Respond to issues that arise as quickly as possible, using consultative decision making as a tool in all matters.
- Be fully conscious, fully present with each other.
- Maintain some time alone for each of us as individuals.
- Ensure we spend time together as a couple on a regular basis.

- Cherish, honor, and respect our children by nurturing bonds of communication and love with them.
- Never argue in front of our children.
- Build and maintain loving and open relationships with all family members.
- Enrich our lives with separate and mutual friendships.
- Demonstrate and accept intimacy from one another regularly.
- Have regular family meetings, including children in the process for problem solving and planning.
- Pray and read scripture separately and together every day.
- Be involved in regular service to each other, our families, friends, and communities.
- Be playful, have fun, and incorporate humor into daily life.
- Choose to speak positive words about each other both to one another and to others.
- Hug and kiss one another every day.
- Act with integrity in all things, including in our finances, our work, and our service commitments.
- Engage in ongoing learning of new information and skills, as well as development of our characters and talents.
- Encourage each other's talents and skills.
- Compliment and praise one another and our children every day. Ensure that for any negative comment, three to five positive ones are offered.
- Enrich our lives with the arts.
- Limit our television or computer time to a moderate amount.
- Regularly participate in religious activities.
- Help one another through difficult times.
- Accompany each other in preparing for passing when end-of-life time arrives.
- Be patient, accepting, and nurturing, maintaining the constancy of our relationship through times of adversity and when we are not being our best selves.

Specifically writing down your intentions makes it more likely that you will fulfill them. There is significant power in commitment. This is one of the quotations that inspired us to make our commitments:

"Until one is committed, there is hesitancy, the chance to draw back, always ineffectiveness. Concerning all acts of initiative (and creation), there is one elementary truth, the ignorance of which kills countless ideas and splendid plans: that the moment one definitely commits oneself, then Providence moves too. All sorts of things occur to help one that would never otherwise have occurred. A whole stream of events issues from the decision, raising in one's favor all manner of unforeseen incidents and meetings and material assistance, which no man could have dreamt would have come his way."[1]

Commitment is a significant part of marriage. Being specific about what you are actually committed and intentional about creating within a marriage together has tremendous power.

1 W. H. Murray, *The Scottish Himalayan Expedition,* pp. 6-7

Susanne M. Alexander is a Relationship and Marriage Coach. She loves watching and participating in the creative process that is released when people make commitments. (www.marriagetranformation.com)

❤ ❤ ❤

Premarital Assessment:
The Importance of Taking an Inventory
Peter J. Larson, Ph.D.

Have you ever been told that eating right and exercising are good for your health? Of course you have, as we've all heard this. But just hearing good advice doesn't always lead to action or lasting change.

The same is true in marriage preparation. Couples who are seriously courting one another and talking about marrying, or engaged couples, are often love struck, unrealistic, and consumed with wedding planning. Bringing them together for a general presentation about healthy relationships may sound like a good idea, but the chances of the good advice leading to the couple taking action or implementing lasting change are small. Relationship inventories/assessments are proven to be far more effective.

Addicted to Love?

Science is beginning to explain the phenomenon of being love struck. One article[1] summarized several intriguing findings on the topic. Helen Fisher, a professor from Rutgers University, used MRI technology to study couples who reported they were "madly in love." While in the MRI machine, subjects were shown two photographs: one neutral and the other of their loved one. The results showed that the pictures of the loved ones evoked a powerful chemical reaction in the pleasure centers of the brain, lighting up the neural receptors for a neurotransmitter called *dopamine*. Dopamine is associated with intense energy, focused attention, exhilaration, and motivation. Certain addictive drugs, such as cocaine, can activate the same regions and chemicals in the brain. In other words, brain physiology suggests couples can feel "addicted to love."

Obsessed with One Another?

Italian researcher Donatella Marazziti explored the similarities between being passionately in love and obsessive compulsive disorder (OCD). The neurotransmitter serotonin seems to be the culprit in OCD. Marazziti looked at three groups of subjects: one group of lovers, one group suffering from OCD, and another group free of mental illness and not experiencing passionate love. Results showed that the levels of serotonin in both the OCD group's blood and the lovers' blood were 40 percent lower than in the normal subjects. In other words, there were similar chemical markers in OCD and being madly in love. We've all seen couples who seem to be obsessed with one another. Perhaps their apparent imbalance is caused by more than just powerful feelings of love.

What's the Problem with Infatuation?

While the phenomenon of being love struck is quite normal, it can also be a setup to experience extremes. Some couples move too quickly toward engagement and marriage, not allowing themselves time to really get to know one another. Others believe they've found their true soulmate, only to question their choice the first time they experience a challenge or conflict. After the wedding day, most married couples are forced to realize that no relationship and no partner are perfect. Ideally, they become more realistic about their relationship as their love matures into something less obsessive and more committed. Those who don't accept the limitations of infatuation, and who are unable to make the shift into mature love, will likely divorce and look elsewhere on a pointless pursuit of short-lived romantic relationships and affairs. One of the key goals of marriage preparation is to help couples engage their minds to balance out some of the "in love" phenomena reported above.

Case Study

Maya and Ricardo, an engaged couple, took the PREPARE-ENRICH relationship inventory four months before their wedding date. A happy and idealistic couple in their early twenties, they were somewhat surprised with the results. While they possessed several strengths, financial management was rated as a relationship growth area. "What do you mean?" reacted Ricardo. "We don't have any problems managing our individual finances. We have no major debts or credit problems."

Their facilitator helped them explore this area further. The couple quickly realized that they had not discussed finances at all. Money issues had not yet led to overt conflict, but Maya and Ricardo had never agreed upon a plan for spending, saving, and budgeting after the wedding. During the discussion, Maya shared some concerns she had about Ricardo's spending habits.

The inventory results effectively directed their attention to an area that needed to be discussed and worked on. They started strengthening this aspect of their relationship with additional resources from the couple's workbook used in combination with the inventory. After an additional meeting with the facilitator and working on their own in between, they had identified three joint financial goals, a savings plan, and a budget they both agreed to abide by in their marriage.

The Goals of a Premarital Inventory

Inventories help the couple:

1. Move past generic good advice and take an in-depth look at their own relationship.

2. Identify their relationship strengths and growth areas (issues), piquing their curiosity, and priming them for feedback from the facilitator, who is usually a trained counselor, marriage educator, clergyperson, or Mentor Couple.

3. Personalize marriage preparation to their actual needs.

4. Hold productive and insightful conversations leading to action and change.

5. Use the inventory results as a bridge to needed skill-building activities.

6. Be proactive and not wait for problems to become serious before dealing with them.

Wise couples will use a premarital inventory and will find it affordable, accessible, and helpful.

1 Slater, L. (2006). True Love. *National Geographic.* February, 32-49.

> **Peter J. Larson**, Ph.D., is the President of Life Innovations, the international headquarters of the PREPARE-ENRICH Program (www.prepare-enrich.com). He is a licensed Psychologist, receiving his doctorate in Clinical Psychology and an M.A. in Theology from Fuller Graduate School of Psychology in Pasadena, California. Before joining Life Innovations, he specialized in premarital counseling and couples therapy as the Director of Research and Clinical Services for the Smalley Relationship Center. Dr. Larson is the co-developer of the Couple Checkup inventory and a co-developer of the *Customized Version* of *PREPARE-ENRICH*. He has published numerous journal articles and has co-authored the *Couple Checkup* book (2008), the *PREPARE to Last* program (2007), and the *PREPARE-ENRICH Marriage Mentor Program* (2009). Peter and Heather Larson have been married fourteen years, and they have three children.

❤ ❤ ❤

Focused Case Study: PREPARE-ENRICH's Development of Premarital Assessments
Peter J. Larson, Ph.D.

The PREPARE-ENRICH inventories began their development over thirty years ago. In some ways, community groups in Minneapolis and St. Paul were ahead of their time in the late 1970s, sponsoring a premarital lecture series run by experts in the field. The ten-week series included financial advisors presenting on money management, counselors teaching about communication, and clergy presenting on the importance of a spiritual foundation. Hundreds of couples had been attending these cutting-edge, community-based marriage preparation programs. With great expectations that they were on to something powerful, the leaders of this program invited

Dr. David Olson and his team of doctoral students from the University of Minnesota's Social Sciences department to study the impact they were having.

The research team set out to measure three areas: knowledge gain, attitude change, and behavior change. An in-depth study was undertaken involving comprehensive surveys, observation, and video and audio taping of couples interacting before and after the program. The research team analyzed a huge amount of data. Finally, the day came to present the results. Dr. Olson still recalls the discomfort he felt standing before a group of fifty community leaders and telling them their program was having absolutely no effect!

In conducting exit interviews with the couples, most said the lectures were good or entertaining, but "they didn't really apply to us." These engaged couples were no different than the norm.

The research did reveal an important insight. As the team discussed their observations regarding the study process, they noticed an interesting side effect of asking couples to fill out surveys on their relationship. The couples were curious—so curious they often had to be separated while they completed the process. They wanted to know what their partner was saying about their relationship, family, personality, and so on. Unlike the canned lectures of good advice they felt didn't apply to them, couples took a very personal interest in the results of the surveys they completed. When offered the chance to receive feedback on their survey results, over 90 percent of the couples came back.

Dr. Olson's team received a grant and set out to develop a premarital inventory that would not only provide solid research-based information about a couple's relationship health, but also promote curiosity and discussion as they received results. After developing the first version of PREPARE and testing it with local clergy, the time came for the study to end, but those who had used the inventory with couples as part of the study demanded ongoing access to it. For the first time, they had solid direction in working with their engaged couples. Couples, too, were more invested in the process.

Since that time, PREPARE-ENRICH has grown into a comprehensive set of relationship inventories designed for both premarital and married couples. Millions around the world have gone through the program, which combines assessment with feedback and skill-building exercises. Several research studies have shown the assessment can effectively predict marital outcomes and dramatically increase the power of marriage and premarital education programs.[1]

1 Fowers, Montel, & Olson, 1996; Olson & Knutson 2003, Larson et al., 2007

Peter J. Larson, Ph.D., is the President of Life Innovations, the international headquarters of the PREPARE-ENRICH Program (www.prepare-enrich.com). He is a licensed Psychologist, receiving his doctorate in Clinical Psychology and an M.A. in Theology from Fuller Graduate School of Psychology in Pasadena, California. Before joining Life Innovations, he specialized in premarital counseling and couples therapy as the Director of Research and Clinical Services for the Smalley Relationship Center. Dr. Larson is the co-developer of the Couple Checkup inventory and a co-developer of the *Customized Version* of *PREPARE-ENRICH*. He has published numerous journal articles and has co-authored the *Couple Checkup* book (2008), the *PREPARE to Last* program (2007), and the *PREPARE-ENRICH Marriage Mentor Program* (2009). Peter and Heather Larson have been married fourteen years, and they have three children.

Chapter Twenty
Planning the Wedding
~ ~

Wedding planning resources are abundant, so our goal here in this final chapter is not to help with the practical details of planning your ceremony and reception. We want to help you understand some of the myriad of emotions that are arising at this stage. You may wish to know more about creating your own wedding vows, and you can benefit from learning how to maximize enjoyment from your wedding night.

Remember that the wedding is a transition point into a new and different life. This book is about helping you plan for your long-term marriage, not just the few hours that a ceremony and celebration take. Be cautious about spending so much time planning your *wedding* that you neglect to plan for your *marriage*. This is by far the greater investment in your long-term happiness and marital success. We trust that the whole book has helped you do just that.

❤ ❤ ❤

Handling the Feelings About Transitioning to Marriage
Sheryl Paul

Does it really have to be this hard? A typical client will come to me full of anxiety and doubt, confusion, and loneliness. She wants to know if this means she's not supposed to get married, and she takes immense comfort in learning she's not alone in feeling anything other than pure joy in the months before and after their wedding. But as she struggles with the various manifestations of grief and fear, she continually wonders if it's supposed to be this hard. She begins to think the struggle and difficult feelings mean she might be making a mistake with marrying.

The Image and the Reality

Our culture conditions you to believe that the wedding transition, from engagement and on into the first year of marriage, should be the most blissful, exciting, magical time of your lives. The planning process and everyone involved are supposed to be perfect, and you, as the couple, continuously filled with unequivocal joy.

So when the fear of marriage hollows your bellies, and the grief of letting go of being single shimmies up your back, you may wonder what's wrong. Surely it's not supposed to be this hard, right?

Wrong! Actually, it *is* supposed to be this hard. Here's the truth that belies the images we've all ingested from every available media source: Transitions are hard; adolescence is hard; leaving home for the first time is hard; becoming a parent is hard; and job changes, midlife, empty nest, retiring, old age are all hard. That doesn't mean there isn't great joy inherent in all of these transitions. However, before we can truly receive the joy, we have to be willing to let go of the old life, to confront our fears, and to tolerate the uncomfortable in-between zone when the familiar stage of life is over, and the new stage and identity have yet to be born.

Transitions render us vulnerable and inspire us to evaluate who we are and what's important to us. They carry the capacity to *increase* our joy, self-respect, self-trust, and general state of ease. But the positive aspects of transition cannot occur without trudging through the muck that defines the early stages of letting go of the old life. What makes it so hard to accept that the wedding and all that surrounds it is challenging, is that we don't expect it. At least in this culture, muck and weddings just don't go together.

It's the expectations that are so damaging for women and men on the threshold of marriage. Because the engaged couple expects bliss and perfection, you may be completely thrown when the other feelings invade your days and nights. The wedding is the transformational transition day and, as such, is the portal we walk through to become a wife or husband. But the months preceding and following the wedding are often fraught with an array of emotions that span the gamut from depression to exhilaration and everything in between.

Examining the Fears

There are two types of fear that arise during engagements: The first is a signal that there's a serious red-flag issue in the relationship, and the second is a signal that you're about to make the biggest commitment of your life—and, yes, it's scary.

What are some of the key red-flag issues I'm referring to? Consider these:

- An untreated addiction issue (alcohol, drugs, work, gambling)
- Betrayal or trust issues that haven't been healed
- Incompatibilities regarding core values like having children or religion
- Others that might be less blatant: serious control issues with no willingness to address; you're too young (early twenties) and aren't ready to commit to one person; more in love with the fantasy or idea of love than really loving each other

The second type of fear is being scared of the unknown. You feel scared of jumping off the cliff of the familiar life and landing in new and unfamiliar territory. You may be scared of committing to one person forever. Getting married is enormously scary, and to say otherwise is to avoid a basic truth about this significant life transition.

Once you determine that there are no serious red-flag issues in the relationship, you can begin to accept that fear about this major transition is normal. You can learn how to make room for the fear during the engagement without letting it run the show.

The thoughts and feelings that typically create engagement, wedding, and marriage anxiety include:

- Grief about letting go of the single identity and lifestyle
- Fears about making the commitment of marrying one person
- Confusion about how to separate from family of origin
- Uncertainty about walking toward the unknown of marriage
- A recurring sense of loss about deceased relatives, past relationships, or previous transitions

In other words, oftentimes the anxiety that arises during an engagement has nothing to do with one's partner. The emotions from major transitions are often stored in the body, and facing a new transition can cause old emotions to arise. People you wished were at your wedding cannot come, and this prompts new feelings of grief. Significant events often remind you of memories of past events.

Memories of a Previous Partner

Thinking about an ex and many aspects of the past is a normal part of being engaged. As we spiral into deeper layers of transitions, our past comes floating to the surface of our thoughts, dreams, and emotional life. For some people, the past includes thoughts or feelings about unfinished transitions like leaving home for the first time, their parents' divorce, the end of a friendship or relationship, or the loss of a loved one. As you move together toward your wedding day, you may re-live the loss associated with the previous transition. The more conscious you both are about these feelings, the more you will recognize that loss is an inherent—and important—part of any transition. Both separately and together, you can then allow yourselves to process the sadness as best as you can. If the pain is significant, you may also need to seek assistance from a counselor, coach, or clergy member.

Since your thoughts during this transition will, at times, involve another man or woman, it's often a lot more challenging to accept it, make sense of it, and move on without feeling guilty or questioning your decision to marry. The thoughts then inevitably become drenched in anxiety. As is so often the case with anxiety, it's not the thoughts or feelings themselves that are a problem; it's the meaning we ascribe to the thoughts that create the pit in our stomachs, the furrowed brow, or the hidden tears. So, remember it's normal, and begin to let the anxiety go.

When you decide to marry one person, you have to say goodbye to every other possible life partner. With billions of members of the opposite sex on this planet, that's a lot of goodbyes! So instead of grieving about every single other option, the mind focuses on the one option that usually represents the polar opposite of the person you're marrying. Where your husband-to-be is responsible and reliable, the ex on the brain is irresponsible and unreliable. Of course, those aren't the characteristics you're focusing on; all you can think about is how spontaneous and fun the person was! But it's important to reel the mind back in and say to yourself, "Yes, he was spontaneous and fun, and sometimes my groom isn't those things, but along with those qualities came an irresponsibility that never would have worked as a life partner." Then, allow yourself to grieve that no one is perfect, and no matter who you marry, you will have to accept their imperfections and limitations.

Considering the Wedding

It's okay not to look forward to your wedding. It's okay to struggle before and after the big day. It doesn't mean you're making a mistake. It doesn't mean there's something wrong with you. It means you're in the midst of an enormous life transition, one in which your previously solid ground is shifting beneath your feet. It means you haven't distracted yourself by obsessively planning an impossibly perfect wedding. Without this distraction, you're left feeling the normal and necessary feelings that define this transition. It means you're being courageous and honest and daring to break the steel-clad cultural taboo that says that struggle and weddings don't go together. It means you're striving to be a conscious bride and groom, which will inevitably help you become a conscious wife and husband and have an honest, real, meaningful marriage. Congratulations!

Sheryl Paul, M.A., pioneered the field of bridal counseling in 1998. She has since counseled thousands of people worldwide through her private practice, her best-selling books, *The Conscious Bride* and *The Conscious Bride's Wedding Planner*, and her website, www.consciousweddings.com. She's regarded as the international expert on the wedding transition and has appeared several times on *The Oprah Winfrey Show*, as well as on *Good Morning America* and other top television and radio shows and in newspapers around the globe. She lives in Boulder, Colorado, with her husband and two young sons. Phone sessions are available worldwide by calling 303-474-4786. Her blog is http://myconscioustransitions.com.

© 2010 S. Paul

❤ ❤ ❤

Creating Your Own Wedding Vows
Linda Bloom and Charlie Bloom

As you discuss marrying one another, you are likely including the topic of your vows. Taking vows is a practice that defines the context, expectations, and values of the marriage. Vows are the cornerstone of the foundation of the marriage.

Although all marriages include marital vows, many of them are not personalized to the specific intentions of each partner. Even where there is a requirement by a marriage officiant that a certain vow be part of the ceremony, most will agree to allow the couple to say their own personal vows in addition.

Every marriage has three components: mine, yours, and ours. The three sets of vows have to do with what you are vowing to me, what I am vowing to you, and what we each are vowing to contribute to the marriage itself. The generic, off-the-rack vows aren't adequate, because they don't reflect each partner's personal vision and unique needs or the mutual commitments of the couple. Only when a couple personalizes their vows are their deepest desires and intentions illuminated. When the declarations are a personal expression of the couple, there tends to be a stronger commitment to carry out the spirit and declarations of the vows.

At times, a couple may decide that each person individually writes a vow, and the partner does not hear it until the wedding. While this may seem romantic, the process of formulating vows together is an essential aspect of the marriage itself. In this process of discussing the content of the vows as a couple, it will become evident where you both are in alignment on what you will commit to create in your marriage, and where there is misalignment. The vow-making process will shed light on any places where partners might not see eye to eye. This is not necessarily a problem, but it will almost certainly become a problem if the differences are not honestly acknowledged and addressed.

The wedding is a public declaration of those agreements that represent the couple's deepest vision and mutual intentions. It's a time to honor their shared commitment to evolve, through the process of marriage, into their greatest selves. And that is an occasion for a wonderful celebration!

Linda Bloom, L.C.S.W., and **Charlie Bloom**, M.S.W., are Psychotherapists and Marriage Counselors who teach communication seminars and relationship workshops throughout the world. They are co-authors of the best-selling book, *101 Things I Wish I Knew When I Got Married, Simple Lessons to Make Love Last,* and *Secrets of Great Marriages: Real Truths from Real Couples About Lasting Love,* published in 2010. They offer educational and counseling services to individuals, couples, and organizations. Their website is www.bloomwork.com, and they can be reached at 831-421-9822 or by email at lcbloom@bloomwork.com. They live and practice in Santa Cruz, California.

❤ ❤ ❤

Ensuring Wedding Night Bliss
James E. Sheridan

They had anticipated *the moment* ever since they became engaged. And, now they were finally alone after all the endless planning and arranging, the rehearsal, the rehearsal dinner, the ceremony, and the reception, with the food, the cake, the dancing, Uncle Ed playing the accordion, and Aunt Martha kissing everyone after her fourth glass of wine.

He carried her over the threshold into the bridal suite to their new beginning. The couple had agreed to remain abstinent until after the wedding; they kept their promise. It was to be a night they'd never forget, and they wanted to be ready. So, they each emotionally prepared for the moment in their own ways.

Unfortunately, it was, indeed, a night they'd never forget, but, not for the reasons they had thought. Within minutes of closing the door, they had a horrible fight that would haunt their relationship for years.

The bride had been told by her married friends that the wedding day would be an incredibly exciting and emotionally draining day. They warned her that she would be completely exhausted. They were right. When the bride saw the bed, all she could think of was sleep. Forget undressing; just let her get horizontal and leave her alone.

The groom had been told by his married buddies that this would be a night of the most passionate sex he'd ever have. All day, he'd watched the clock, counting the minutes until he'd finally have his bride alone and ready. When the groom saw the bed, all he could think about was the glorious sexual adventure he and his blushing bride were about to experience.

They had planned everything else about the day. But, they had not thought about this. It was so obvious to the bride that she'd be exhausted that there was no need to talk about it. It was so obvious to the groom that he was sexually ready that there was no need to explain it.

The bride lay down on the bed and rolled over to go to sleep. The groom exploded, and the fight was on. It lasted for nearly an hour. The wounds lasted for years.

The wedding night is filled with high expectations. Unfortunately, the expectations of the bride and the groom are often very different. Try the tips below for the best ways to make the wedding night and the honeymoon the wonderful experiences they should be.

Have sex or sleep? Whether you have sex on your wedding night when you're able to finally do what you've wanted for so long, or you wait until the next day when you're both awake and refreshed, is something only you as a couple can decide. If one of you gets tired easily, sex on the first night may be disappointing. Still, as one woman told me emphatically: "I've been a virgin for twenty-six years. Once I'm married, I am not waiting another day!" The main point is: Talk about your expectations and agree on an approach. Let your fiancé know your concerns, your hopes, and your desires.

Choreograph the first few minutes. Whether you have sex the first night or wait until the next day, there are still issues to discuss. You may agree on sex as soon as you're alone. But she might assume that means she will disappear into the bathroom, freshen up, put on a sheer, white negligee, and then re-enter the bridal chamber. In the meantime, she thinks her beloved will change into white, silk boxers, turn the lights low, spread rose pedals on the bed, and put on soft, romantic music. When she comes out, they will dance together to their favorite love song, and then recline to slowly make passionate love.

He assumes that sex as soon as they're alone means once the door is shut, they'll rip each other's clothes off, and if they make it to the bed, fine, but the floor is just as good!

If it is sex the next morning, does that include time for teeth brushing, using the toilet, taking a shower, or combing hair? Or does it mean as soon as we wake up and forget the niceties?

Don't guess about what you'll do! Choreograph the first few minutes after you close the door behind you, and how you want sex to happen if you delay it. Talk it out in advance. This is a topic that most couples have a lot of fun planning prior to the wedding.

If you've been sexually active before the wedding, it is still important to choreograph the first few minutes of your marital sex life. Talk about things you have not done together, perhaps some secret fantasies that are doable. (Anything that gets you arrested or hurt is not "doable.") Plan a time for specials or acting out a fantasy. Don't let your wedding night become just another night. With planning, you can make it something that will be a source of memorable joy for the rest of your lives.

Don't overdo on the big day. Your wedding day is a major life event, but be sensible. Avoid planning so many things that the day becomes highly stressful. Plan well for what you do include, and allow enough time for each. Delegate some tasks to trusted and capable family members and friends. Then don't be surprised when everything doesn't go as expected. That rarely happens anyway. Don't make what doesn't go well a source of conflict. The missteps become part of the adventure, which will make interesting stories for you to tell over time.

Limit alcohol consumption. Alcohol is a depressant. If you serve it at your reception, leave it for the others to drink. If there are champagne toasts, a sip is enough. You'll be sufficiently tired without drinking something that will make you all the more sleepy when you're finally alone.

Go slow and keep your expectations realistic. If this is the first time you're having sex, go slow and don't expect fireworks to go off. Women often require time and experiences to adjust to sexual relations before becoming orgasmic. Focus on the closeness, the warmth of being intimate, and the joy of joining together. Take your time with lots of loving words, caressing, kissing, and touching instead of trying to attempt intercourse without preamble. Remember to have fun exploring and learning where and how you both enjoy being touched. You can use your wedding night, your honeymoon, and the months that follow to experiment with your hands and mouths in new ways. Learn through experimenting and communicating what works best for both of you.

Make all first-night plans tentative. No matter what you plan, whether it's sex or sleep the first night, be prepared for last-minute changes. You may have decided on sex, but if one of you is too tired or not feeling well due to the emotional stress, too much wedding cake, or too many toasts, it is important that you have a Plan B. Or, you may decide to wait, only to realize you both have more than enough emotional energy and physical desire to have a wonderful experience.

If you're thinking about Plan B, it may include setting an alarm and sleeping for a few hours or sleeping through the night and having sex in the morning. Again, choreograph the first few minutes of Plan B.

Usually, it is the bride who will experience an emotional letdown and energy drain that leaves her exhausted, but it could be the groom, so don't make assumptions. Before the big day, make sure you've given each other consent to call a delay of game and a move to Plan B, even at the last minute.

Do your best to be honest with each other about how you are feeling.

The primary way to avoid a wedding night fight or serious disappointment is to recognize the potential issue ahead of time and talk it out. You want the start of your married life to be a source of joy and fond memories. By having a Plan A and a Plan B, both with choreographed openings, you greatly increase the chances that you will both be happy with the outcome.

James Sheridan, author of *A Blessing for the Heart, God's Beautiful Plan for Marital Intimacy*, writes a weekly newspaper column on marriage skills. He also frequently presents before judicial and legislative groups on Marriage and Public Policy. He regularly speaks for couples' retreats and banquets on a variety of subjects, including Sex & Romance in the Biblical Marriage, 10 Things Every Married Couple Should Know About Sex, and Using Rituals to Strengthen Your Marriage. He is a regular presenter at the international Smart Marriages® and Happy Families Conference. Contact information: www.marriagedoneright.com, email: jsheridan@marriagedoneright.com.

❤ ❤ ❤

A Prayer For Us
Raphaella Vaisseau

May our hearts be blessed with love
May our spirits sing in tune
May the moments we're together
be like flowers in full bloom

May we nurture in each other
understanding of ourselves
May we sing and dance with freedom
wings and hear the Holy Bells

May God support and guide us
as we open to our love
May we soar to that place inside us
Where there waits a golden dove

May the peace we find together
spread through grace across the land
May each heart that hears our laughter
awaken as it can

May these things to us be granted
as it is for the highest good
And may all the gifts we're given
be returned a hundredfold

Raphaella Vaisseau is a prolific artist and writer. Through her company, Heartful Art (www.heartfulart.com), she focuses on providing original art, as well as artfully designed posters and magnets to assist people everywhere to empower themselves and others. Her artwork hangs in collections world-wide and has been licensed for use on music covers, t-shirts, and more. She can also be reached at raphaella@heartfulart.com.

♥ ♥ ♥

Blessed Joining
Susanne Mariella Alexander

What does it mean to join as husband, wife?
Two souls gathered by God's Hands
uniting dreams and thoughts and touch
loving strongly peaceful certainty
that joining is forever blessed

Marriage changes things
no longer dating or engaged
now entered in the fortress for well-being
where pearls of great price must
find a home with dust and scattered socks
where some days doors might slam
and on others "I love you" echoes
richly through the halls

Nurture the best from each other
and on days when you cannot be your best
then be patient and wait
tomorrow will be better

Through the marriage fortress
God has built, not you,
you have the wondrous task
of lighting every hearth
with fires of warmth and joyfulness
and softening the walls with fragrant climbing roses
and throwing windows open wide
to welcome in the sun and filling it each day
with prayer so angels guard and guide you

And then someday it will be blessed again
as God smiles through your lovely children's laughter

Susanne M. Alexander is a Relationship and Marriage Coach with Marriage
Transformation (www.marriagetransformation.com).

❤ ❤ ❤

A Note in Closing

I'm sure at the beginning of this book you had no idea of the wealth of actions you could take to be well prepared for marriage. You now have a wonderfully expanded tool box and set of resources and experts to help you be successful as you go forward with making powerful choices about your future.

My husband and I always prayed for the relationships and marriages of those we worked with and those reading our books. I began praying for yours as I was compiling and writing this book.

Have a great marriage journey!
Susanne M. Alexander

♥ ♥ ♥

Acknowledgements

I thank all of the Expert Contributors with heartfelt gratitude. Without their wisdom, expertise, and commitment to couples and happy, lasting marriages, this book would not exist! Their enthusiasm for this project has been truly inspirational. I appreciated their trust, patience, and confidence in me as their editor.

Bouquets of flowers to my amazing support team: Roger Bascom, Shirley Bascom, Jennifer DeMaria, Jen Griffin, Rodney Grubbs, Kay Reed, David Rikklan, and Jeff Schlesinger and staff at Barringer Publishing for their assistance, flexibility, and dedication to my vision for this book. Autumn Conley also did an outstanding job as the overall book editor.

I appreciate the following people who provided wonderful testimonials: Sherry Amatenstein, Elva Anson, F. D., Elizabeth Doherty Thomas, Jodie Gould, Ralph Jones, K. Jason Krafsky, Kelli Krafsky, Talia Lindsley, Pat Love, Brenda Maxwell, Sharon Naylor, Charles Schmitz, Elizabeth Schmitz, Diane Sollee, Tina Tessina, and Melodie Tucker.

Thank you to my Editorial Review Team. You helped make this a better book! Gratitude to Ann Bivans, Phillipe Copeland, Fanya DeMaria, Jennifer DeMaria, Jane Ives, Talia Lindsley, Kay Muttart, Martha Schweitz, Diane Sollee, Michelle Tashakor, Rory Turnbull, and Brenda Zografov.

And, last, but definitely not least, my overwhelming gratitude to God for sustaining me in all my work. I'm also thankful to my angel Craig hanging out and providing inspiration every day. I love you!

Susanne M. Alexander

Thinking About Marriage?

Take a Moment to Laugh on the Path to a Successful Marriage with Susanne M. Alexander!

A Perfectly Funny Marriage:
A Humorous View of Creating a Successful Marriage

Take a fresh look at how to create a successful marriage with Relationship and Marriage Coach Susanne M. Alexander and several insightful cartoonists. Bring fun and laughter to your marriage preparation process, wedding, or to your marriage through reading and sharing this light-hearted perspective. Each page has a brief statement of what is important in relationships and marriage illustrated by a cartoon.

A Perfectly Funny Marriage will help you to explore the stages of self-discovery, friendship, relationship building, and marriage. It is ideal for singles to learn about relationships, wedding parties to use as a favor or gift, married couples to lighten up their relationship, or groups to use for playful learning. Couples will enjoy this book as a great wedding shower, wedding, or anniversary gift.

"This delightful book shows how the path to a splendid marriage can be both meaningful and fun! Every couple, from their first date to their 50th wedding anniversary, should have it close at hand."

Scott Haltzman, M.D., Author of *The Secrets of Happily Married Men* and *The Secrets of Happily Married Women*

Get your copy today!
www.marriagetransformation.com/store_FunnyMarriage.htm
or www.amazon.com
Marriage Transformation LLC, 800-501-6682

LaVergne, TN USA
30 June 2010
187953LV00003B/2/P